PhD

PHANTASY DEGREE

3

Episode 3: Swordmaster Chun-Lang

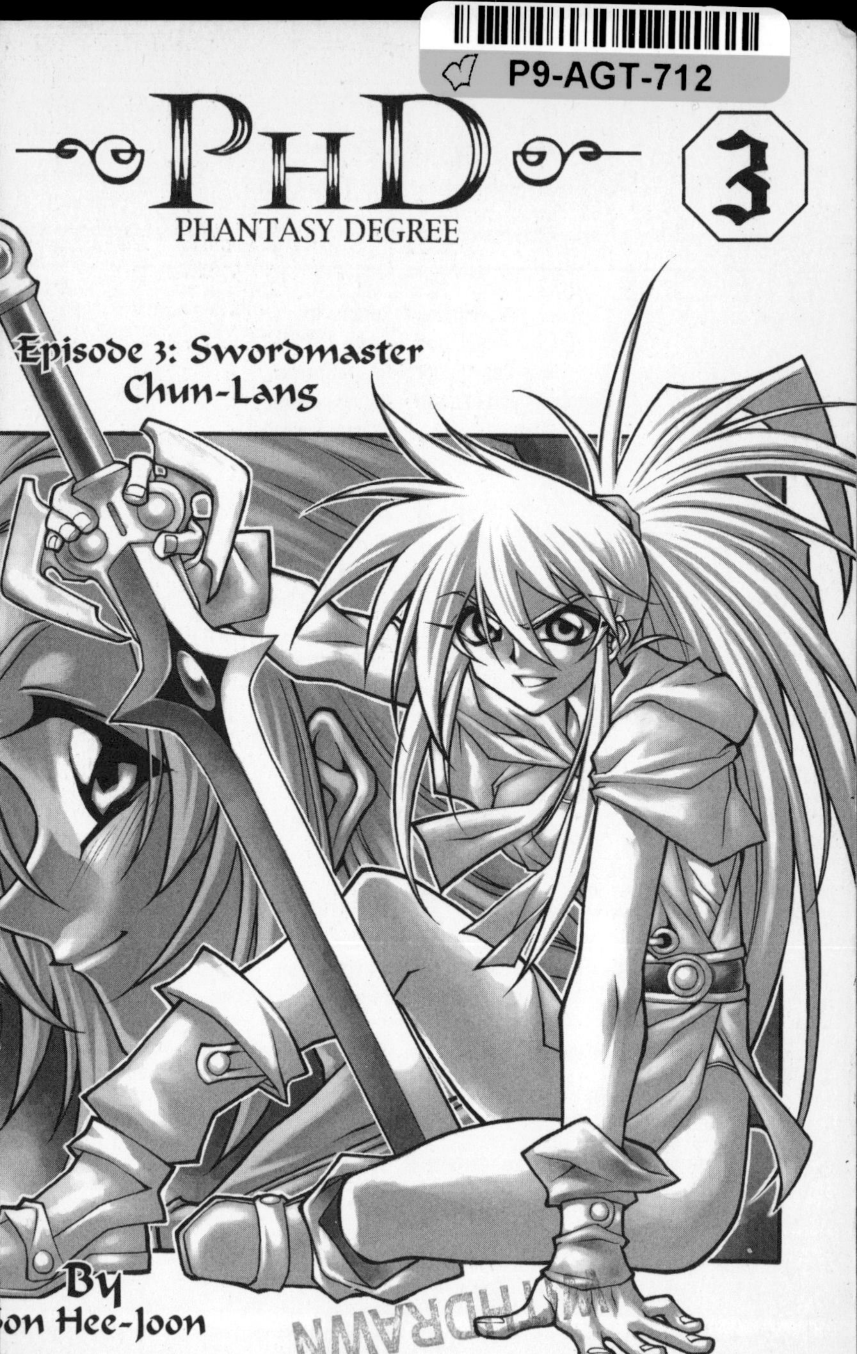

By
Son Hee-Joon

PhD: Phantasy Degree Vol. 3
Created by Son Hee-Joon

Translation - Sarah Kim
English Adaptation - Adam Arnold
Copy Editor - Aaron Sparrow
Retouch and Lettering - Adriana Rivera
Production Artist - James Dashiell
Cover Design - Seth Cable

Editor - Paul Morrissey
Digital Imaging Manager - Chris Buford
Pre-Press Manager - Antonio DePietro
Production Managers - Jennifer Miller and Mutsumi Miyazaki
Art Director - Matt Alford
Managing Editor - Jill Freshney
VP of Production - Ron Klamert
Editor-in-Chief - Mike Kiley
President and C.O.O. - John Parker
Publisher and C.E.O. - Stuart Levy

A ⬤ TOKYOPOP® Manga

TOKYOPOP Inc.
5900 Wilshire Blvd. Suite 2000
Los Angeles, CA 90036

E-mail: info@TOKYOPOP.com
Come visit us online at www.TOKYOPOP.com

ISBN: 1-59532-321-X

First TOKYOPOP printing: July 2005
10 9 8 7 6 5 4 3 2 1
Printed in the USA

PHANTASY DEGREE

Volume 3

By
SON HEE-JOON

HAMBURG // LONDON // LOS ANGELES // TOKYO

Previously in...

PHD
PHANTASY DEGREE

MOST MUMMIES I'VE SEEN ARE ROTTING IN SARCOPHAGUSES, AND THEY'RE LIVELIER THAN YOU! DO MUMMIES EVEN EAT FLESH? I THOUGHT THAT'S WHAT ZOMBIES DID. AT LEAST ZOMBIES CAN INSPIRE SOME FEAR.
HEY, YOU! WITH THE BABY FANGS! YOU'RE NOT EVEN A PURE-BLOODED VAMPIRE, ARE YOU? I BET YOU WERE BITTEN BY ANOTHER VAMPIRE, RIGHT?
Mm-hmm.
AND YOU, GOAT BOY! ARE YOU SUPPOSED TO BE A DEMON? WITH HORNS THAT STUBBY, YOU'RE NOTHING BUT AN IMPOTENT IMP! HONESTLY, ARE YOU EVEN CAPABLE OF CASTING MAGIC?
WHAT A BUNCH OF SAD SACKS! PATHETIC!
YOU'RE A BUNCH OF DEMON SCHOOL SLACKERS, AREN'T YOU? JUST A GROUP OF BELOW-AVERAGE BEELZEBUBS! AM I RIGHT?

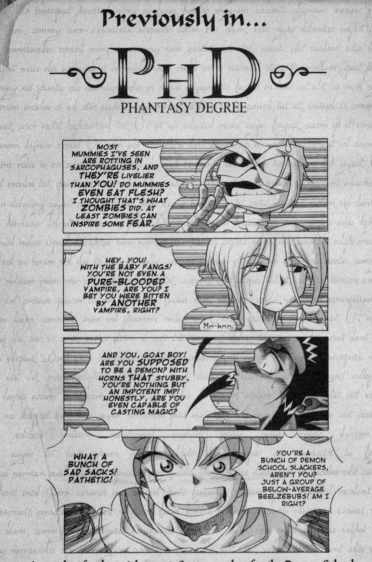

A spunky, fearless girl named Sang searches for the Demon School Hades...and a legendary ring contained within its walls. When she encounters a group of misfit monsters that are playing hooky from school, her hunt is over. They reluctantly take her to Hades, where Sang meets Notra, a female monster who's wearing a very special ring! But before Sang can snatch Notra's ring, a group of humans from the Madosa Guild attack the school! A deadly battle ensues, and Sang fights alongside her new beastly buddies...

PhD
PHANTASY DEGREE

Table of Contents

Swordmaster Chun-Lang

Quest 22

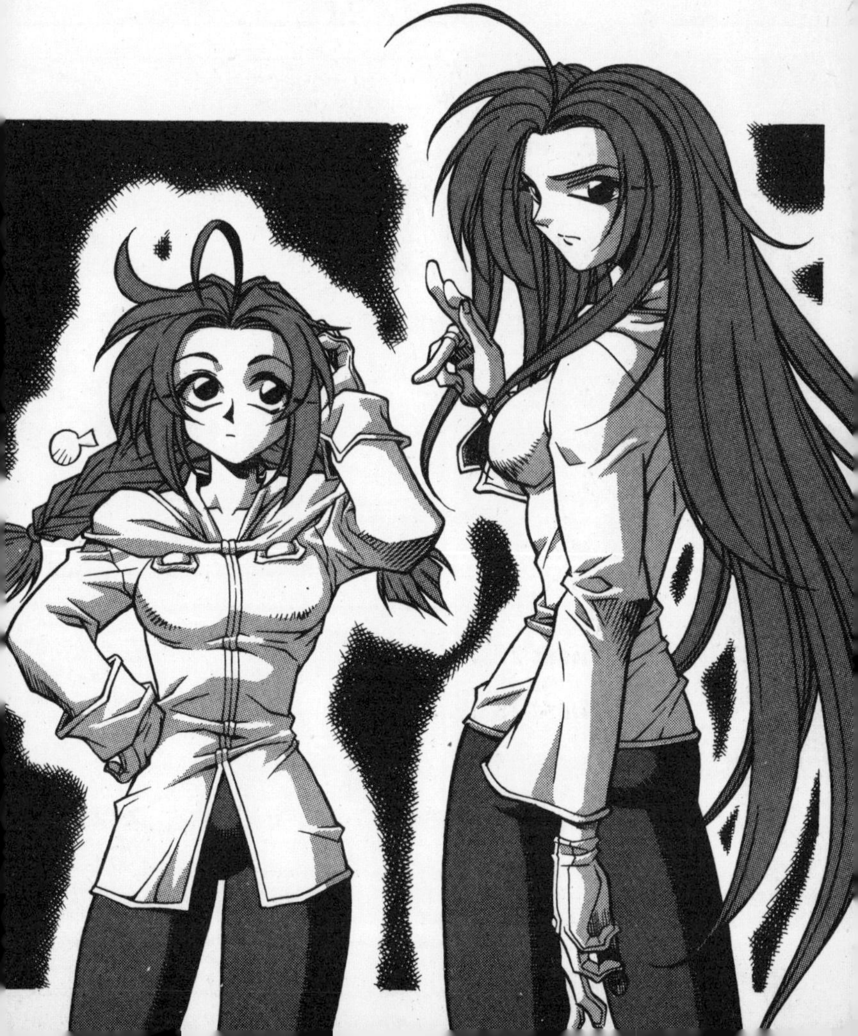

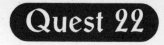

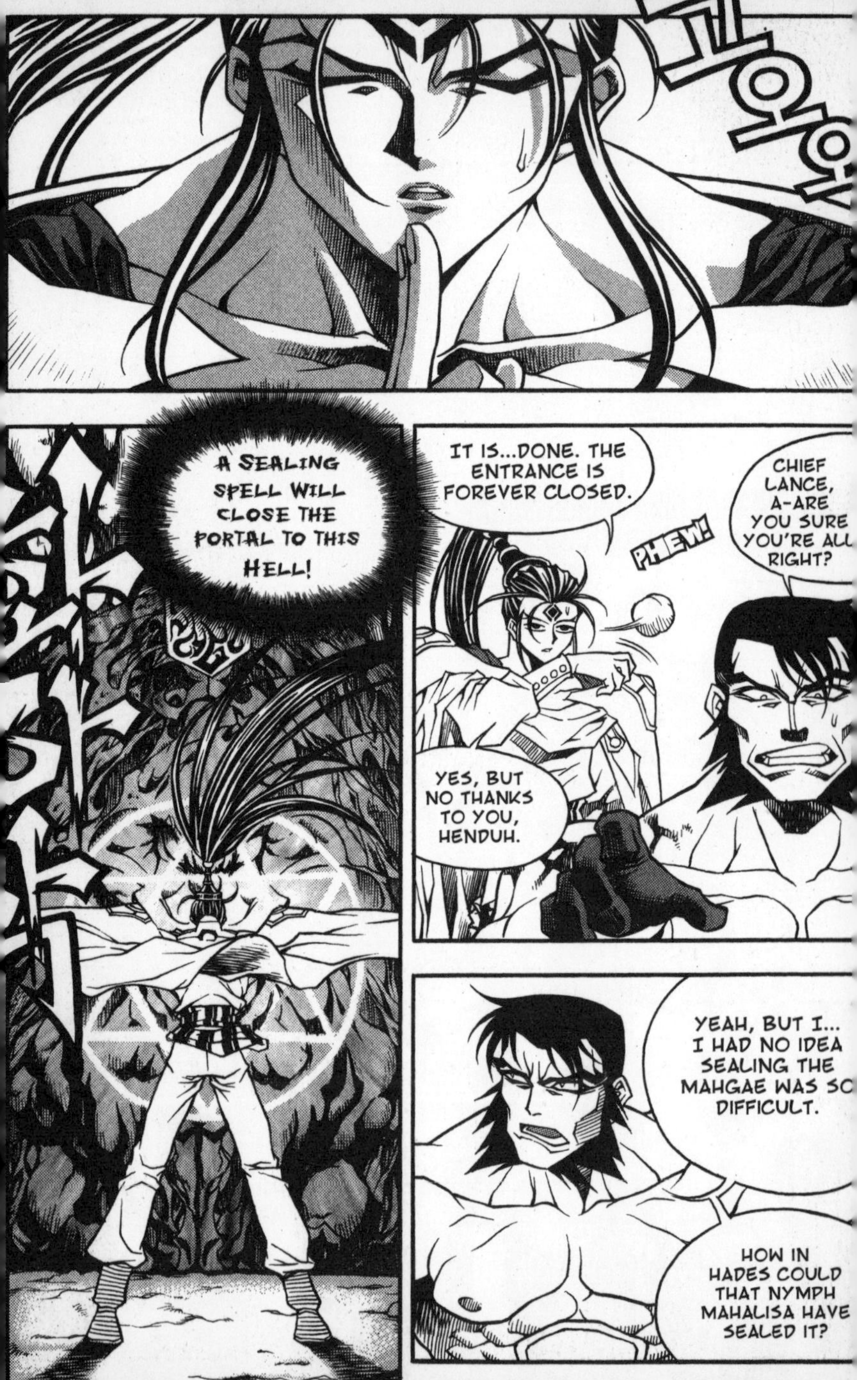
A SEALING SPELL WILL CLOSE THE PORTAL TO THIS HELL!
IT IS...DONE. THE ENTRANCE IS FOREVER CLOSED.
PHEW!
CHIEF LANCE, A-ARE YOU SURE YOU'RE ALL RIGHT?
YES, BUT NO THANKS TO YOU, HENDUH.
YEAH, BUT I... I HAD NO IDEA SEALING THE MAHGAE WAS SO DIFFICULT.
HOW IN HADES COULD THAT NYMPH MAHALISA HAVE SEALED IT?

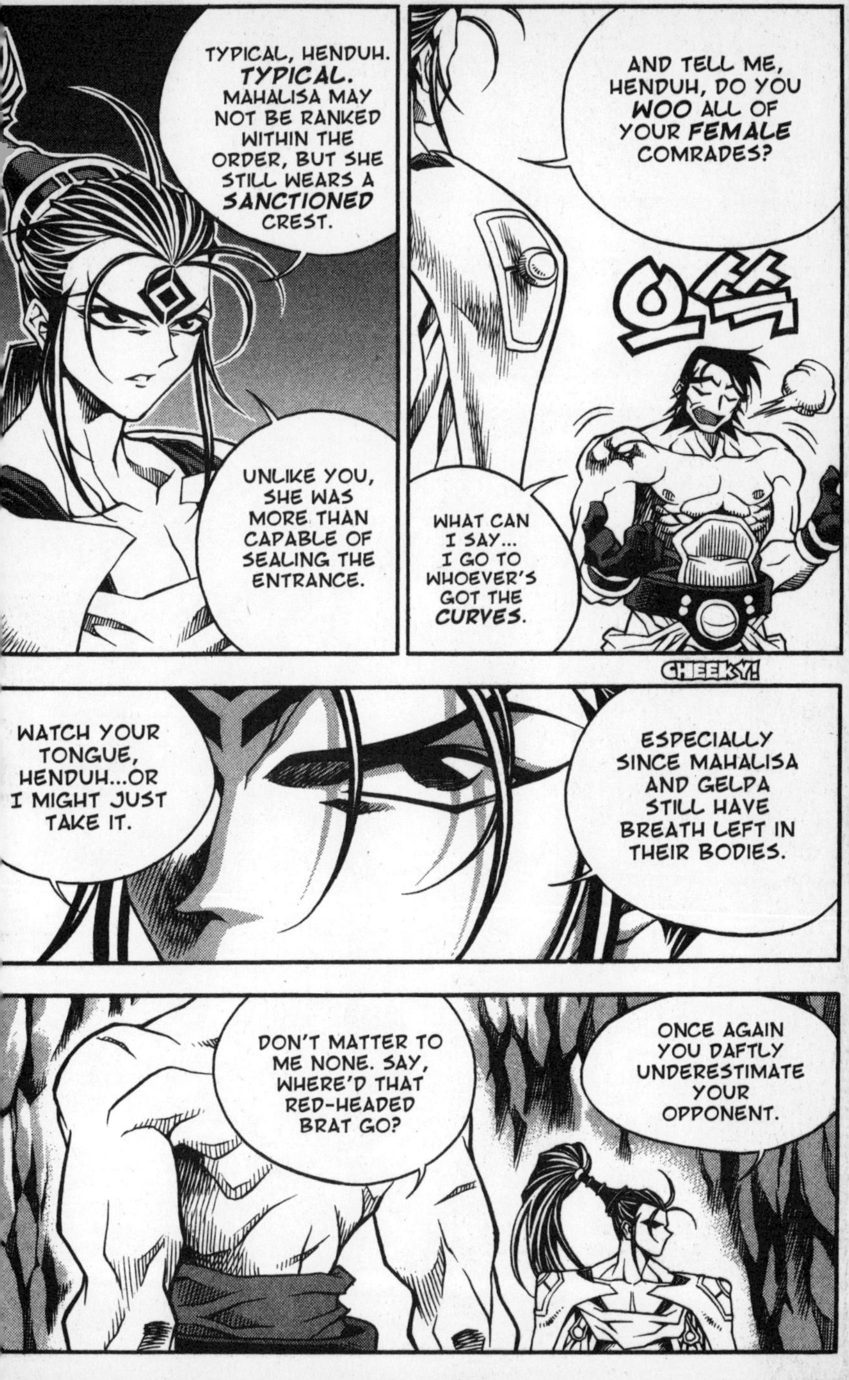
TYPICAL, HENDUH. TYPICAL. MAHALISA MAY NOT BE RANKED WITHIN THE ORDER, BUT SHE STILL WEARS A SANCTIONED CREST.
UNLIKE YOU, SHE WAS MORE THAN CAPABLE OF SEALING THE ENTRANCE.
AND TELL ME, HENDUH, DO YOU WOO ALL OF YOUR FEMALE COMRADES?
으쓱
WHAT CAN I SAY... I GO TO WHOEVER'S GOT THE CURVES.
CHEEKY!
WATCH YOUR TONGUE, HENDUH...OR I MIGHT JUST TAKE IT.
ESPECIALLY SINCE MAHALISA AND GELPA STILL HAVE BREATH LEFT IN THEIR BODIES.
DON'T MATTER TO ME NONE. SAY, WHERE'D THAT RED-HEADED BRAT GO?
ONCE AGAIN YOU DAFTLY UNDERESTIMATE YOUR OPPONENT.

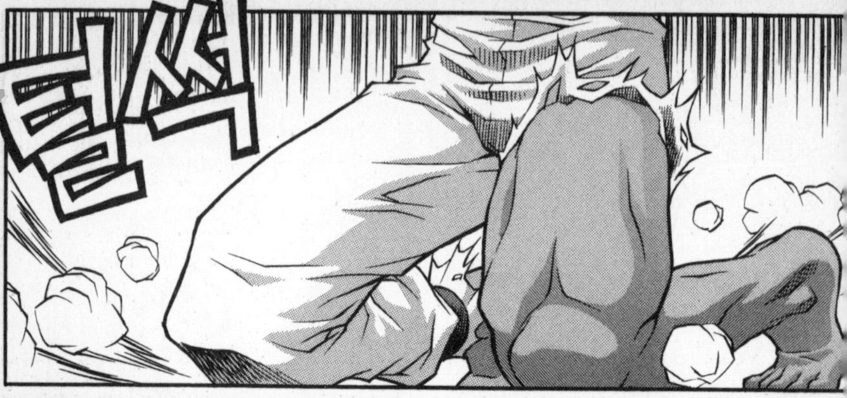
털썩

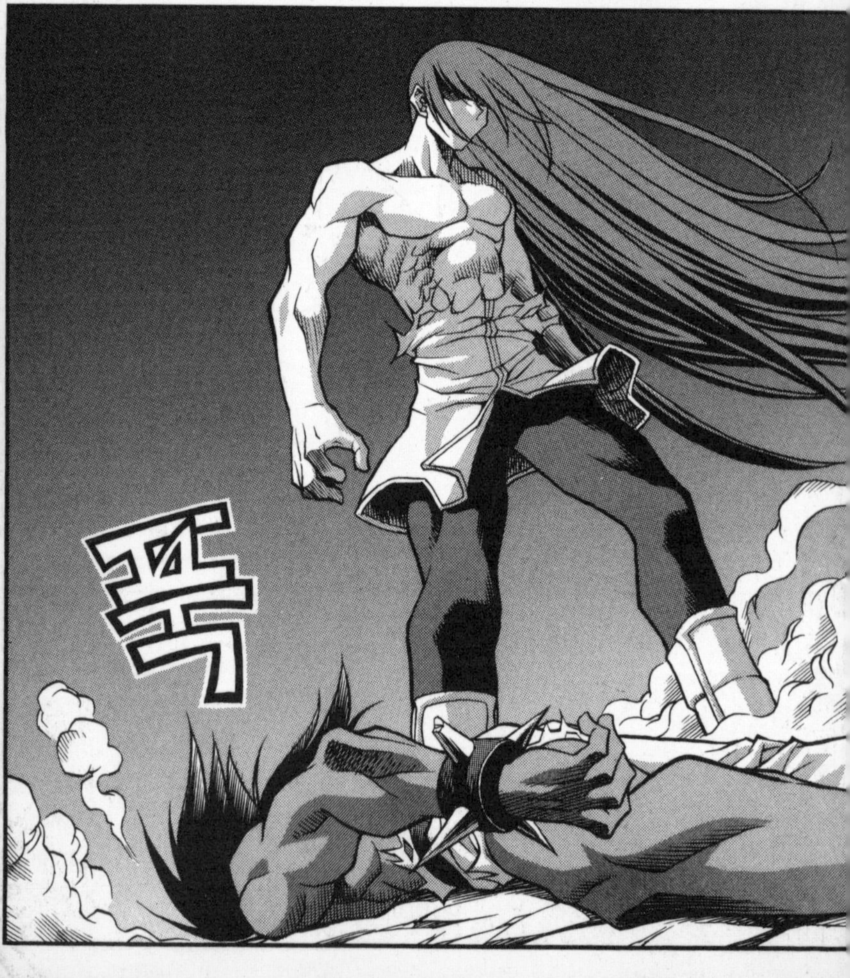
푹

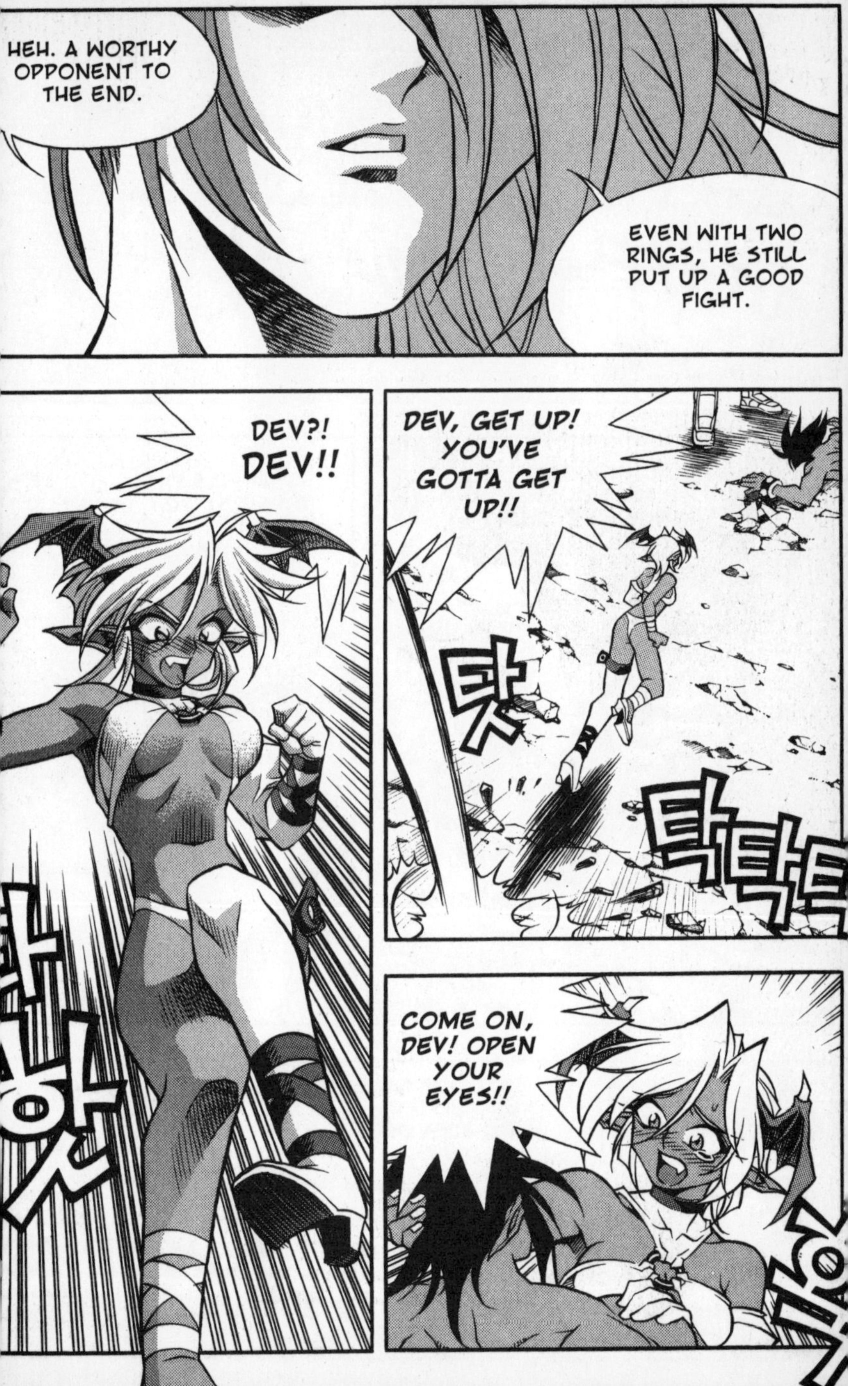
HEH. A WORTHY OPPONENT TO THE END.
EVEN WITH TWO RINGS, HE STILL PUT UP A GOOD FIGHT.
DEV?! DEV!!
DEV, GET UP! YOU'VE GOTTA GET UP!!
COME ON, DEV! OPEN YOUR EYES!!

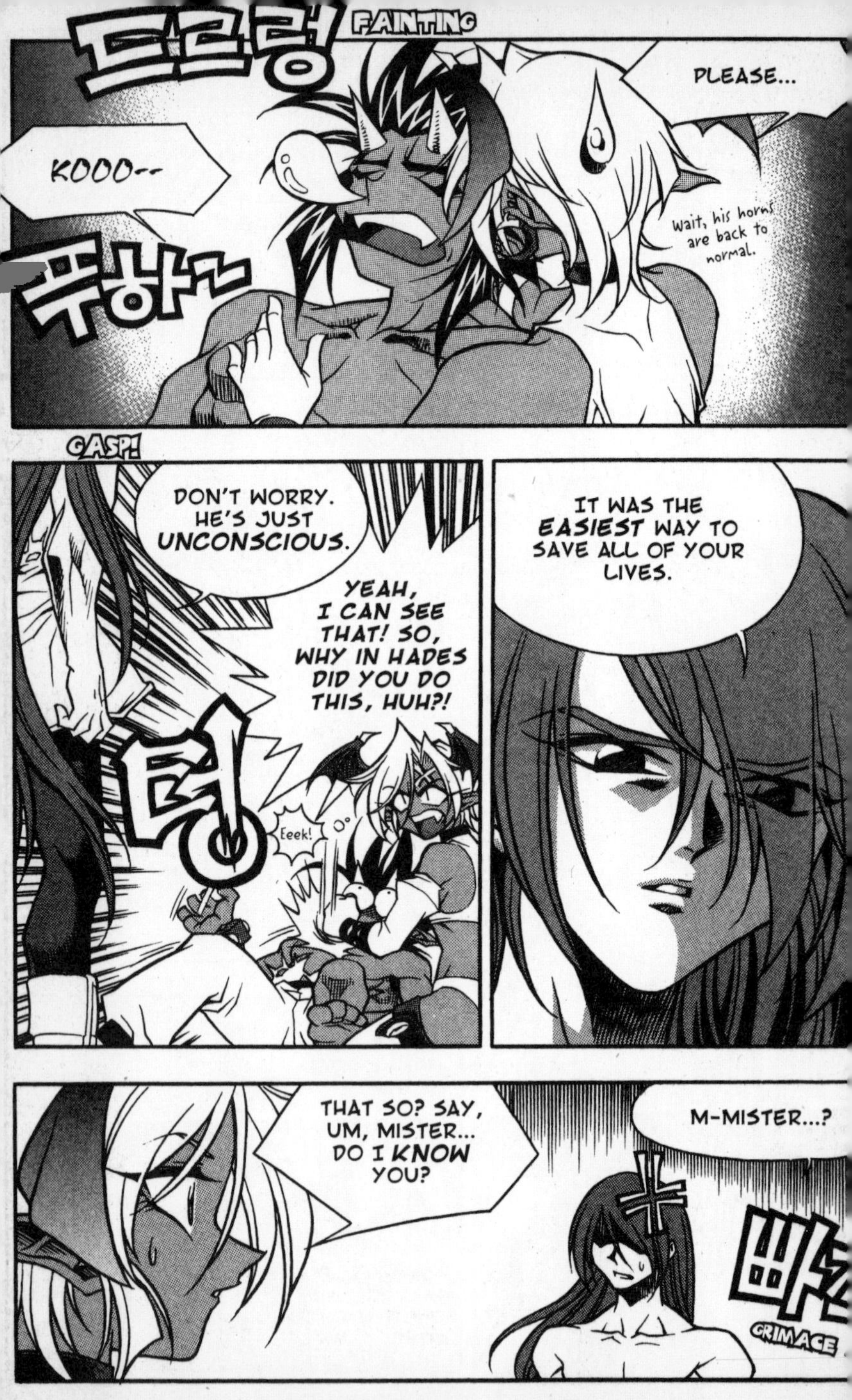
드르렁
FAINTING
KOOO--
PLEASE...
푸하
Wait, his horns are back to normal.
GASP!
DON'T WORRY. HE'S JUST **UNCONSCIOUS.**
YEAH, I CAN SEE THAT! SO, WHY IN HADES DID YOU DO THIS, HUH?!
턱
Eeek!
IT WAS THE **EASIEST** WAY TO SAVE ALL OF YOUR LIVES.
THAT SO? SAY, UM, MISTER... DO I **KNOW** YOU?
M-MISTER...?
빠
GRIMACE

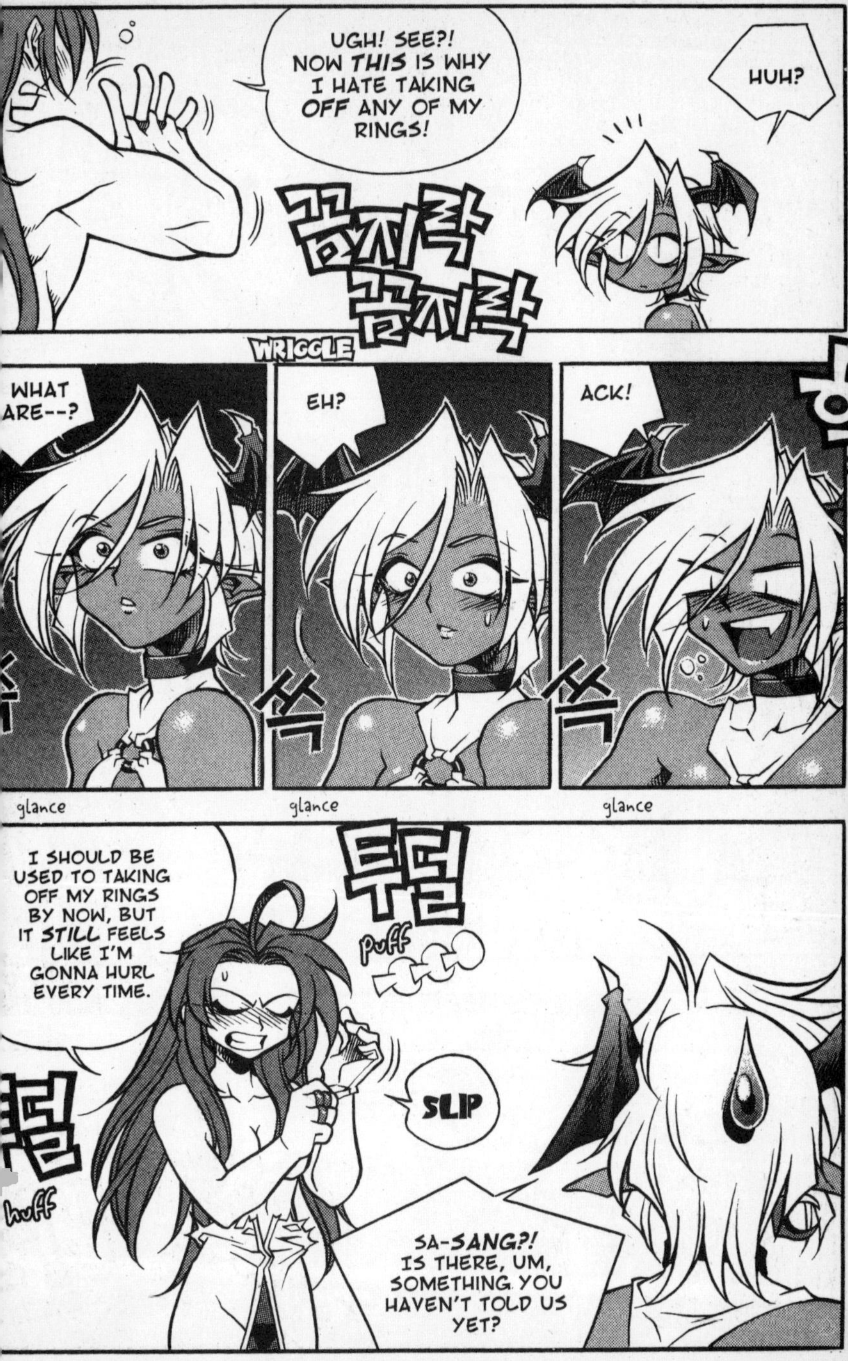

UGH! SEE?! NOW THIS IS WHY I HATE TAKING OFF ANY OF MY RINGS!
HUH?
WRIGGLE
WHAT ARE--?
glance
EH?
쓱
glance
ACK!
쓱
glance
I SHOULD BE USED TO TAKING OFF MY RINGS BY NOW, BUT IT STILL FEELS LIKE I'M GONNA HURL EVERY TIME.
투덜
puff
huff
SLIP
SA-SANG?! IS THERE, UM, SOMETHING YOU HAVEN'T TOLD US YET?

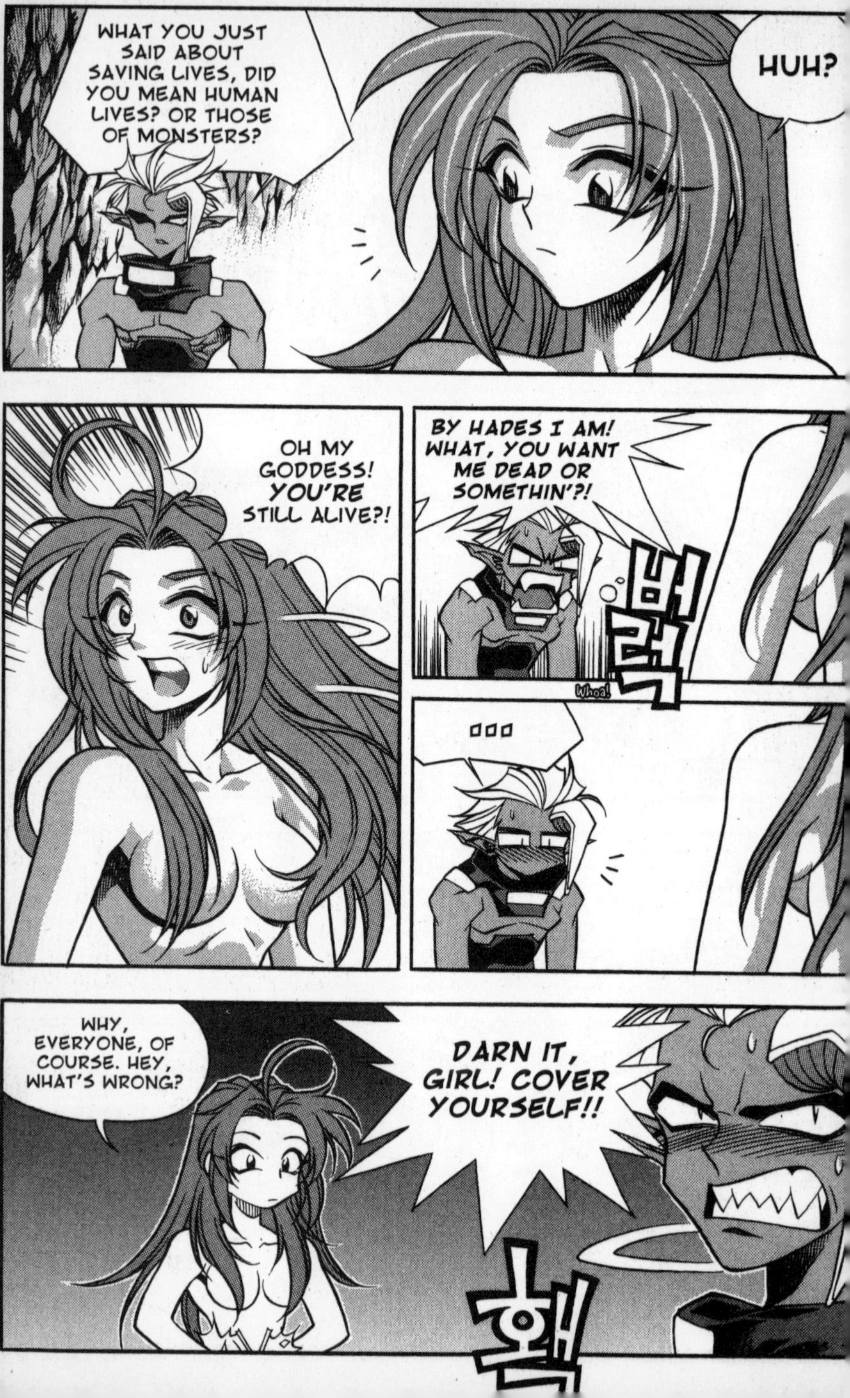
WHAT YOU JUST SAID ABOUT SAVING LIVES, DID YOU MEAN HUMAN LIVES? OR THOSE OF MONSTERS?
HUH?
OH MY GODDESS! YOU'RE STILL ALIVE?!
BY HADES I AM! WHAT, YOU WANT ME DEAD OR SOMETHIN'?!
Whoa!
□□□
WHY, EVERYONE, OF COURSE. HEY, WHAT'S WRONG?
DARN IT, GIRL! COVER YOURSELF!!

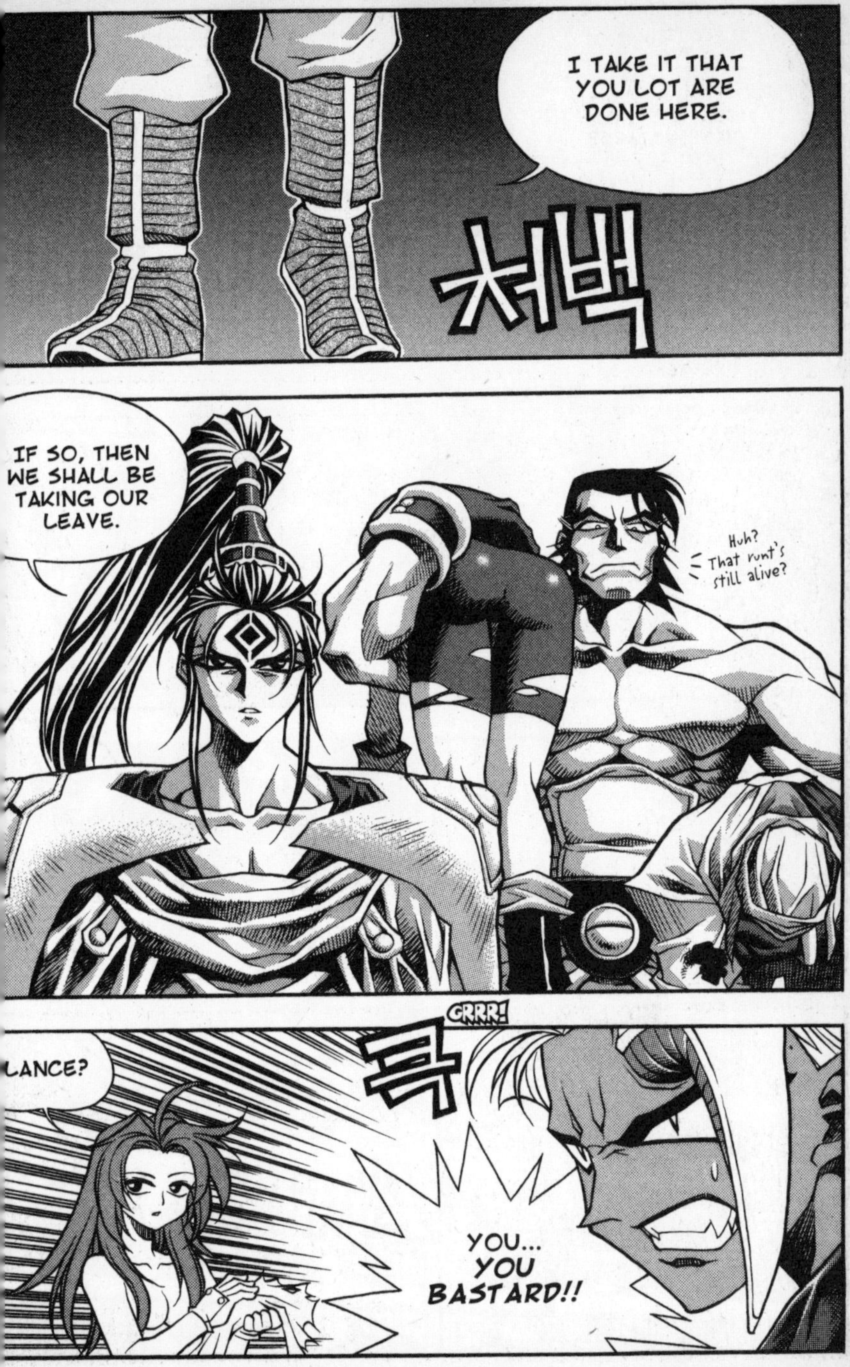
I TAKE IT THAT YOU LOT ARE DONE HERE.
처벅
IF SO, THEN WE SHALL BE TAKING OUR LEAVE.
Huh? That runt's still alive?
GRRR!
크
LANCE?
YOU... YOU BASTARD!!

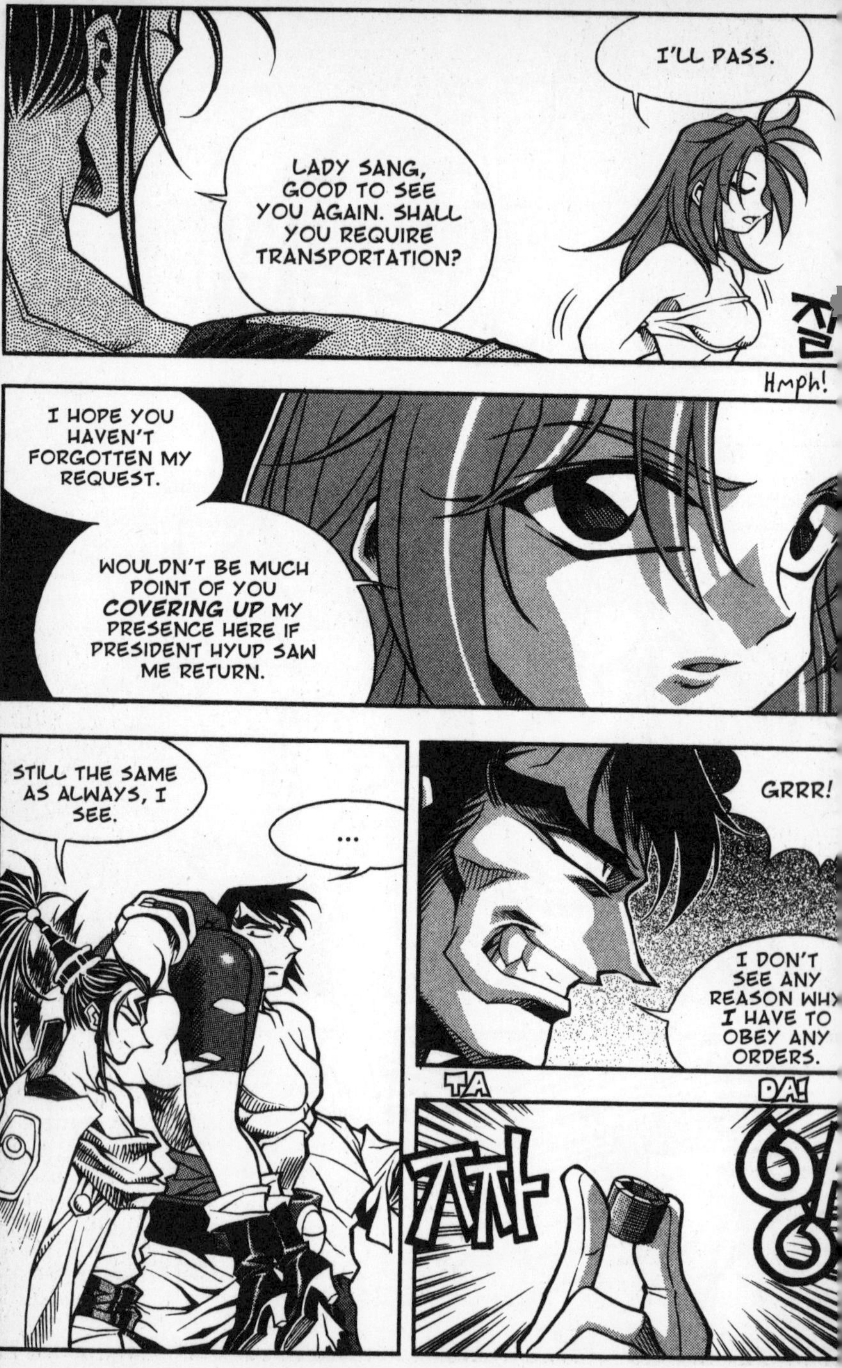
LADY SANG, GOOD TO SEE YOU AGAIN. SHALL YOU REQUIRE TRANSPORTATION?
I'LL PASS.
Hmph!
I HOPE YOU HAVEN'T FORGOTTEN MY REQUEST.
WOULDN'T BE MUCH POINT OF YOU COVERING UP MY PRESENCE HERE IF PRESIDENT HYUP SAW ME RETURN.
STILL THE SAME AS ALWAYS, I SEE.
...
GRRR!
I DON'T SEE ANY REASON WH I HAVE TO OBEY ANY ORDERS.
TA
DA!

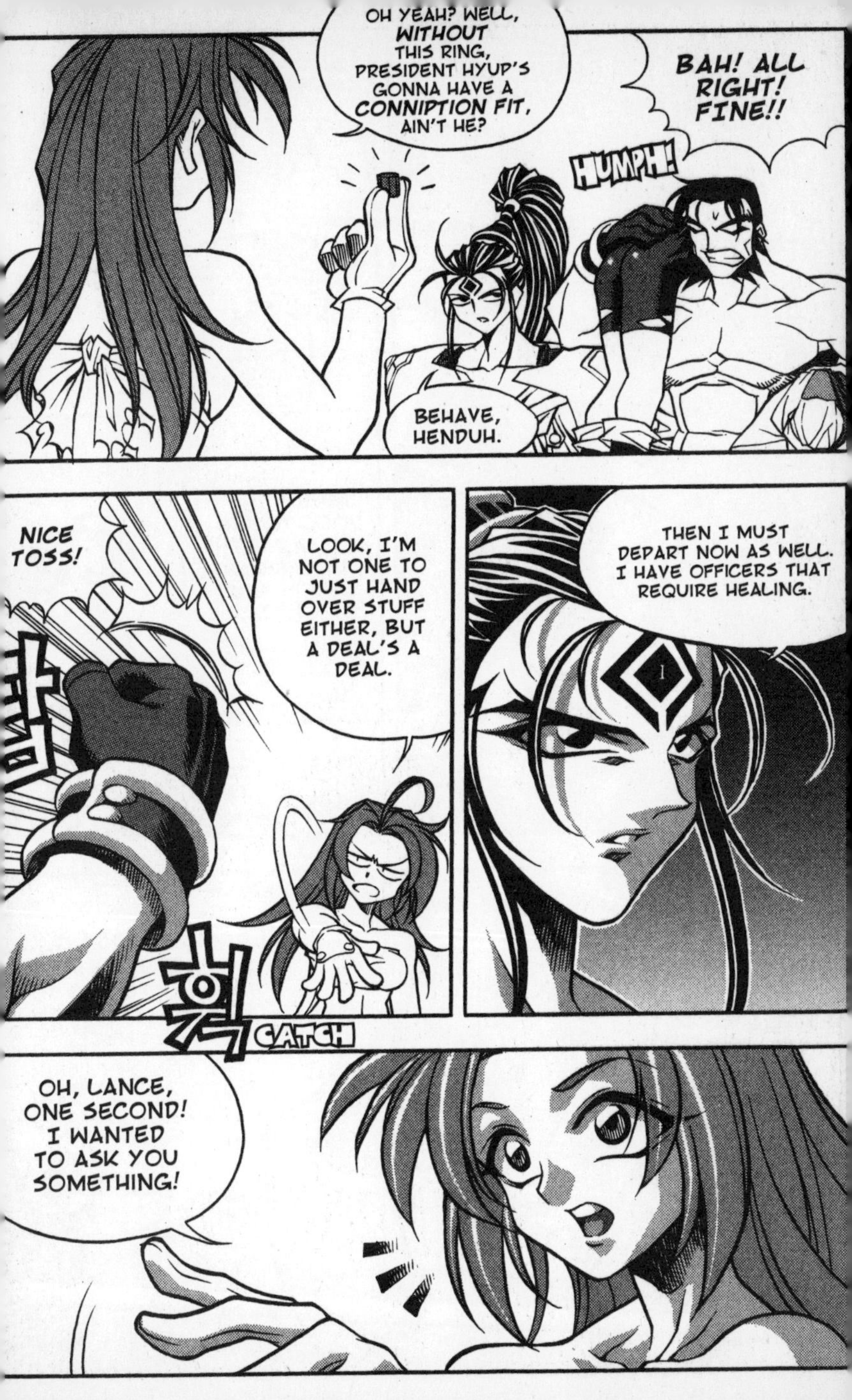
OH YEAH? WELL, WITHOUT THIS RING, PRESIDENT HYUP'S GONNA HAVE A CONNIPTION FIT, AIN'T HE?
BAH! ALL RIGHT! FINE!!
HUMPH!
BEHAVE, HENDUH.
NICE TOSS!
LOOK, I'M NOT ONE TO JUST HAND OVER STUFF EITHER, BUT A DEAL'S A DEAL.
CATCH
THEN I MUST DEPART NOW AS WELL. I HAVE OFFICERS THAT REQUIRE HEALING.
OH, LANCE, ONE SECOND! I WANTED TO ASK YOU SOMETHING!

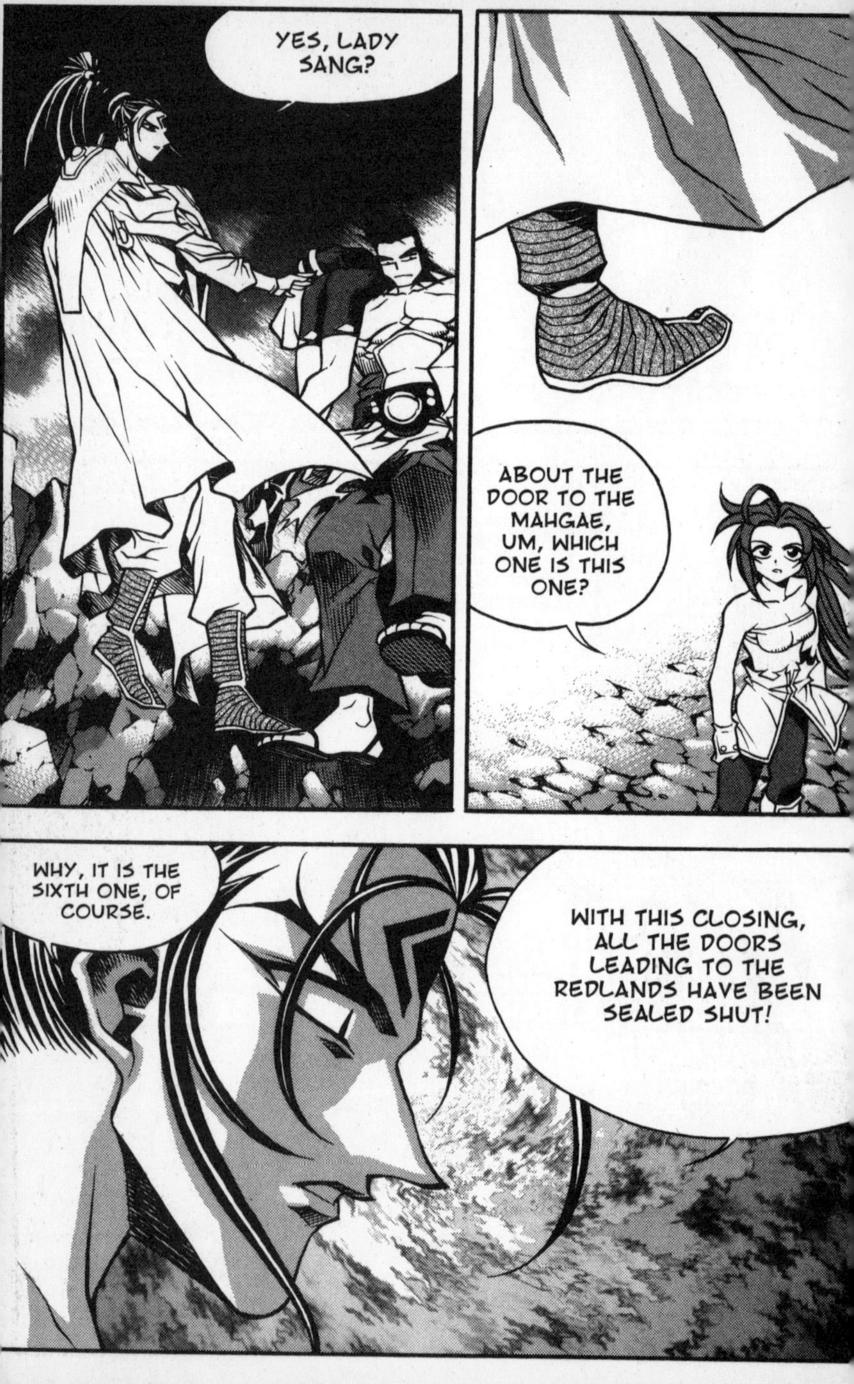
YES, LADY SANG?
ABOUT THE DOOR TO THE MAHGAE, UM, WHICH ONE IS THIS ONE?
WHY, IT IS THE SIXTH ONE, OF COURSE.
WITH THIS CLOSING, ALL THE DOORS LEADING TO THE REDLANDS HAVE BEEN SEALED SHUT!

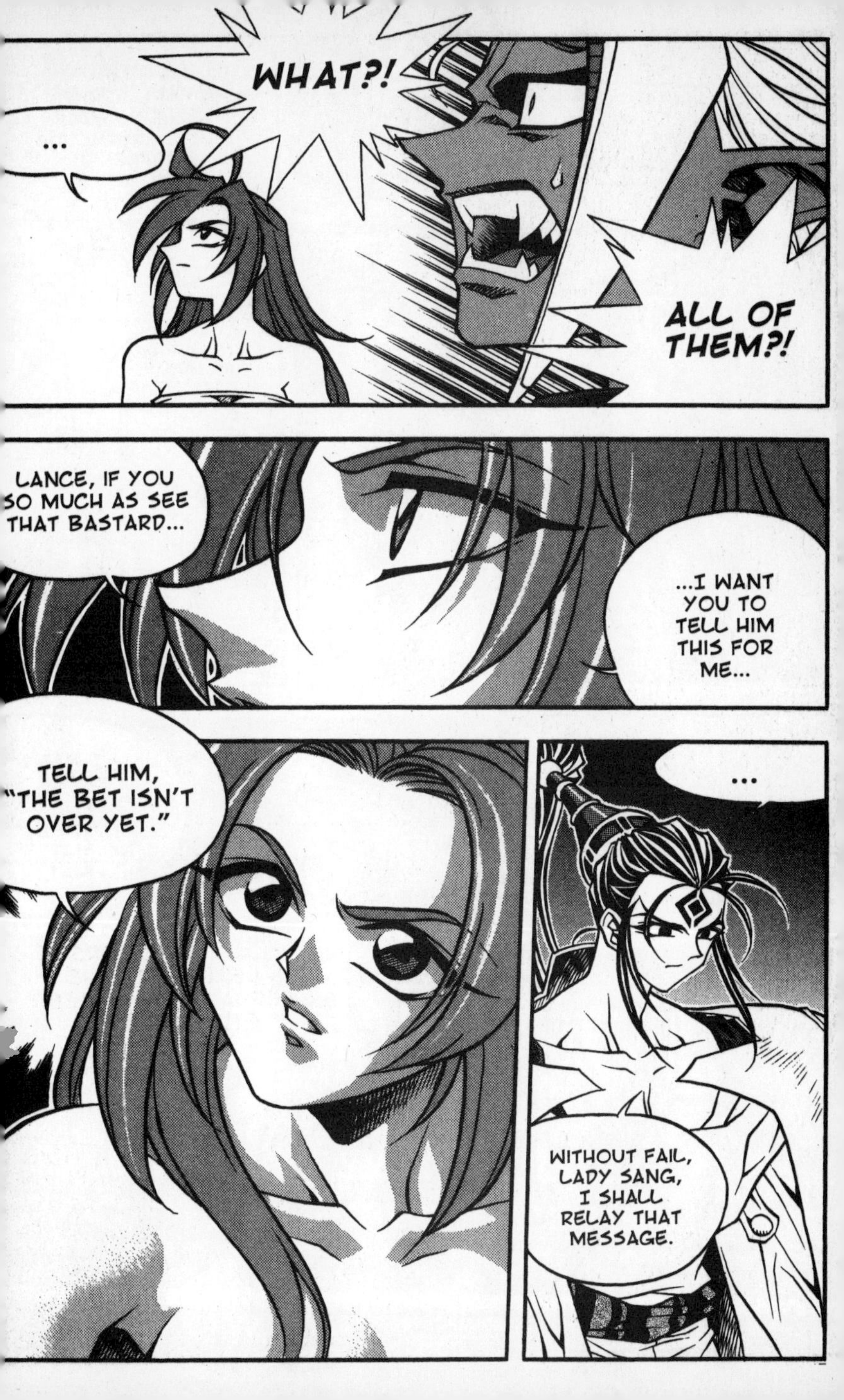
WHAT?!
...
ALL OF THEM?!
LANCE, IF YOU SO MUCH AS SEE THAT BASTARD...
...I WANT YOU TO TELL HIM THIS FOR ME...
TELL HIM, "THE BET ISN'T OVER YET."
...
WITHOUT FAIL, LADY SANG, I SHALL RELAY THAT MESSAGE.

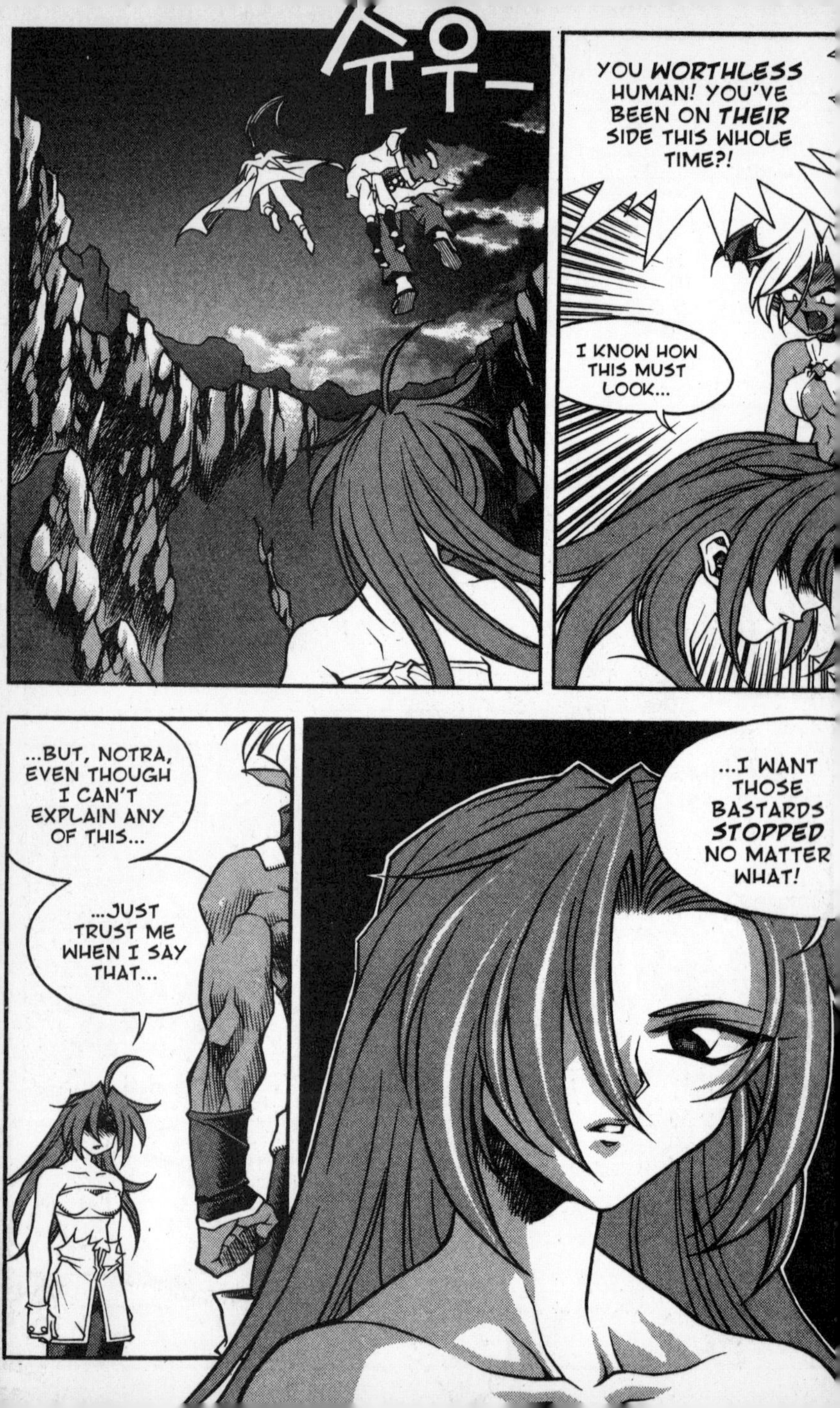
슈우
YOU WORTHLESS HUMAN! YOU'VE BEEN ON THEIR SIDE THIS WHOLE TIME?!
I KNOW HOW THIS MUST LOOK...
...BUT, NOTRA, EVEN THOUGH I CAN'T EXPLAIN ANY OF THIS...
...JUST TRUST ME WHEN I SAY THAT...
...I WANT THOSE BASTARDS STOPPED NO MATTER WHAT!

Quest 23

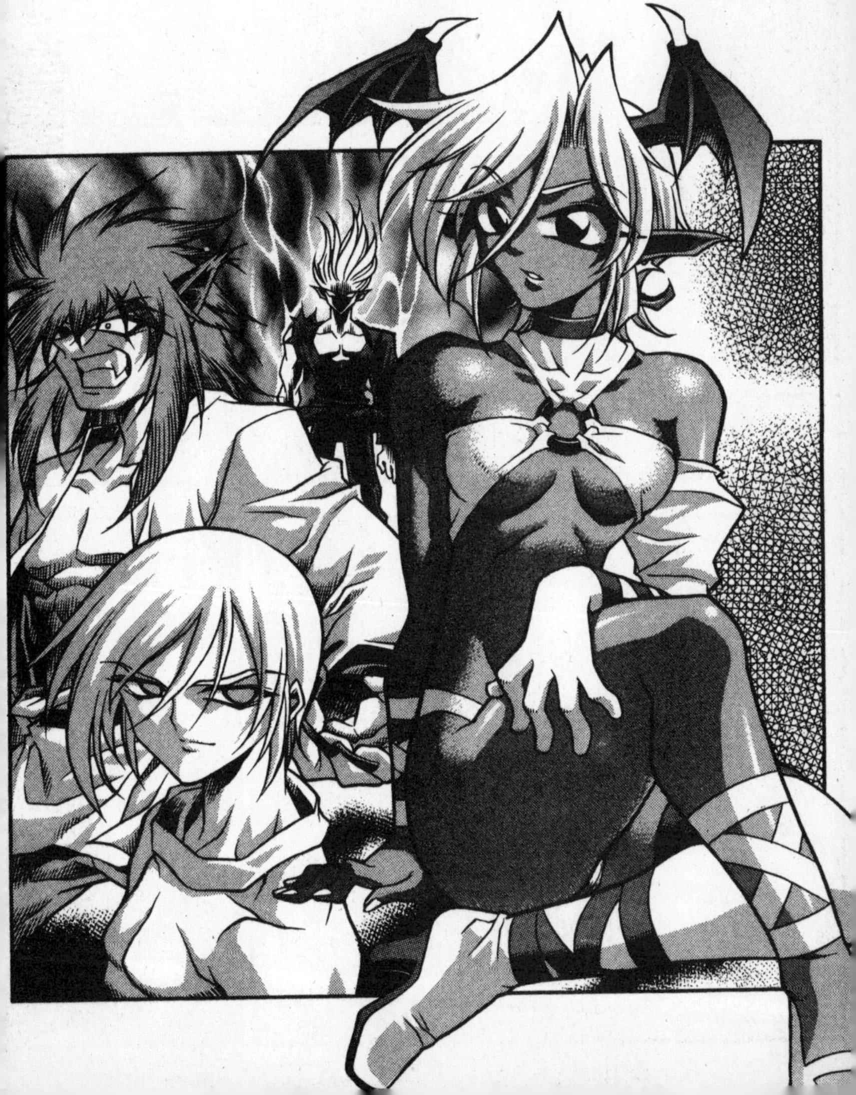

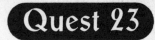

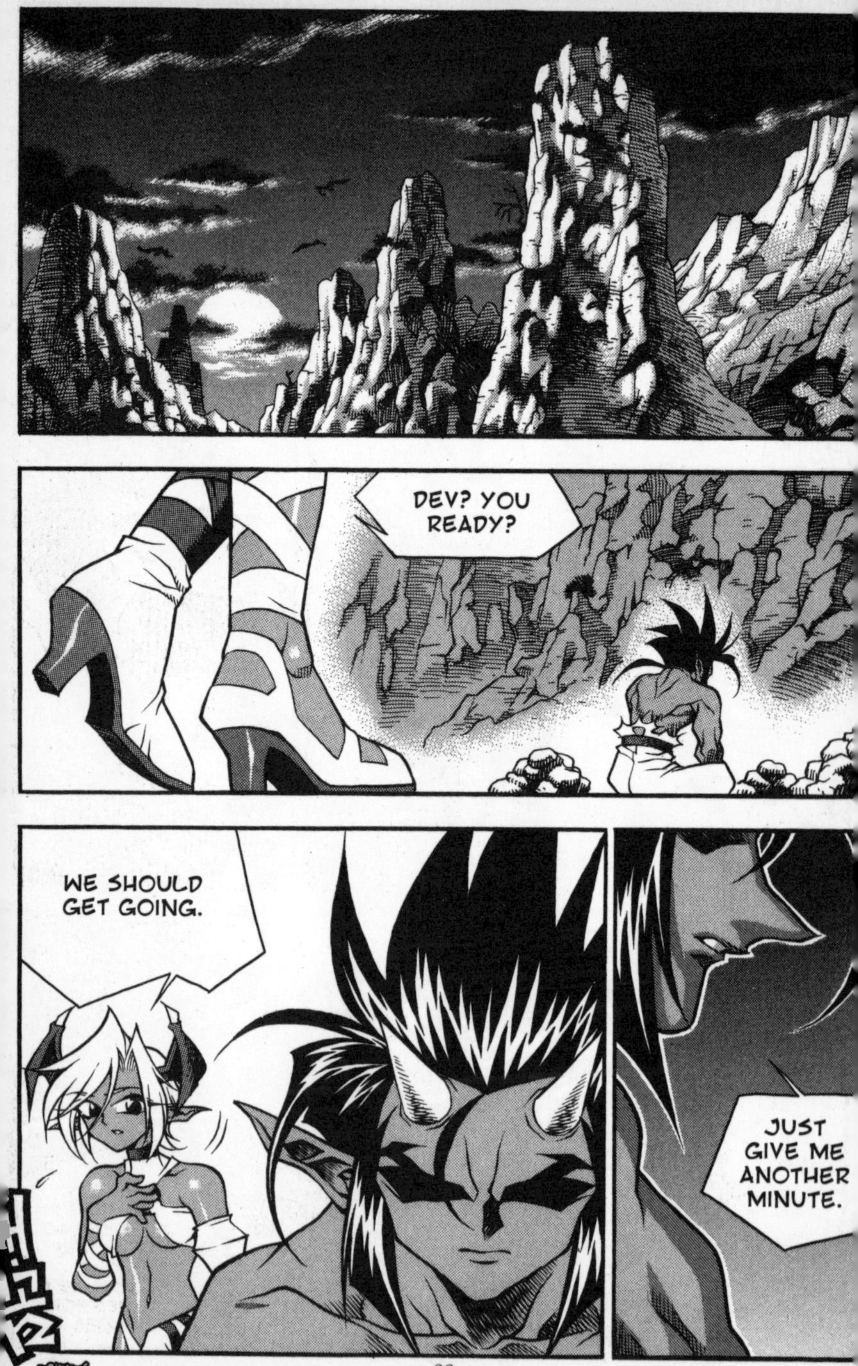
DEV? YOU READY?
WE SHOULD GET GOING.
JUST GIVE ME ANOTHER MINUTE.
nervous

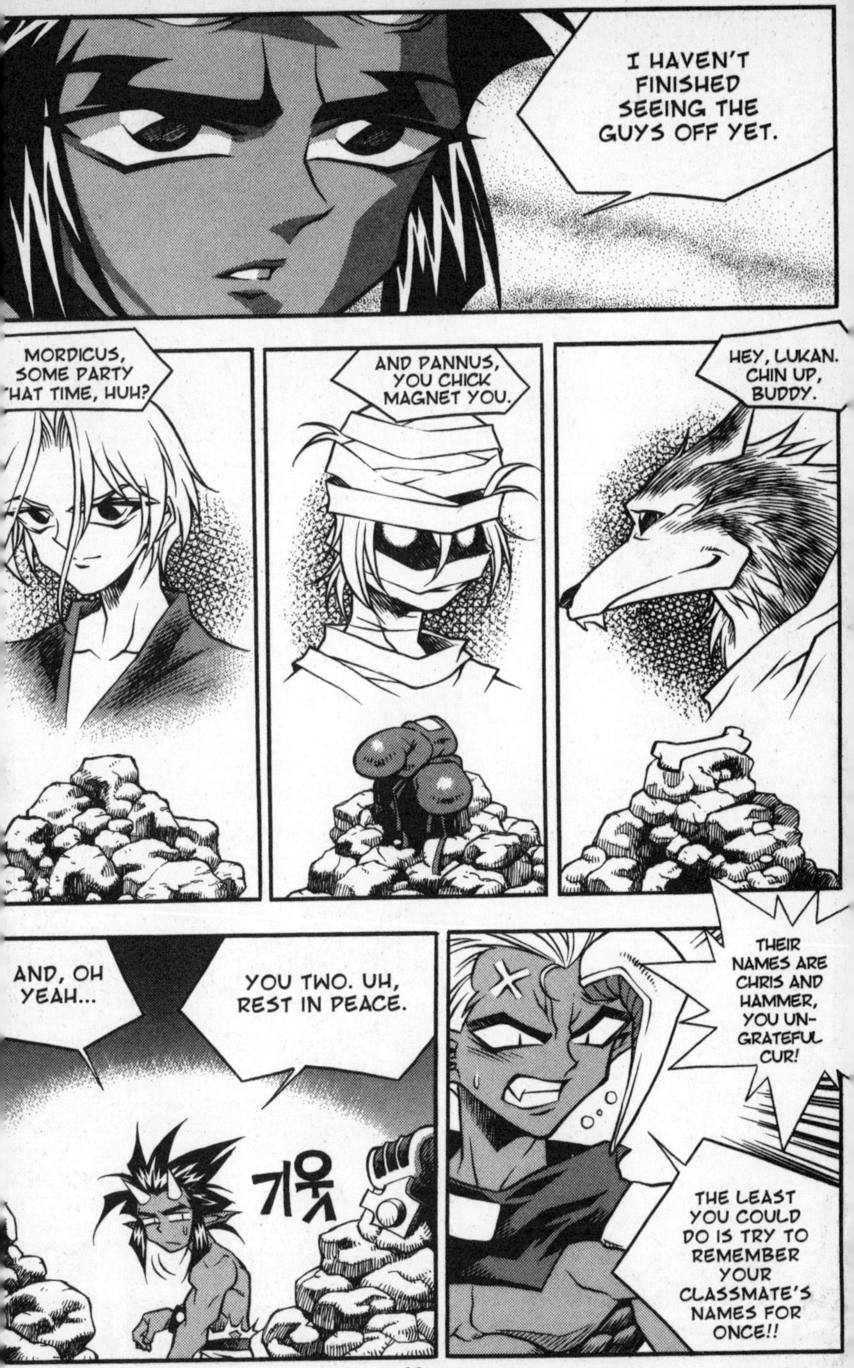
I HAVEN'T FINISHED SEEING THE GUYS OFF YET.
MORDICUS, SOME PARTY THAT TIME, HUH?
AND PANNUS, YOU CHICK MAGNET YOU.
HEY, LUKAN. CHIN UP, BUDDY.
AND, OH YEAH...
YOU TWO. UH, REST IN PEACE.
기우ㅅ
THEIR NAMES ARE CHRIS AND HAMMER, YOU UN-GRATEFUL CUR!
THE LEAST YOU COULD DO IS TRY TO REMEMBER YOUR CLASSMATE'S NAMES FOR ONCE!!

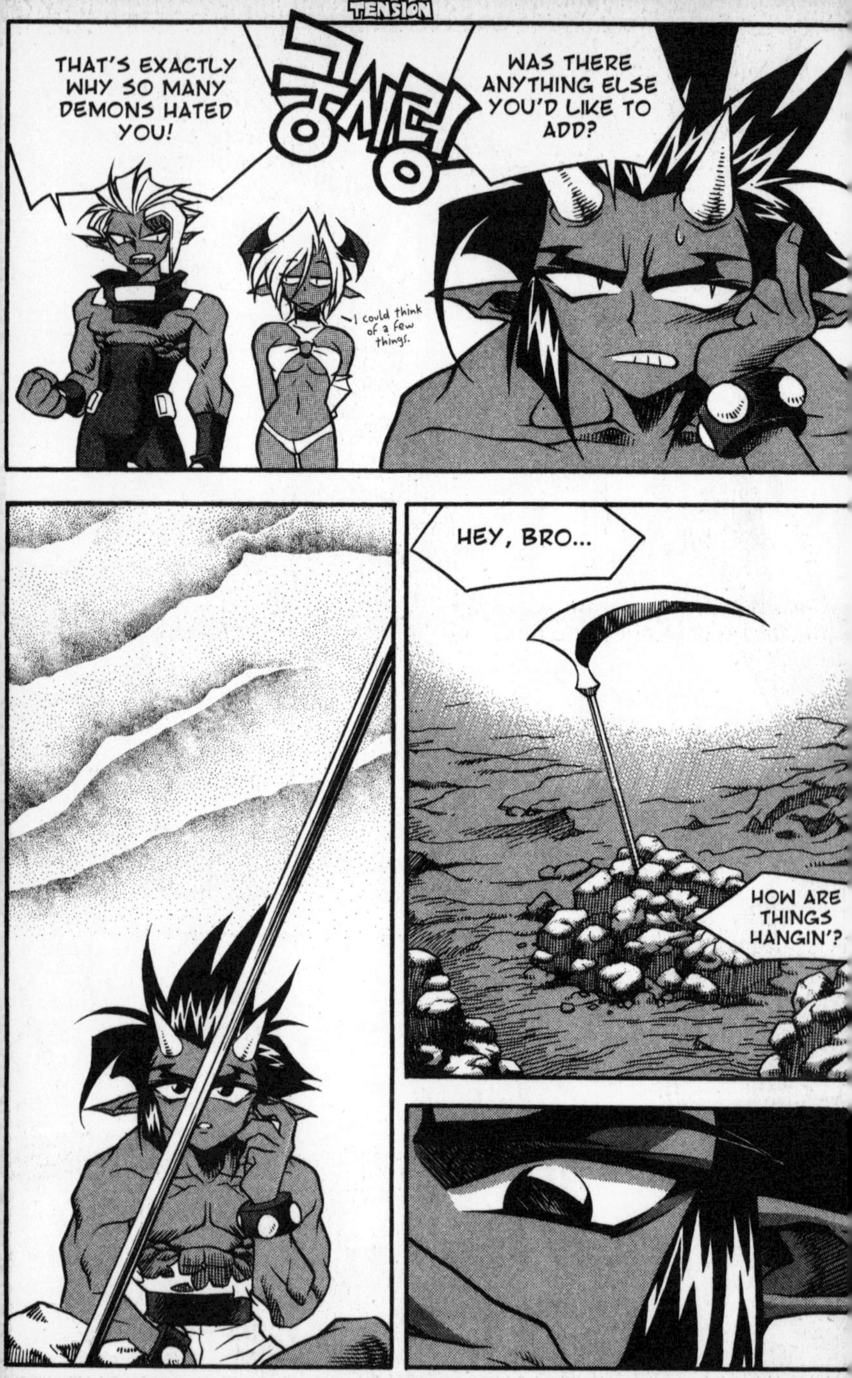
TENSION
THAT'S EXACTLY WHY SO MANY DEMONS HATED YOU!
I could think of a few things.
WAS THERE ANYTHING ELSE YOU'D LIKE TO ADD?
HEY, BRO...
HOW ARE THINGS HANGIN'?

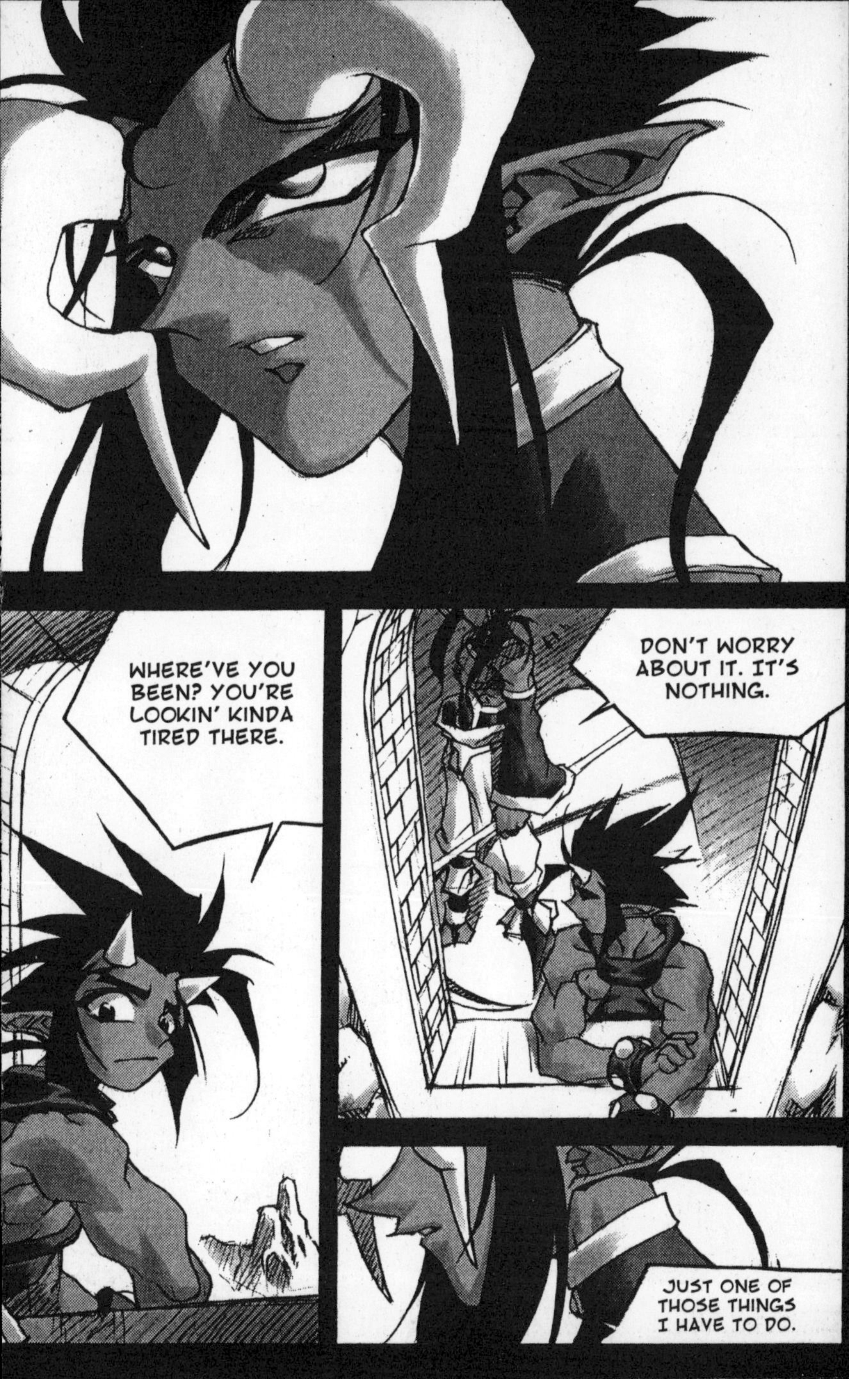
WHERE'VE YOU BEEN? YOU'RE LOOKIN' KINDA TIRED THERE.
DON'T WORRY ABOUT IT. IT'S NOTHING.
JUST ONE OF THOSE THINGS I HAVE TO DO.

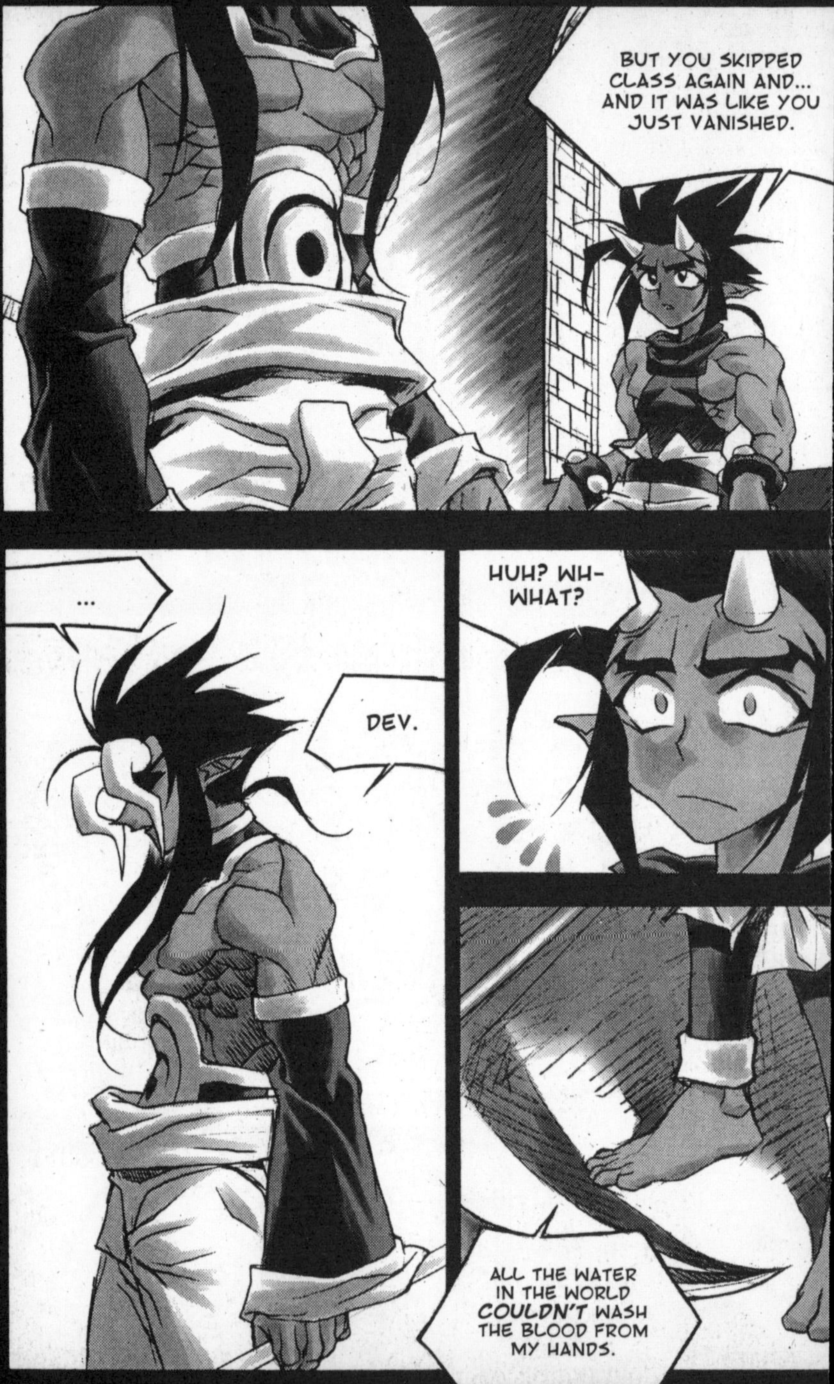
BUT YOU SKIPPED CLASS AGAIN AND... AND IT WAS LIKE YOU JUST VANISHED.
...
DEV.
HUH? WH- WHAT?
ALL THE WATER IN THE WORLD *COULDN'T* WASH THE BLOOD FROM MY HANDS.

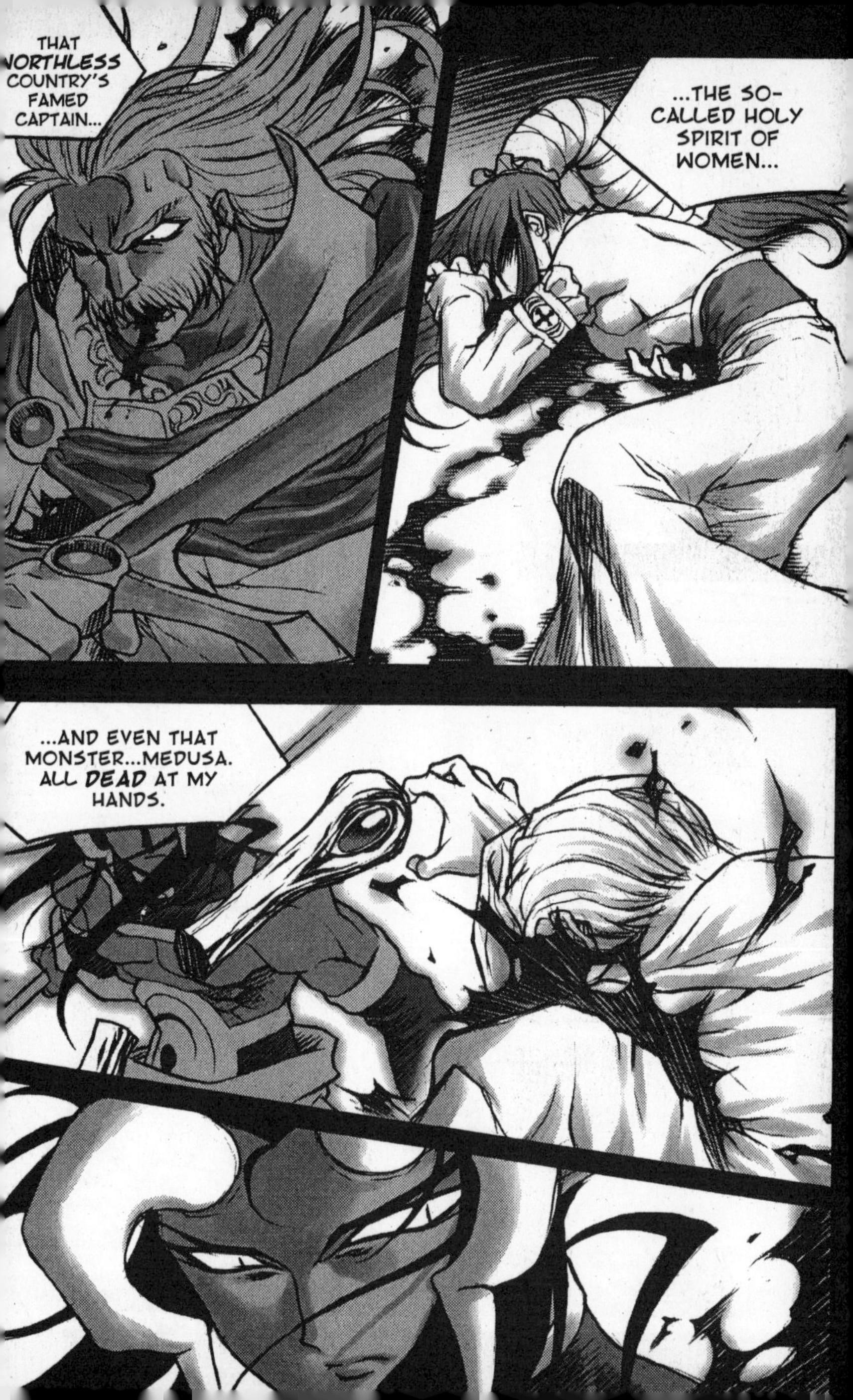
THAT WORTHLESS COUNTRY'S FAMED CAPTAIN...
...THE SO-CALLED HOLY SPIRIT OF WOMEN...
...AND EVEN THAT MONSTER...MEDUSA. ALL DEAD AT MY HANDS.

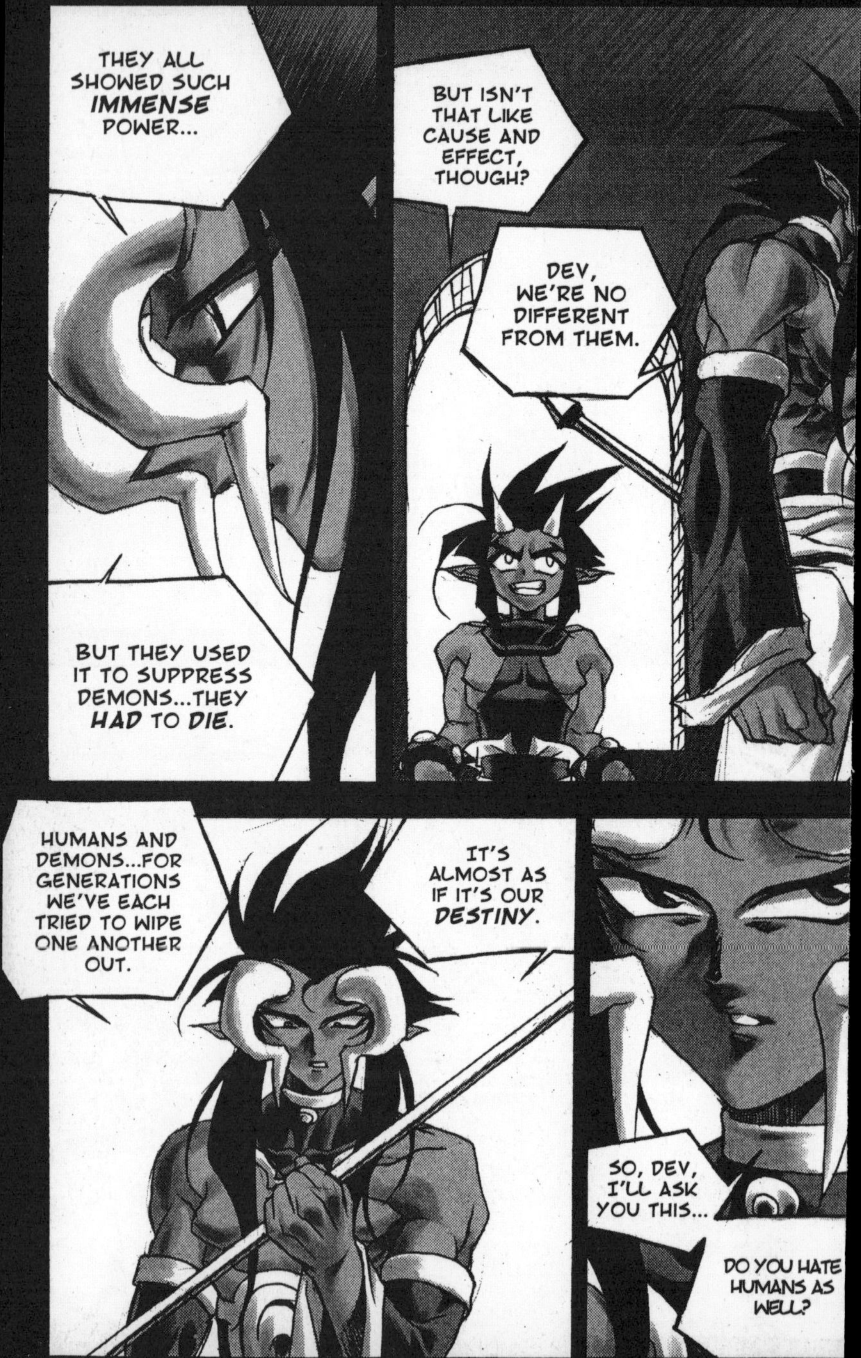
THEY ALL SHOWED SUCH IMMENSE POWER...
BUT THEY USED IT TO SUPPRESS DEMONS...THEY HAD TO DIE.
BUT ISN'T THAT LIKE CAUSE AND EFFECT, THOUGH?
DEV, WE'RE NO DIFFERENT FROM THEM.
HUMANS AND DEMONS...FOR GENERATIONS WE'VE EACH TRIED TO WIPE ONE ANOTHER OUT.
IT'S ALMOST AS IF IT'S OUR DESTINY.
SO, DEV, I'LL ASK YOU THIS...
DO YOU HATE HUMANS AS WELL?

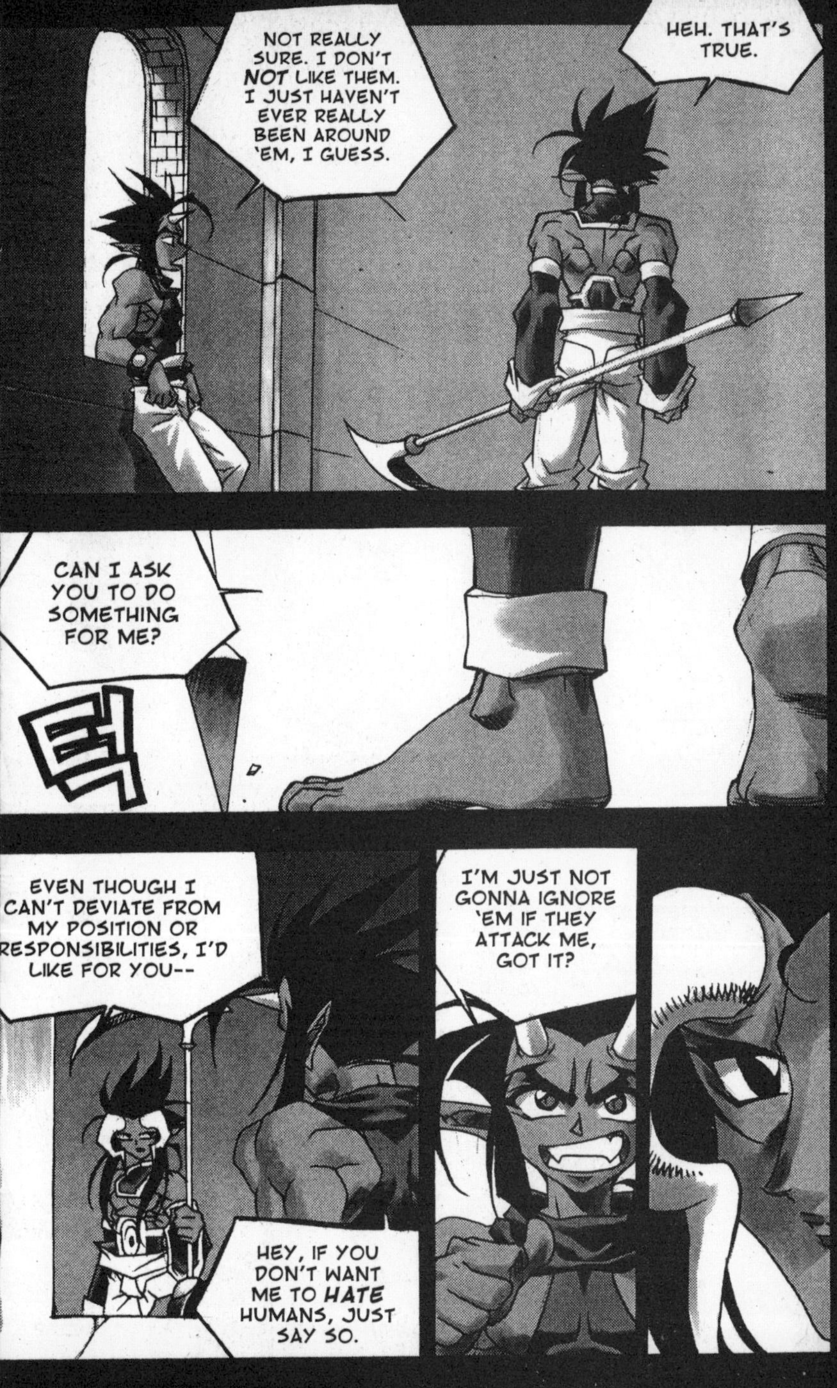
NOT REALLY SURE. I DON'T NOT LIKE THEM. I JUST HAVEN'T EVER REALLY BEEN AROUND 'EM, I GUESS.
HEH. THAT'S TRUE.
CAN I ASK YOU TO DO SOMETHING FOR ME?
EVEN THOUGH I CAN'T DEVIATE FROM MY POSITION OR RESPONSIBILITIES, I'D LIKE FOR YOU--
HEY, IF YOU DON'T WANT ME TO HATE HUMANS, JUST SAY SO.
I'M JUST NOT GONNA IGNORE 'EM IF THEY ATTACK ME, GOT IT?

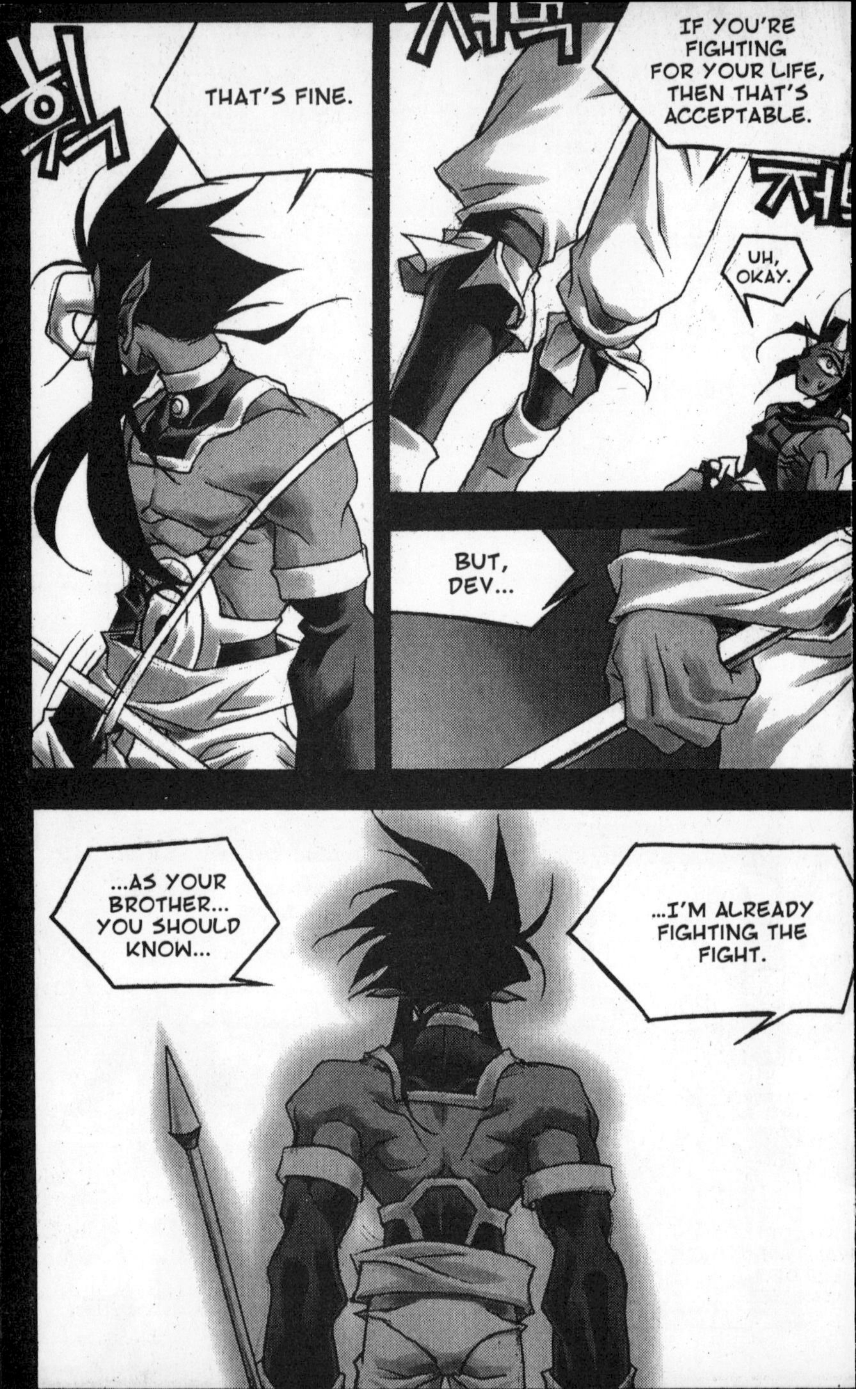
THAT'S FINE.
IF YOU'RE FIGHTING FOR YOUR LIFE, THEN THAT'S ACCEPTABLE.
UH, OKAY.
BUT, DEV...
...AS YOUR BROTHER... YOU SHOULD KNOW...
...I'M ALREADY FIGHTING THE FIGHT.

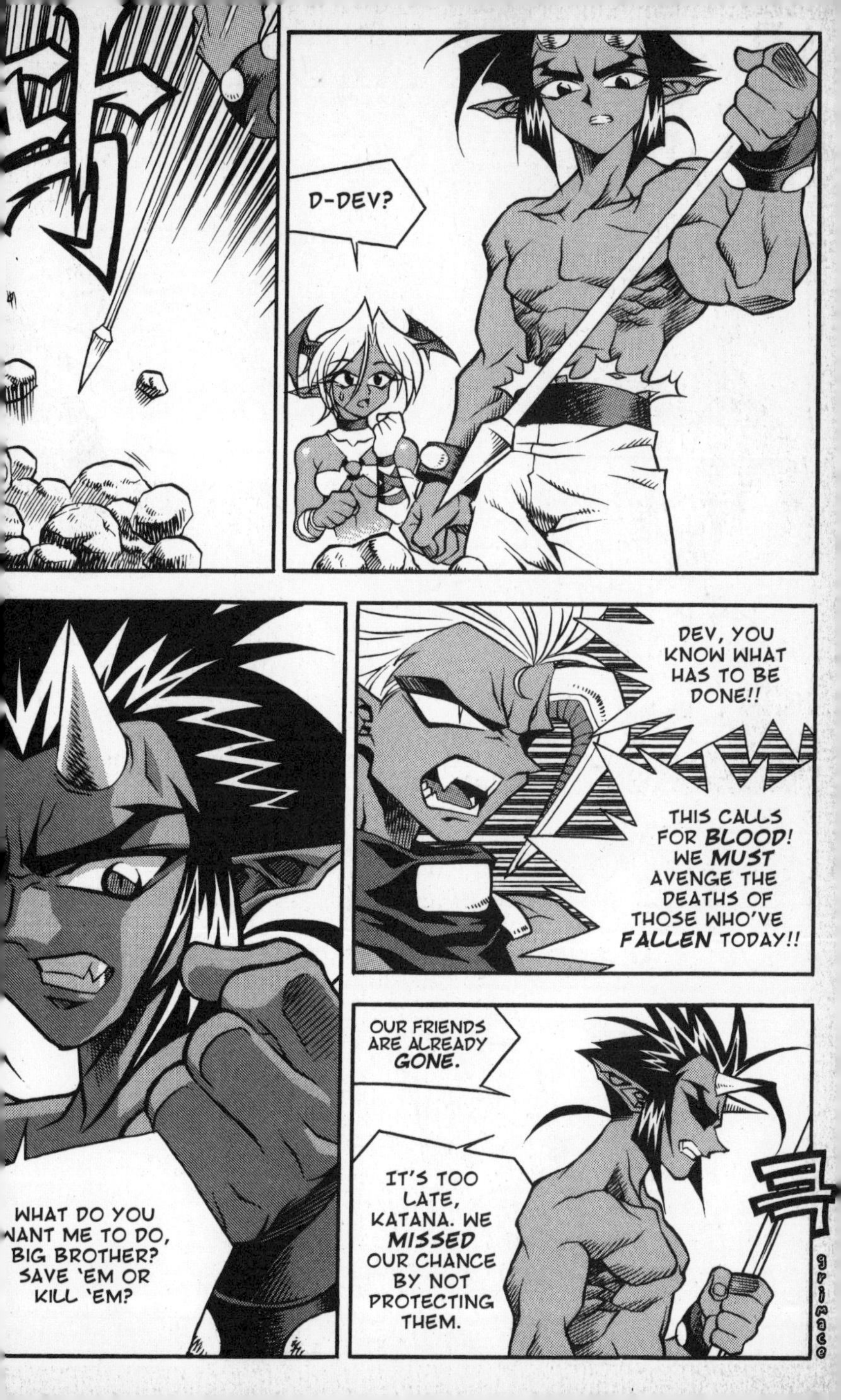

D-DEV?
WHAT DO YOU WANT ME TO DO, BIG BROTHER? SAVE 'EM OR KILL 'EM?
DEV, YOU KNOW WHAT HAS TO BE DONE!!
THIS CALLS FOR **BLOOD**! WE **MUST** AVENGE THE DEATHS OF THOSE WHO'VE **FALLEN** TODAY!!
OUR FRIENDS ARE ALREADY **GONE**.
IT'S TOO LATE, KATANA. WE **MISSED** OUR CHANCE BY NOT PROTECTING THEM.
grimace

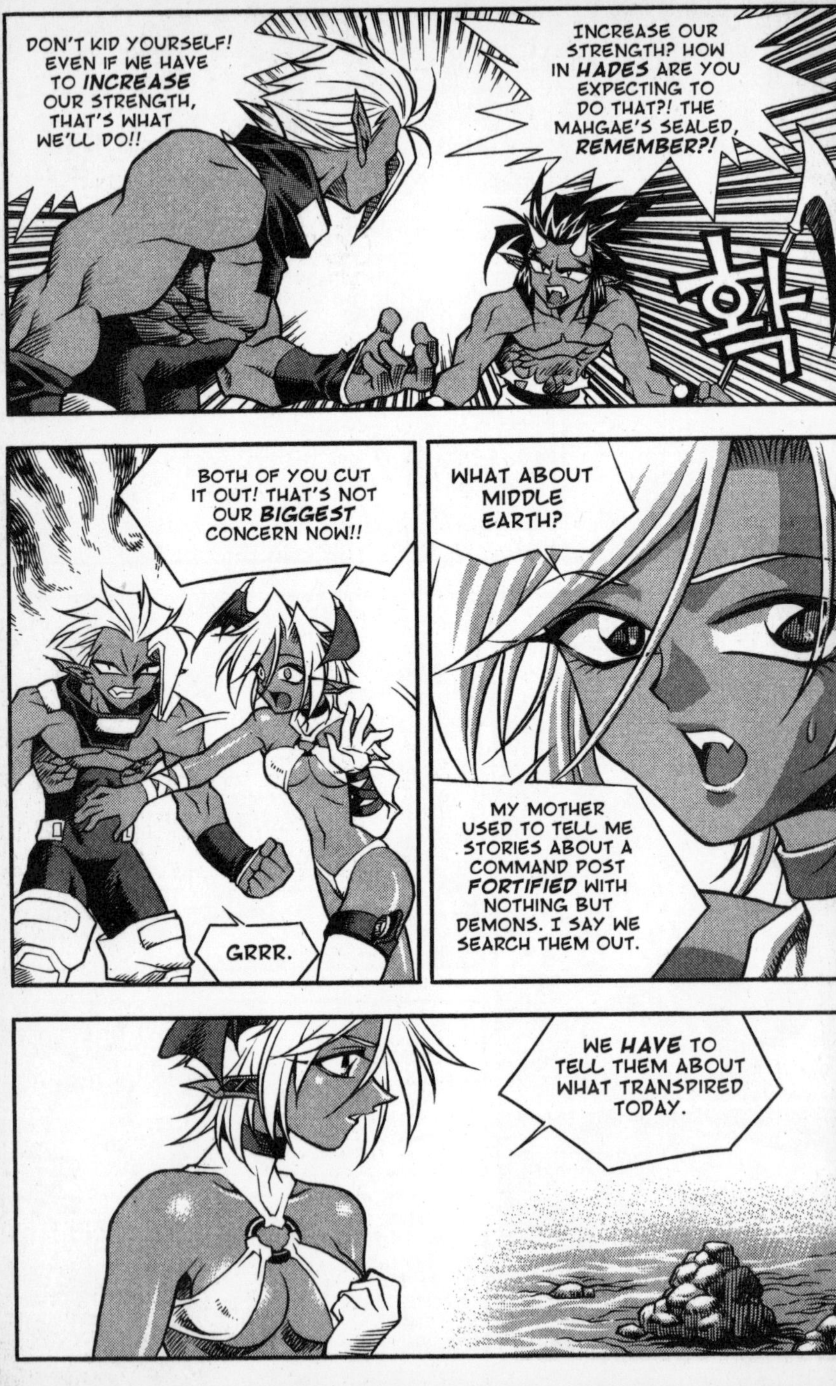
DON'T KID YOURSELF! EVEN IF WE HAVE TO *INCREASE* OUR STRENGTH, THAT'S WHAT WE'LL DO!!
INCREASE OUR STRENGTH? HOW IN *HADES* ARE YOU EXPECTING TO DO THAT?! THE MAHGAE'S SEALED, *REMEMBER?!*
BOTH OF YOU CUT IT OUT! THAT'S NOT OUR *BIGGEST* CONCERN NOW!!
GRRR.
WHAT ABOUT MIDDLE EARTH?
MY MOTHER USED TO TELL ME STORIES ABOUT A COMMAND POST *FORTIFIED* WITH NOTHING BUT DEMONS. I SAY WE SEARCH THEM OUT.
WE *HAVE* TO TELL THEM ABOUT WHAT TRANSPIRED TODAY.

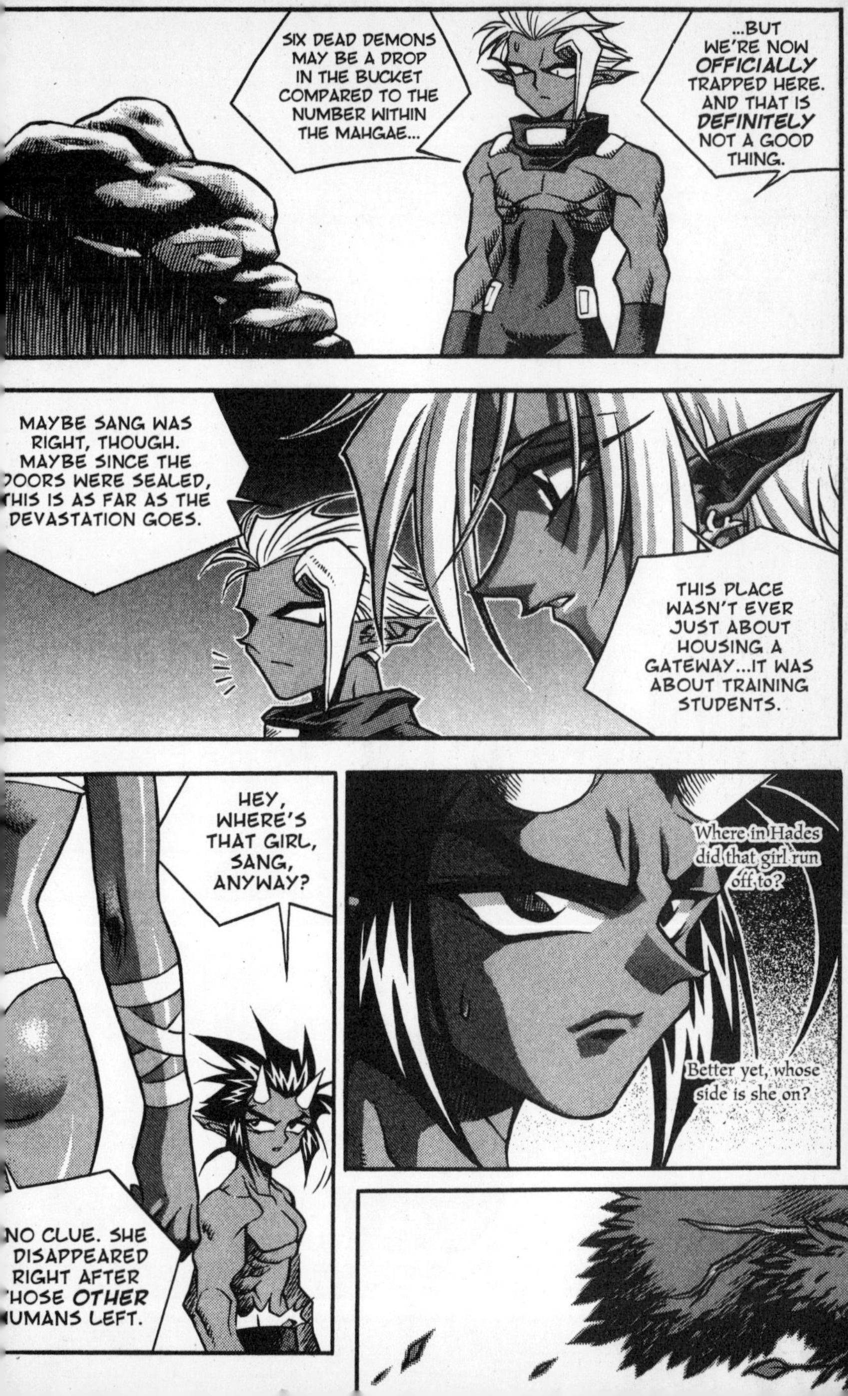
SIX DEAD DEMONS MAY BE A DROP IN THE BUCKET COMPARED TO THE NUMBER WITHIN THE MAHGAE...
...BUT WE'RE NOW *OFFICIALLY* TRAPPED HERE. AND THAT IS *DEFINITELY* NOT A GOOD THING.
MAYBE SANG WAS RIGHT, THOUGH. MAYBE SINCE THE OORS WERE SEALED, THIS IS AS FAR AS THE DEVASTATION GOES.
THIS PLACE WASN'T EVER JUST ABOUT HOUSING A GATEWAY...IT WAS ABOUT TRAINING STUDENTS.
HEY, WHERE'S THAT GIRL, SANG, ANYWAY?
NO CLUE. SHE DISAPPEARED RIGHT AFTER HOSE *OTHER* UMANS LEFT.
Where in Hades did that girl run off to?
Better yet, whose side is she on?

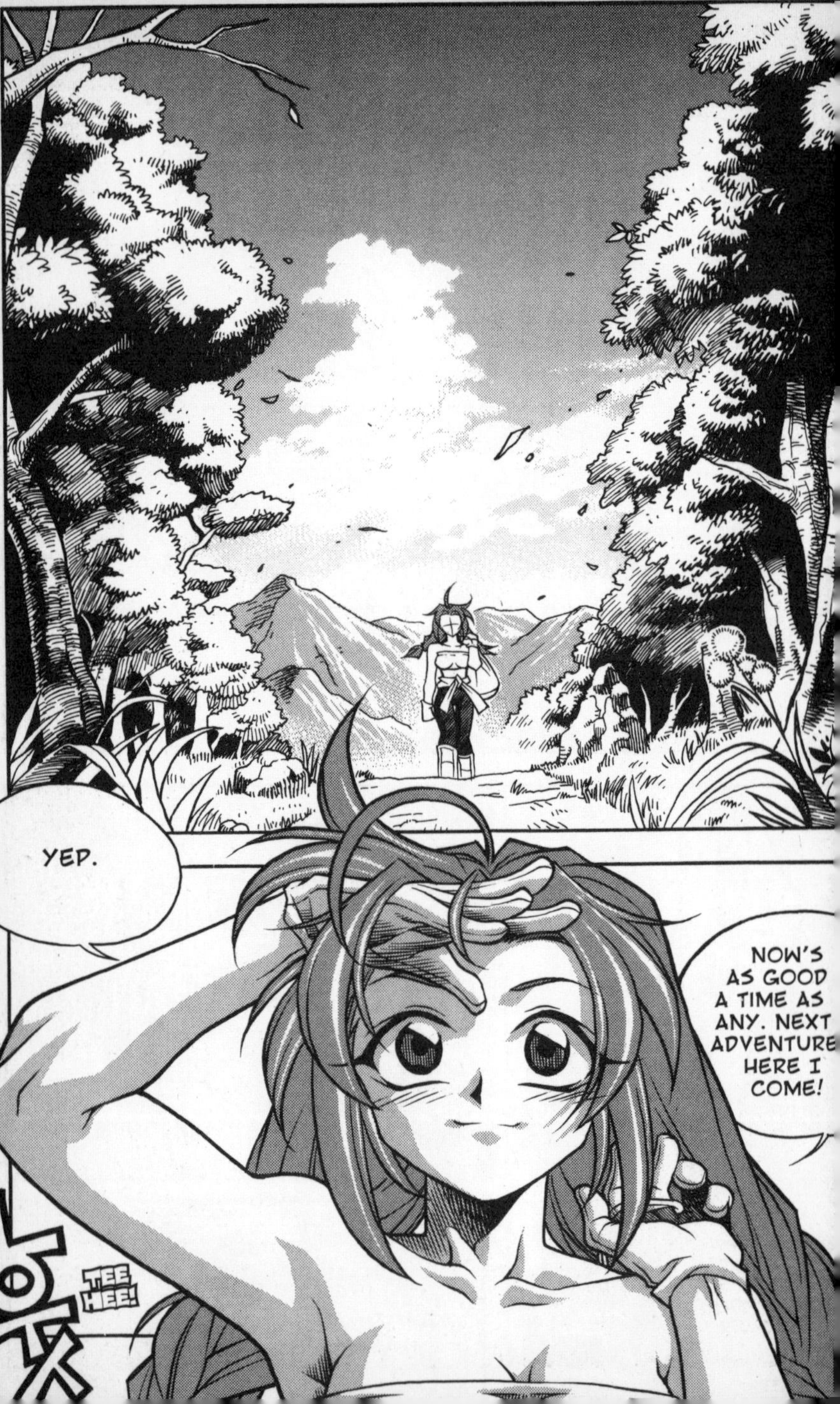
YEP.
NOW'S AS GOOD A TIME AS ANY. NEXT ADVENTURE HERE I COME!
TEE HEE!

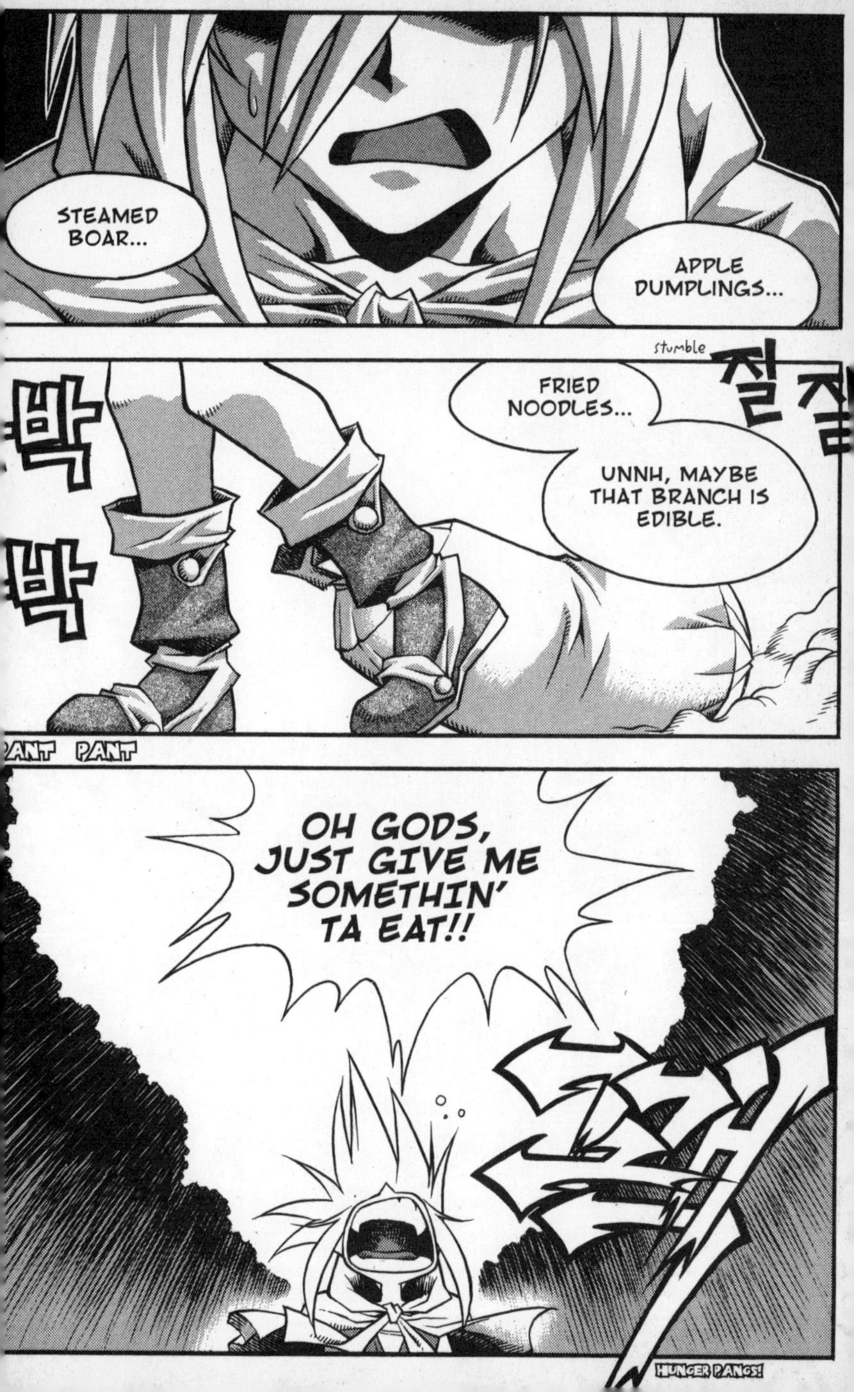

STEAMED BOAR...
APPLE DUMPLINGS...
박
박
FRIED NOODLES...
stumble
절 절
UNNH, MAYBE THAT BRANCH IS EDIBLE.
PANT PANT
OH GODS, JUST GIVE ME SOMETHIN' TA EAT!!
HUNGER PANGS!

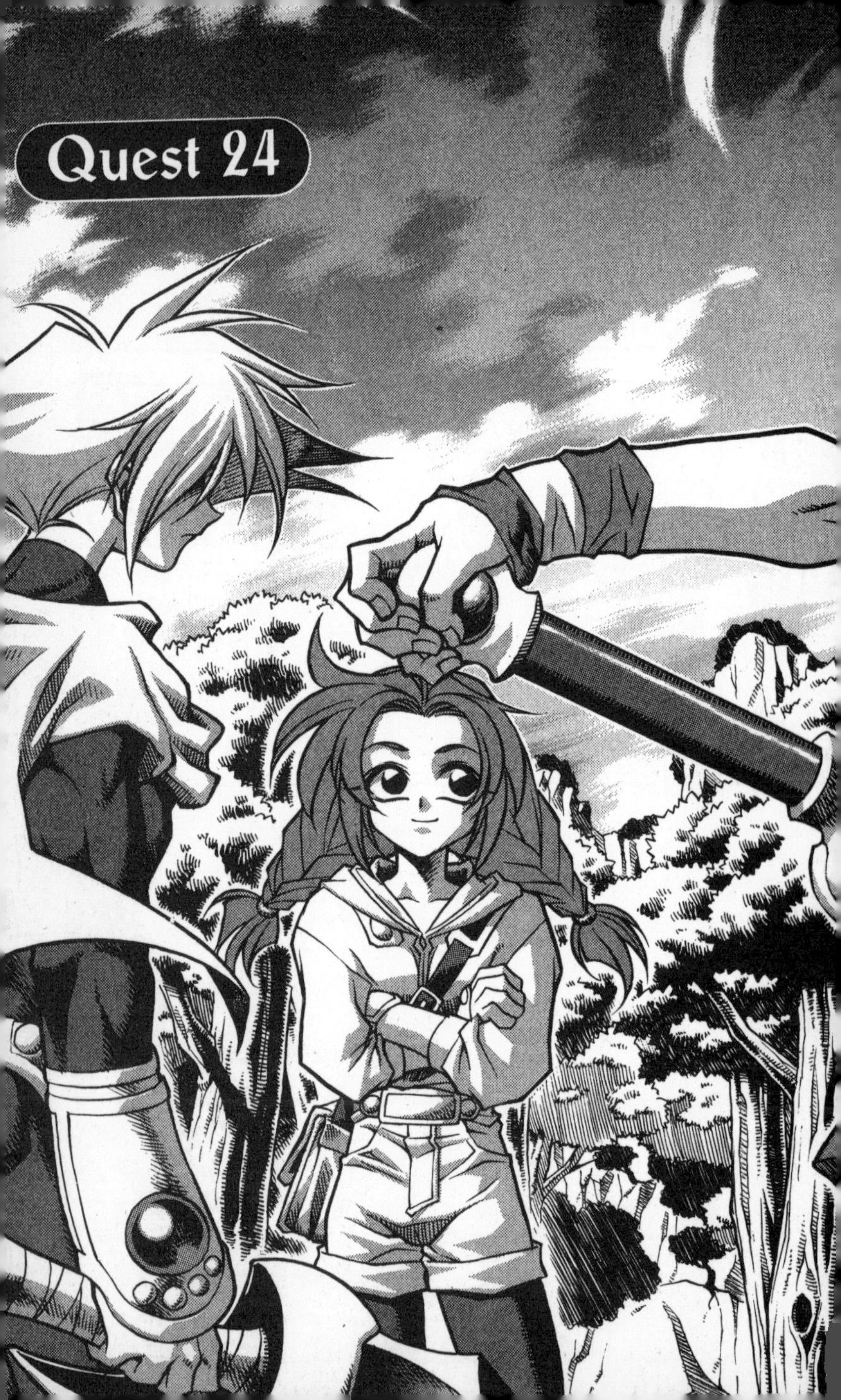
Quest 24

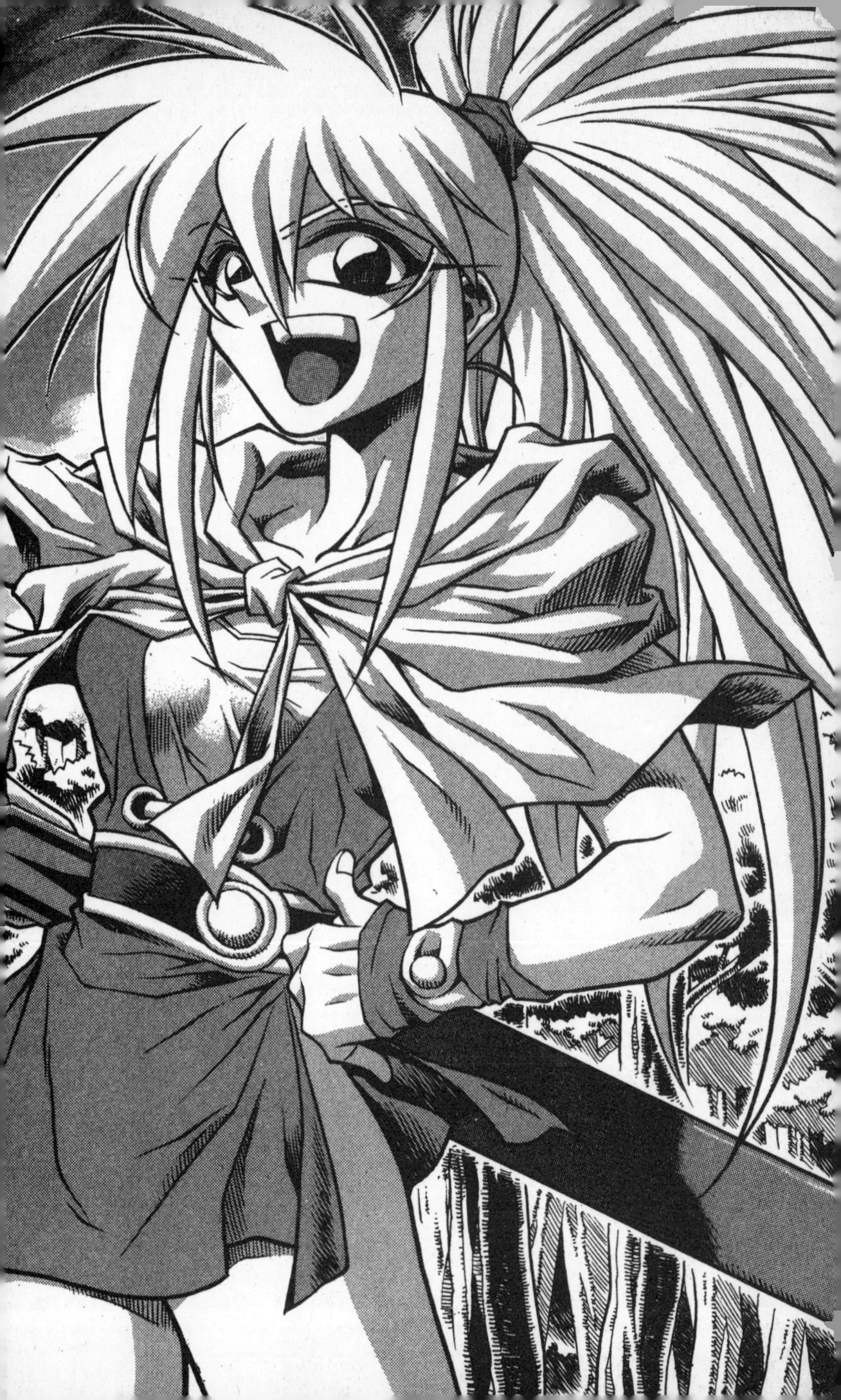

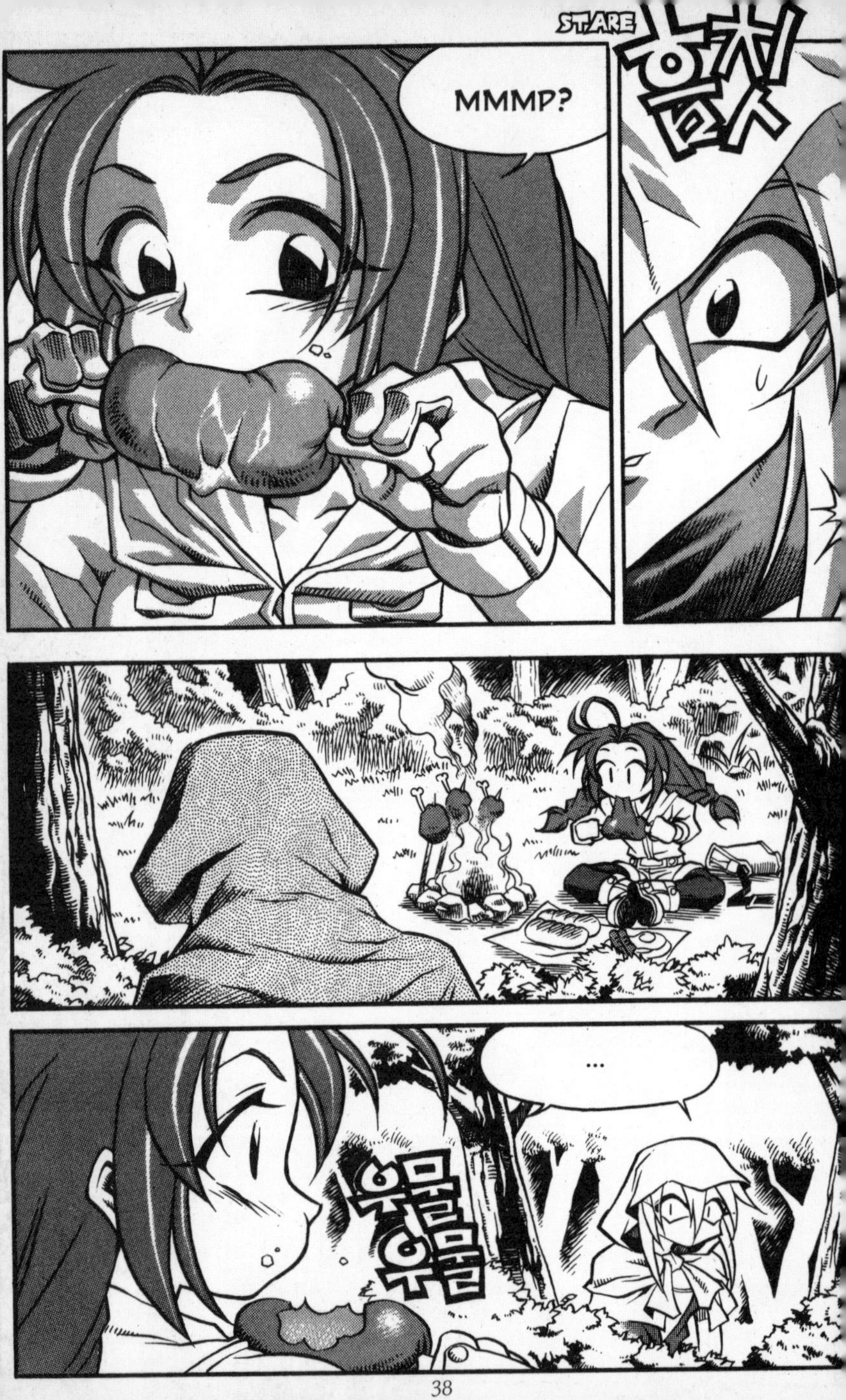
MMMP?
STARE
...

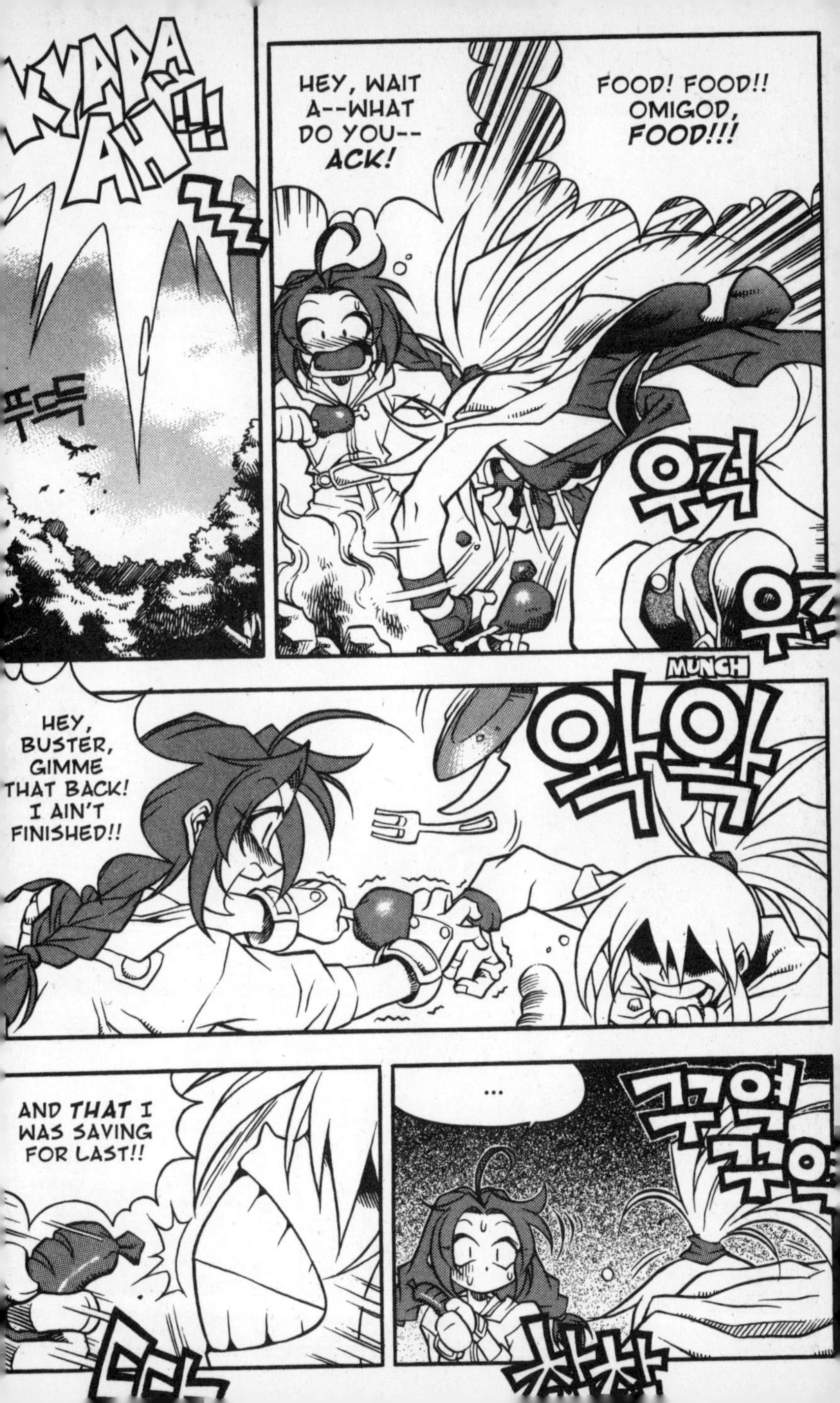
KYAPAAAH!!!
HEY, WAIT A--WHAT DO YOU-- ACK!
FOOD! FOOD!! OMIGOD, FOOD!!!
HEY, BUSTER, GIMME THAT BACK! I AIN'T FINISHED!!
MUNCH
AND THAT I WAS SAVING FOR LAST!!
...

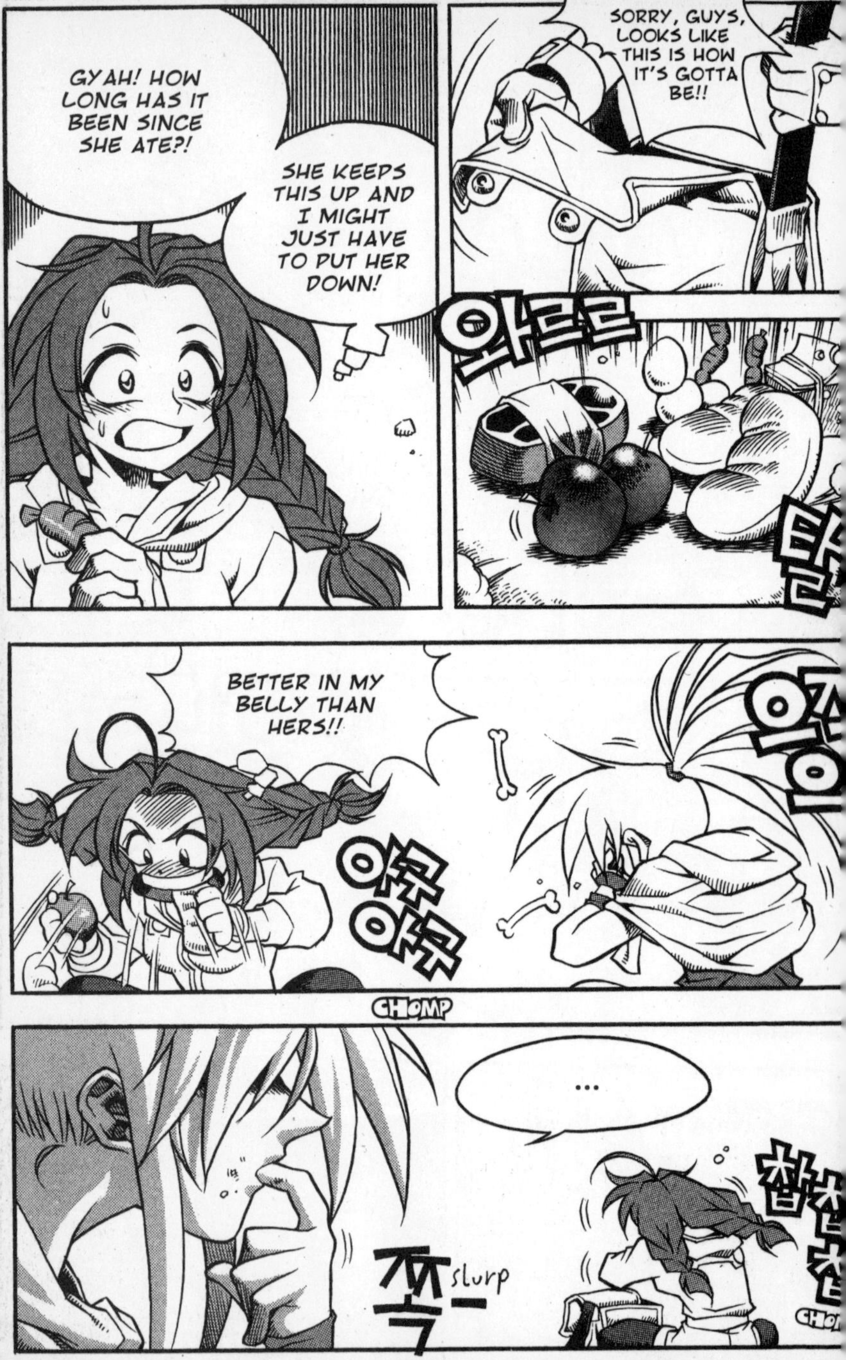
GYAH! HOW LONG HAS IT BEEN SINCE SHE ATE?!
SHE KEEPS THIS UP AND I MIGHT JUST HAVE TO PUT HER DOWN!
SORRY, GUYS, LOOKS LIKE THIS IS HOW IT'S GOTTA BE!!
와르르
BETTER IN MY BELLY THAN HERS!!
와구 와구
CHOMP
...
slurp

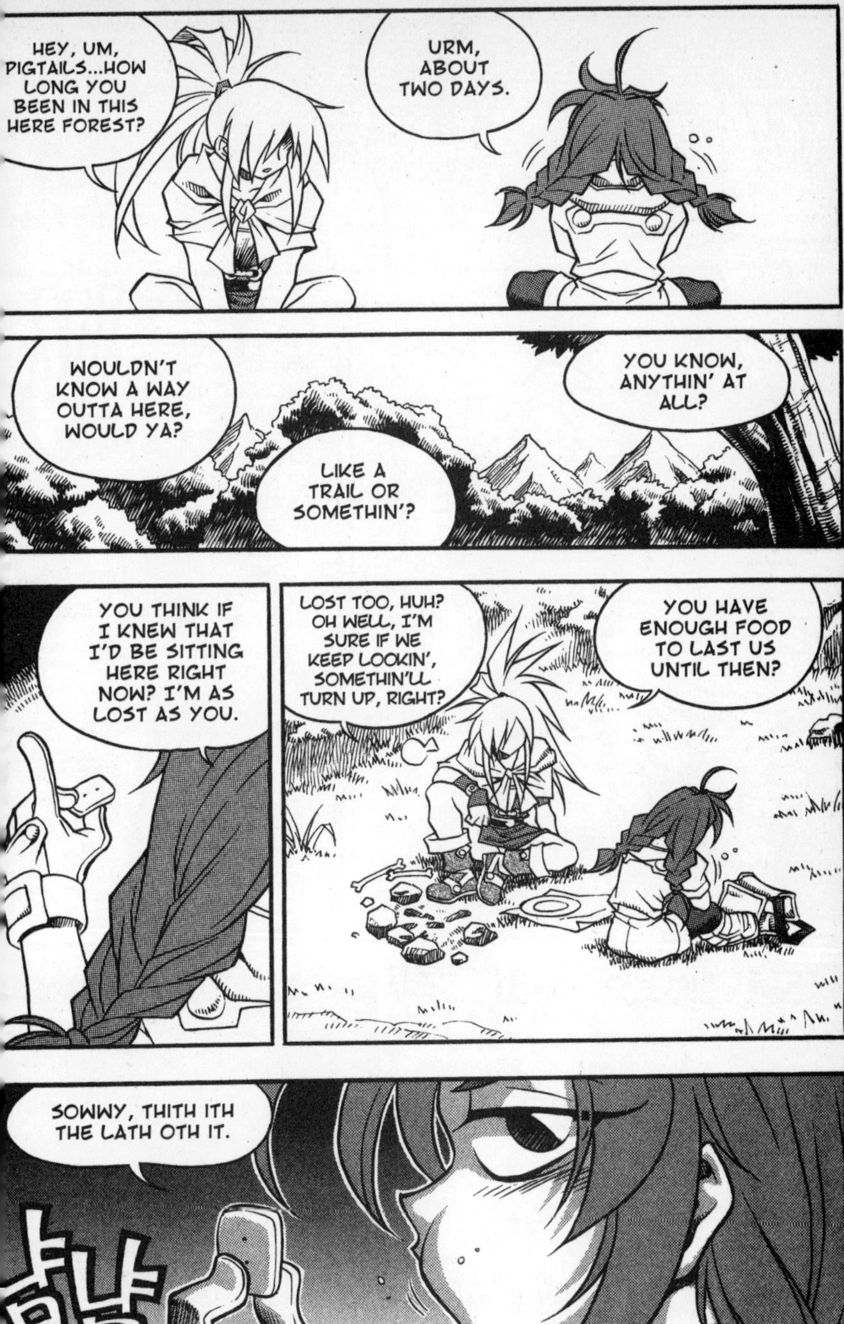
HEY, UM, PIGTAILS...HOW LONG YOU BEEN IN THIS HERE FOREST?
URM, ABOUT TWO DAYS.
WOULDN'T KNOW A WAY OUTTA HERE, WOULD YA?
LIKE A TRAIL OR SOMETHIN'?
YOU KNOW, ANYTHIN' AT ALL?
YOU THINK IF I KNEW THAT I'D BE SITTING HERE RIGHT NOW? I'M AS LOST AS YOU.
LOST TOO, HUH? OH WELL, I'M SURE IF WE KEEP LOOKIN', SOMETHIN'LL TURN UP, RIGHT?
YOU HAVE ENOUGH FOOD TO LAST US UNTIL THEN?
SOWWY, THITH ITH THE LATH OTH IT.
MNNCH MNNCH

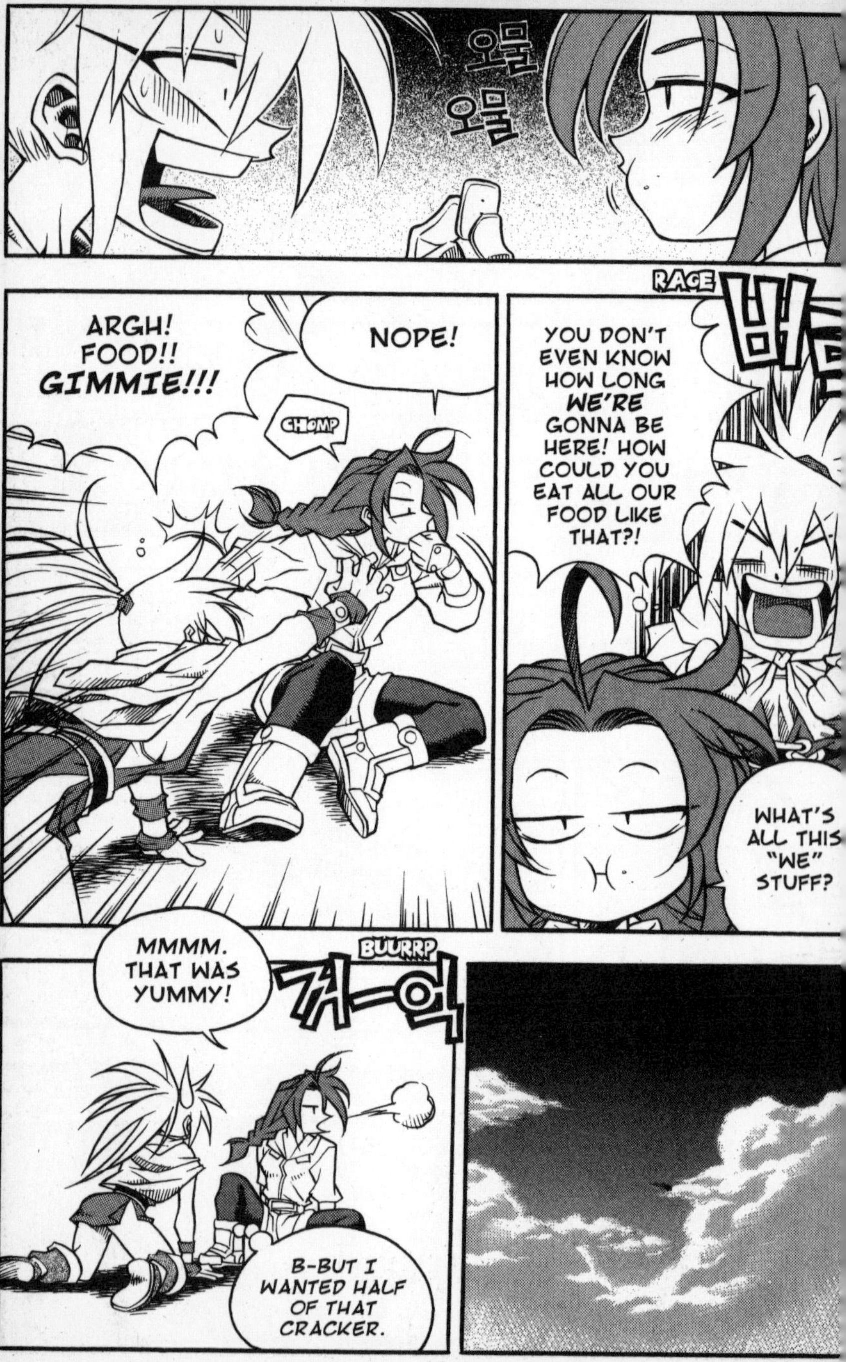
오물
오물
ARGH! FOOD!! GIMMIE!!!
NOPE!
CHOMP
RAGE
YOU DON'T EVEN KNOW HOW LONG WE'RE GONNA BE HERE! HOW COULD YOU EAT ALL OUR FOOD LIKE THAT?!
WHAT'S ALL THIS "WE" STUFF?
MMMM. THAT WAS YUMMY!
BUURRP
꺼-억
B-BUT I WANTED HALF OF THAT CRACKER.

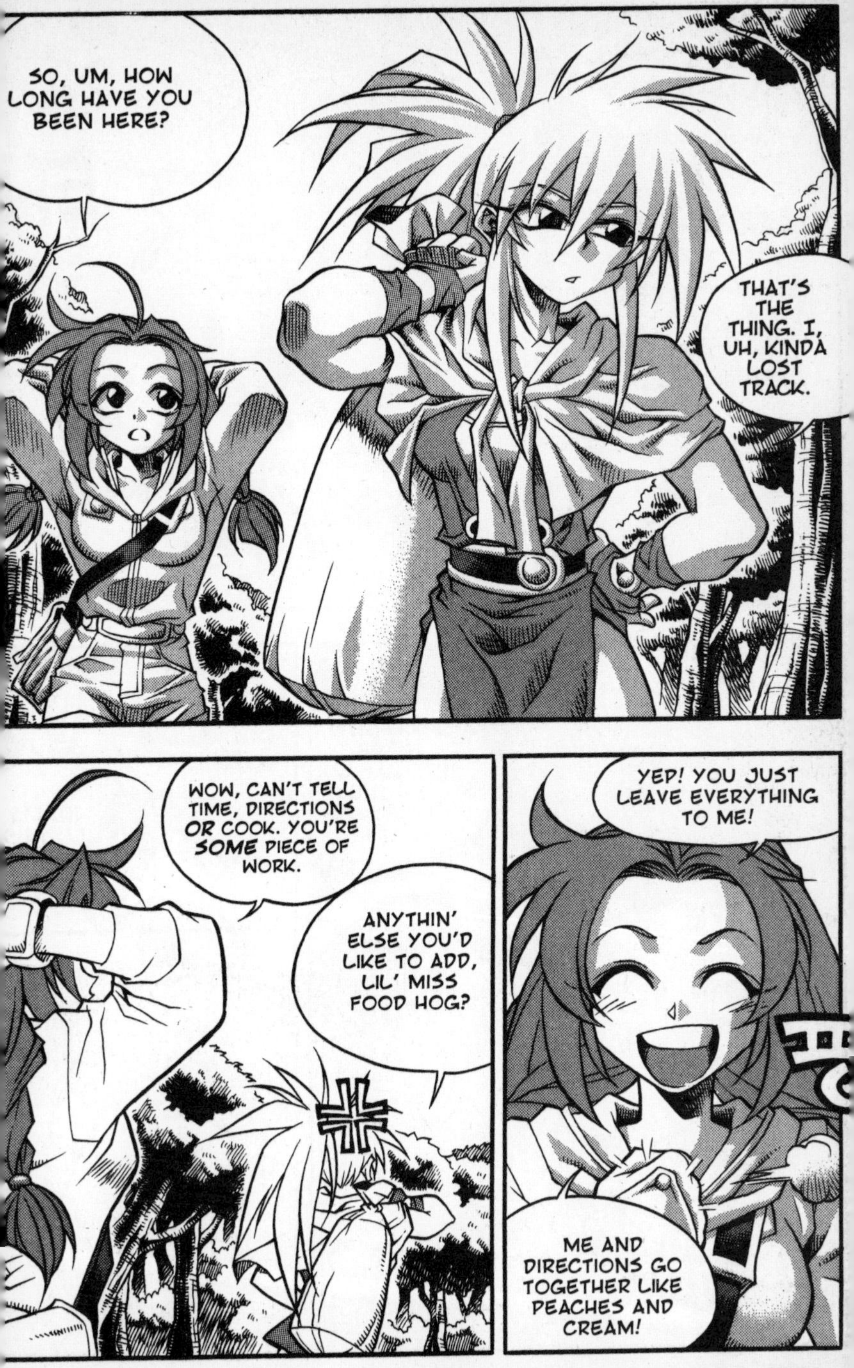
SO, UM, HOW LONG HAVE YOU BEEN HERE?
THAT'S THE THING. I, UH, KINDA LOST TRACK.
WOW, CAN'T TELL TIME, DIRECTIONS OR COOK. YOU'RE SOME PIECE OF WORK.
ANYTHIN' ELSE YOU'D LIKE TO ADD, LIL' MISS FOOD HOG?
YEP! YOU JUST LEAVE EVERYTHING TO ME!
ME AND DIRECTIONS GO TOGETHER LIKE PEACHES AND CREAM!

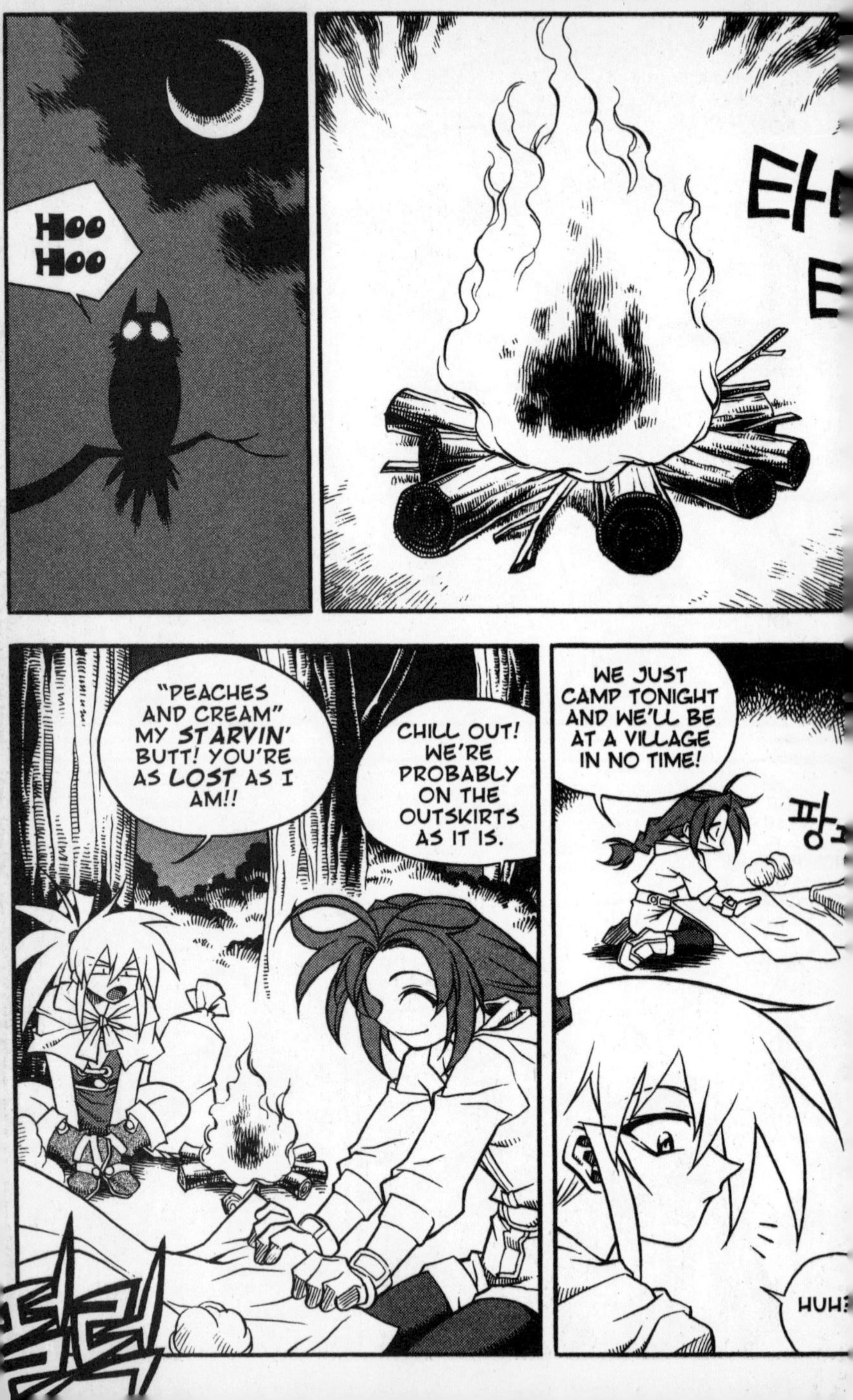
HOO HOO
"PEACHES AND CREAM" MY STARVIN' BUTT! YOU'RE AS LOST AS I AM!!
CHILL OUT! WE'RE PROBABLY ON THE OUTSKIRTS AS IT IS.
WE JUST CAMP TONIGHT AND WE'LL BE AT A VILLAGE IN NO TIME!
HUH?

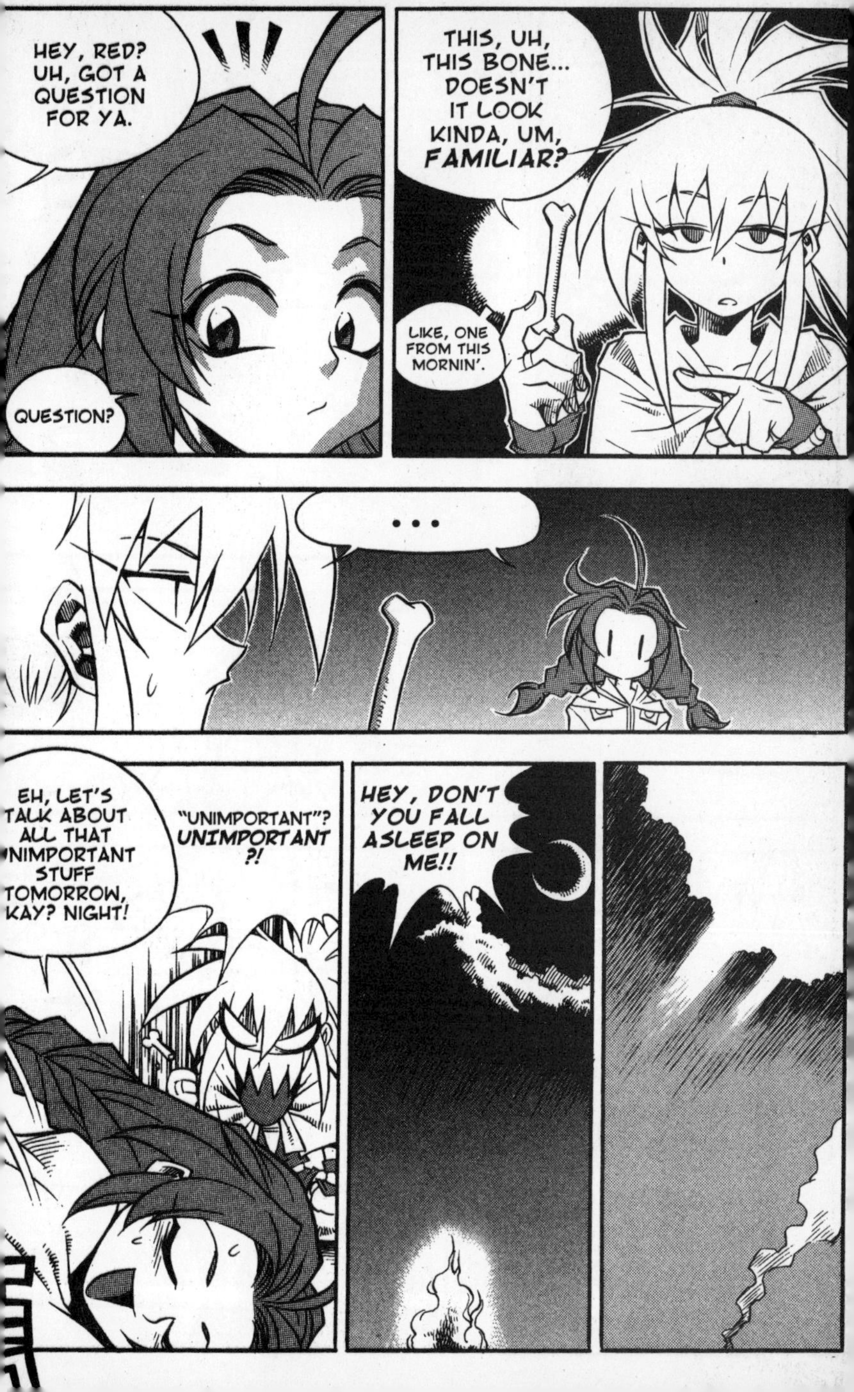

HEY, RED? UH, GOT A QUESTION FOR YA.
QUESTION?
THIS, UH, THIS BONE... DOESN'T IT LOOK KINDA, UM, FAMILIAR?
LIKE, ONE FROM THIS MORNIN'.
...
EH, LET'S TALK ABOUT ALL THAT UNIMPORTANT STUFF TOMORROW, KAY? NIGHT!
"UNIMPORTANT"? UNIMPORTANT?!
HEY, DON'T YOU FALL ASLEEP ON ME!!

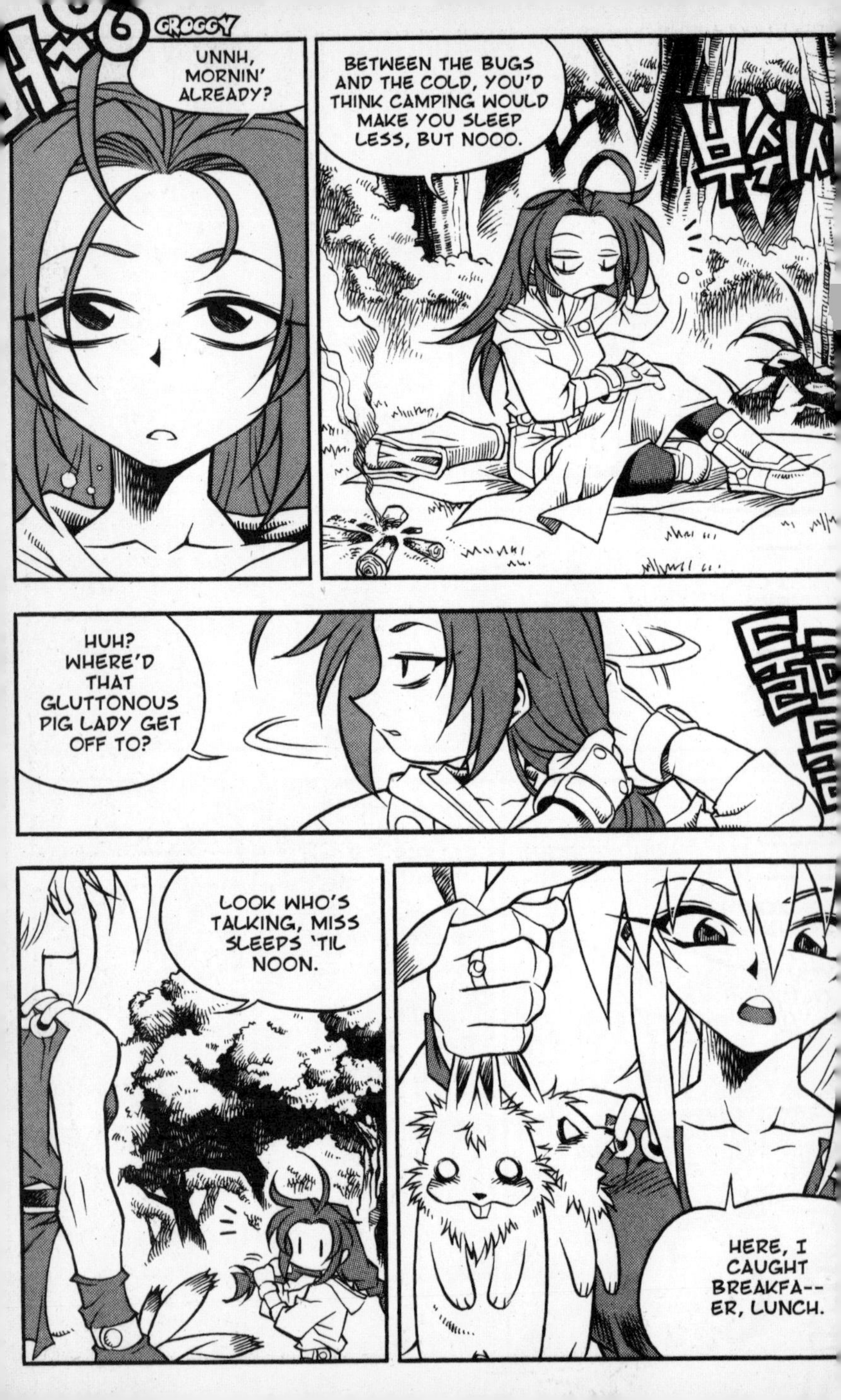
GROGGY
UNNH, MORNIN' ALREADY?
BETWEEN THE BUGS AND THE COLD, YOU'D THINK CAMPING WOULD MAKE YOU SLEEP LESS, BUT NOOO.
HUH? WHERE'D THAT GLUTTONOUS PIG LADY GET OFF TO?
LOOK WHO'S TALKING, MISS SLEEPS 'TIL NOON.
HERE, I CAUGHT BREAKFA-- ER, LUNCH.

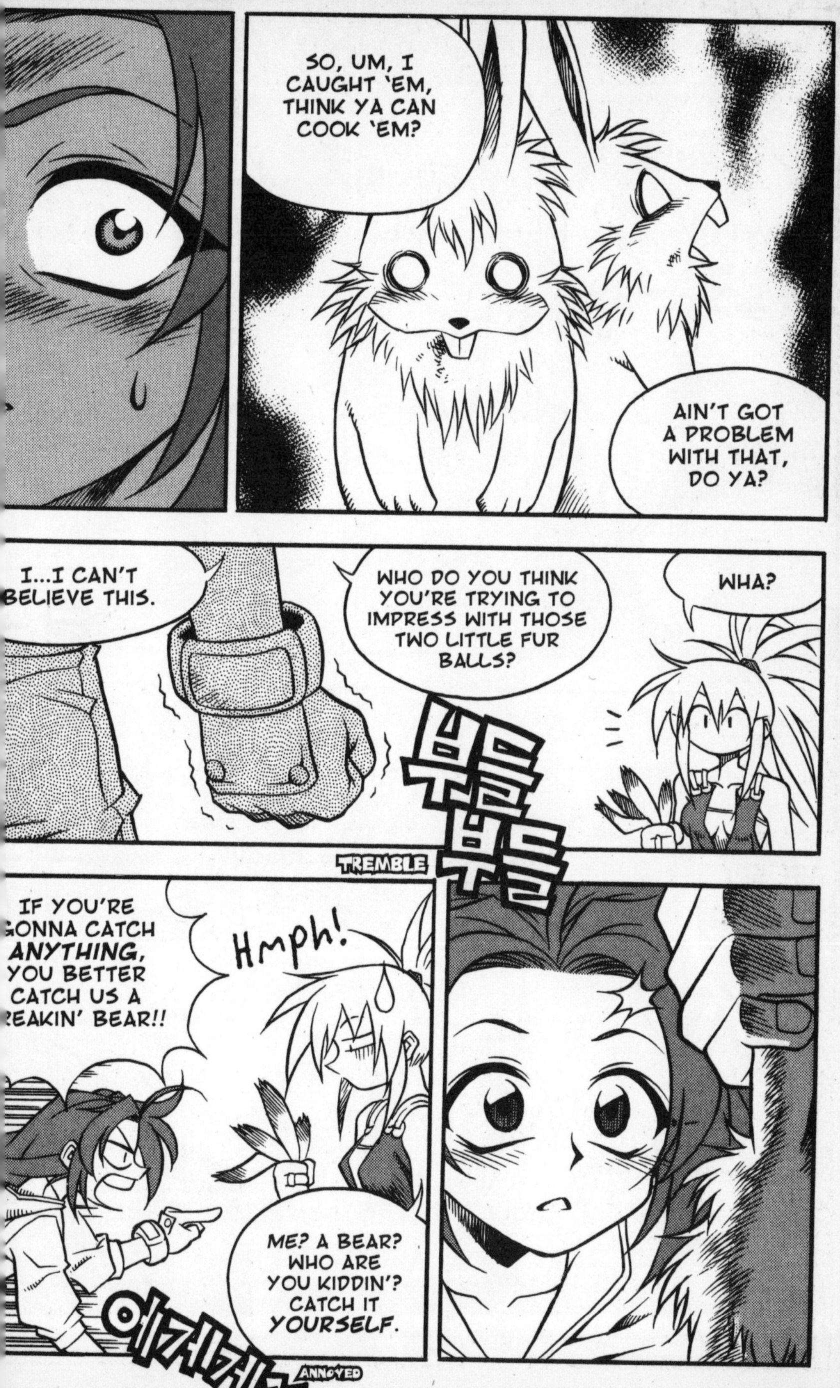

SO, UM, I CAUGHT 'EM, THINK YA CAN COOK 'EM?
AIN'T GOT A PROBLEM WITH THAT, DO YA?
I...I CAN'T BELIEVE THIS.
WHO DO YOU THINK YOU'RE TRYING TO IMPRESS WITH THOSE TWO LITTLE FUR BALLS?
WHA?
부들부들
TREMBLE
IF YOU'RE GONNA CATCH ANYTHING, YOU BETTER CATCH US A REAKIN' BEAR!!
Hmph!
ME? A BEAR? WHO ARE YOU KIDDIN'? CATCH IT YOURSELF.
ANNOYED

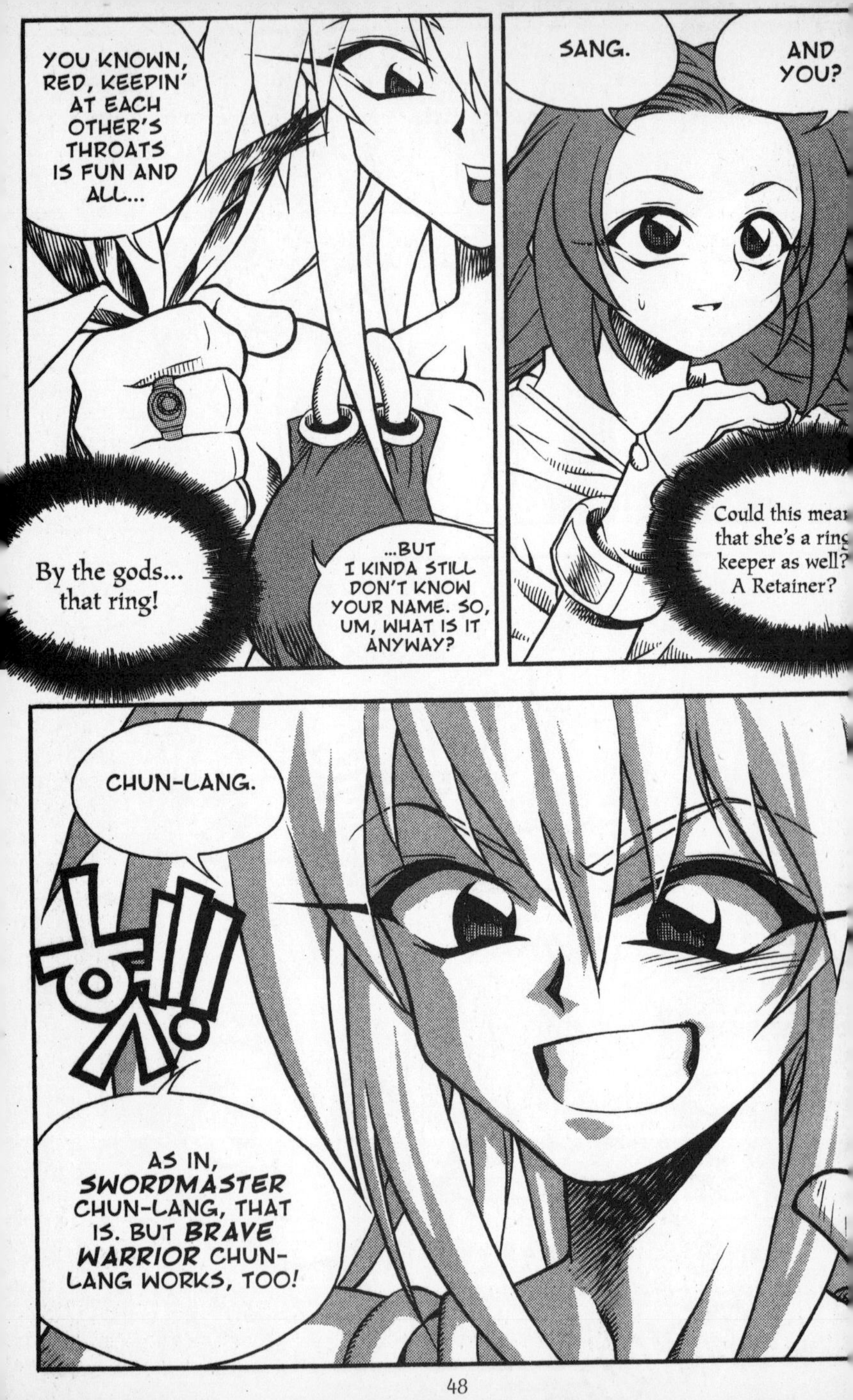
YOU KNOWN, RED, KEEPIN' AT EACH OTHER'S THROATS IS FUN AND ALL...
By the gods... that ring!
...BUT I KINDA STILL DON'T KNOW YOUR NAME. SO, UM, WHAT IS IT ANYWAY?
SANG.
AND YOU?
Could this mea that she's a ring keeper as well? A Retainer?
CHUN-LANG.
AS IN, *SWORDMASTER* CHUN-LANG, THAT IS. BUT *BRAVE WARRIOR* CHUN-LANG WORKS, TOO!

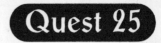

Quest 25

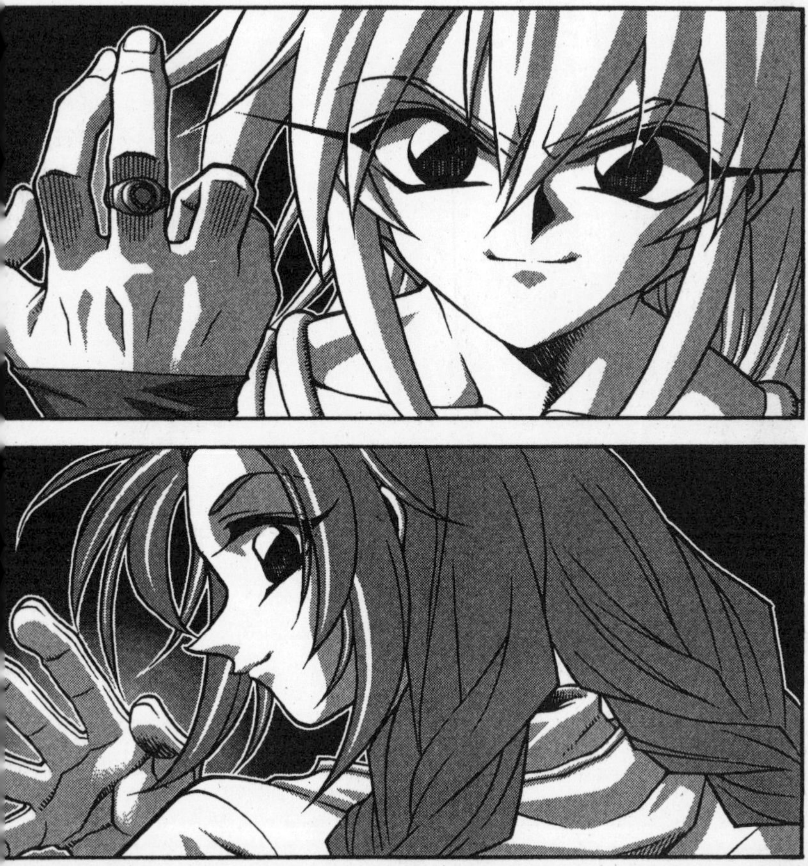

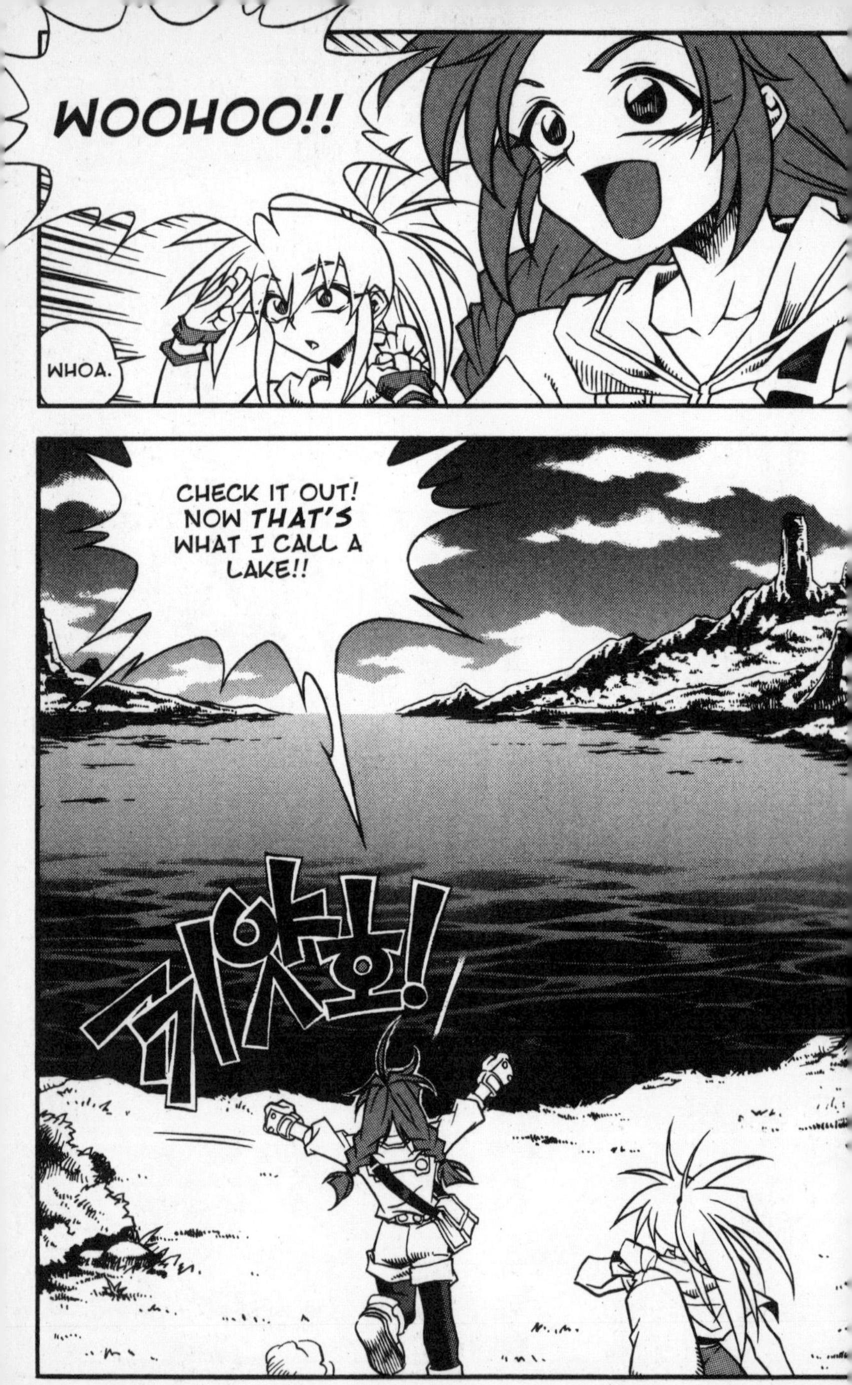
WOOHOO!!
WHOA.
CHECK IT OUT! NOW THAT'S WHAT I CALL A LAKE!!
야호!

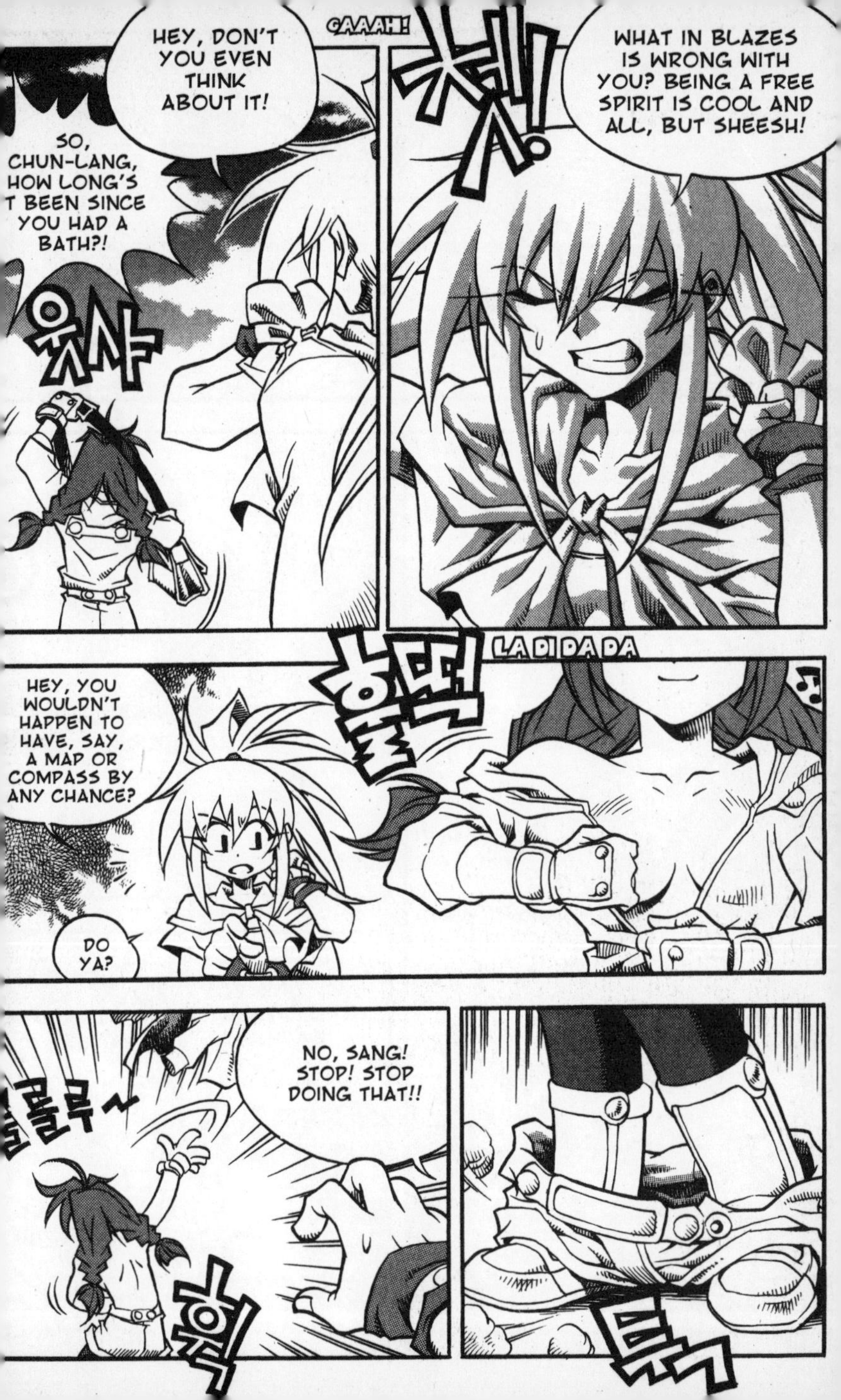
SO, CHUN-LANG, HOW LONG'S IT BEEN SINCE YOU HAD A BATH?!
HEY, DON'T YOU EVEN THINK ABOUT IT!
읏샤
GAAAH!
WHAT IN BLAZES IS WRONG WITH YOU? BEING A FREE SPIRIT IS COOL AND ALL, BUT SHEESH!
HEY, YOU WOULDN'T HAPPEN TO HAVE, SAY, A MAP OR COMPASS BY ANY CHANCE?
DO YA?
LA DI DA DA
NO, SANG! STOP! STOP DOING THAT!!

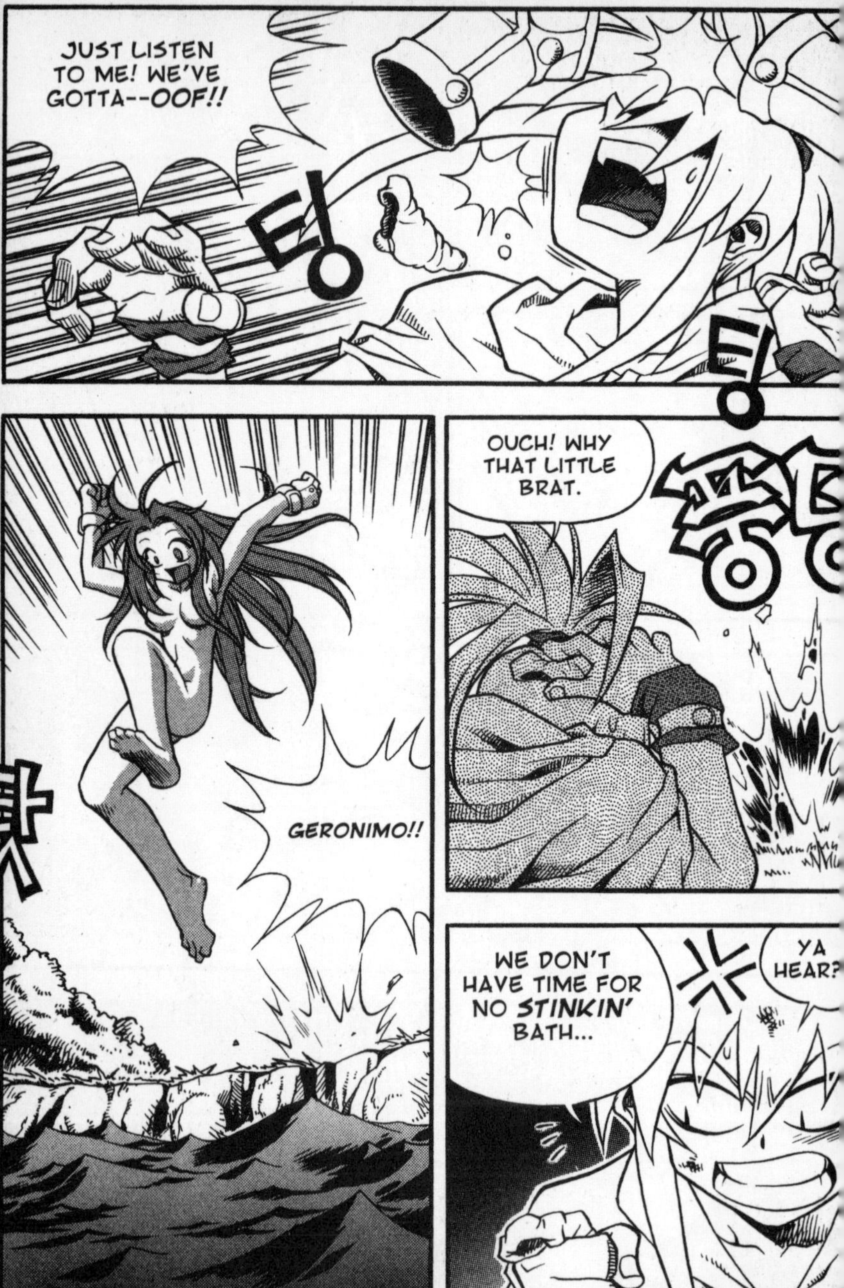
JUST LISTEN TO ME! WE'VE GOTTA--OOF!!
GERONIMO!!
OUCH! WHY THAT LITTLE BRAT.
WE DON'T HAVE TIME FOR NO STINKIN' BATH...
YA HEAR?

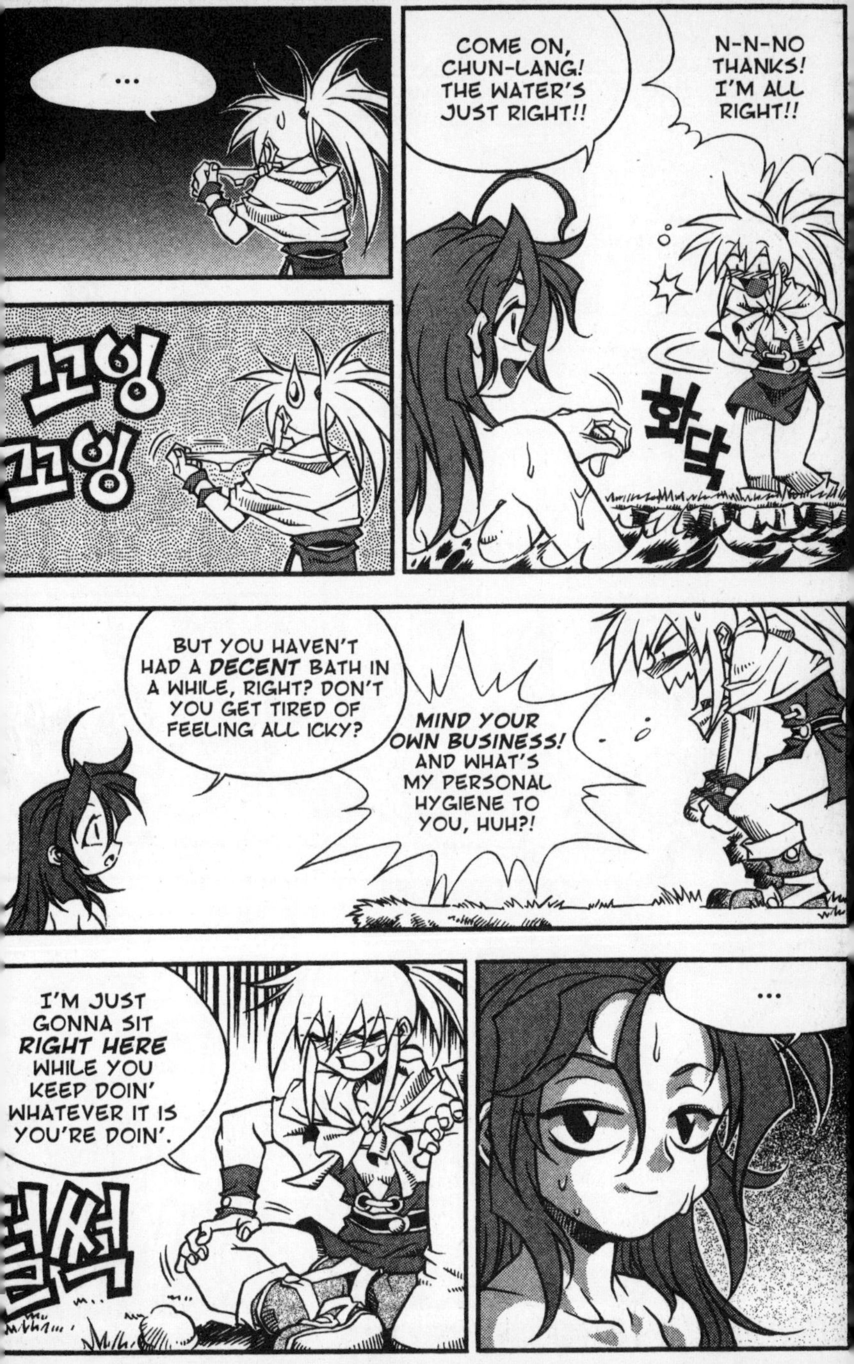
...
COME ON, CHUN-LANG! THE WATER'S JUST RIGHT!!
N-N-NO THANKS! I'M ALL RIGHT!!
화닥
BUT YOU HAVEN'T HAD A *DECENT* BATH IN A WHILE, RIGHT? DON'T YOU GET TIRED OF FEELING ALL ICKY?
MIND YOUR OWN BUSINESS! AND WHAT'S MY PERSONAL HYGIENE TO YOU, HUH?!
I'M JUST GONNA SIT *RIGHT HERE* WHILE YOU KEEP DOIN' WHATEVER IT IS YOU'RE DOIN'.
...

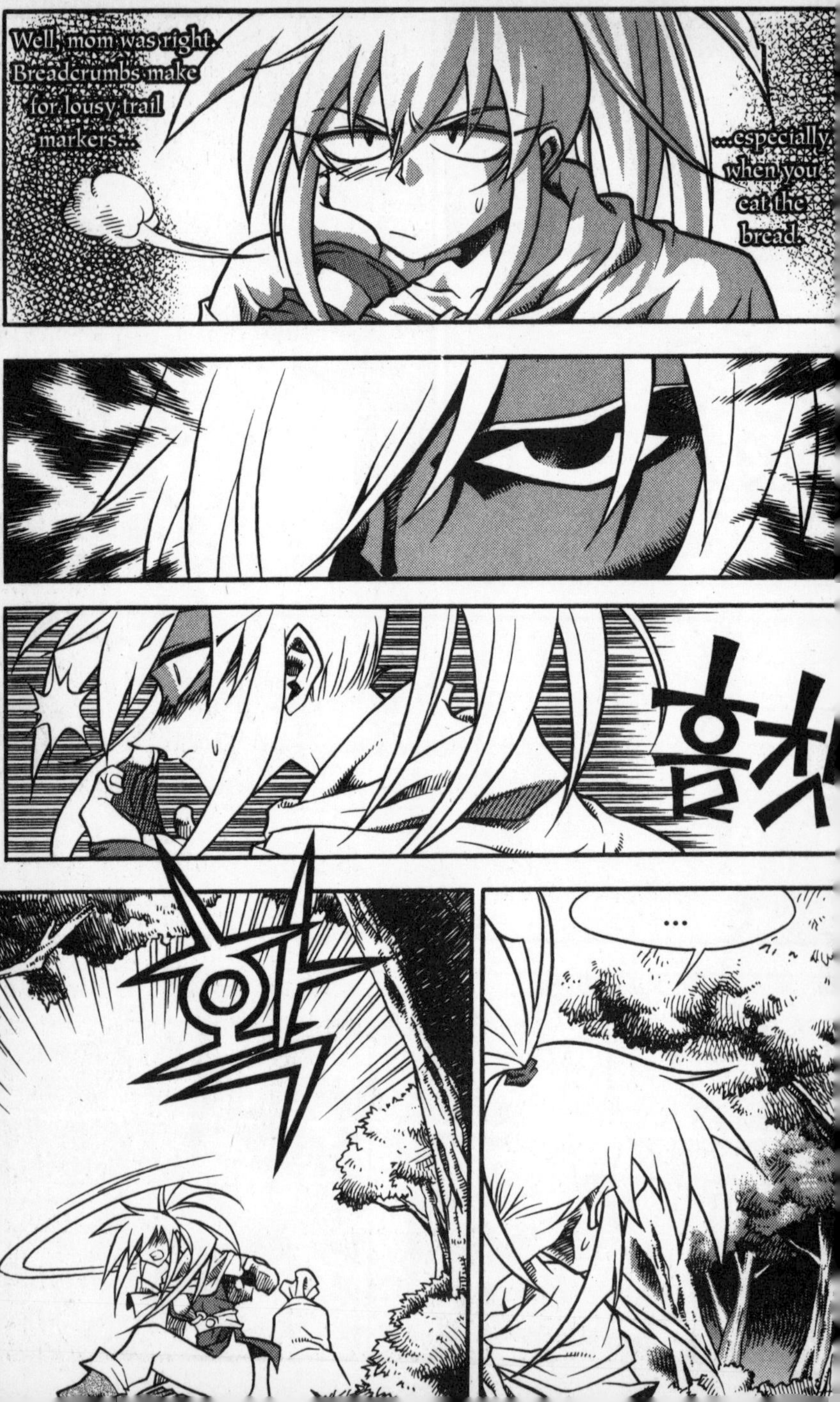
Well, mom was right. Breadcrumbs make for lousy trail markers...
...especially when you eat the bread.
흠칫
왁
...

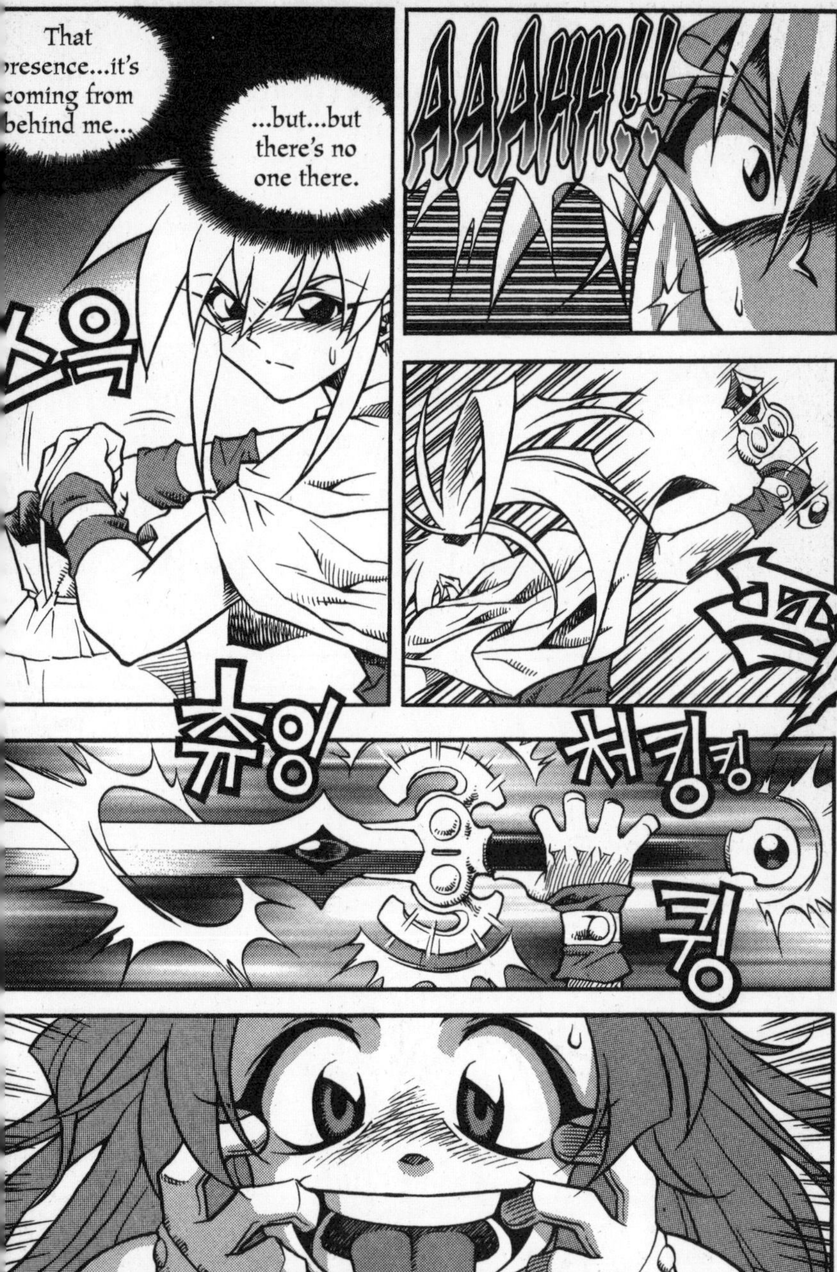
That presence...it's coming from behind me...
...but...but there's no one there.
AAAHH!!
츄잉!
쿵!

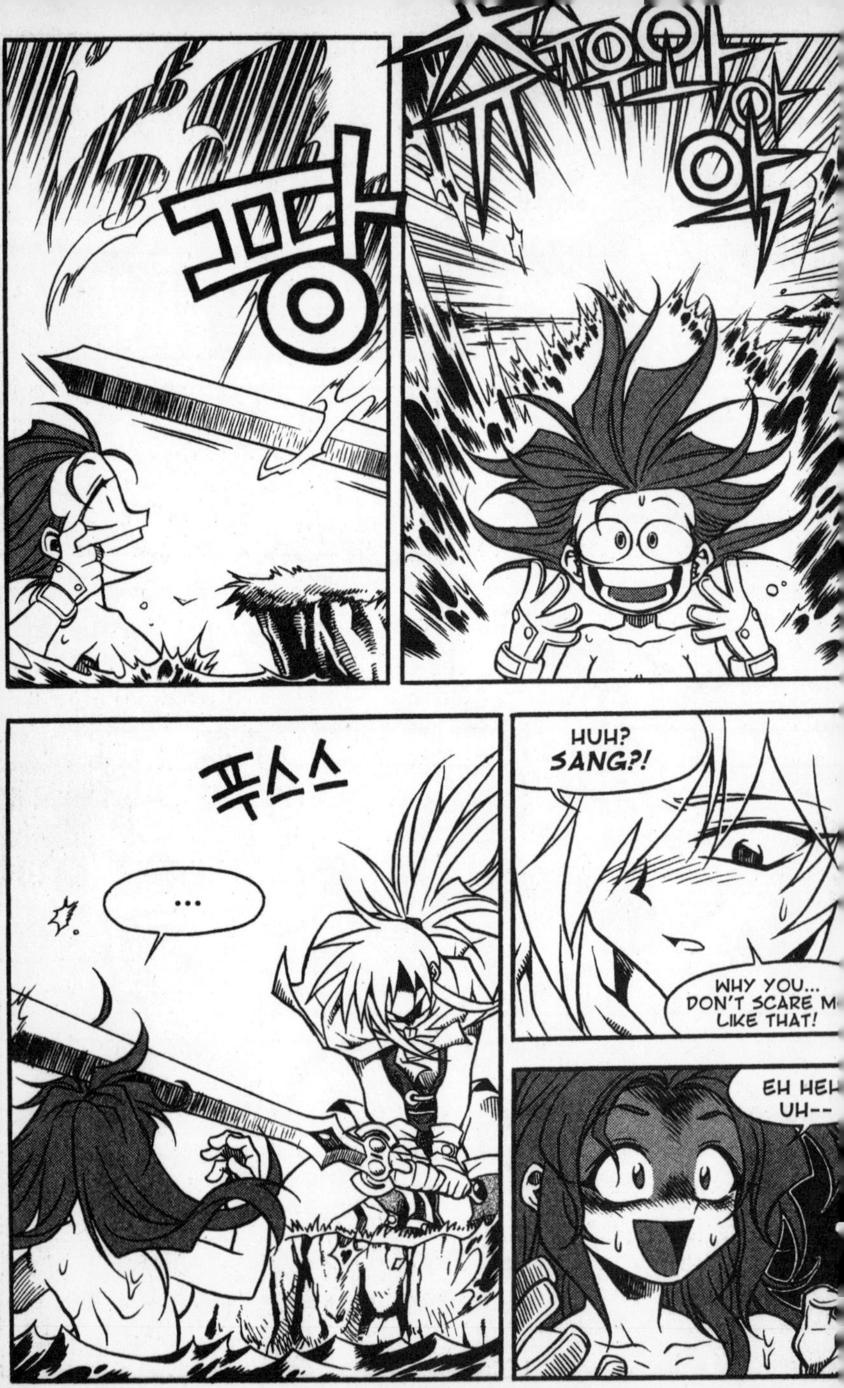

푸스스
...
HUH? SANG?!
WHY YOU... DON'T SCARE M LIKE THAT!
EH HEH UH--

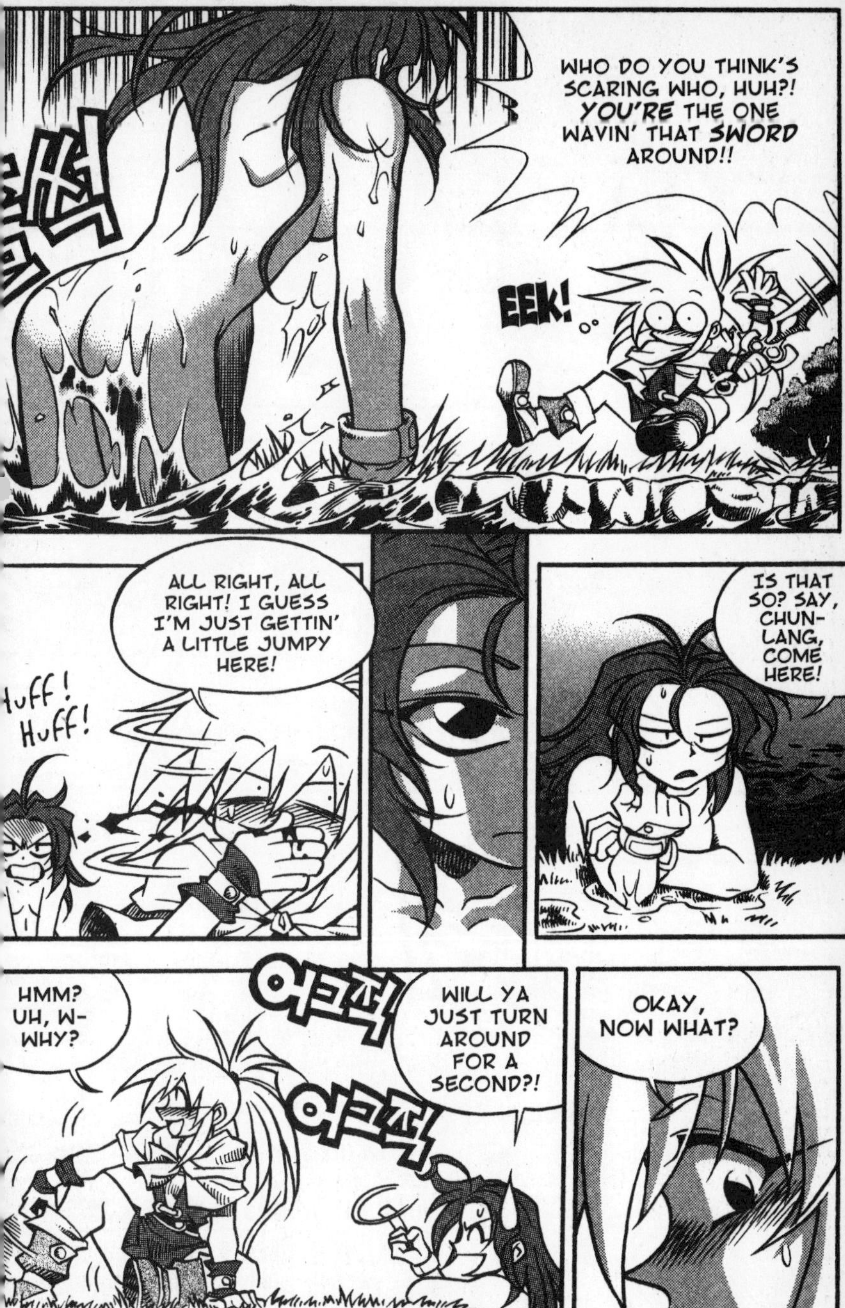
WHO DO YOU THINK'S SCARING WHO, HUH?! ***YOU'RE*** THE ONE WAVIN' THAT ***SWORD*** AROUND!!
EEK!
ALL RIGHT, ALL RIGHT! I GUESS I'M JUST GETTIN' A LITTLE JUMPY HERE!
Huff! Huff!
IS THAT SO? SAY, CHUN-LANG, COME HERE!
HMM? UH, W-WHY?
WILL YA JUST TURN AROUND FOR A SECOND?!
OKAY, NOW WHAT?

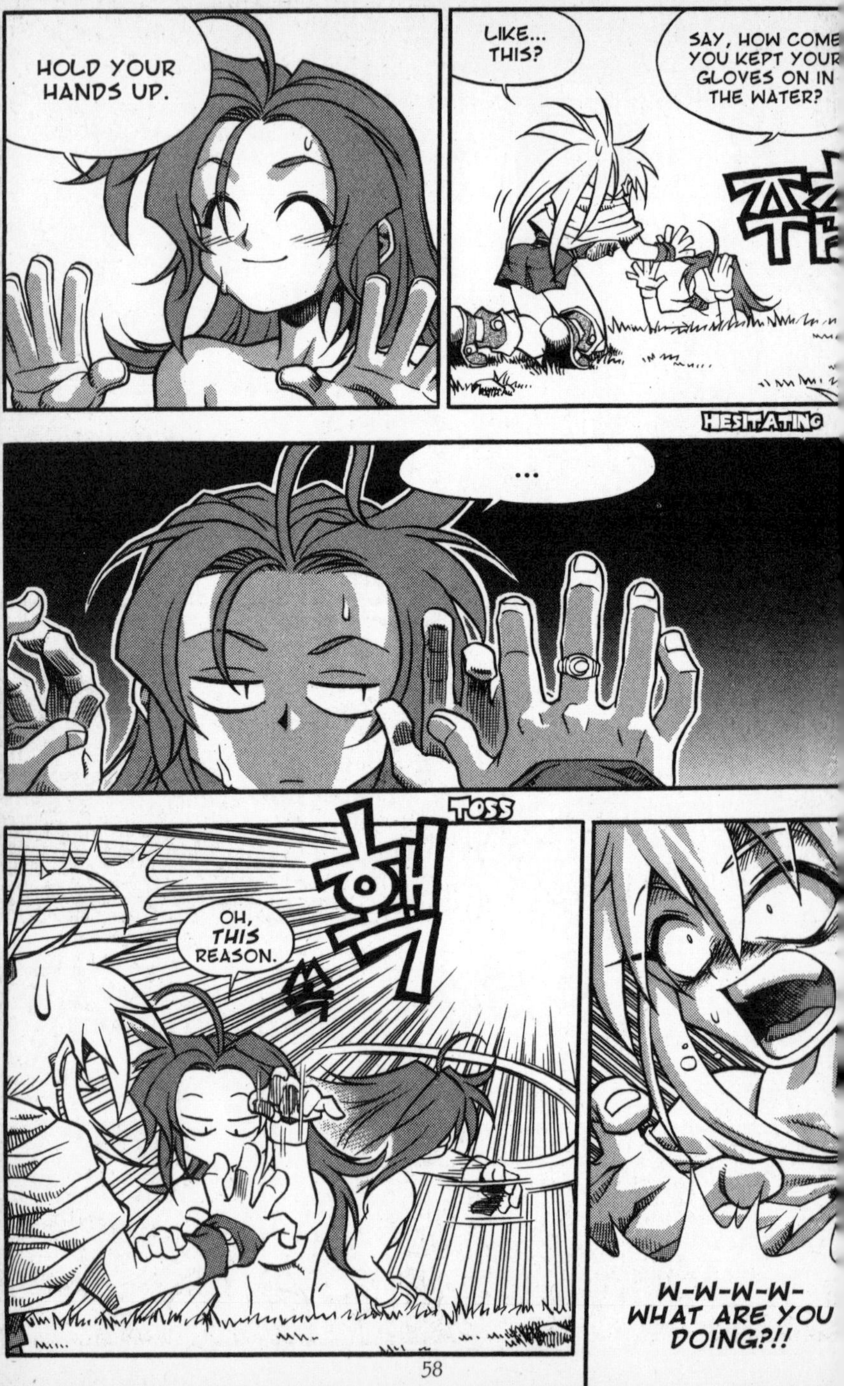
HOLD YOUR HANDS UP.
LIKE... THIS?
SAY, HOW COME YOU KEPT YOUR GLOVES ON IN THE WATER?
HESITATING
...
TOSS
OH, THIS REASON.
W-W-W-W- WHAT ARE YOU DOING?!!

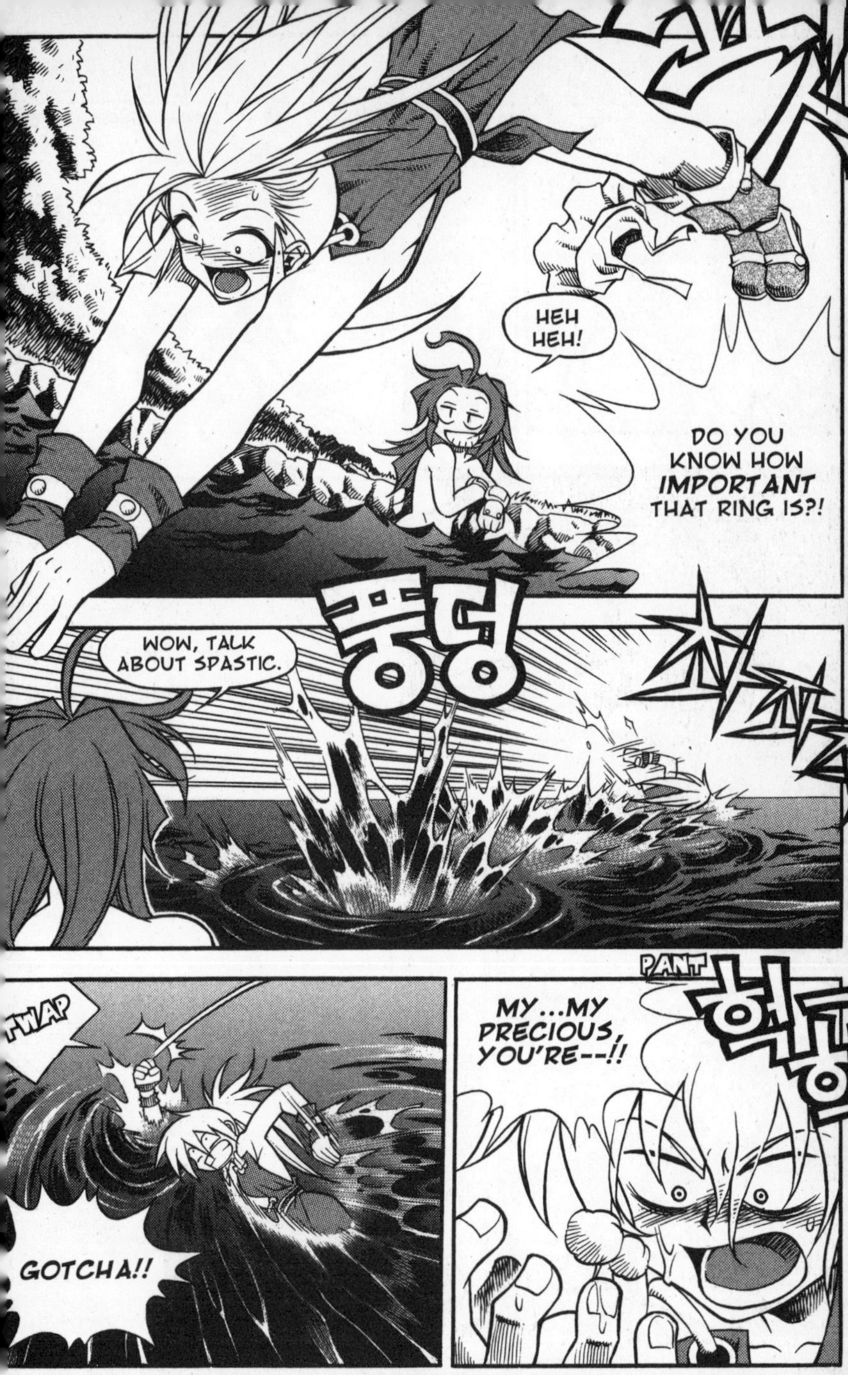
HEH HEH!
DO YOU KNOW HOW IMPORTANT THAT RING IS?!
WOW, TALK ABOUT SPASTIC.
풍덩
GOTCHA!!
PANT
MY...MY PRECIOUS, YOU'RE--!!

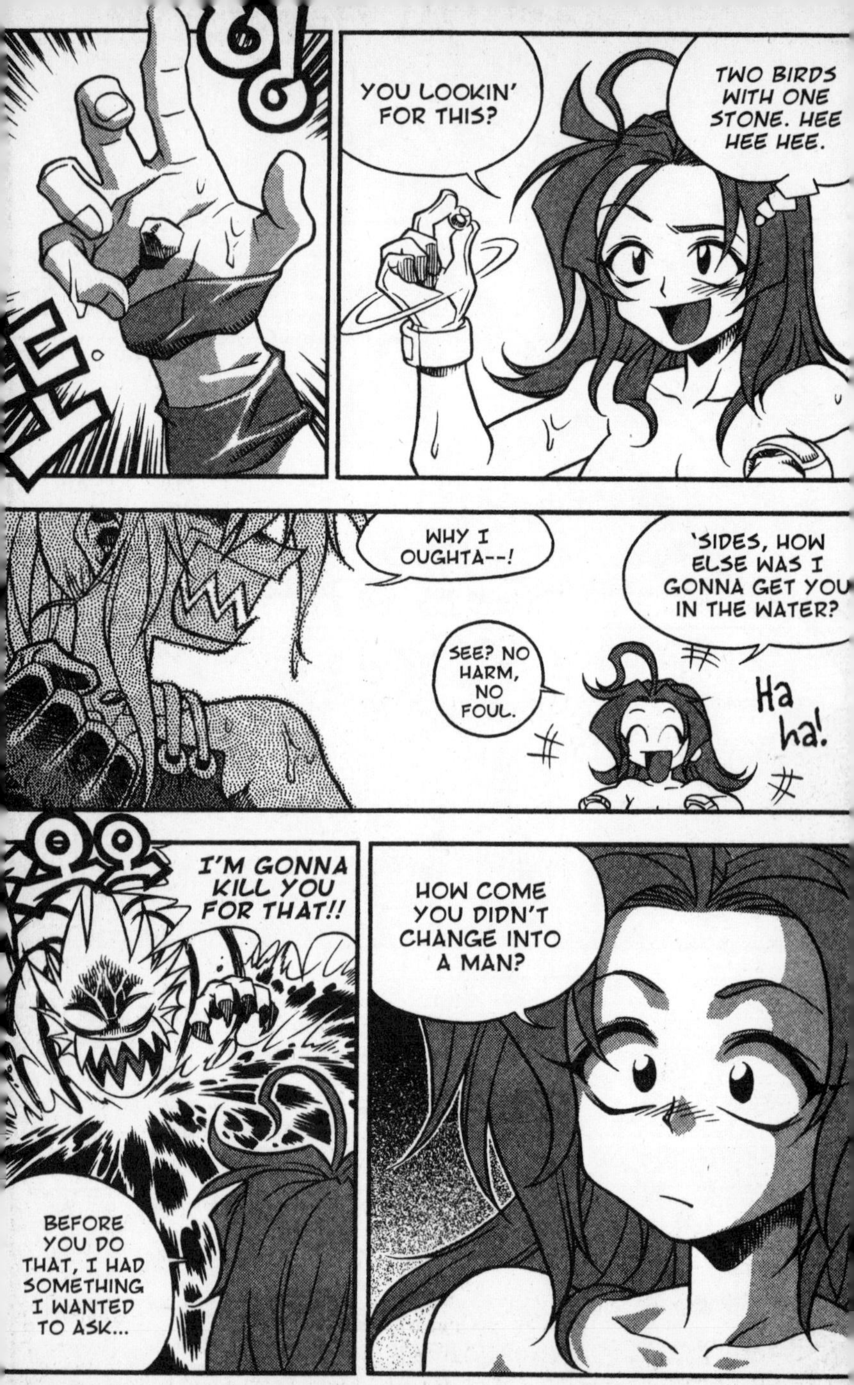
YOU LOOKIN' FOR THIS?
TWO BIRDS WITH ONE STONE. HEE HEE HEE.
WHY I OUGHTA--!
'SIDES, HOW ELSE WAS I GONNA GET YOU IN THE WATER?
SEE? NO HARM, NO FOUL.
Ha ha!
I'M GONNA KILL YOU FOR THAT!!
BEFORE YOU DO THAT, I HAD SOMETHING I WANTED TO ASK...
HOW COME YOU DIDN'T CHANGE INTO A MAN?

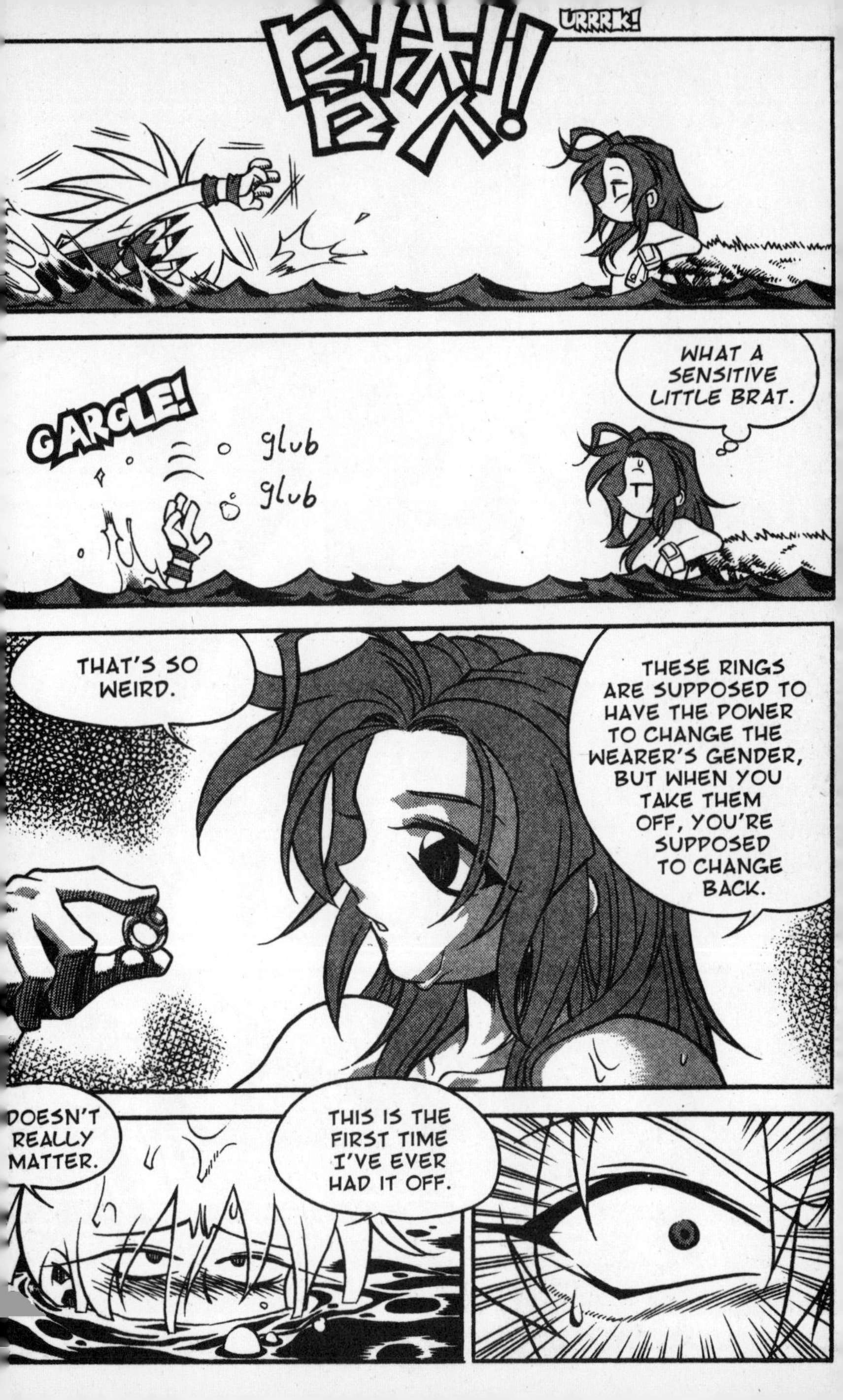
URRRK!
GARGLE!
glub
glub
WHAT A SENSITIVE LITTLE BRAT.
THAT'S SO WEIRD.
THESE RINGS ARE SUPPOSED TO HAVE THE POWER TO CHANGE THE WEARER'S GENDER, BUT WHEN YOU TAKE THEM OFF, YOU'RE SUPPOSED TO CHANGE BACK.
DOESN'T REALLY MATTER.
THIS IS THE FIRST TIME I'VE EVER HAD IT OFF.

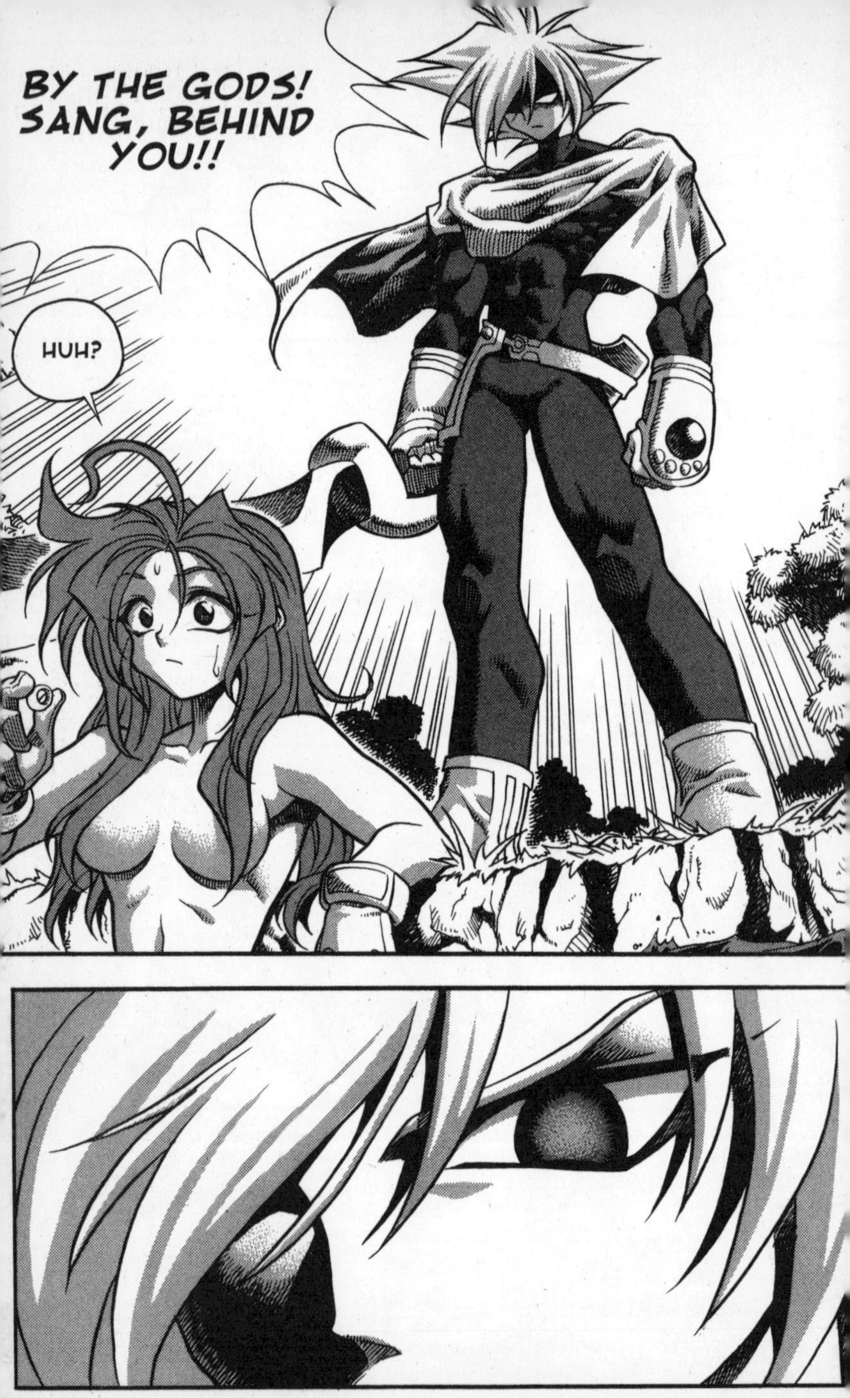
BY THE GODS! SANG, BEHIND YOU!!
HUH?

Quest 26

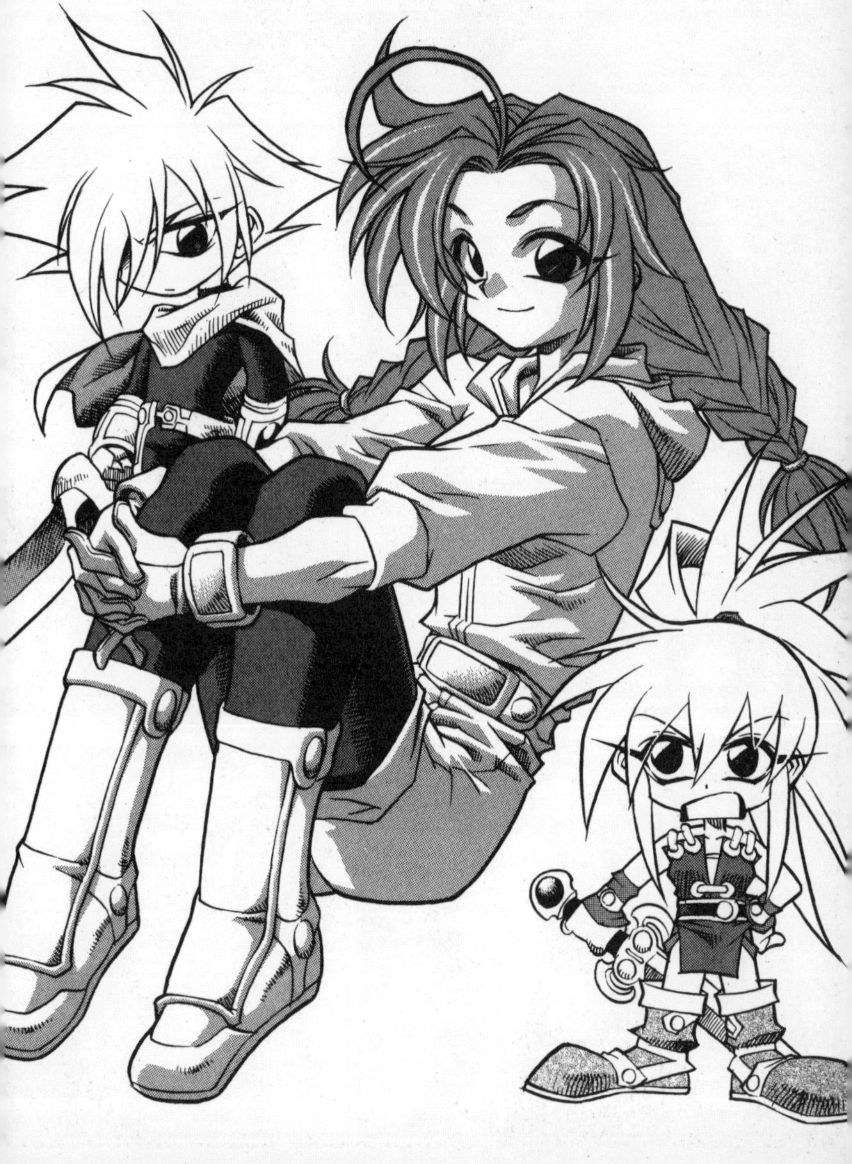

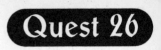

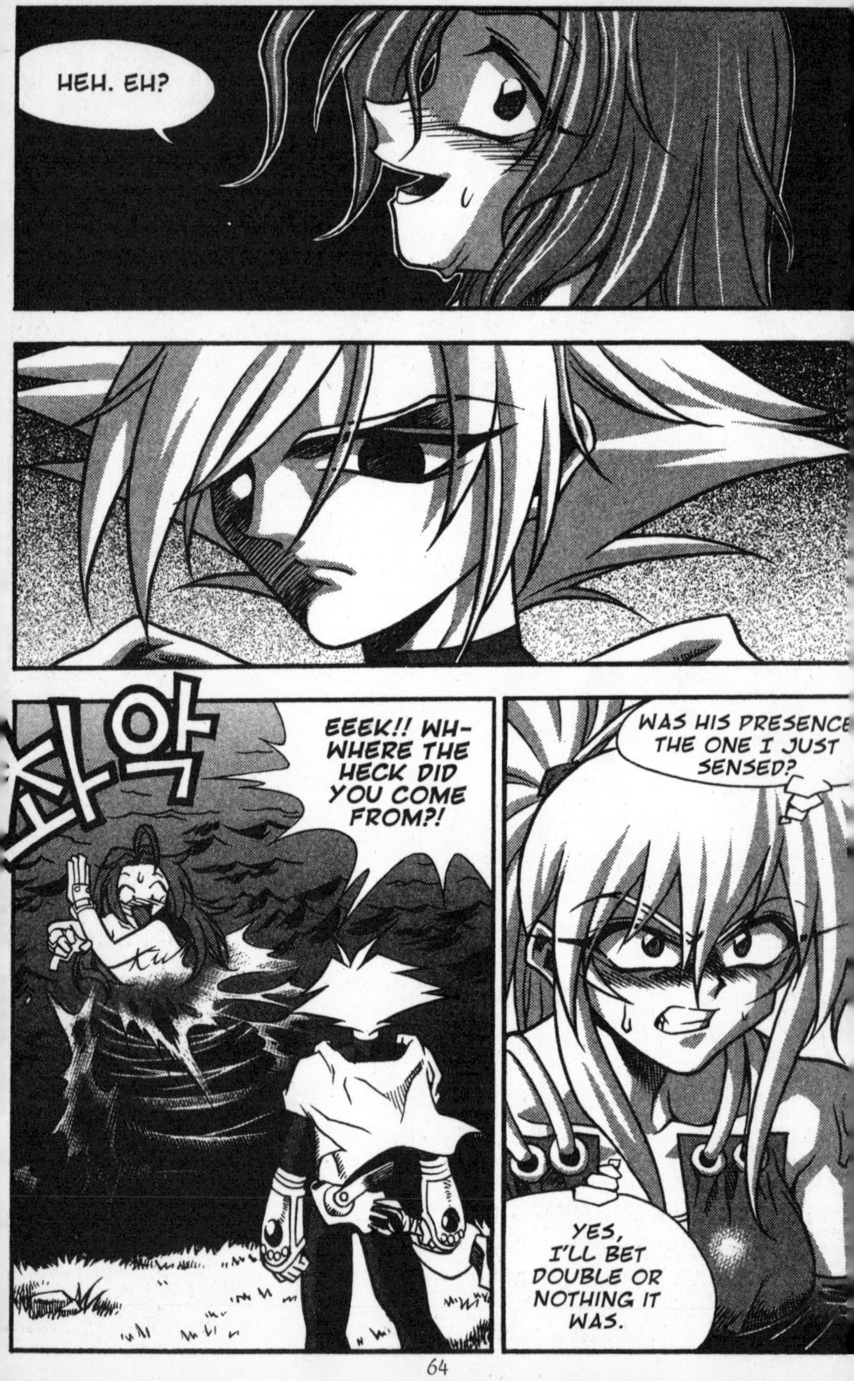
HEH. EH?
EEEK!! WH- WHERE THE HECK DID YOU COME FROM?!
WAS HIS PRESENCE THE ONE I JUST SENSED?
YES, I'LL BET DOUBLE OR NOTHING IT WAS.

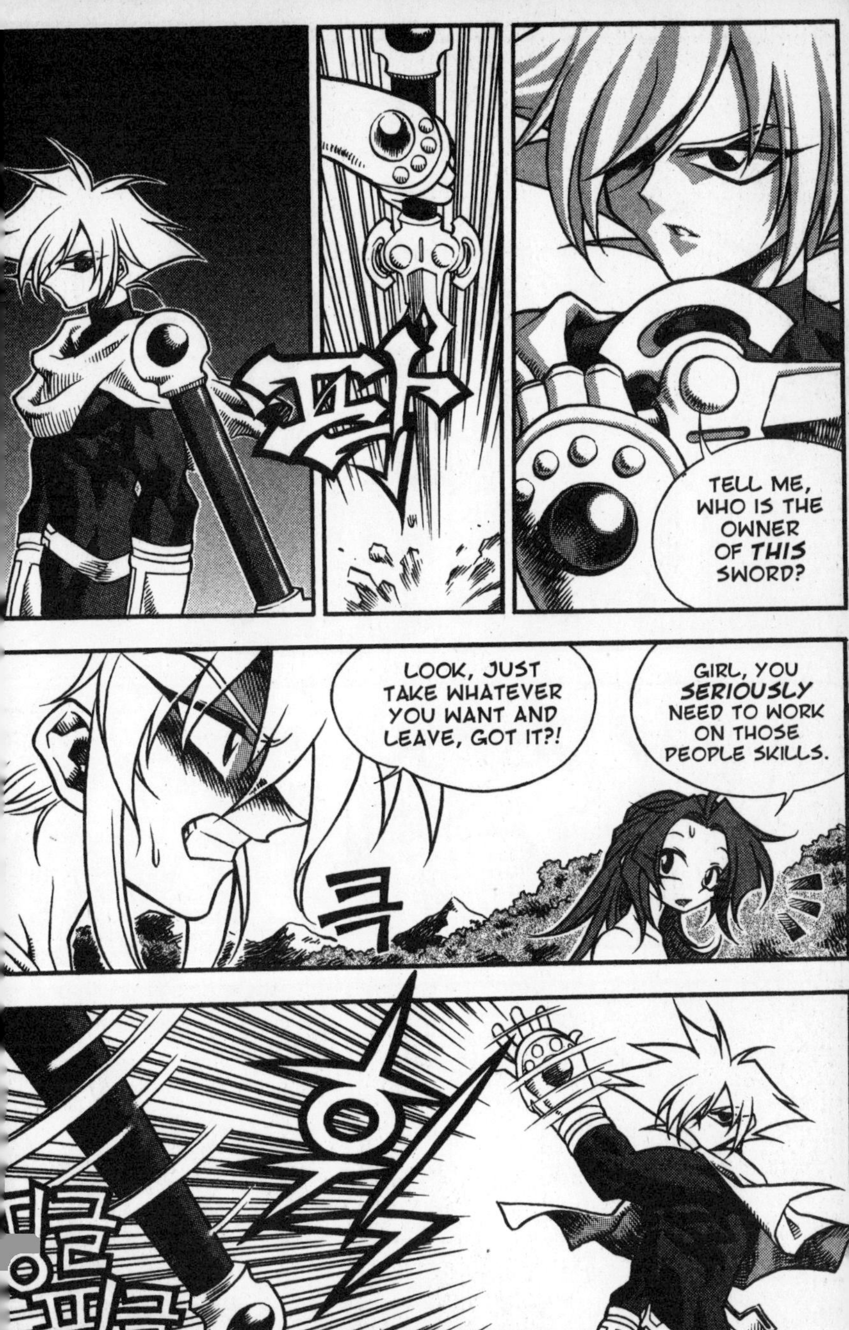
TELL ME, WHO IS THE OWNER OF *THIS* SWORD?
LOOK, JUST TAKE WHATEVER YOU WANT AND LEAVE, GOT IT?!
GIRL, YOU ***SERIOUSLY*** NEED TO WORK ON THOSE PEOPLE SKILLS.
크

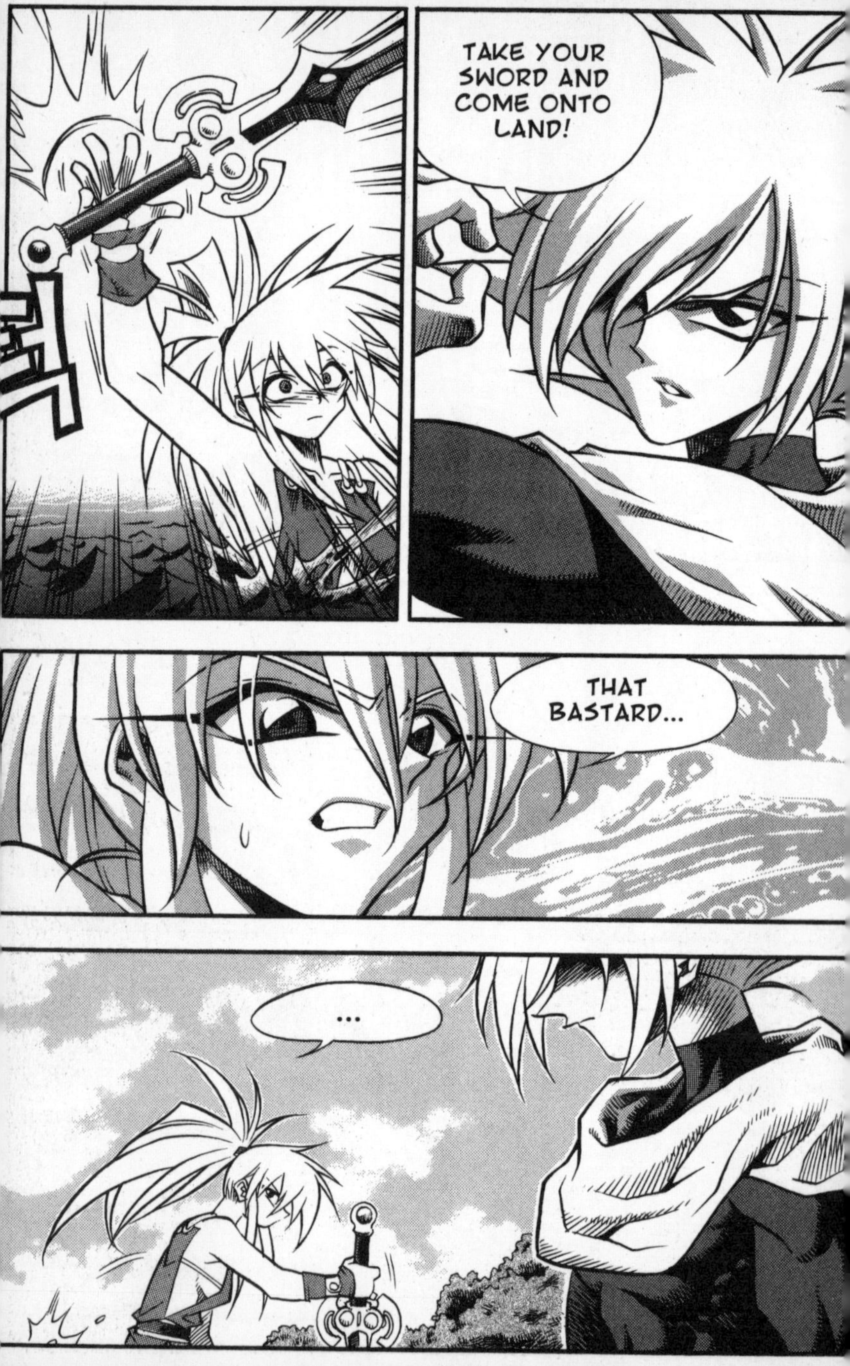
TAKE YOUR SWORD AND COME ONTO LAND!
THAT BASTARD...
...

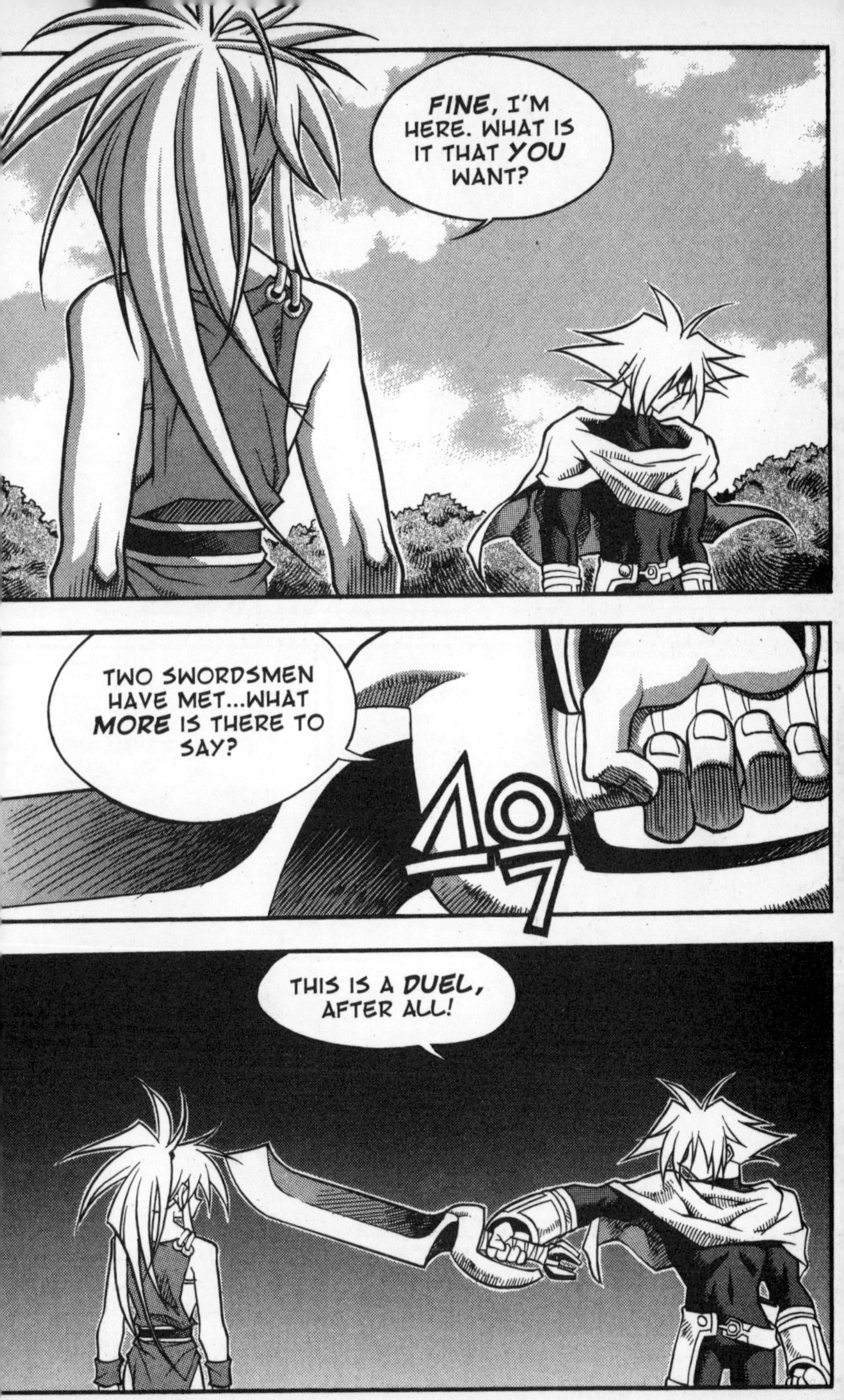
FINE, I'M HERE. WHAT IS IT THAT YOU WANT?
TWO SWORDSMEN HAVE MET...WHAT MORE IS THERE TO SAY?
THIS IS A DUEL, AFTER ALL!

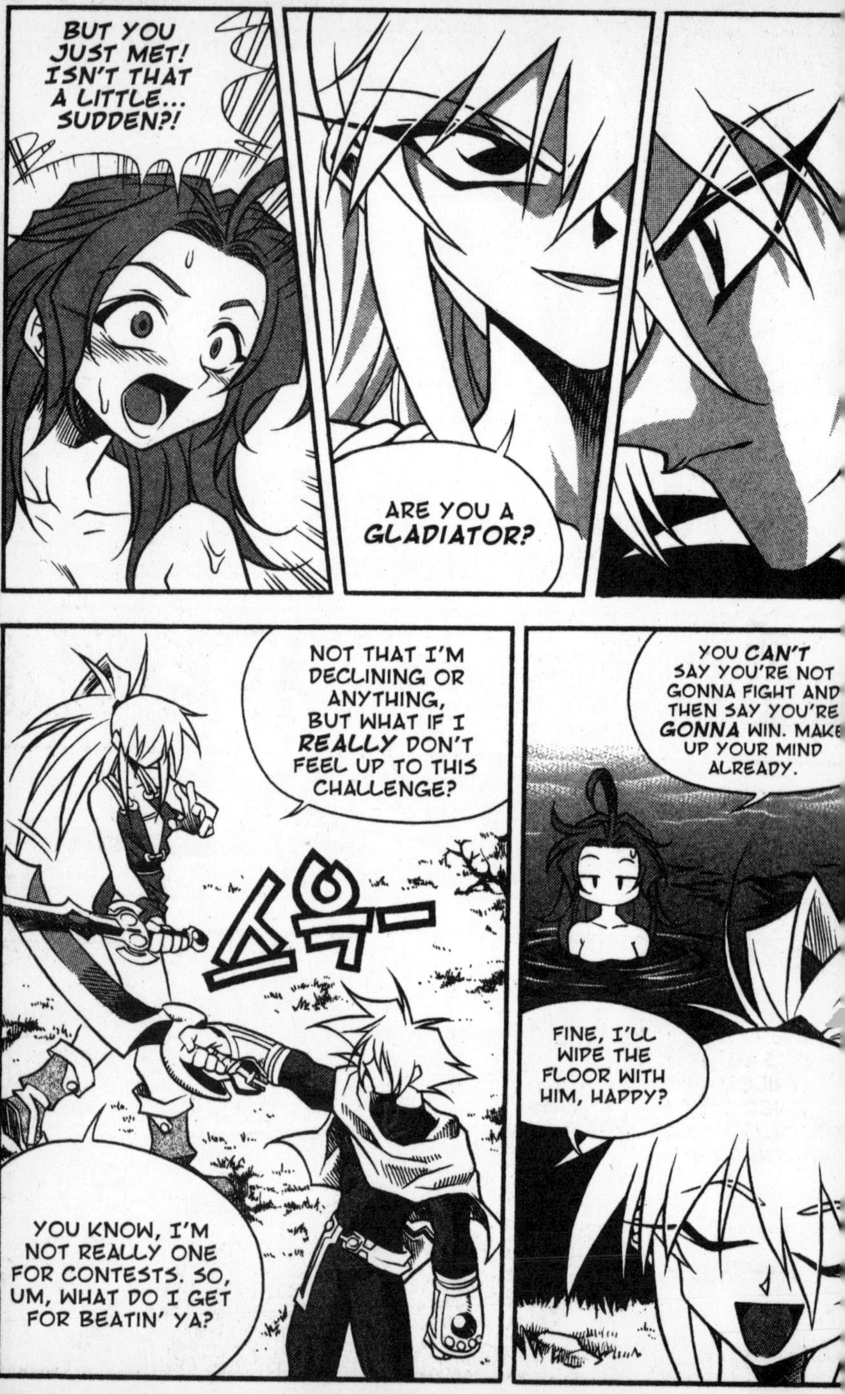
BUT YOU JUST MET! ISN'T THAT A LITTLE... SUDDEN?!
ARE YOU A GLADIATOR?
NOT THAT I'M DECLINING OR ANYTHING, BUT WHAT IF I REALLY DON'T FEEL UP TO THIS CHALLENGE?
스윽-
YOU KNOW, I'M NOT REALLY ONE FOR CONTESTS. SO, UM, WHAT DO I GET FOR BEATIN' YA?
YOU CAN'T SAY YOU'RE NOT GONNA FIGHT AND THEN SAY YOU'RE GONNA WIN. MAKE UP YOUR MIND ALREADY.
FINE, I'LL WIPE THE FLOOR WITH HIM, HAPPY?

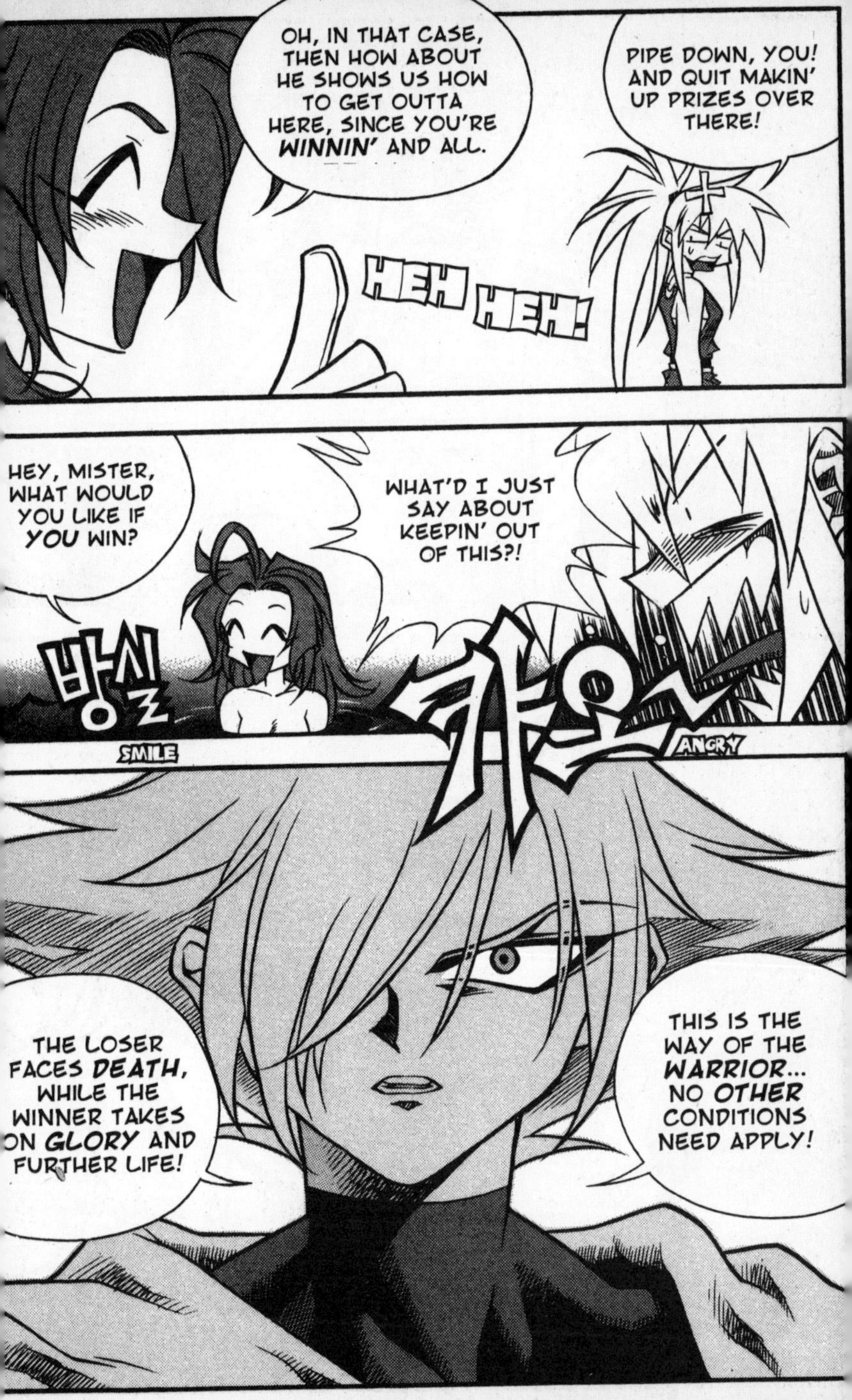
OH, IN THAT CASE, THEN HOW ABOUT HE SHOWS US HOW TO GET OUTTA HERE, SINCE YOU'RE WINNIN' AND ALL.
PIPE DOWN, YOU! AND QUIT MAKIN' UP PRIZES OVER THERE!
HEH HEH!
HEY, MISTER, WHAT WOULD YOU LIKE IF YOU WIN?
WHAT'D I JUST SAY ABOUT KEEPIN' OUT OF THIS?!
방시
SMILE
ANGRY
THE LOSER FACES DEATH, WHILE THE WINNER TAKES ON GLORY AND FURTHER LIFE!
THIS IS THE WAY OF THE WARRIOR... NO OTHER CONDITIONS NEED APPLY!

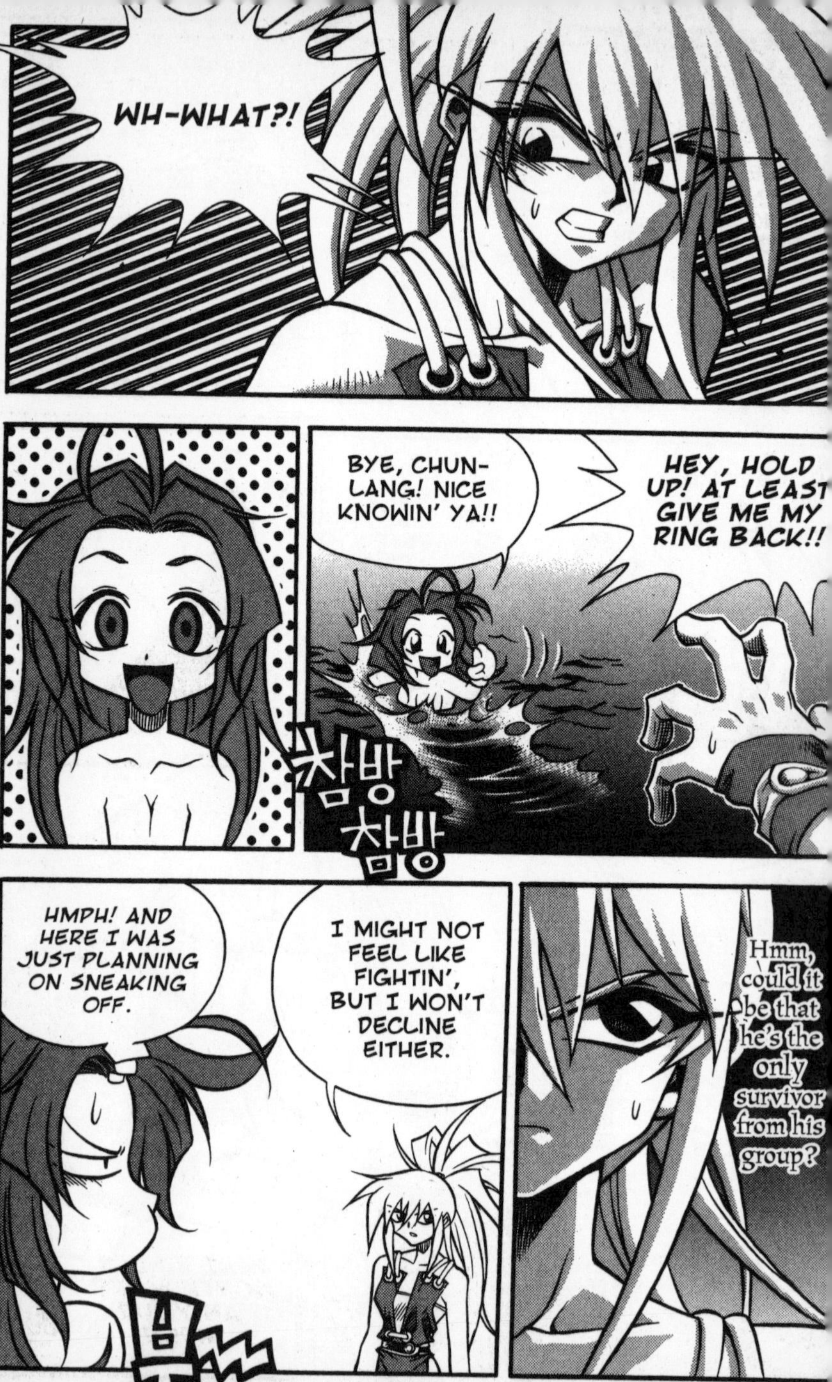
WH-WHAT?!
BYE, CHUN-LANG! NICE KNOWIN' YA!!
HEY, HOLD UP! AT LEAST GIVE ME MY RING BACK!!
참방
참방
HMPH! AND HERE I WAS JUST PLANNING ON SNEAKING OFF.
HUMPH!
I MIGHT NOT FEEL LIKE FIGHTIN', BUT I WON'T DECLINE EITHER.
Hmm, could it be that he's the only survivor from his group?

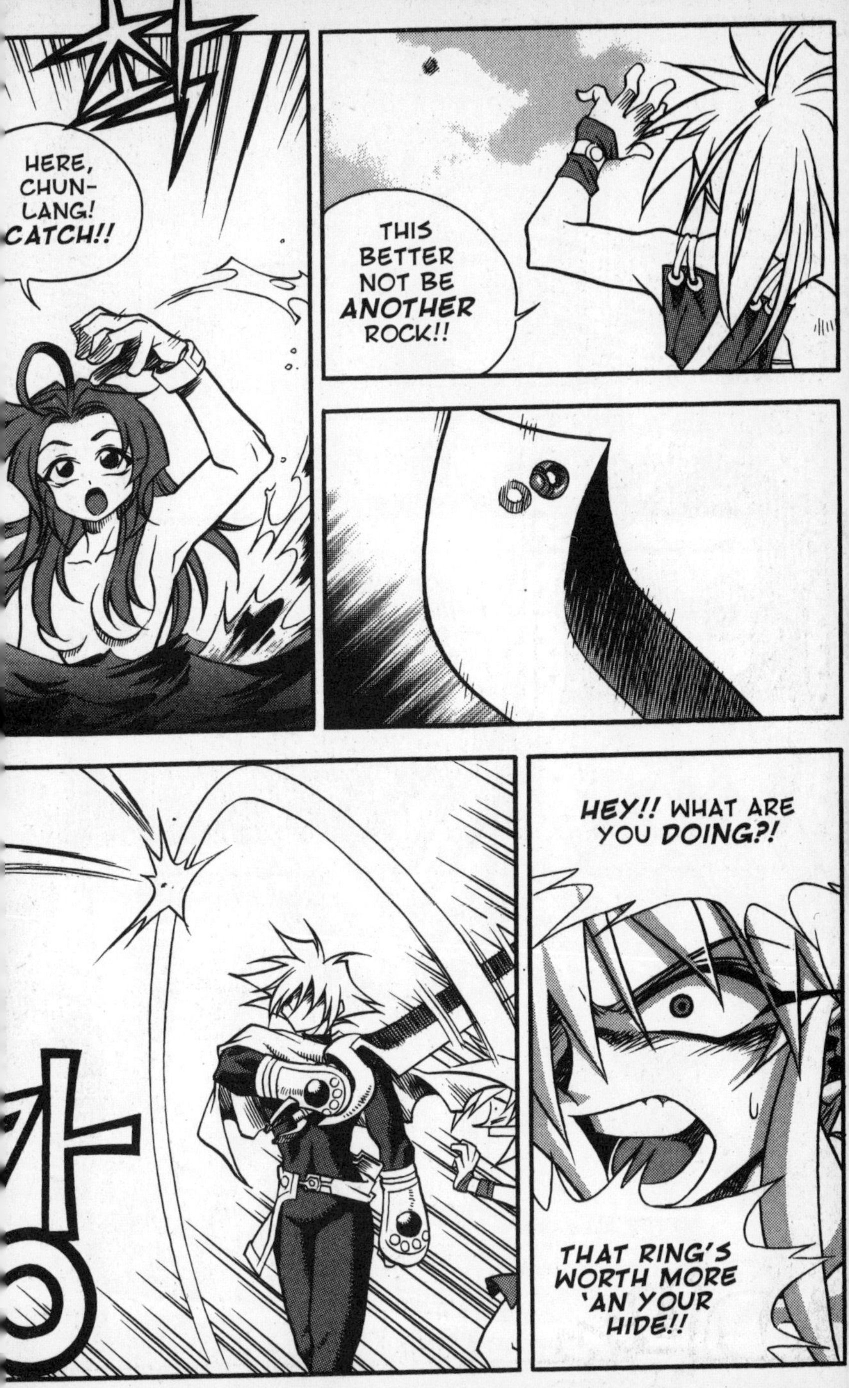
HERE, CHUN-LANG! CATCH!!
THIS BETTER NOT BE ANOTHER ROCK!!
HEY!! WHAT ARE YOU DOING?!
THAT RING'S WORTH MORE 'AN YOUR HIDE!!

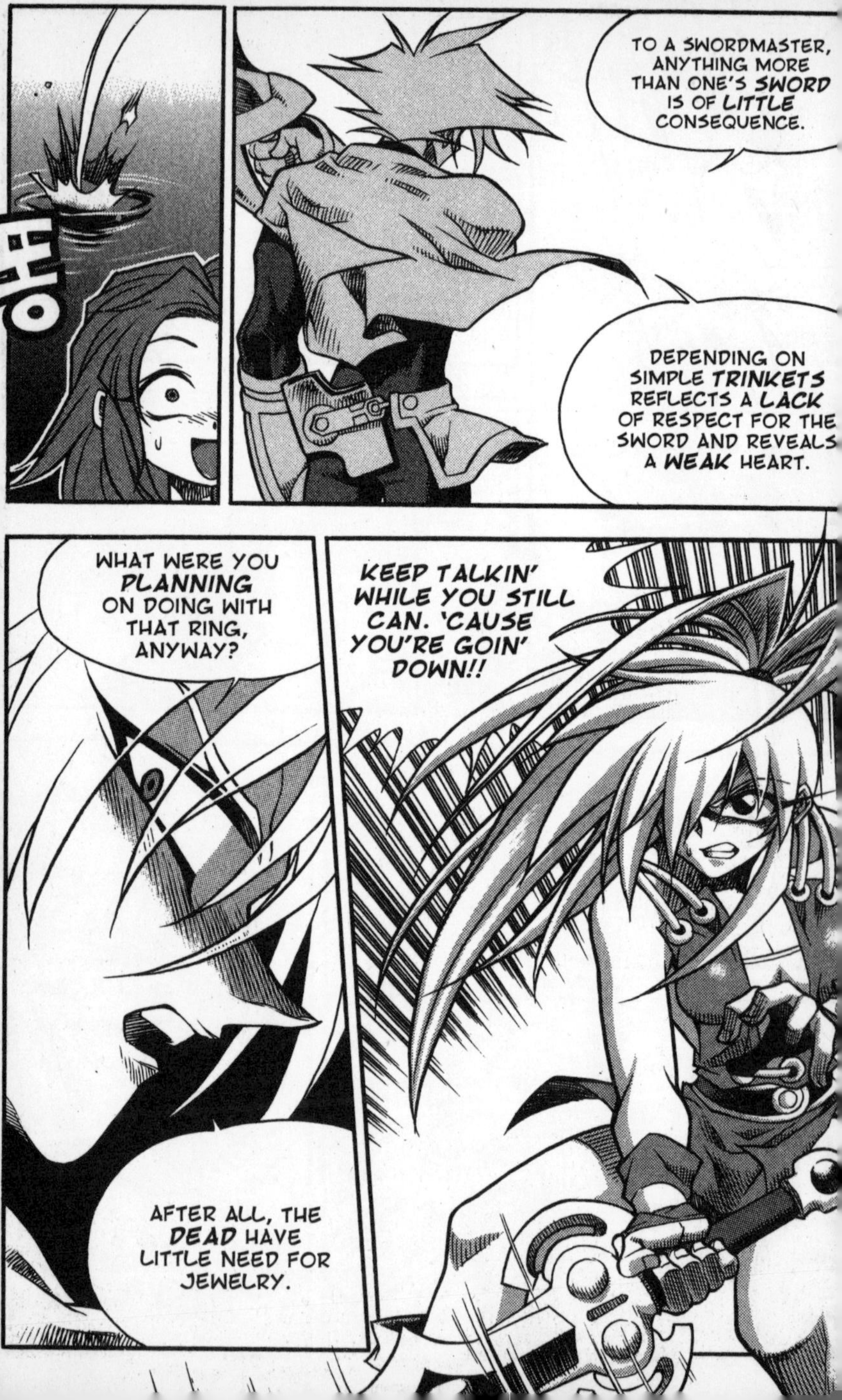
TO A SWORDMASTER, ANYTHING MORE THAN ONE'S SWORD IS OF LITTLE CONSEQUENCE.
DEPENDING ON SIMPLE TRINKETS REFLECTS A LACK OF RESPECT FOR THE SWORD AND REVEALS A WEAK HEART.
WHAT WERE YOU PLANNING ON DOING WITH THAT RING, ANYWAY?
AFTER ALL, THE DEAD HAVE LITTLE NEED FOR JEWELRY.
KEEP TALKIN' WHILE YOU STILL CAN. 'CAUSE YOU'RE GOIN' DOWN!!

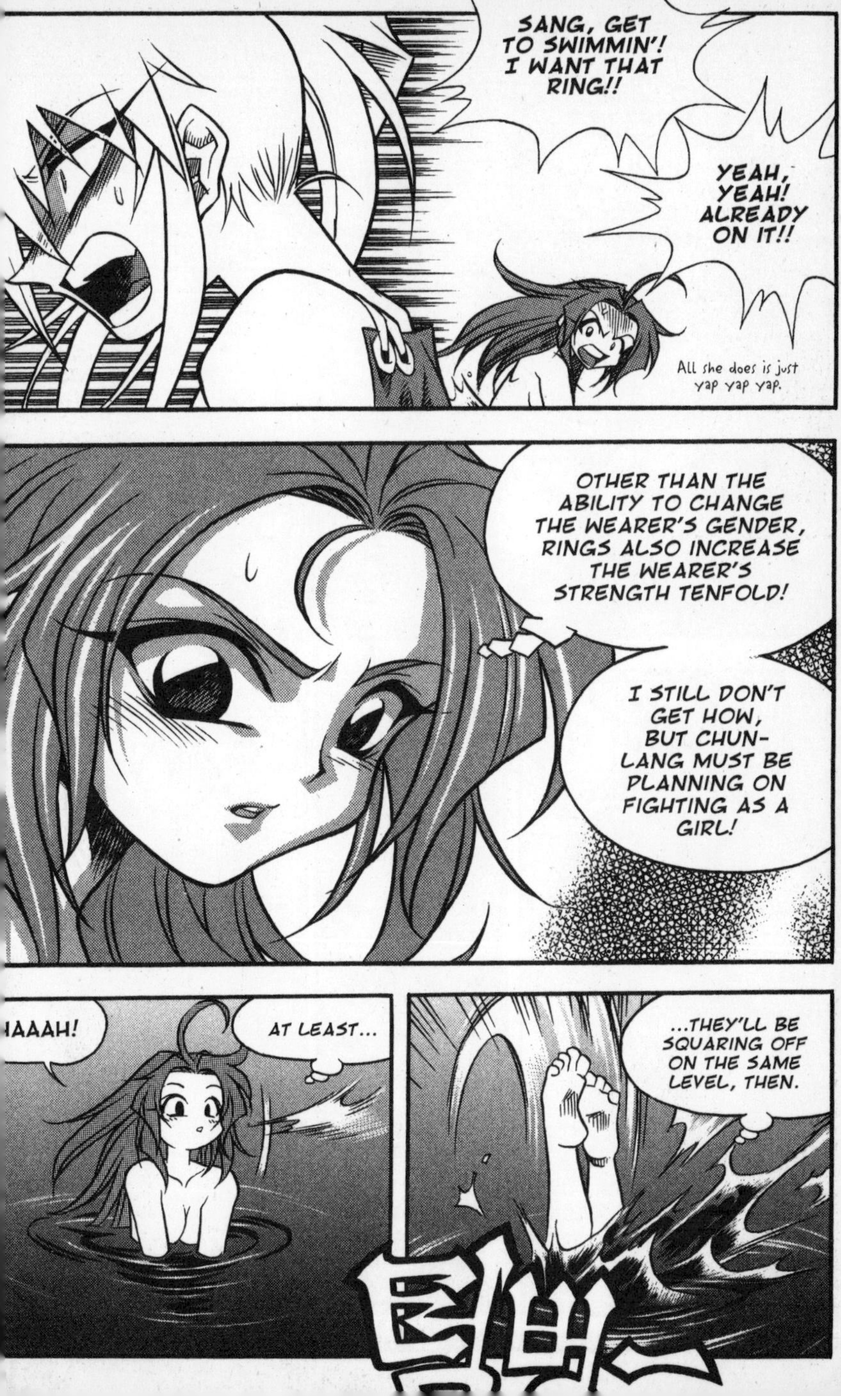
SANG, GET TO SWIMMIN'! I WANT THAT RING!!
YEAH, YEAH! ALREADY ON IT!!
All she does is just yap yap yap.
OTHER THAN THE ABILITY TO CHANGE THE WEARER'S GENDER, RINGS ALSO INCREASE THE WEARER'S STRENGTH TENFOLD!
I STILL DON'T GET HOW, BUT CHUN-LANG MUST BE PLANNING ON FIGHTING AS A GIRL!
HAAAH!
AT LEAST...
...THEY'LL BE SQUARING OFF ON THE SAME LEVEL, THEN.

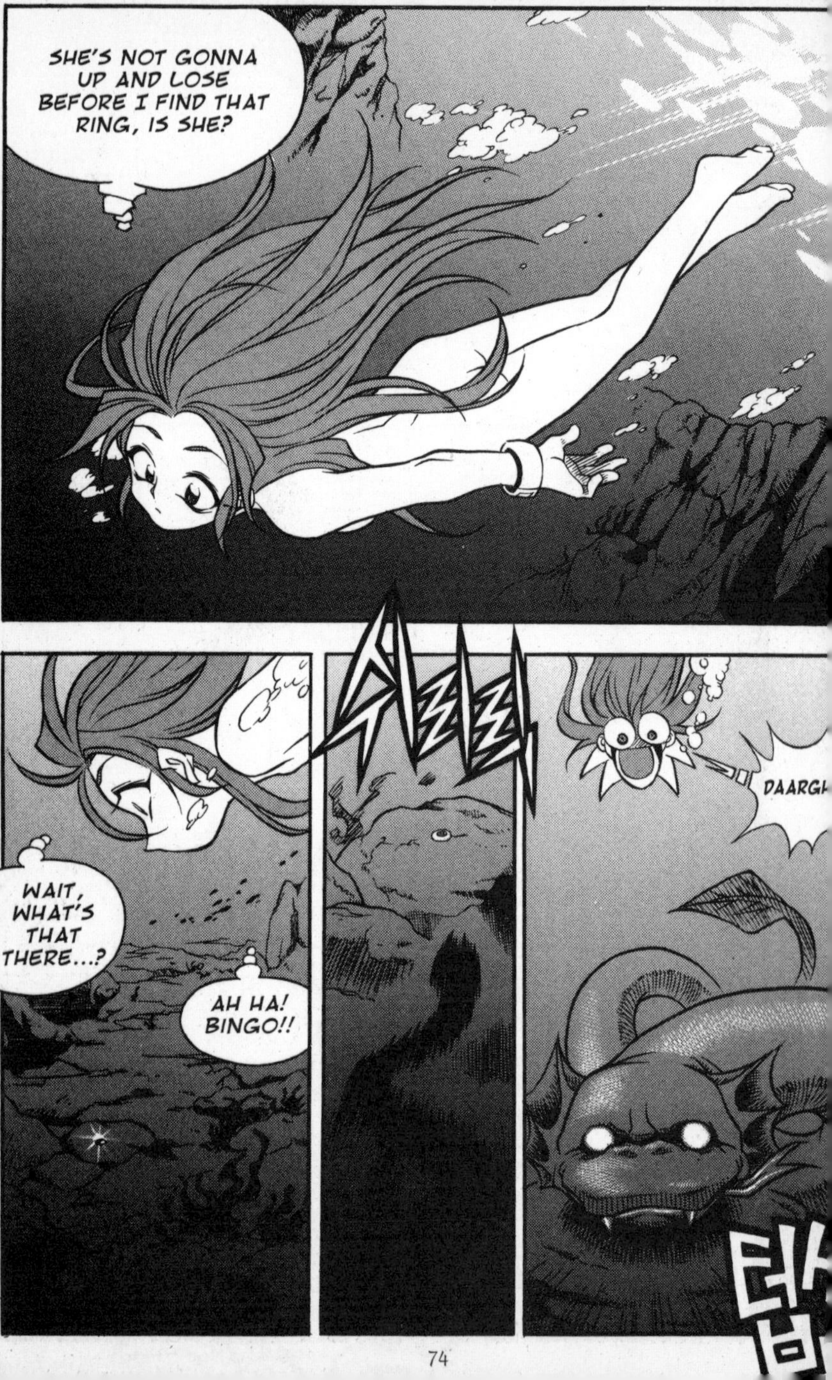
SHE'S NOT GONNA UP AND LOSE BEFORE I FIND THAT RING, IS SHE?
WAIT, WHAT'S THAT THERE...?
AH HA! BINGO!!
DAARG

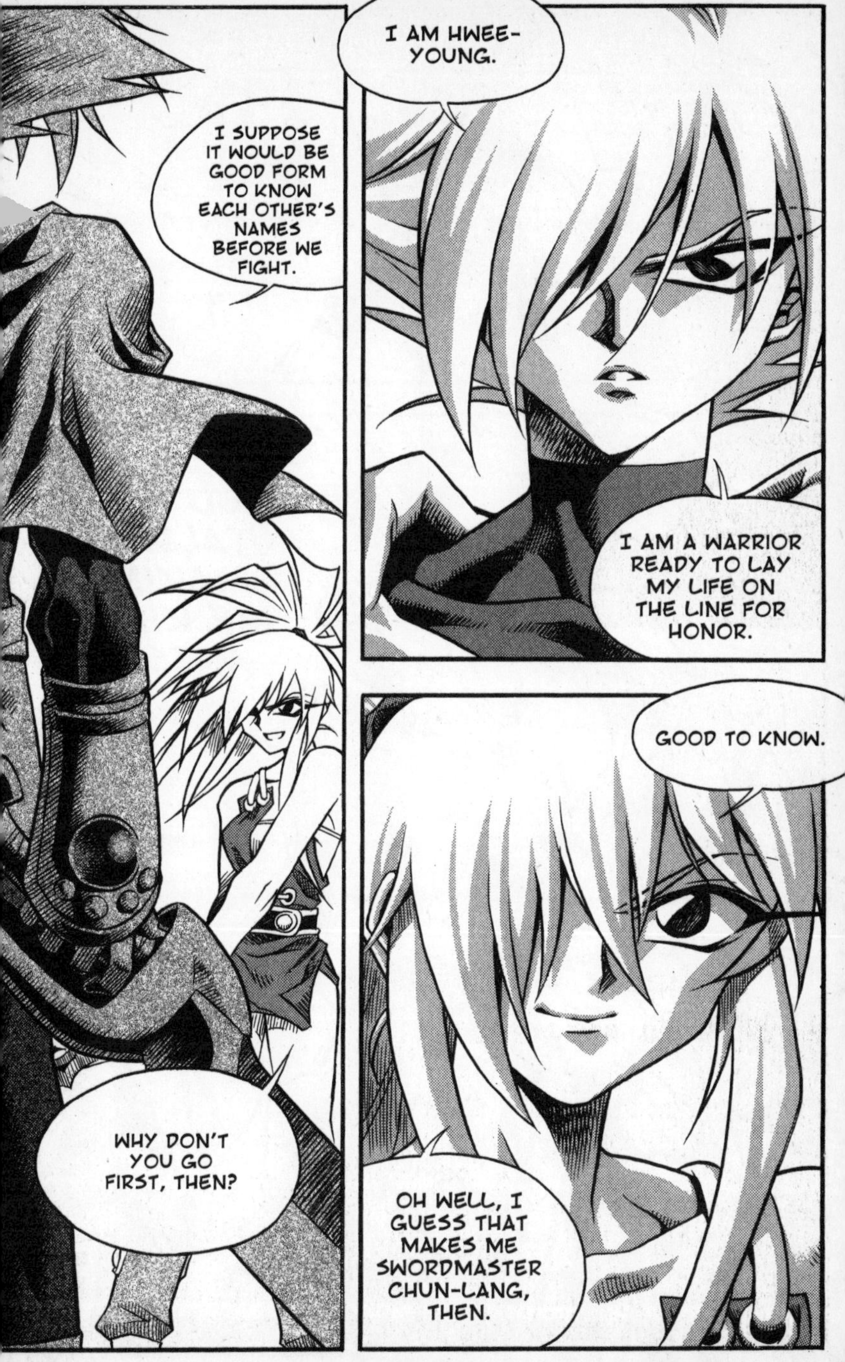
I SUPPOSE IT WOULD BE GOOD FORM TO KNOW EACH OTHER'S NAMES BEFORE WE FIGHT.
WHY DON'T YOU GO FIRST, THEN?
I AM HWEE-YOUNG.
I AM A WARRIOR READY TO LAY MY LIFE ON THE LINE FOR HONOR.
GOOD TO KNOW.
OH WELL, I GUESS THAT MAKES ME SWORDMASTER CHUN-LANG, THEN.

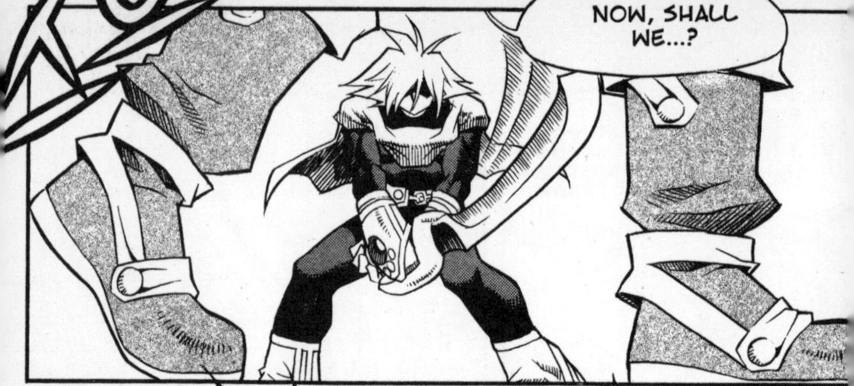
NOW, SHALL WE...?
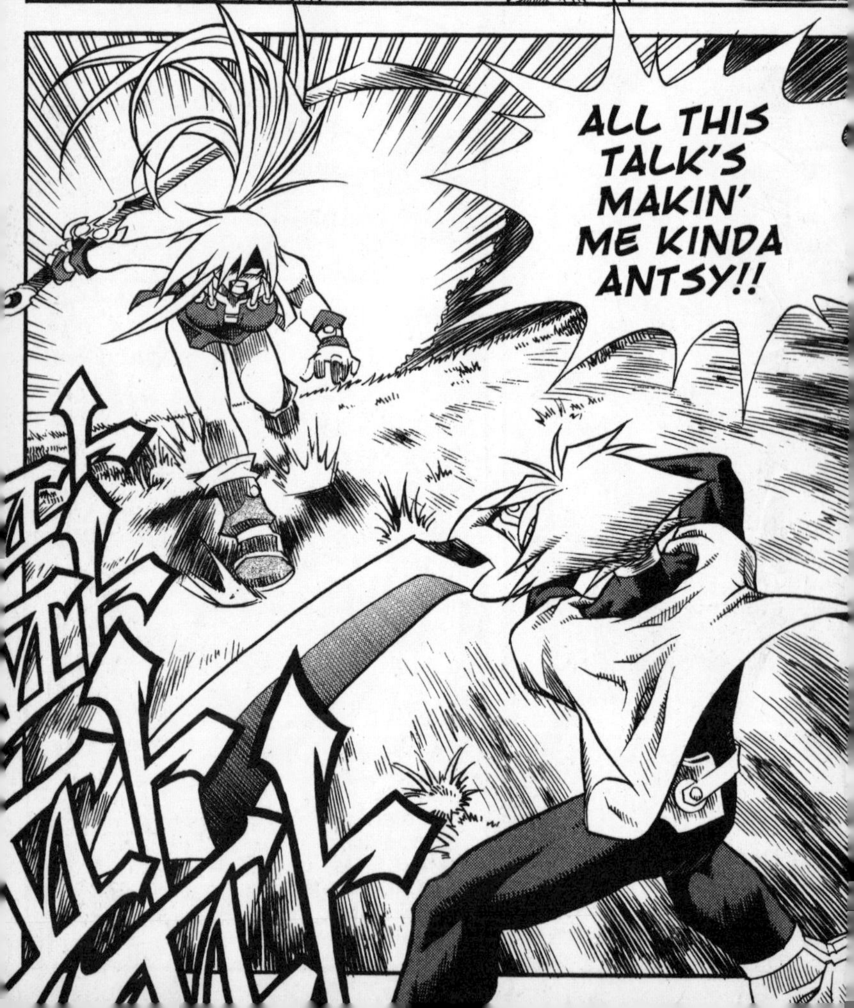
ALL THIS TALK'S MAKIN' ME KINDA ANTSY!!

Quest 27

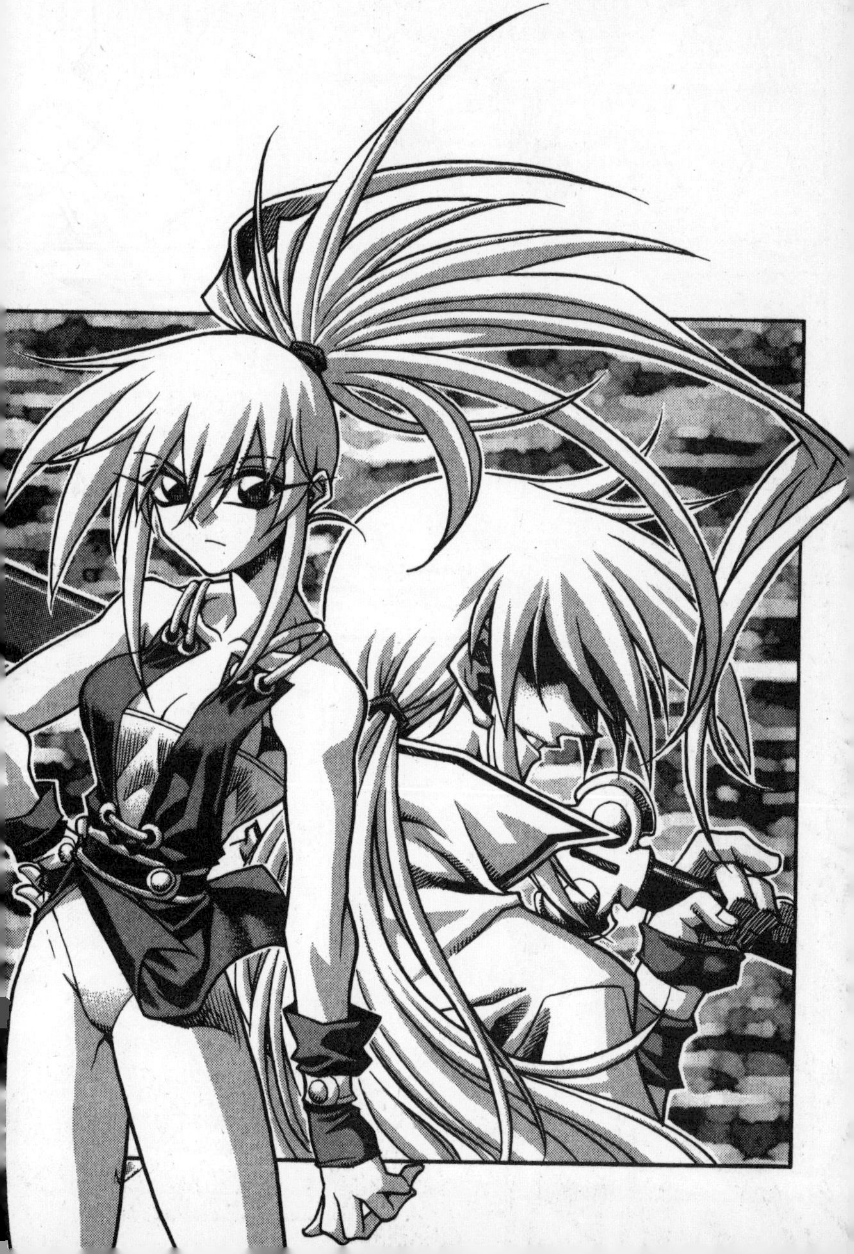

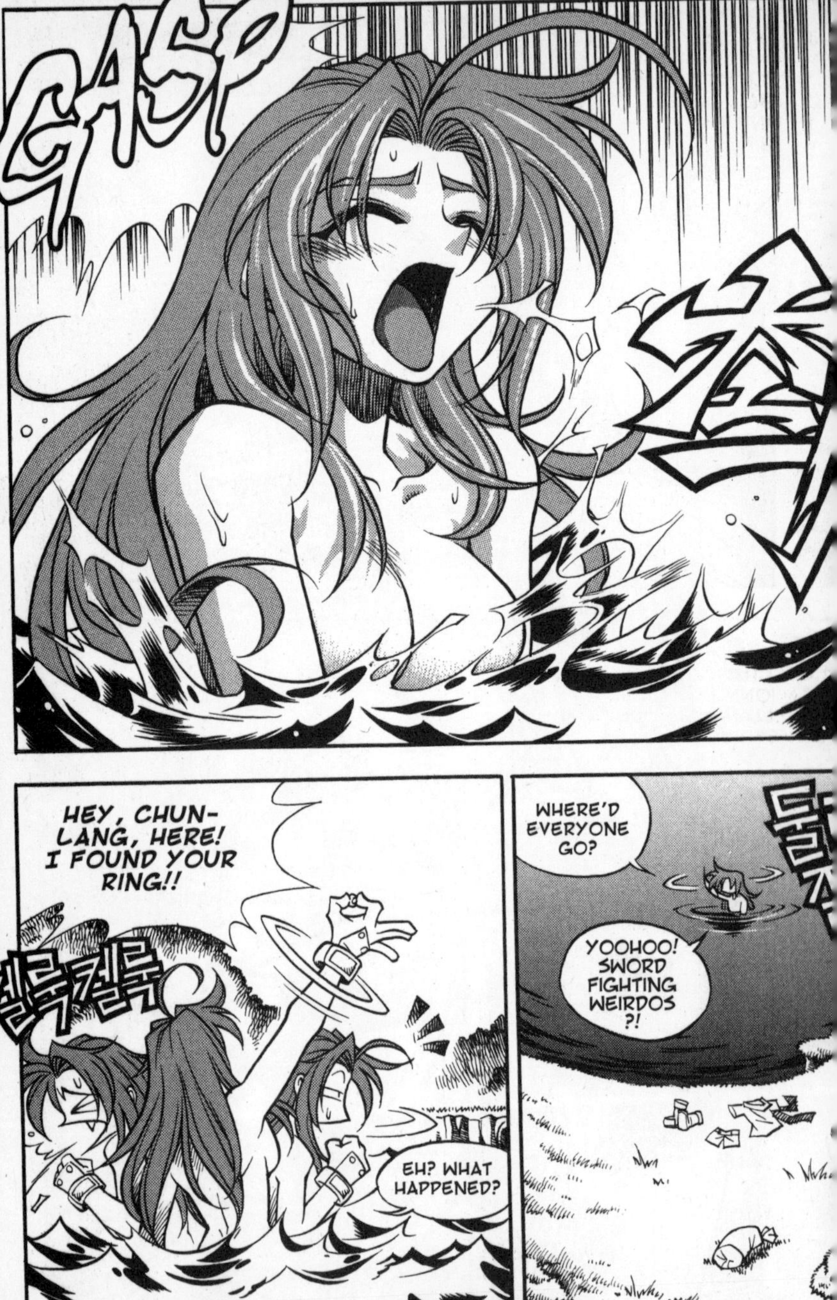
GASP
HEY, CHUN-LANG, HERE! I FOUND YOUR RING!!
EH? WHAT HAPPENED?
WHERE'D EVERYONE GO?
YOOHOO! SWORD FIGHTING WEIRDOS ?!

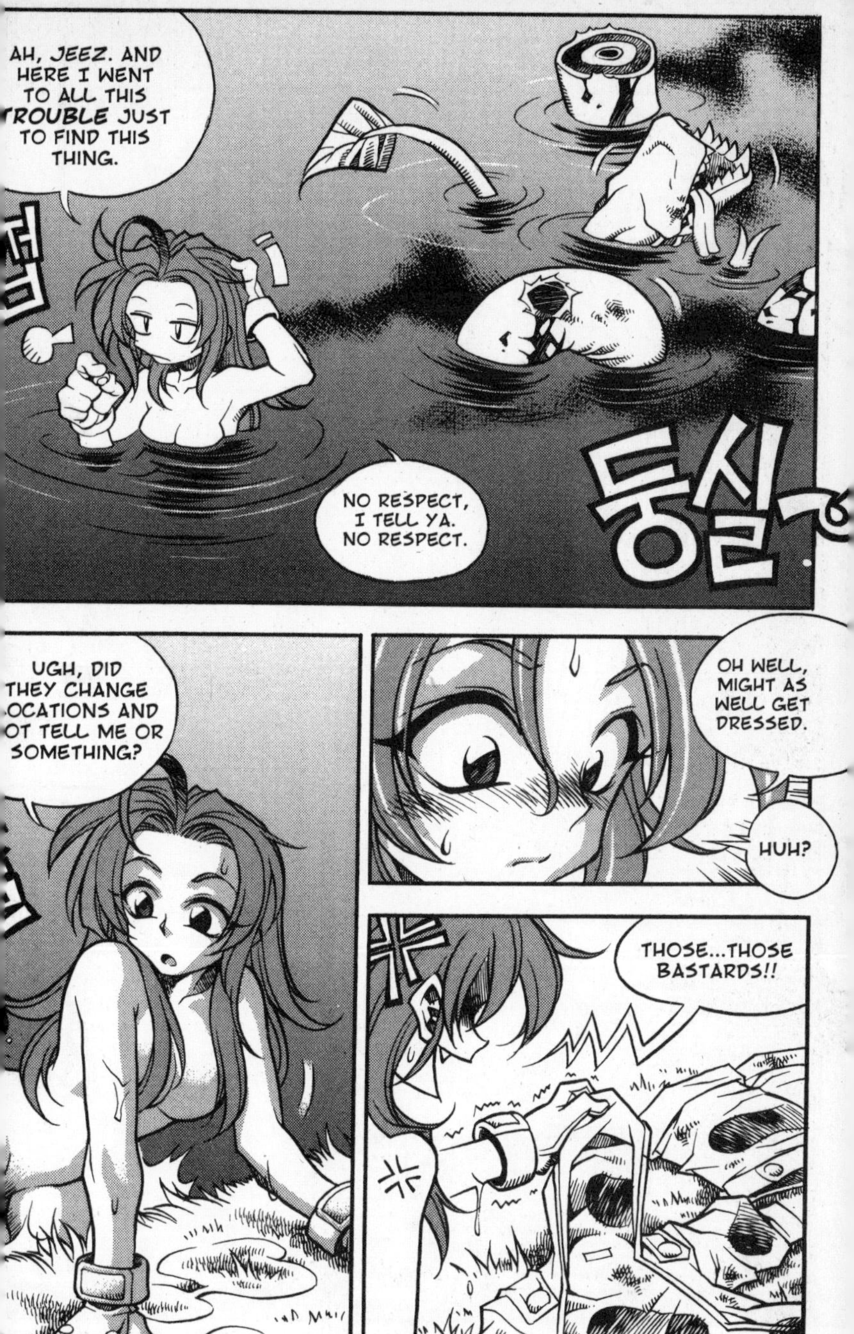
AH, JEEZ. AND HERE I WENT TO ALL THIS TROUBLE JUST TO FIND THIS THING.
NO RESPECT, I TELL YA. NO RESPECT.
둥실~
UGH, DID THEY CHANGE OCATIONS AND OT TELL ME OR SOMETHING?
OH WELL, MIGHT AS WELL GET DRESSED.
HUH?
THOSE...THOSE BASTARDS!!

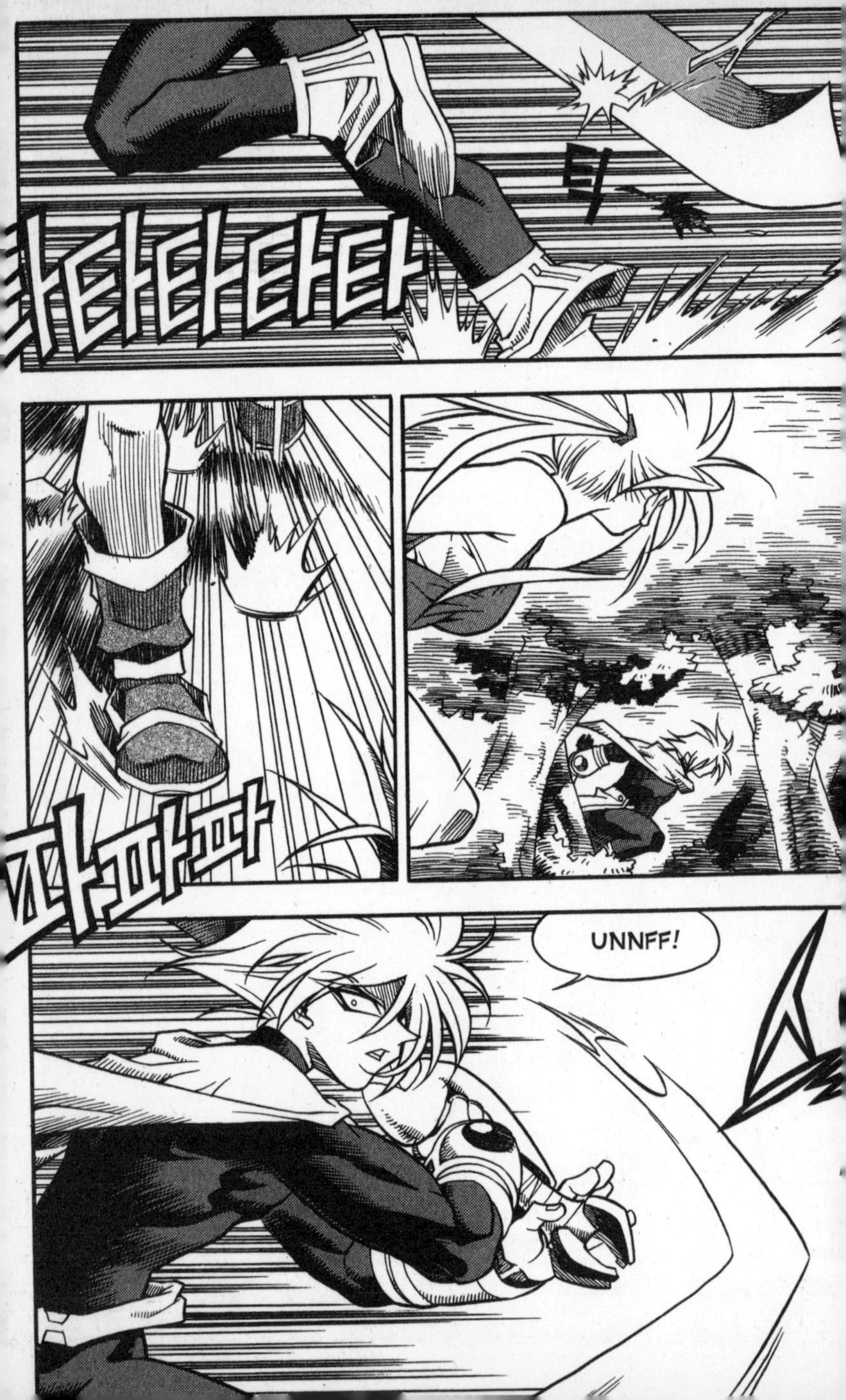
UNNFF!

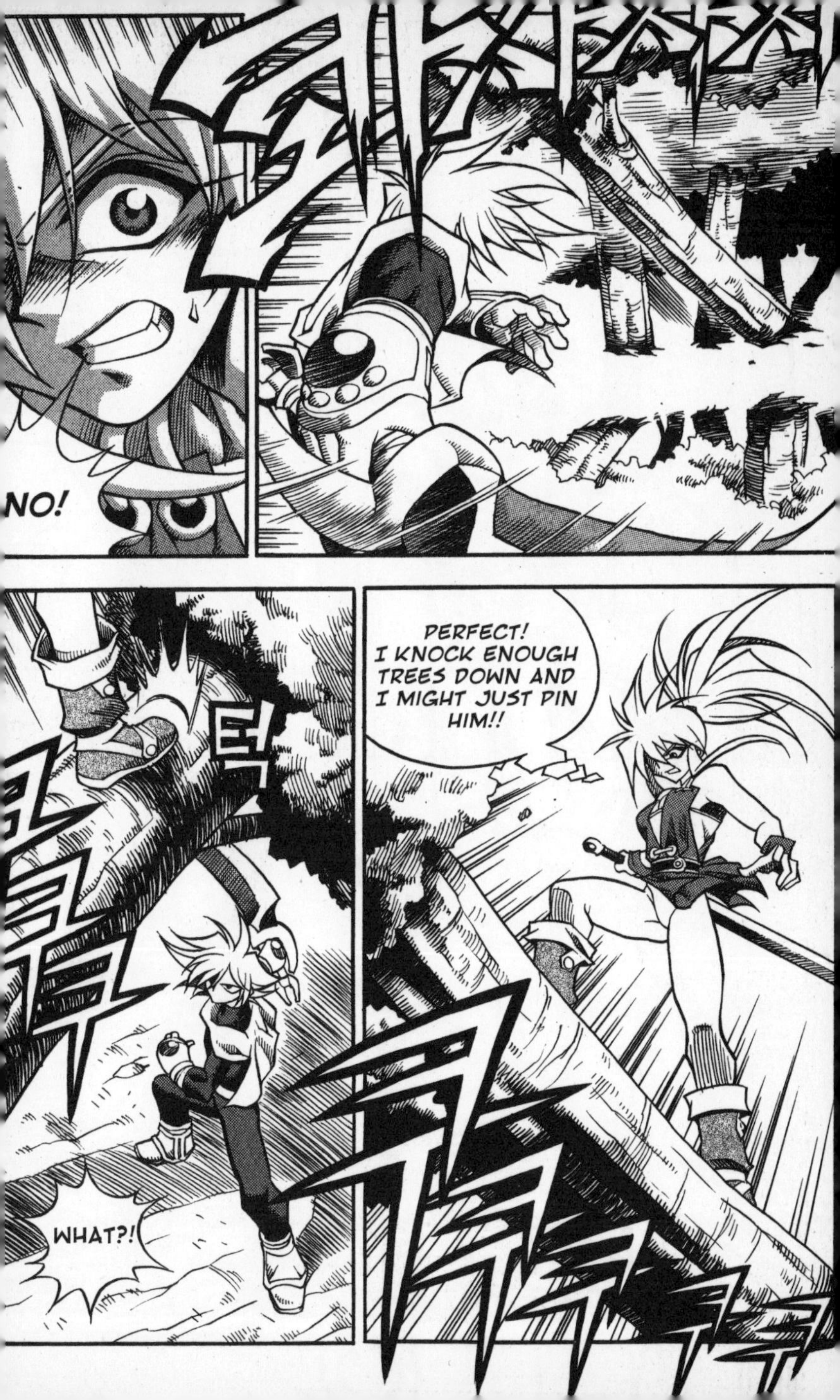
NO!
WHAT?!
PERFECT! I KNOCK ENOUGH TREES DOWN AND I MIGHT JUST PIN HIM!!

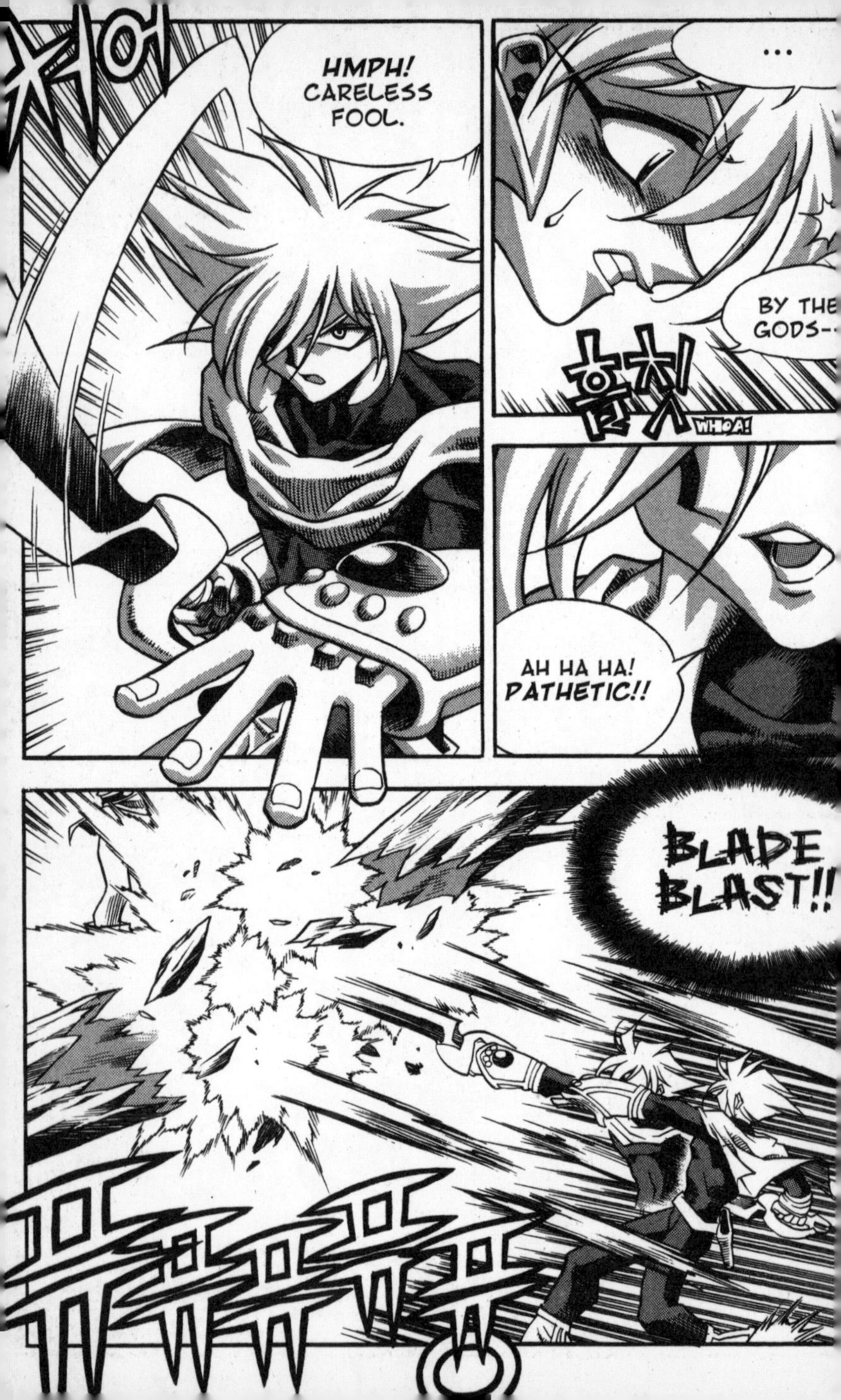
HMPH! CARELESS FOOL.
...
BY THE GODS--
흠칫!
WHOA!
AH HA HA! PATHETIC!!
BLADE BLAST!!

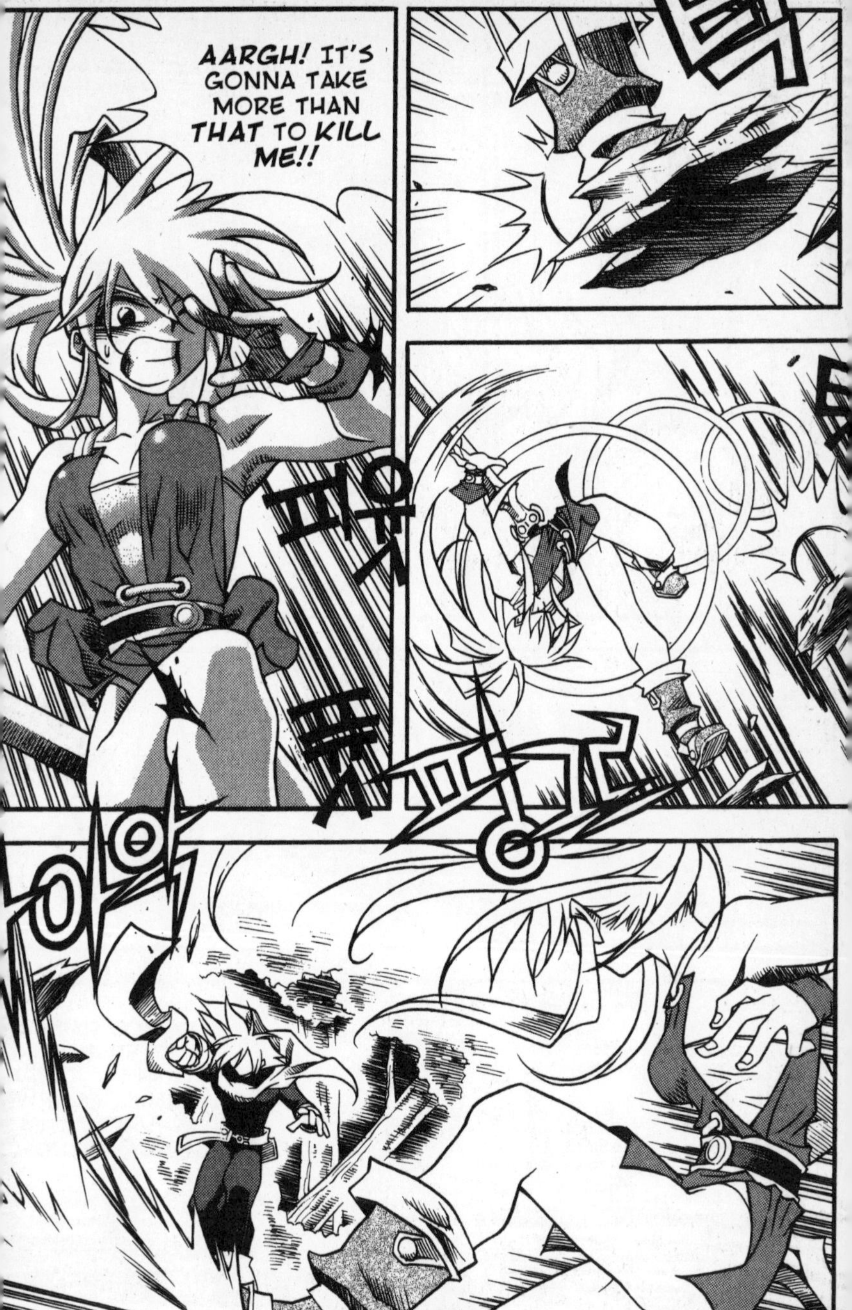
AARGH! IT'S GONNA TAKE MORE THAN THAT TO KILL ME!!

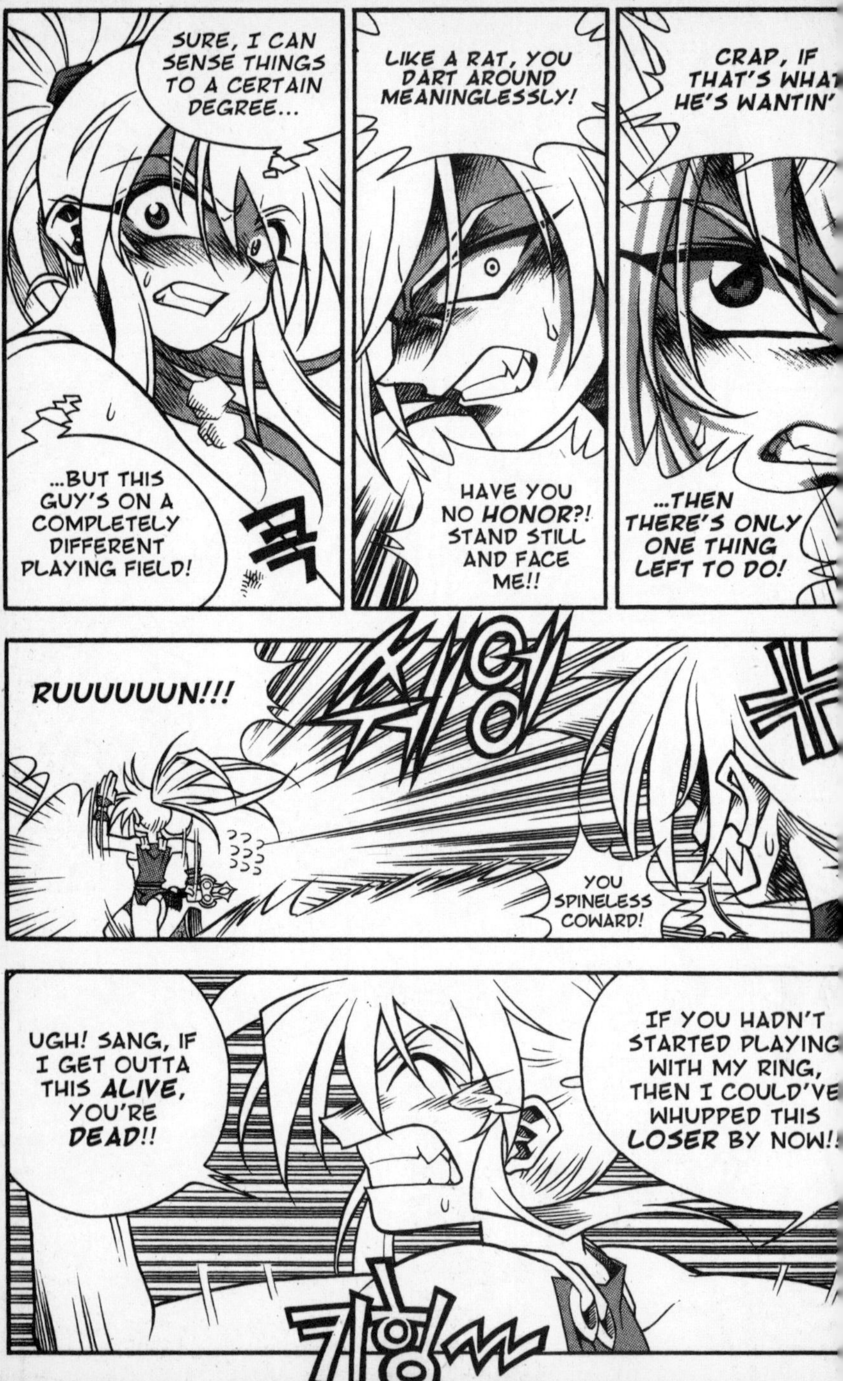
SURE, I CAN SENSE THINGS TO A CERTAIN DEGREE...
...BUT THIS GUY'S ON A COMPLETELY DIFFERENT PLAYING FIELD!
LIKE A RAT, YOU DART AROUND MEANINGLESSLY!
HAVE YOU NO HONOR?! STAND STILL AND FACE ME!!
CRAP, IF THAT'S WHAT HE'S WANTIN'
...THEN THERE'S ONLY ONE THING LEFT TO DO!
RUUUUUUN!!!
YOU SPINELESS COWARD!
UGH! SANG, IF I GET OUTTA THIS ALIVE, YOU'RE DEAD!!
IF YOU HADN'T STARTED PLAYING WITH MY RING, THEN I COULD'VE WHUPPED THIS LOSER BY NOW!!

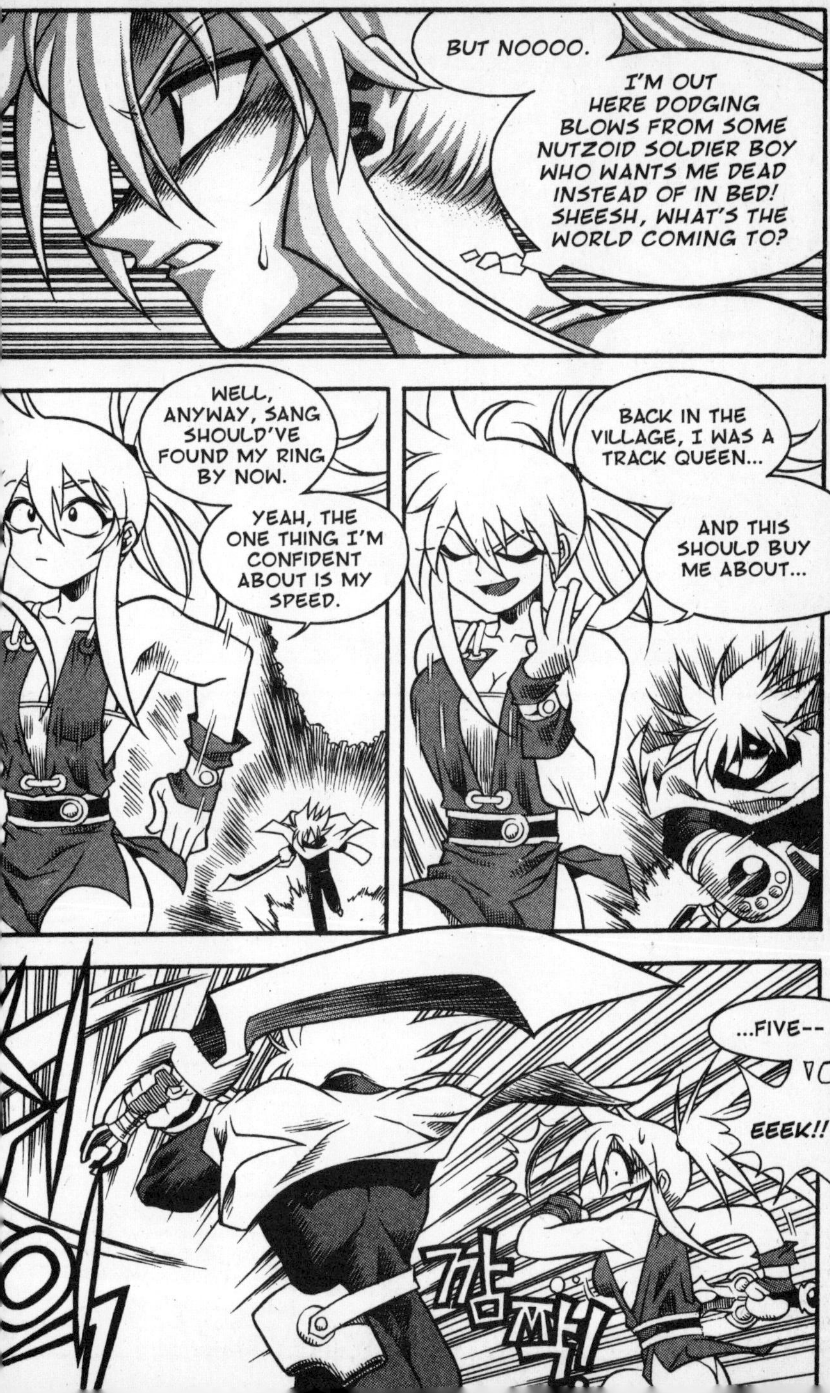
BUT NOOOO.
I'M OUT HERE DODGING BLOWS FROM SOME NUTZOID SOLDIER BOY WHO WANTS ME DEAD INSTEAD OF IN BED! SHEESH, WHAT'S THE WORLD COMING TO?
WELL, ANYWAY, SANG SHOULD'VE FOUND MY RING BY NOW.
YEAH, THE ONE THING I'M CONFIDENT ABOUT IS MY SPEED.
BACK IN THE VILLAGE, I WAS A TRACK QUEEN...
AND THIS SHOULD BUY ME ABOUT...
...FIVE--
EEEK!!
깜짝!

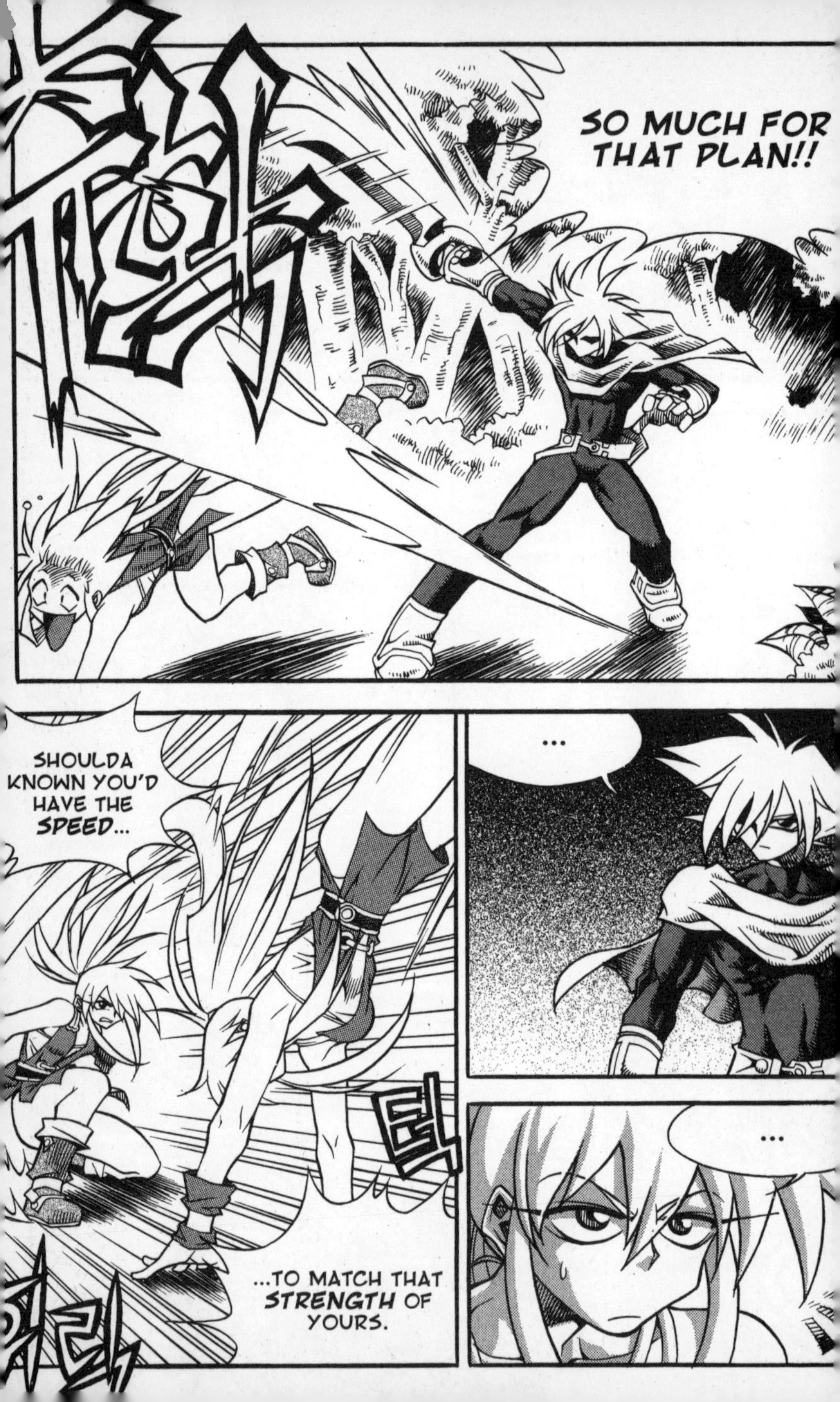
SO MUCH FOR THAT PLAN!!
SHOULDA KNOWN YOU'D HAVE THE SPEED...
...TO MATCH THAT STRENGTH OF YOURS.
...
...

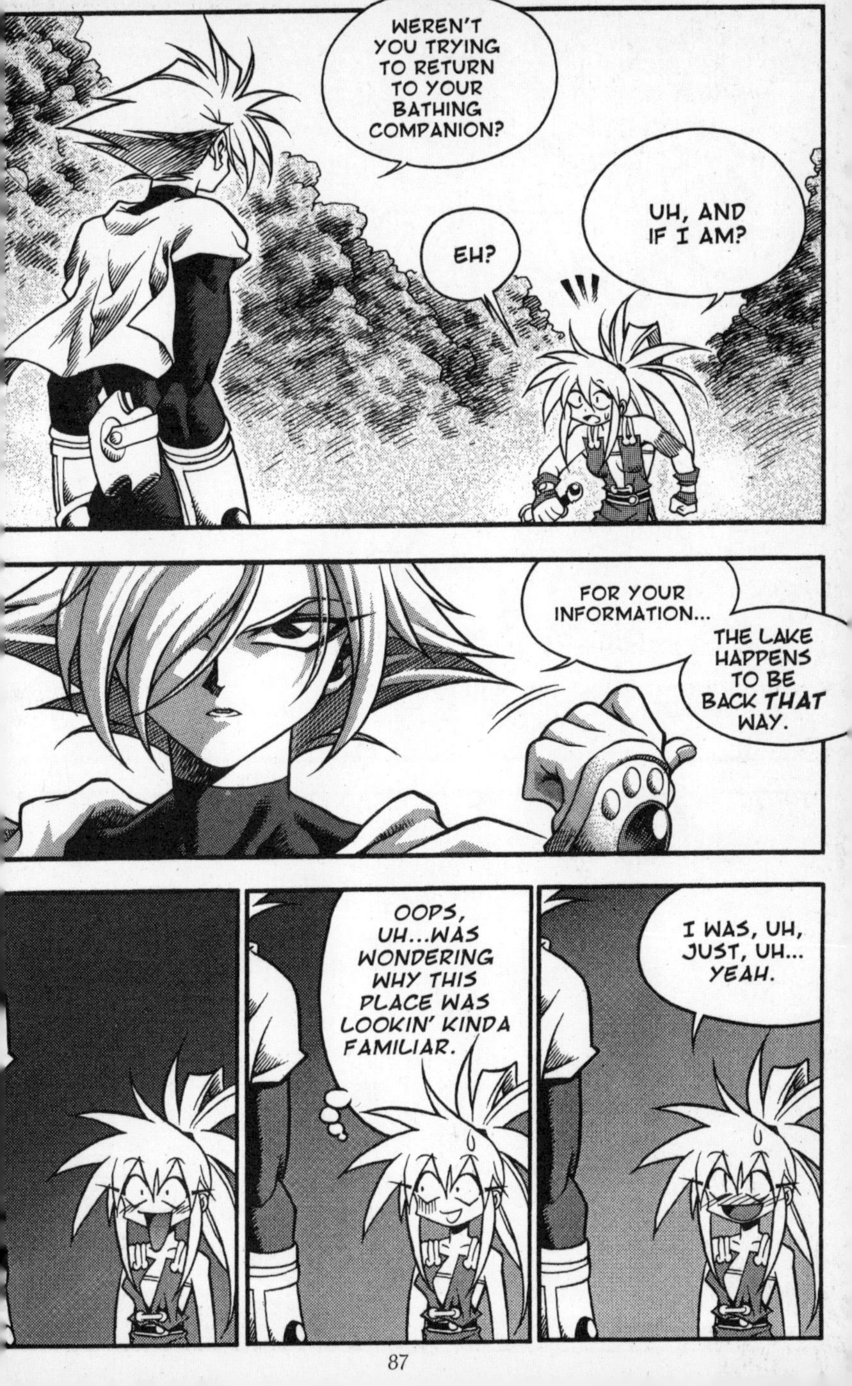
WEREN'T YOU TRYING TO RETURN TO YOUR BATHING COMPANION?
EH?
UH, AND IF I AM?
!!!
FOR YOUR INFORMATION...
THE LAKE HAPPENS TO BE BACK *THAT* WAY.
OOPS, UH...WAS WONDERING WHY THIS PLACE WAS LOOKIN' KINDA FAMILIAR.
I WAS, UH, JUST, UH... YEAH.

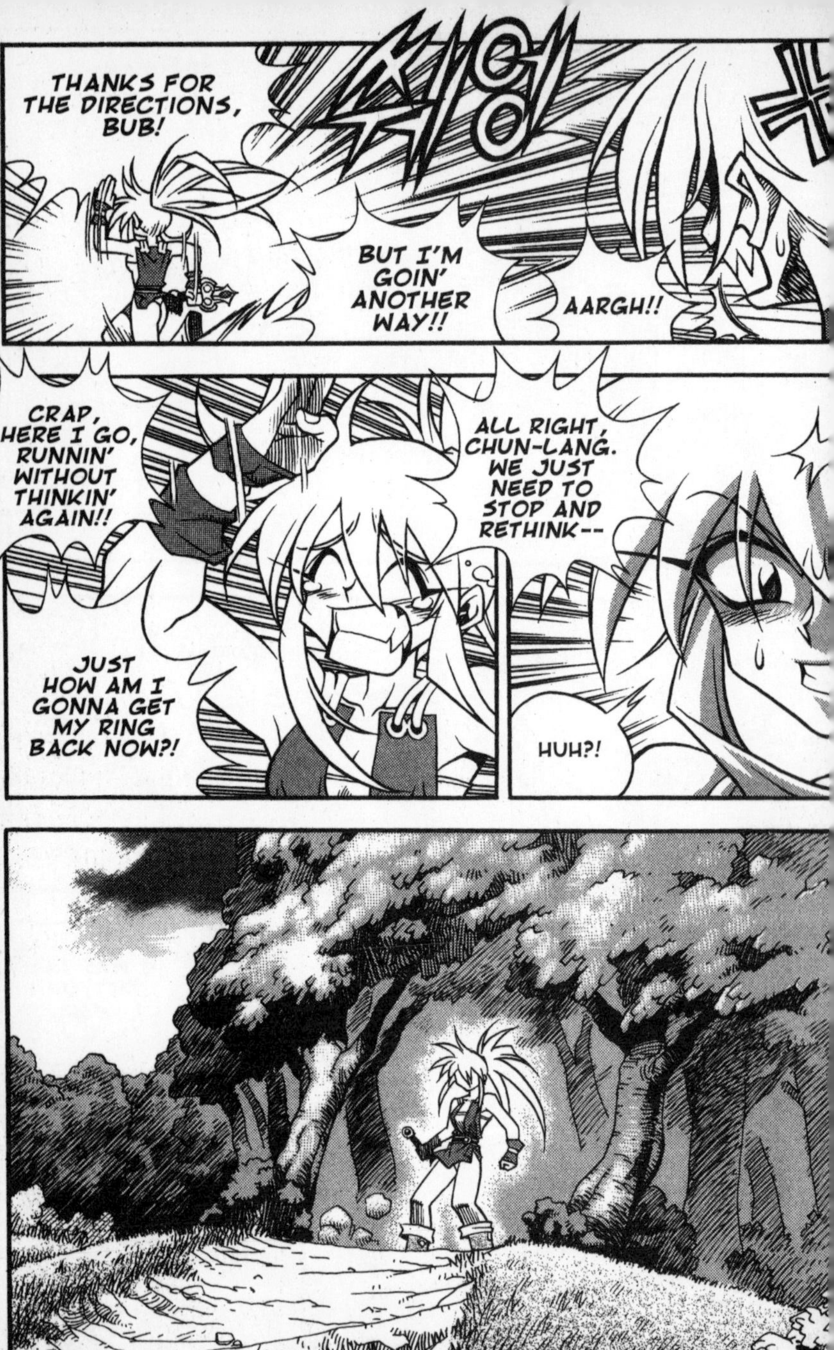
THANKS FOR THE DIRECTIONS, BUB!
BUT I'M GOIN' ANOTHER WAY!!
AARGH!!
CRAP, HERE I GO, RUNNIN' WITHOUT THINKIN' AGAIN!!
JUST HOW AM I GONNA GET MY RING BACK NOW?!
ALL RIGHT, CHUN-LANG. WE JUST NEED TO STOP AND RETHINK--
HUH?!

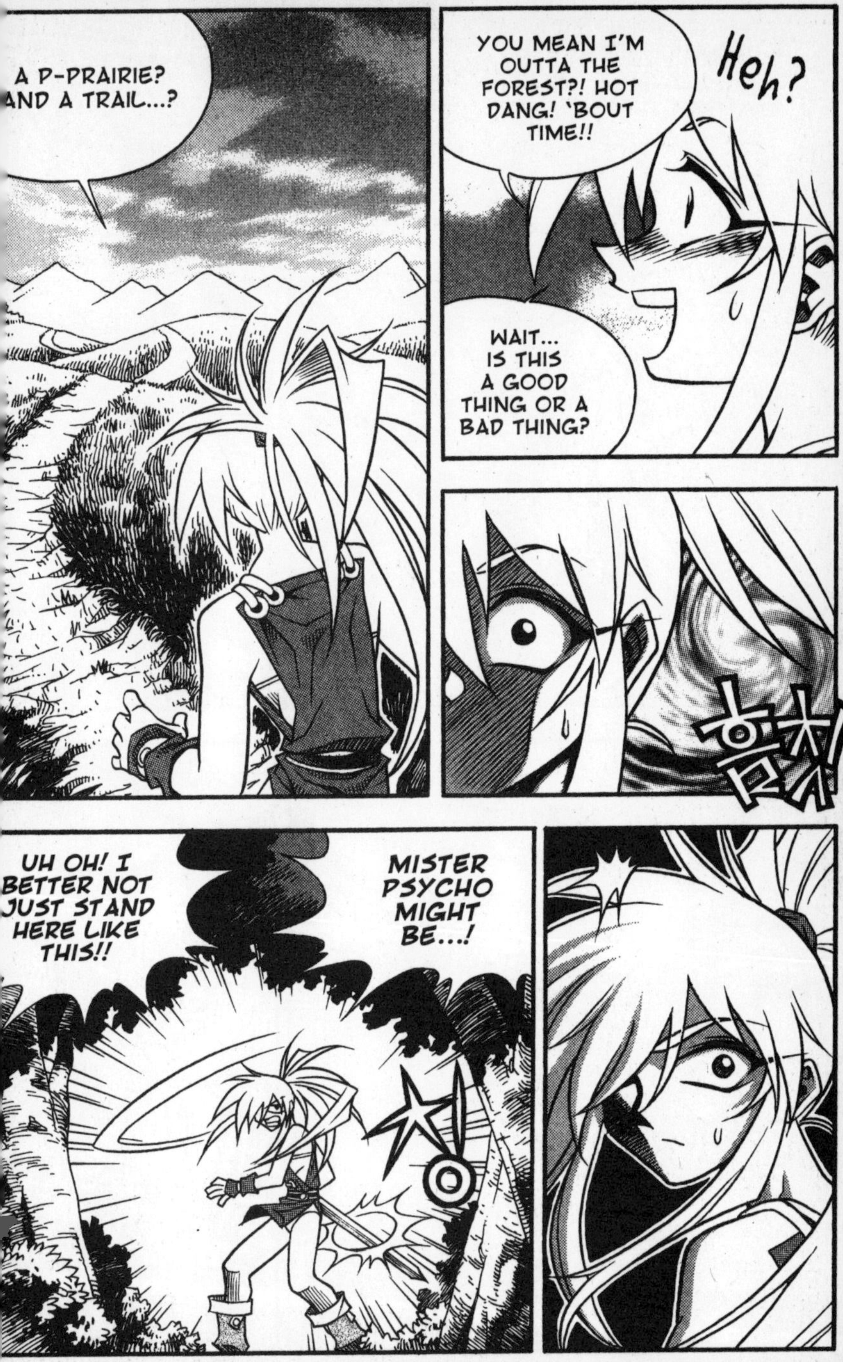
A P-PRAIRIE? AND A TRAIL...?
YOU MEAN I'M OUTTA THE FOREST?! HOT DANG! 'BOUT TIME!!
Heh?
WAIT... IS THIS A GOOD THING OR A BAD THING?
흠칫!
UH OH! I BETTER NOT JUST STAND HERE LIKE THIS!!
MISTER PSYCHO MIGHT BE...!

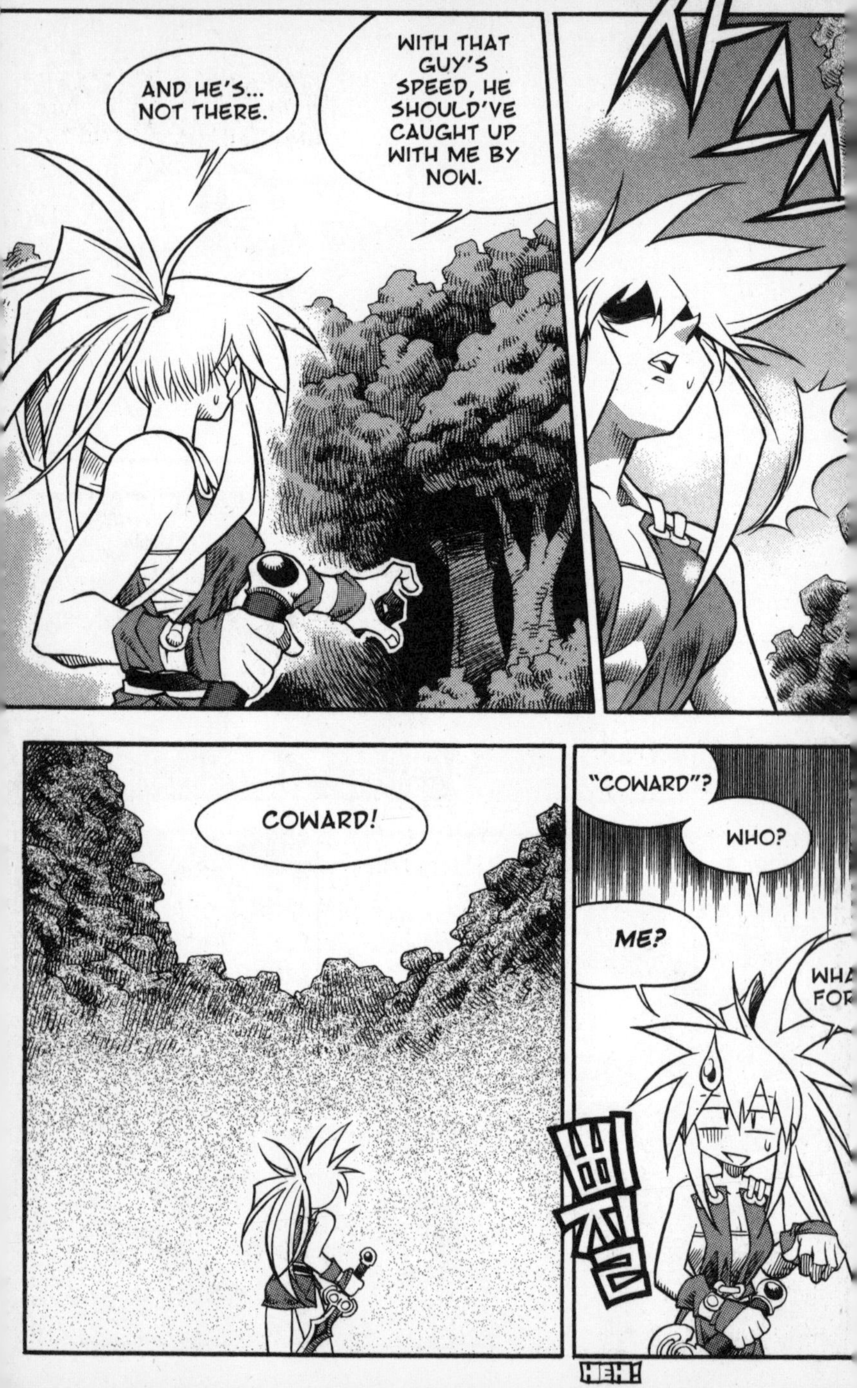
AND HE'S... NOT THERE.
WITH THAT GUY'S SPEED, HE SHOULD'VE CAUGHT UP WITH ME BY NOW.
COWARD!
"COWARD"?
WHO?
ME?
WHA
FOR
HEH!

Quest 28

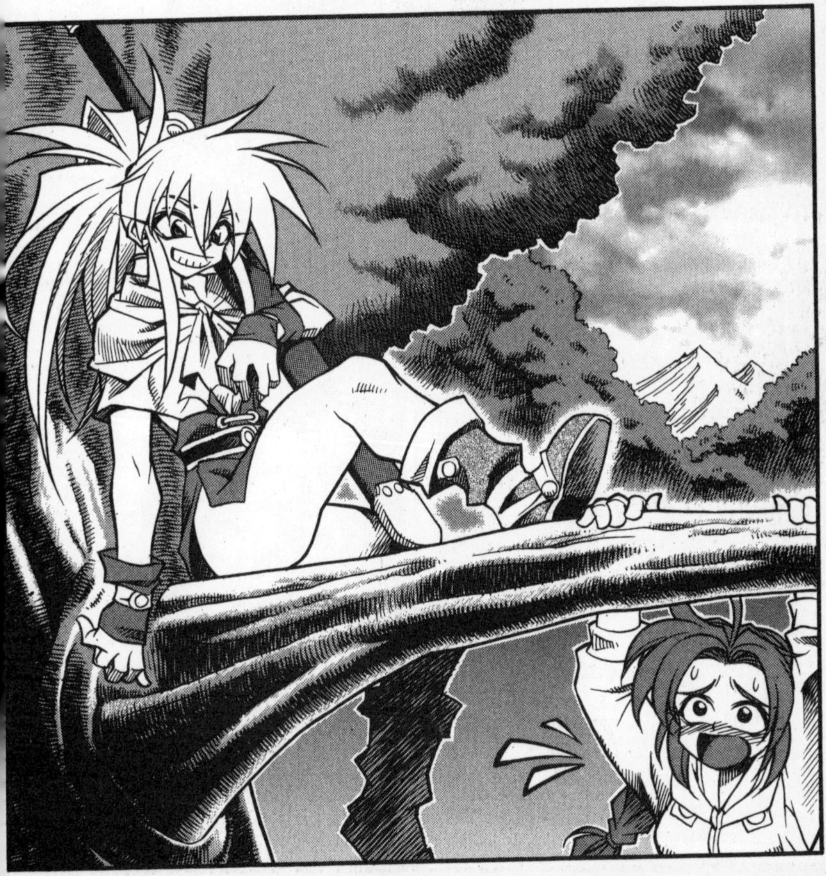

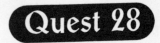

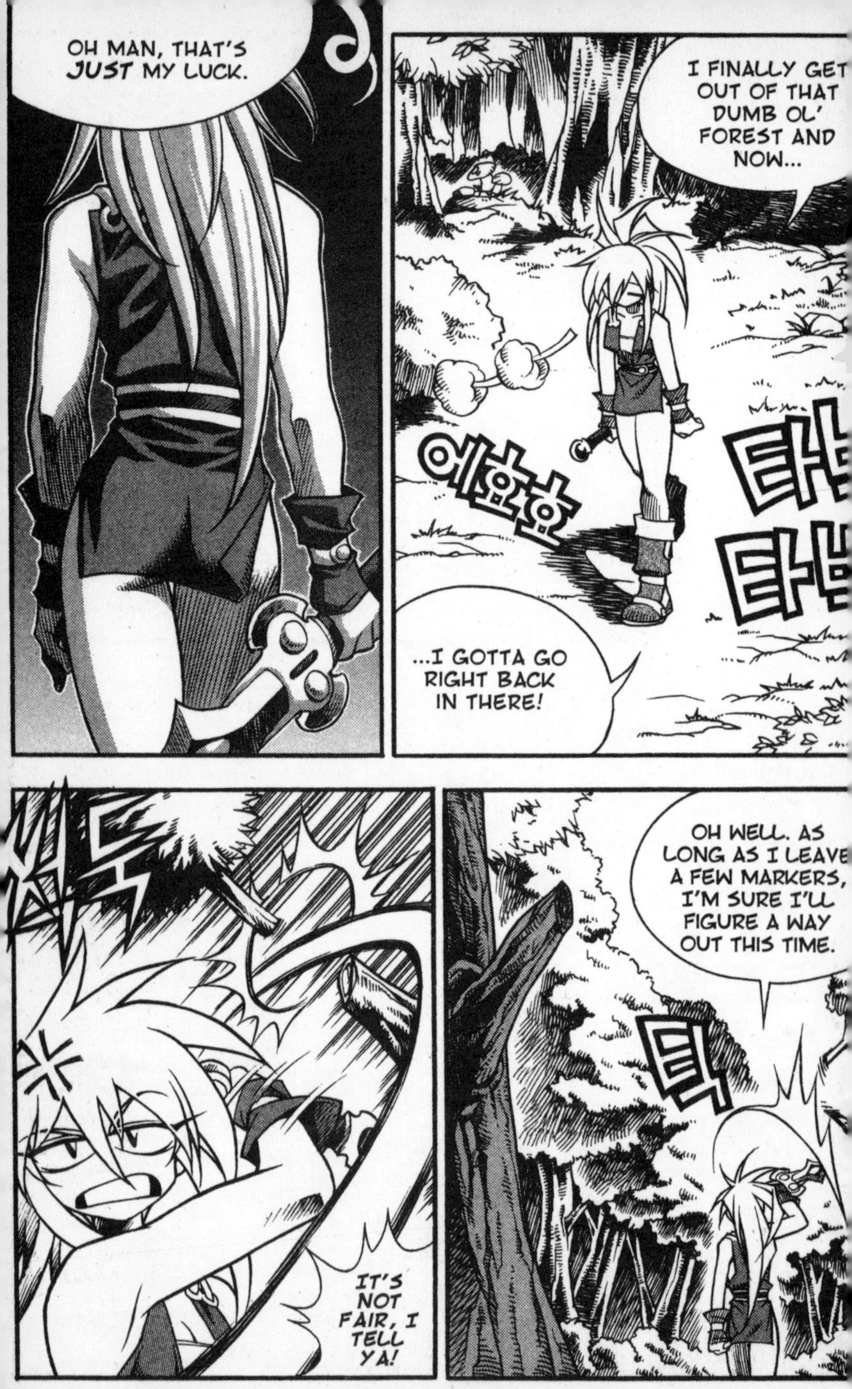
OH MAN, THAT'S JUST MY LUCK.
I FINALLY GET OUT OF THAT DUMB OL' FOREST AND NOW...
...I GOTTA GO RIGHT BACK IN THERE!
IT'S NOT FAIR, I TELL YA!
OH WELL. AS LONG AS I LEAVE A FEW MARKERS, I'M SURE I'LL FIGURE A WAY OUT THIS TIME.

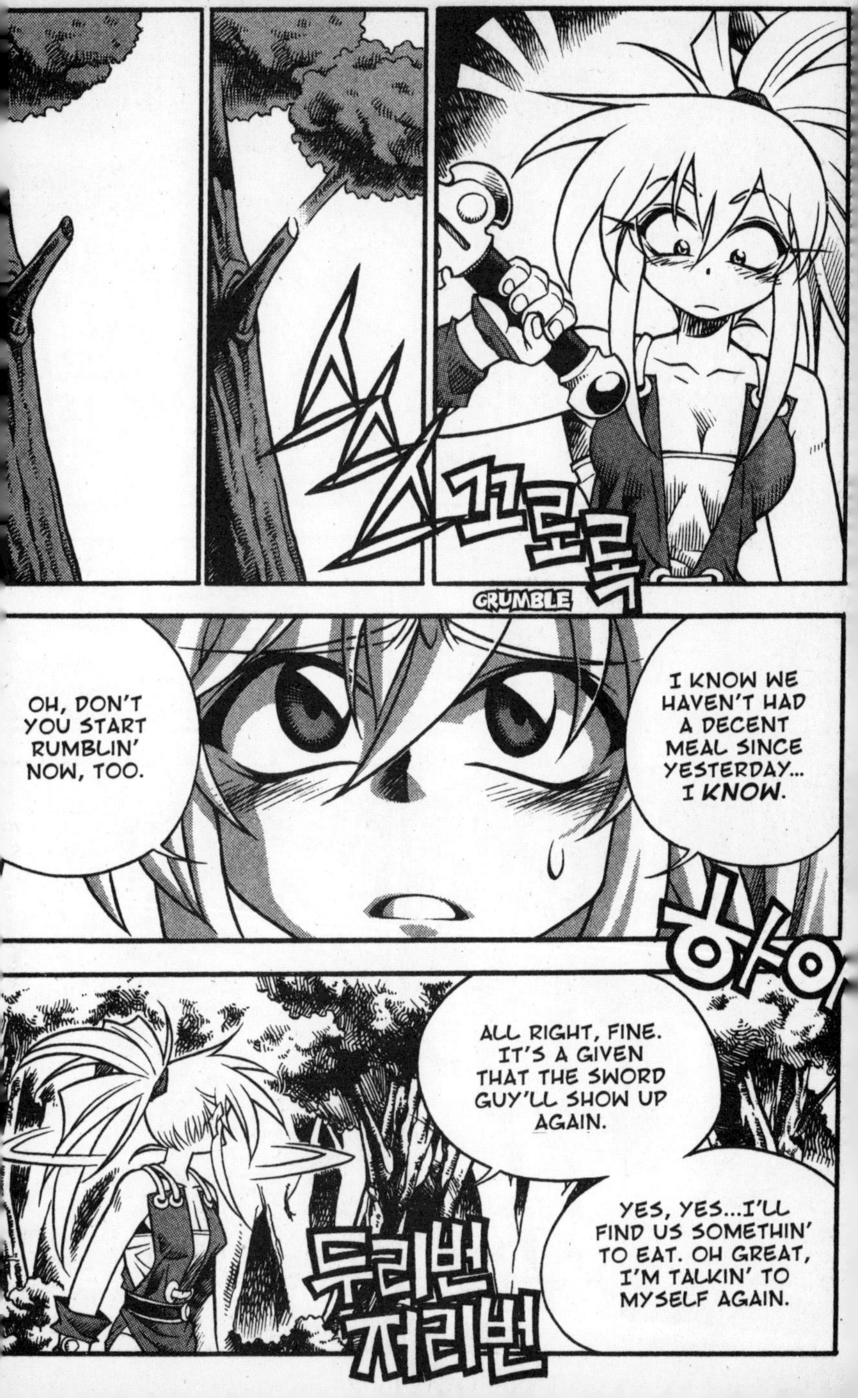
GRUMBLE
OH, DON'T YOU START RUMBLIN' NOW, TOO.
I KNOW WE HAVEN'T HAD A DECENT MEAL SINCE YESTERDAY... I **KNOW**.
ALL RIGHT, FINE. IT'S A GIVEN THAT THE SWORD GUY'LL SHOW UP AGAIN.
YES, YES...I'LL FIND US SOMETHIN' TO EAT. OH GREAT, I'M TALKIN' TO MYSELF AGAIN.

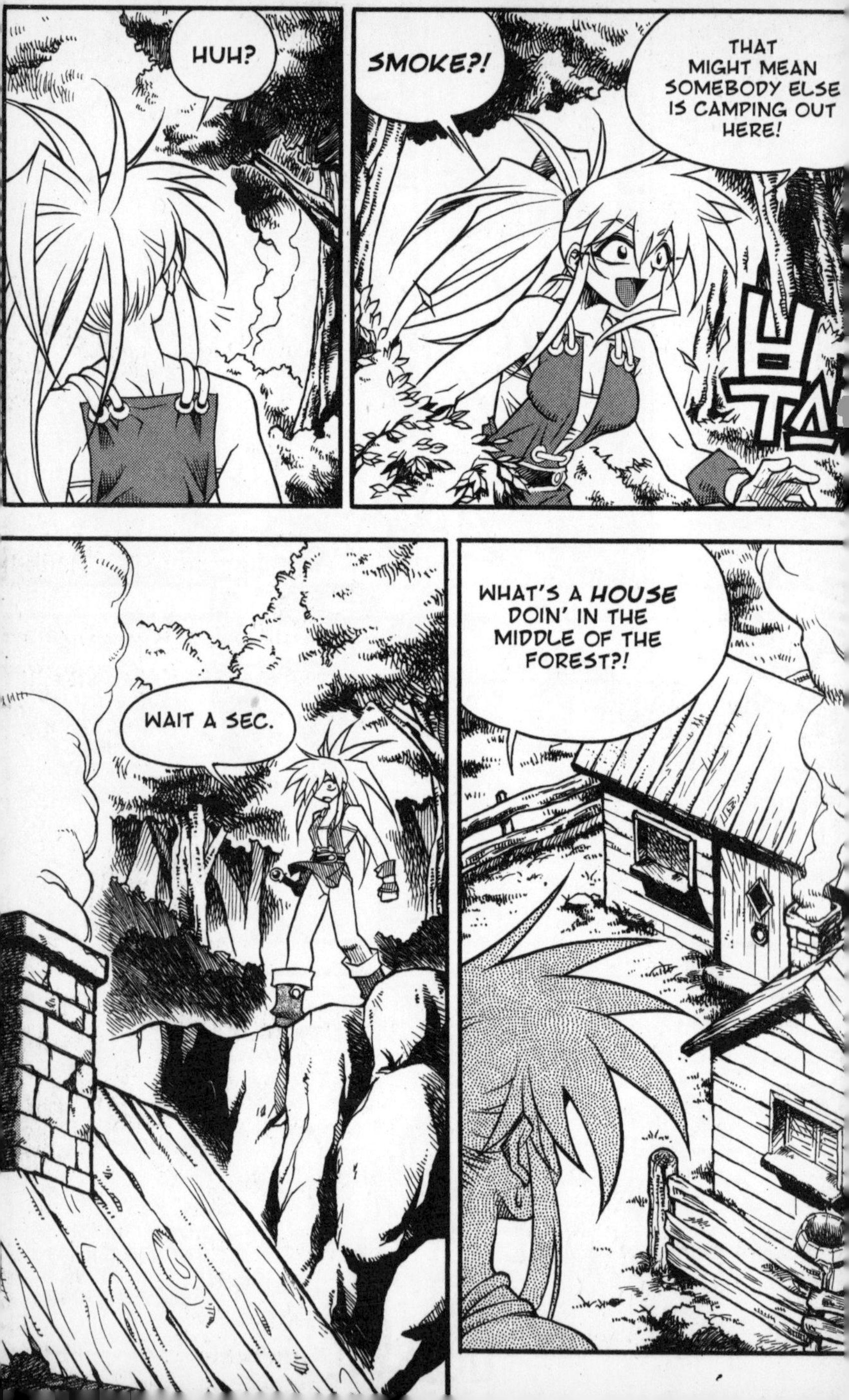
HUH?
SMOKE?!
THAT MIGHT MEAN SOMEBODY ELSE IS CAMPING OUT HERE!
WAIT A SEC.
WHAT'S A HOUSE DOIN' IN THE MIDDLE OF THE FOREST?!

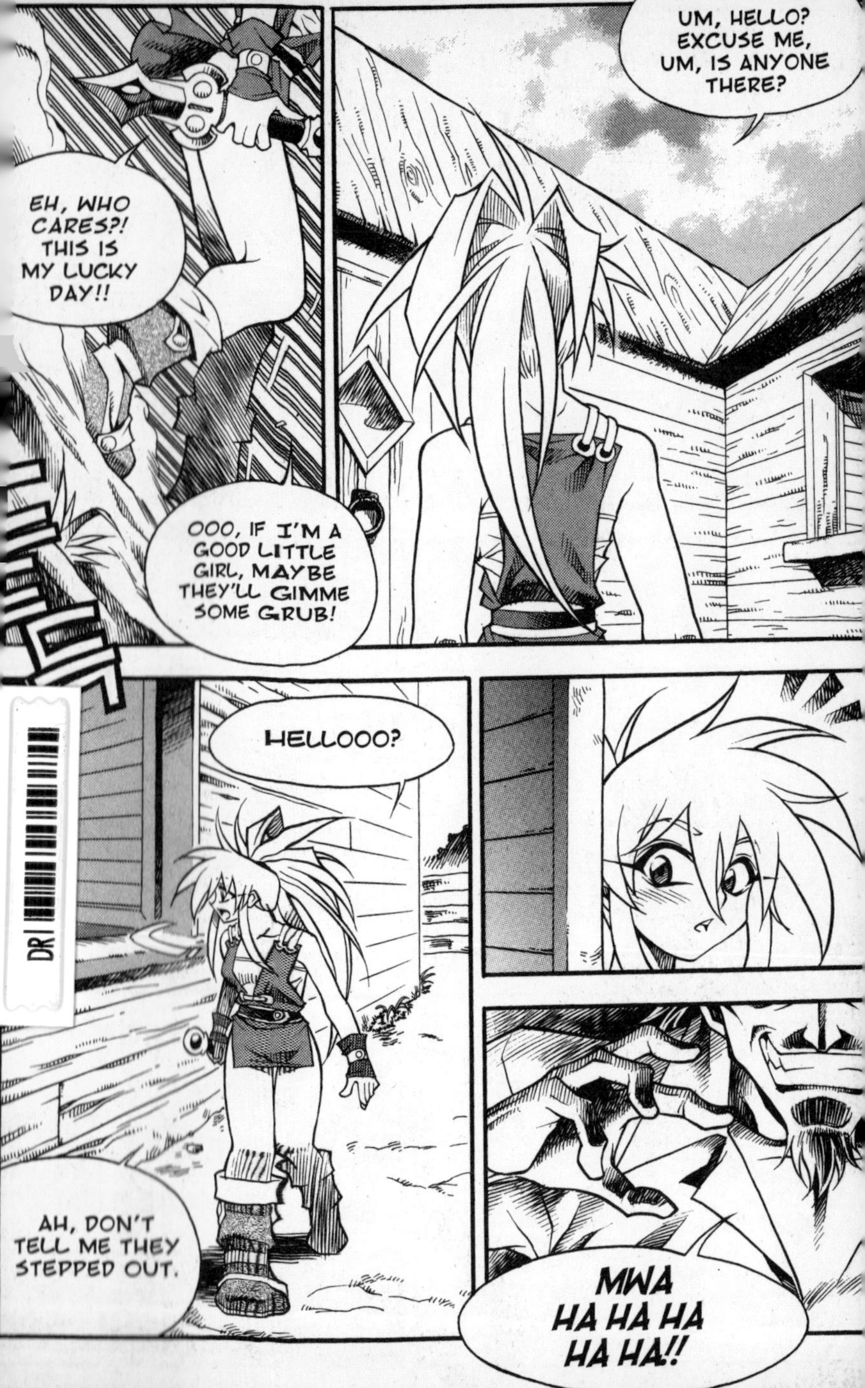

EH, WHO CARES?! THIS IS MY LUCKY DAY!!
OOO, IF I'M A GOOD LITTLE GIRL, MAYBE THEY'LL GIMME SOME GRUB!
UM, HELLO? EXCUSE ME, UM, IS ANYONE THERE?
HELLOOO?
AH, DON'T TELL ME THEY STEPPED OUT.
MWA HA HA HA HA HA!!

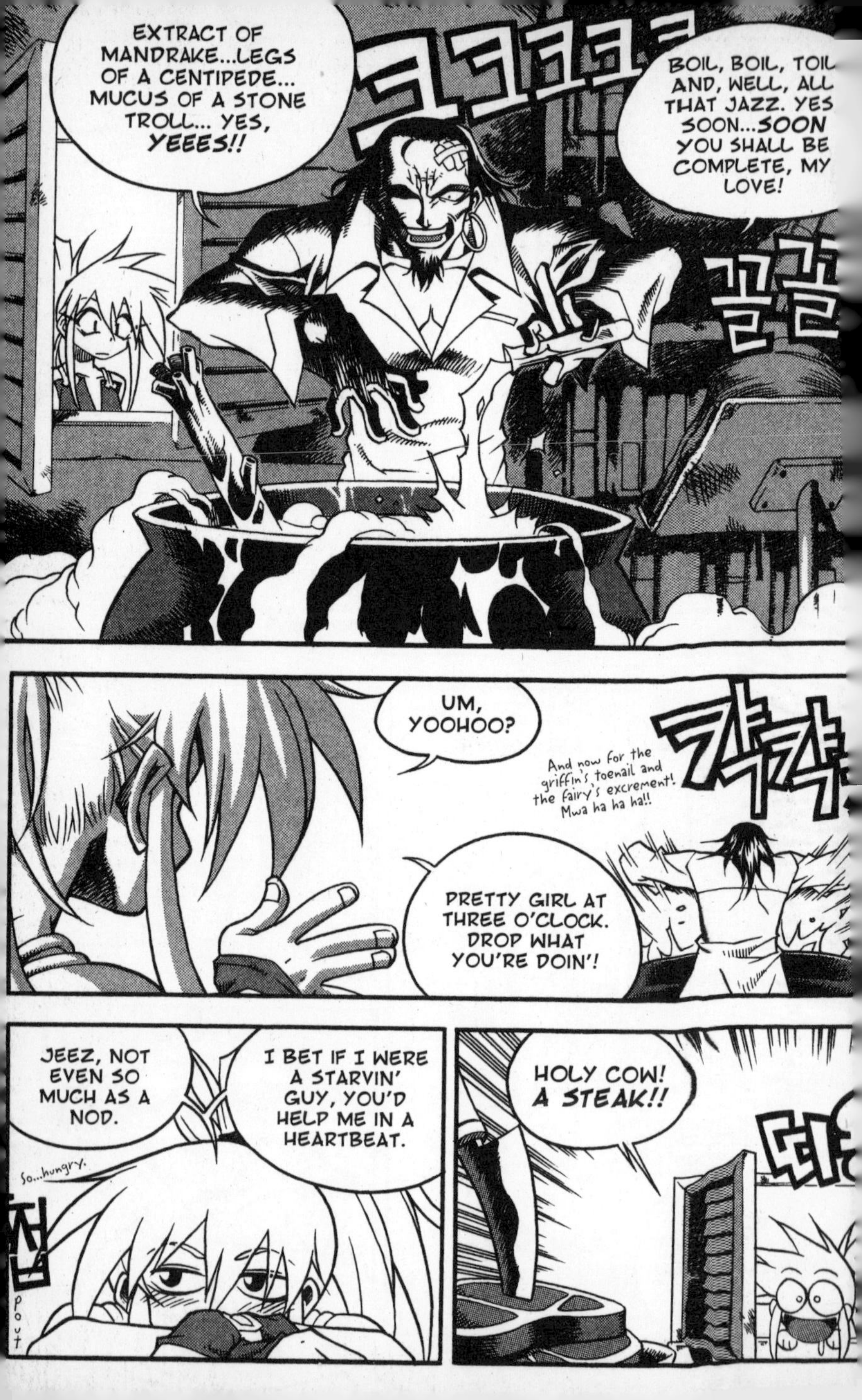
EXTRACT OF MANDRAKE...LEGS OF A CENTIPEDE... MUCUS OF A STONE TROLL... YES, YEEES!!
BOIL, BOIL, TOIL AND, WELL, ALL THAT JAZZ. YES SOON...SOON YOU SHALL BE COMPLETE, MY LOVE!
UM, YOOHOO?
And now for the griffin's toenail and the fairy's excrement! Mwa ha ha ha!!
PRETTY GIRL AT THREE O'CLOCK. DROP WHAT YOU'RE DOIN'!
JEEZ, NOT EVEN SO MUCH AS A NOD.
I BET IF I WERE A STARVIN' GUY, YOU'D HELP ME IN A HEARTBEAT.
So...hungry.
pout
HOLY COW! A STEAK!!

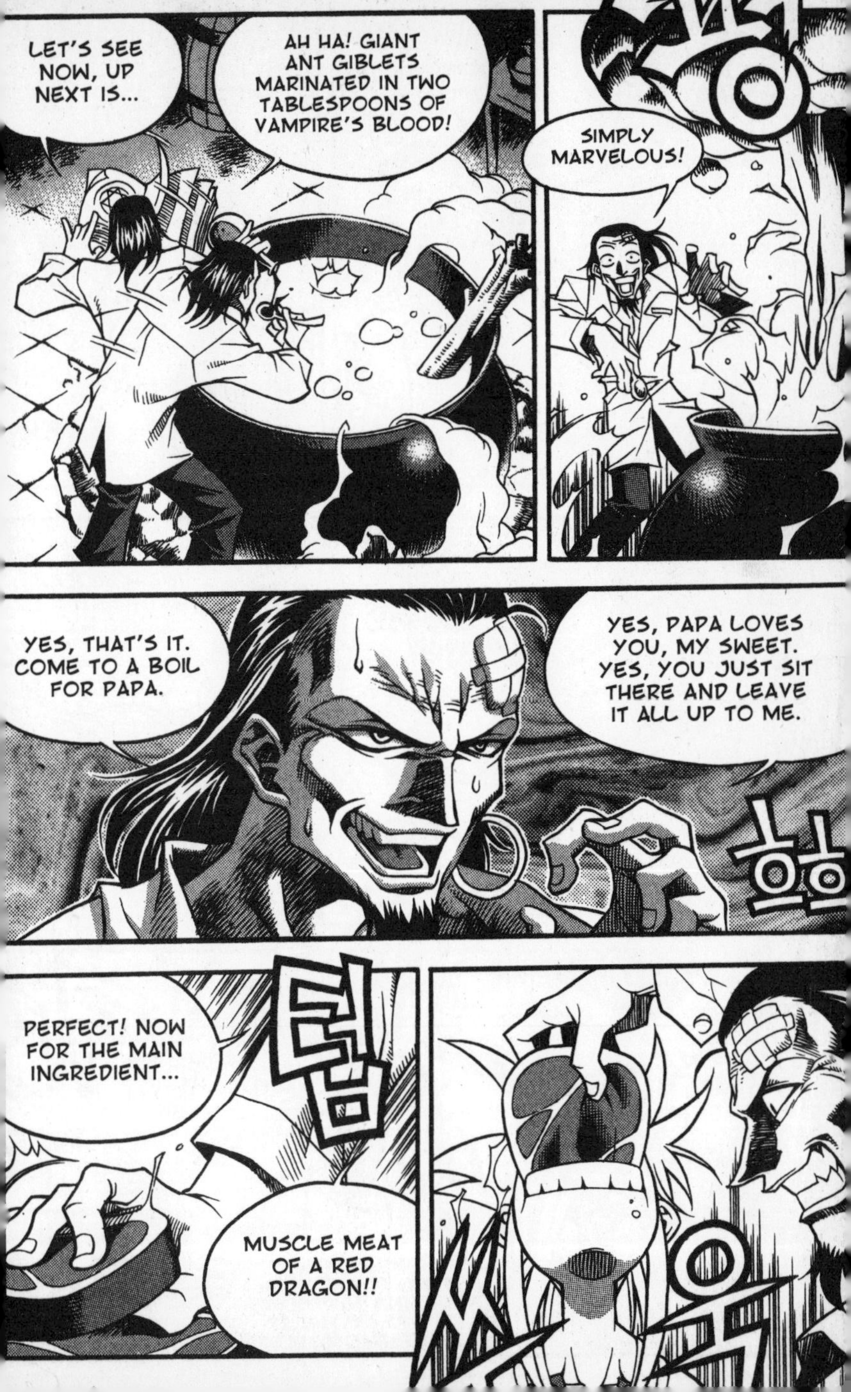
LET'S SEE NOW, UP NEXT IS...
AH HA! GIANT ANT GIBLETS MARINATED IN TWO TABLESPOONS OF VAMPIRE'S BLOOD!
SIMPLY MARVELOUS!
YES, THAT'S IT. COME TO A BOIL FOR PAPA.
YES, PAPA LOVES YOU, MY SWEET. YES, YOU JUST SIT THERE AND LEAVE IT ALL UP TO ME.
PERFECT! NOW FOR THE MAIN INGREDIENT...
MUSCLE MEAT OF A RED DRAGON!!

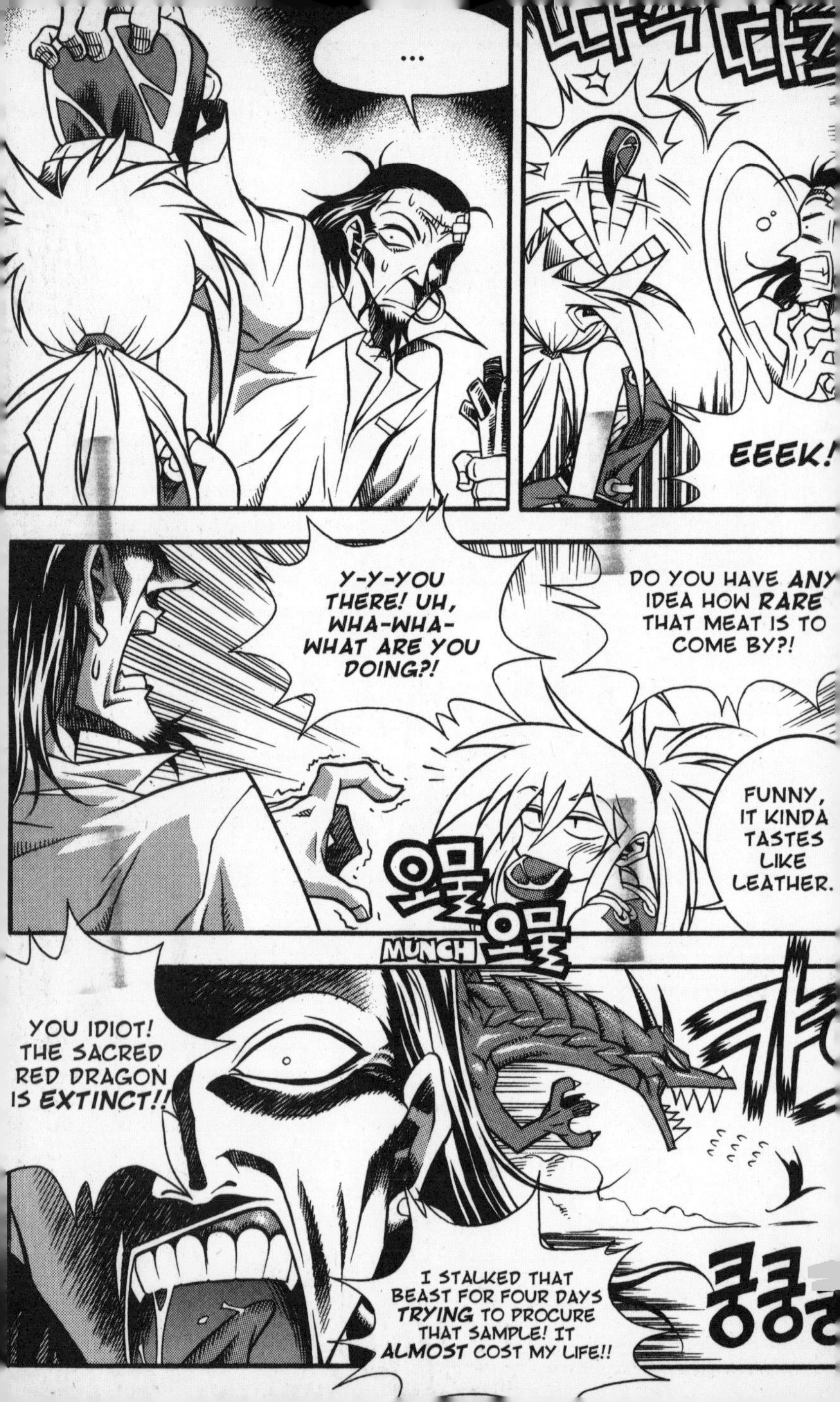
...
EEEK!
Y-Y-YOU THERE! UH, WHA-WHA-WHAT ARE YOU DOING?!
DO YOU HAVE ANY IDEA HOW RARE THAT MEAT IS TO COME BY?!
FUNNY, IT KINDA TASTES LIKE LEATHER.
오물오물
MUNCH
YOU IDIOT! THE SACRED RED DRAGON IS EXTINCT!!
I STALKED THAT BEAST FOR FOUR DAYS TRYING TO PROCURE THAT SAMPLE! IT ALMOST COST MY LIFE!!
쿵쿵

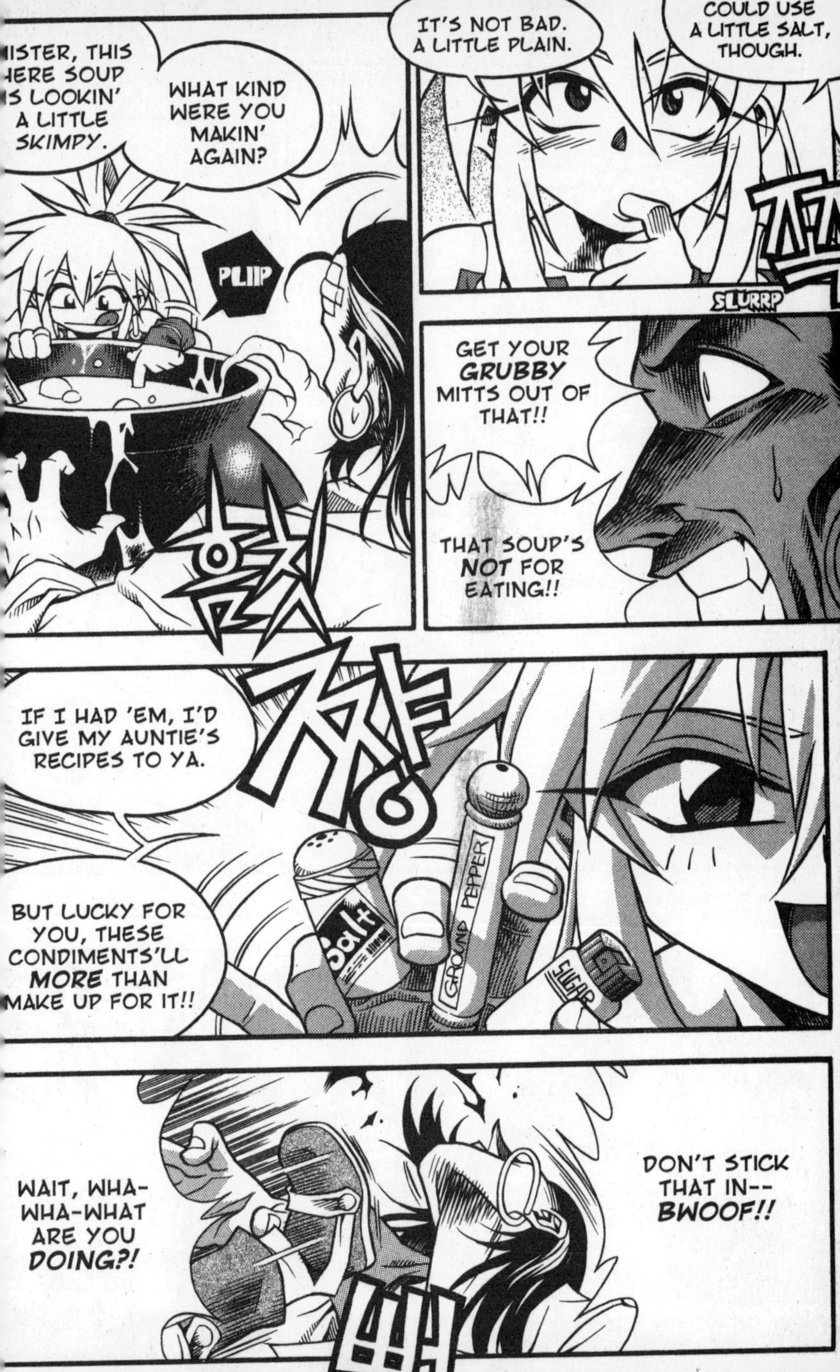
ISTER, THIS HERE SOUP IS LOOKIN' A LITTLE SKIMPY.
WHAT KIND WERE YOU MAKIN' AGAIN?
PLIIP
IT'S NOT BAD. A LITTLE PLAIN.
COULD USE A LITTLE SALT, THOUGH.
SLURRP
GET YOUR *GRUBBY* MITTS OUT OF THAT!!
THAT SOUP'S *NOT* FOR EATING!!
IF I HAD 'EM, I'D GIVE MY AUNTIE'S RECIPES TO YA.
BUT LUCKY FOR YOU, THESE CONDIMENTS'LL *MORE* THAN MAKE UP FOR IT!!
Salt
GROUND PEPPER
SUGAR
WAIT, WHA-WHA-WHAT ARE YOU *DOING?!*
DON'T STICK THAT IN-- *BWOOF!!*

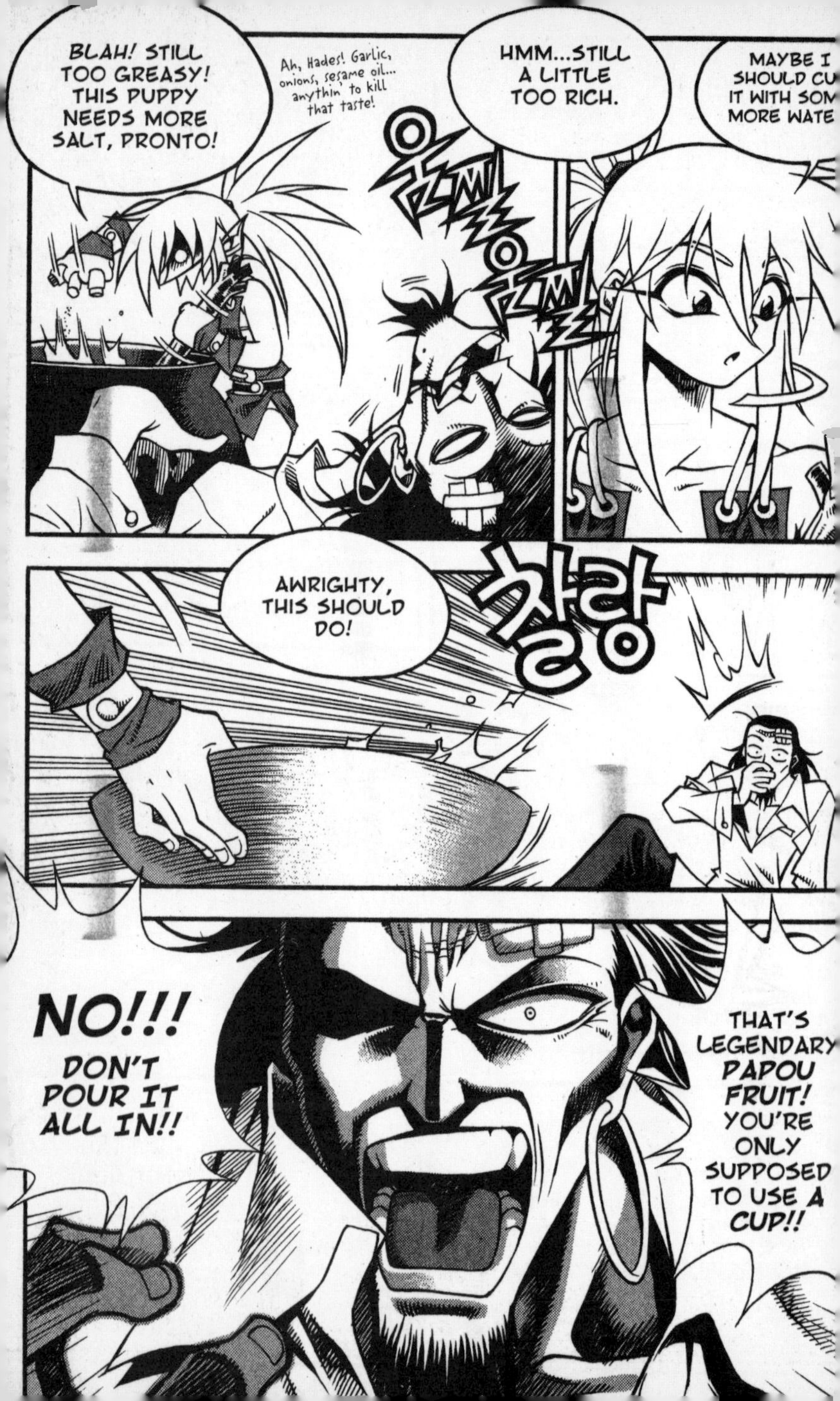
BLAH! STILL TOO GREASY! THIS PUPPY NEEDS MORE SALT, PRONTO!
Ah, Hades! Garlic, onions, sesame oil... anythin' to kill that taste!
HMM...STILL A LITTLE TOO RICH.
움찔
움찔
MAYBE I SHOULD CU IT WITH SOM MORE WATE
AWRIGHTY, THIS SHOULD DO!
찰랑
NO!!! DON'T POUR IT ALL IN!!
THAT'S LEGENDARY PAPOU FRUIT! YOU'RE ONLY SUPPOSED TO USE A CUP!!

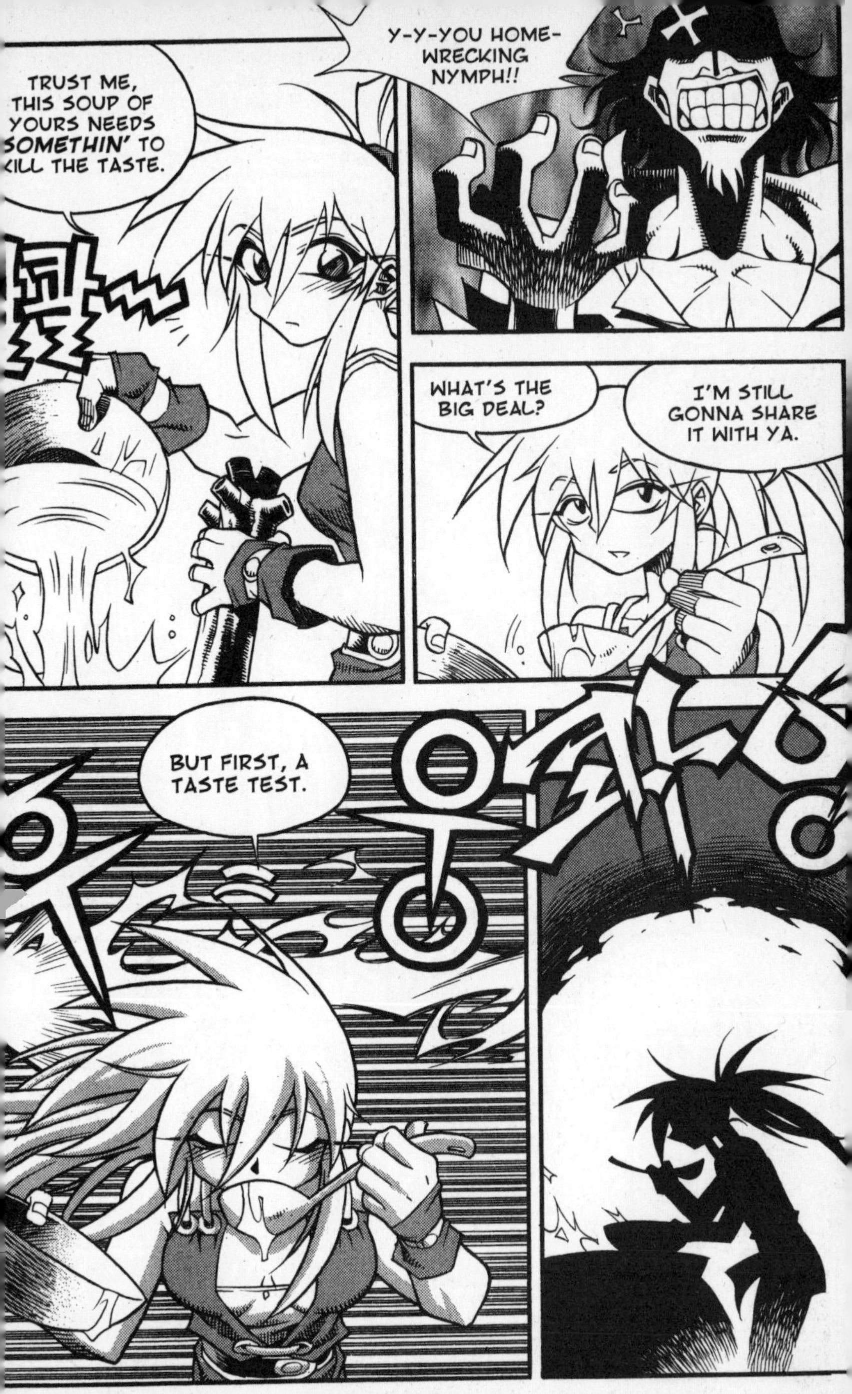
TRUST ME, THIS SOUP OF YOURS NEEDS SOMETHIN' TO KILL THE TASTE.
Y-Y-YOU HOME-WRECKING NYMPH!!
WHAT'S THE BIG DEAL?
I'M STILL GONNA SHARE IT WITH YA.
BUT FIRST, A TASTE TEST.

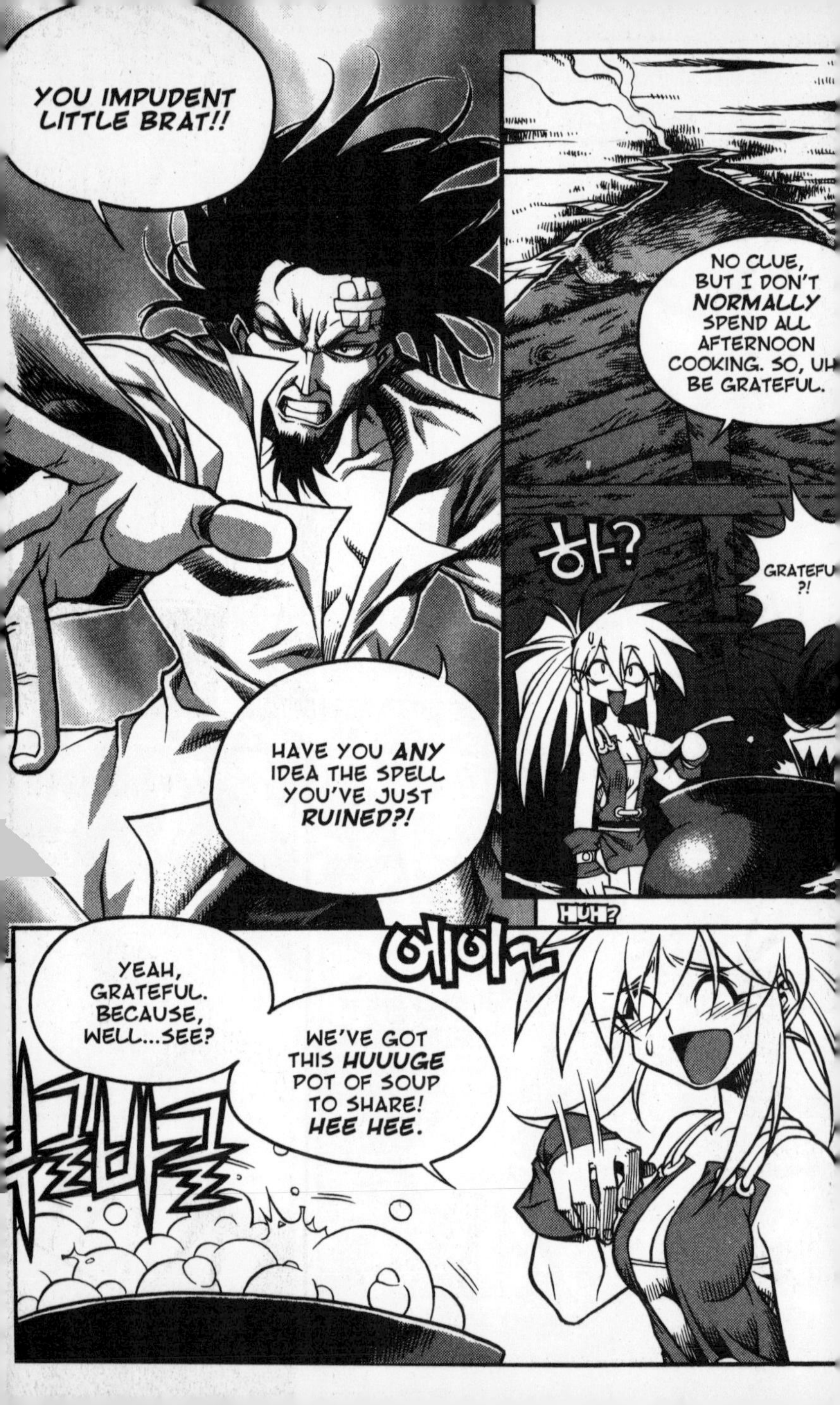
YOU IMPUDENT LITTLE BRAT!!
HAVE YOU ANY IDEA THE SPELL YOU'VE JUST RUINED?!
NO CLUE, BUT I DON'T NORMALLY SPEND ALL AFTERNOON COOKING. SO, UH BE GRATEFUL.
하?
GRATEFU ?!
HUH?
헤이~
YEAH, GRATEFUL. BECAUSE, WELL...SEE?
WE'VE GOT THIS HUUUGE POT OF SOUP TO SHARE! HEE HEE.

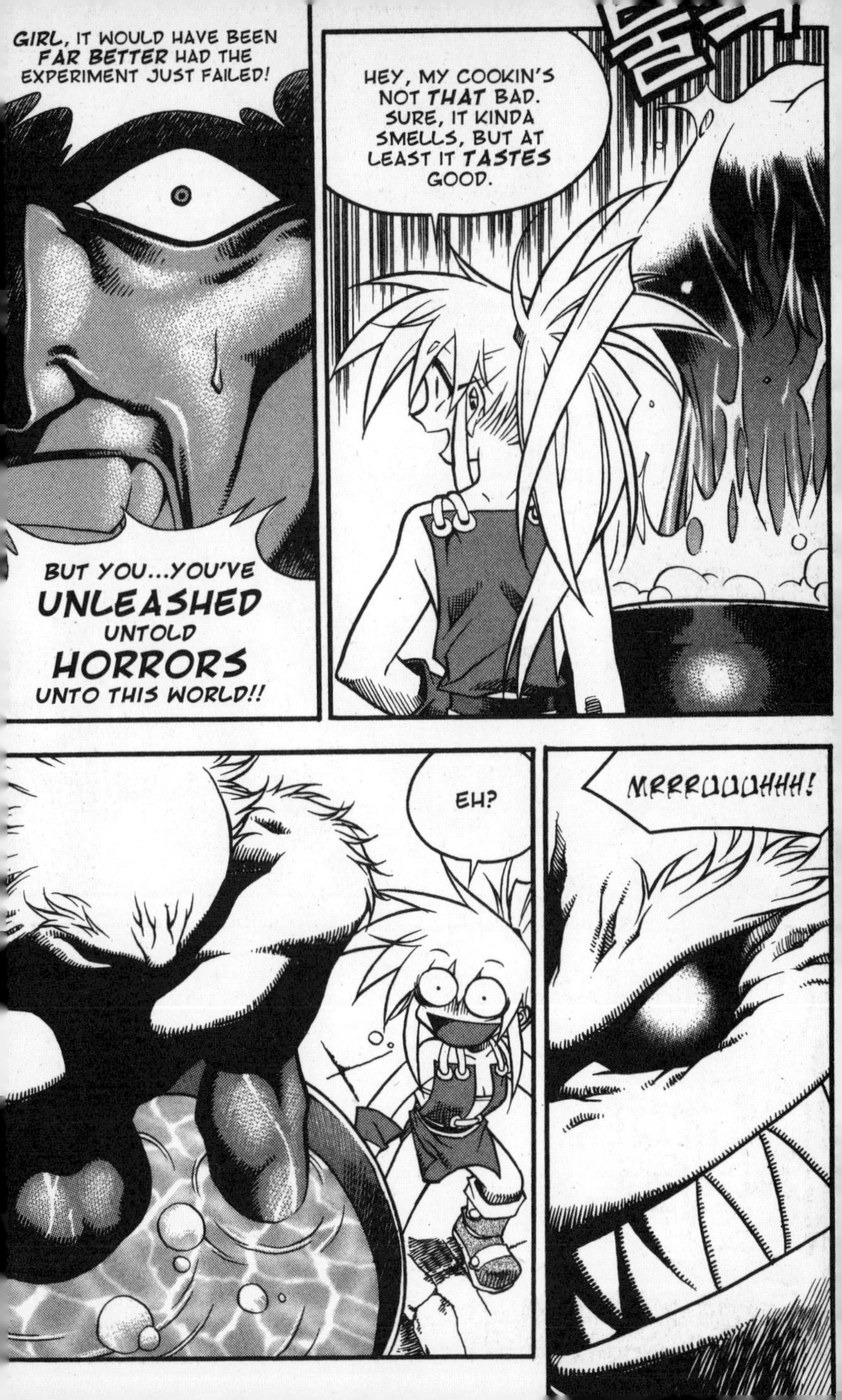
GIRL, IT WOULD HAVE BEEN FAR BETTER HAD THE EXPERIMENT JUST FAILED!
BUT YOU...YOU'VE UNLEASHED UNTOLD HORRORS UNTO THIS WORLD!!
HEY, MY COOKIN'S NOT THAT BAD. SURE, IT KINDA SMELLS, BUT AT LEAST IT TASTES GOOD.
EH?
MRRRUUUHHH!

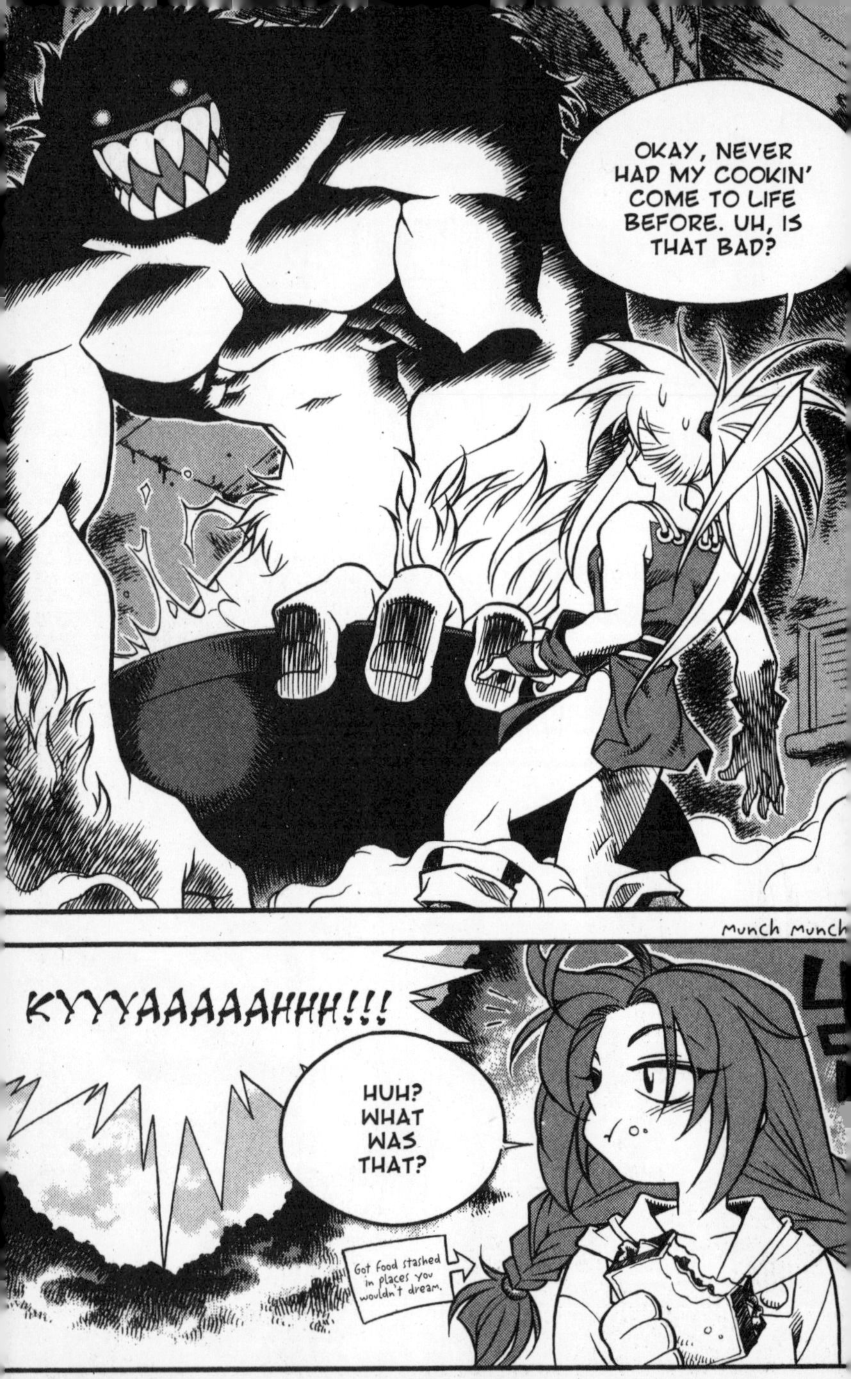
OKAY, NEVER HAD MY COOKIN' COME TO LIFE BEFORE. UH, IS THAT BAD?
Munch Munch
KYYYAAAAAHHH!!!
HUH? WHAT WAS THAT?
Got food stashed in places you wouldn't dream.

Quest 29

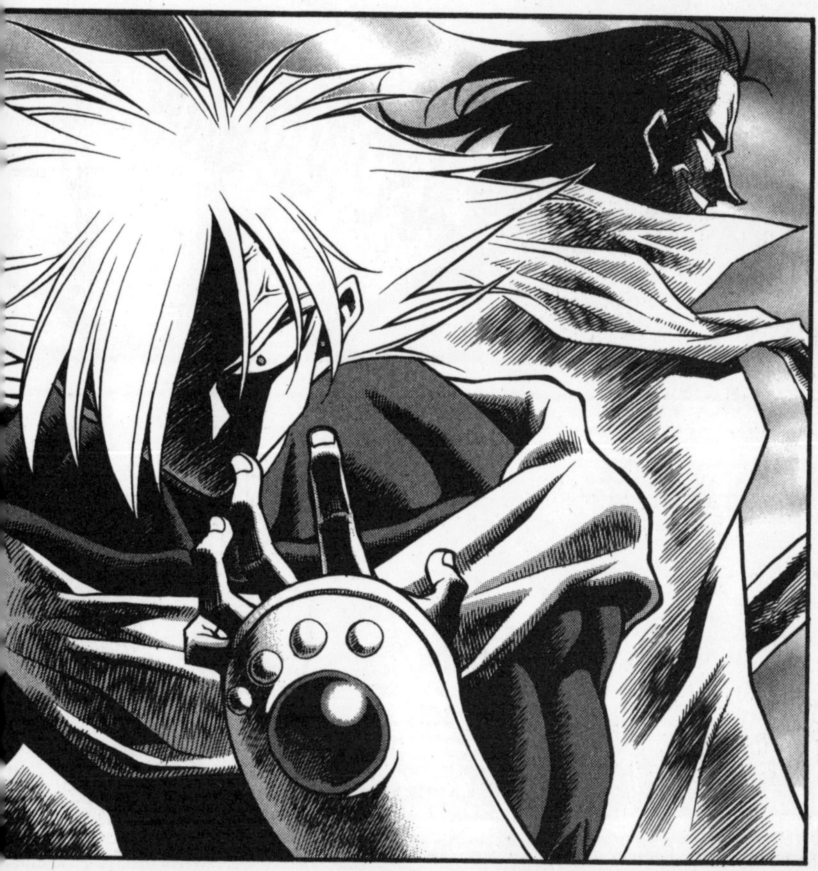

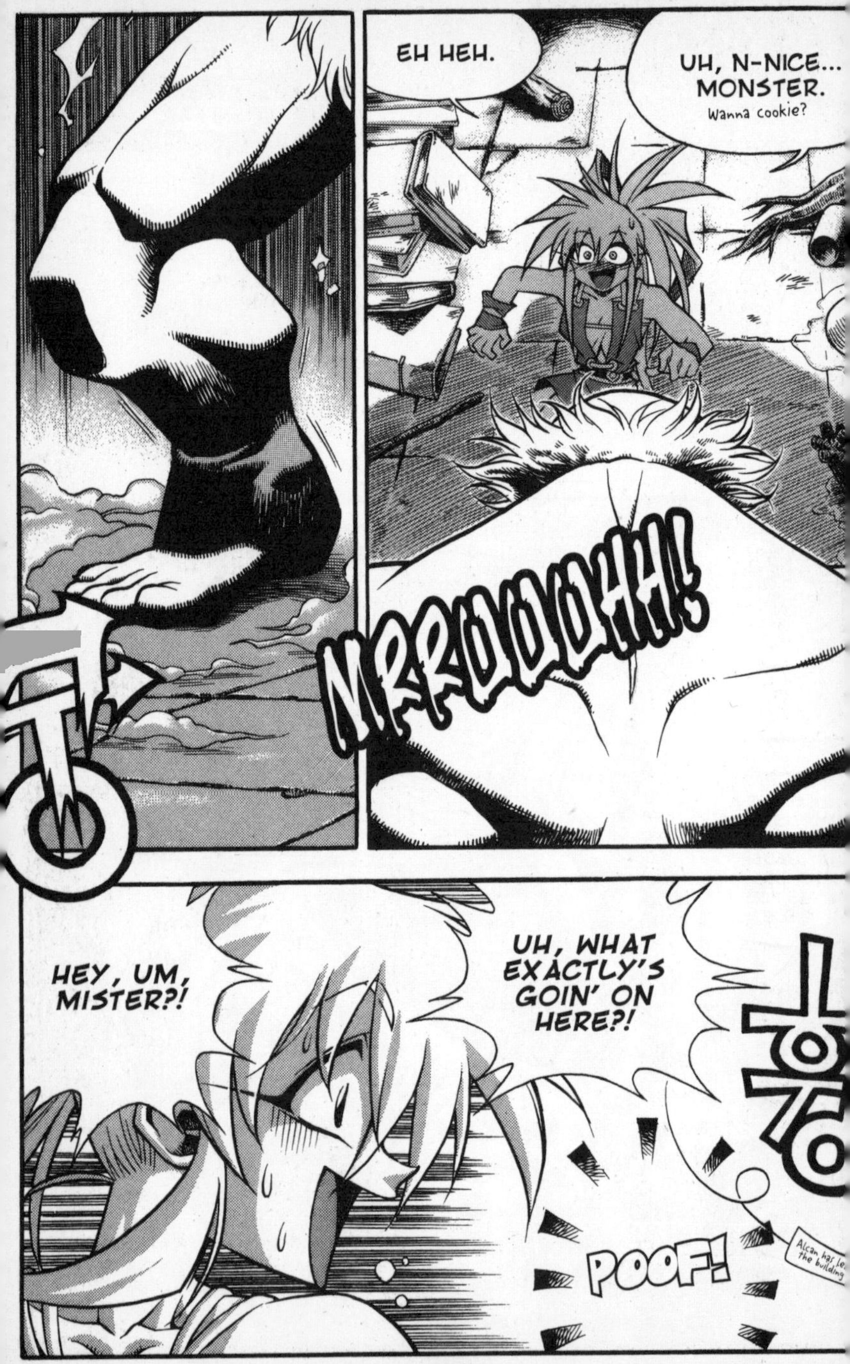
EH HEH.
UH, N-NICE... MONSTER.
Wanna cookie?
MRROOOOHH!!
HEY, UM, MISTER?!
UH, WHAT EXACTLY'S GOIN' ON HERE?!
POOF!
Alcan has le
the building

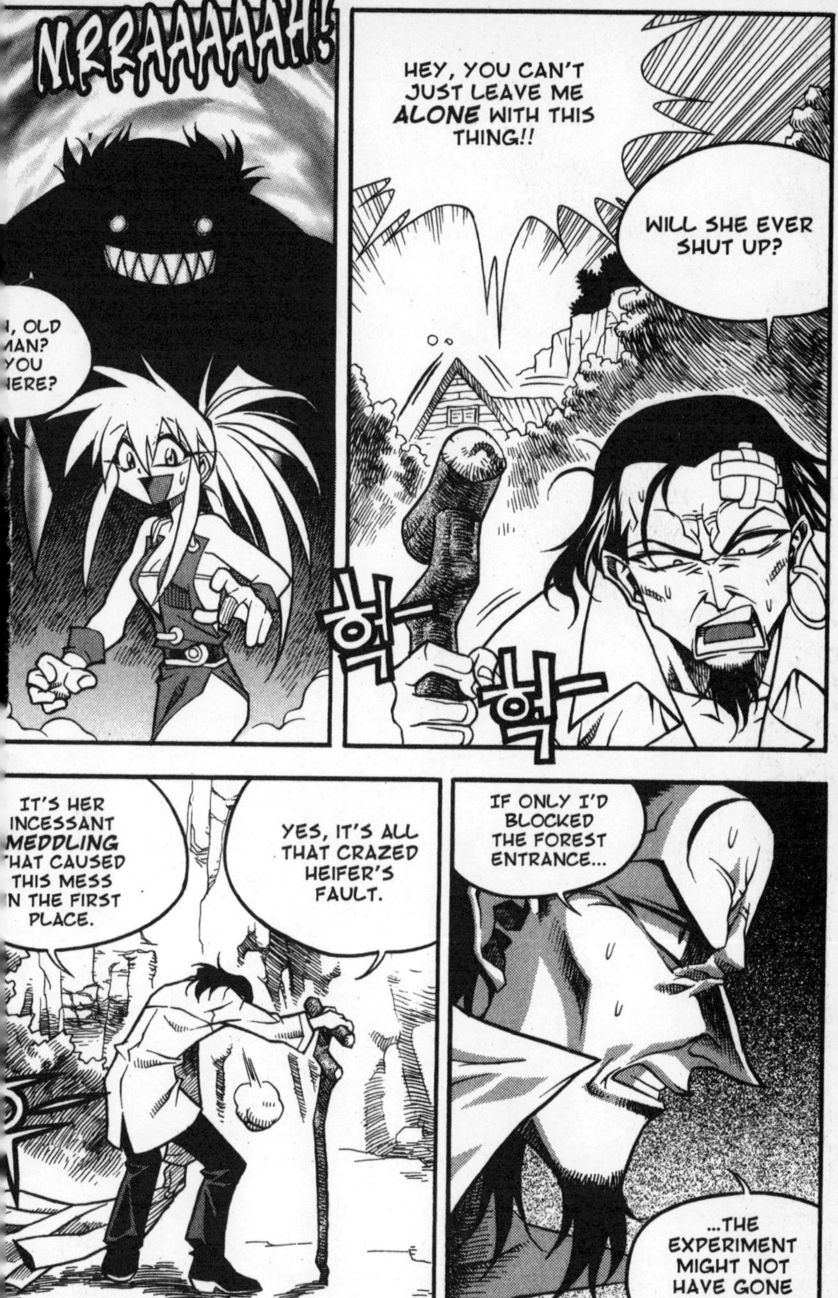
MRRAAAAAH!
OLD MAN? YOU HERE?
HEY, YOU CAN'T JUST LEAVE ME ALONE WITH THIS THING!!
WILL SHE EVER SHUT UP?
헉 헉
IT'S HER INCESSANT MEDDLING THAT CAUSED THIS MESS IN THE FIRST PLACE.
YES, IT'S ALL THAT CRAZED HEIFER'S FAULT.
IF ONLY I'D BLOCKED THE FOREST ENTRANCE...
...THE EXPERIMENT MIGHT NOT HAVE GONE STRAIGHT TO HADES.

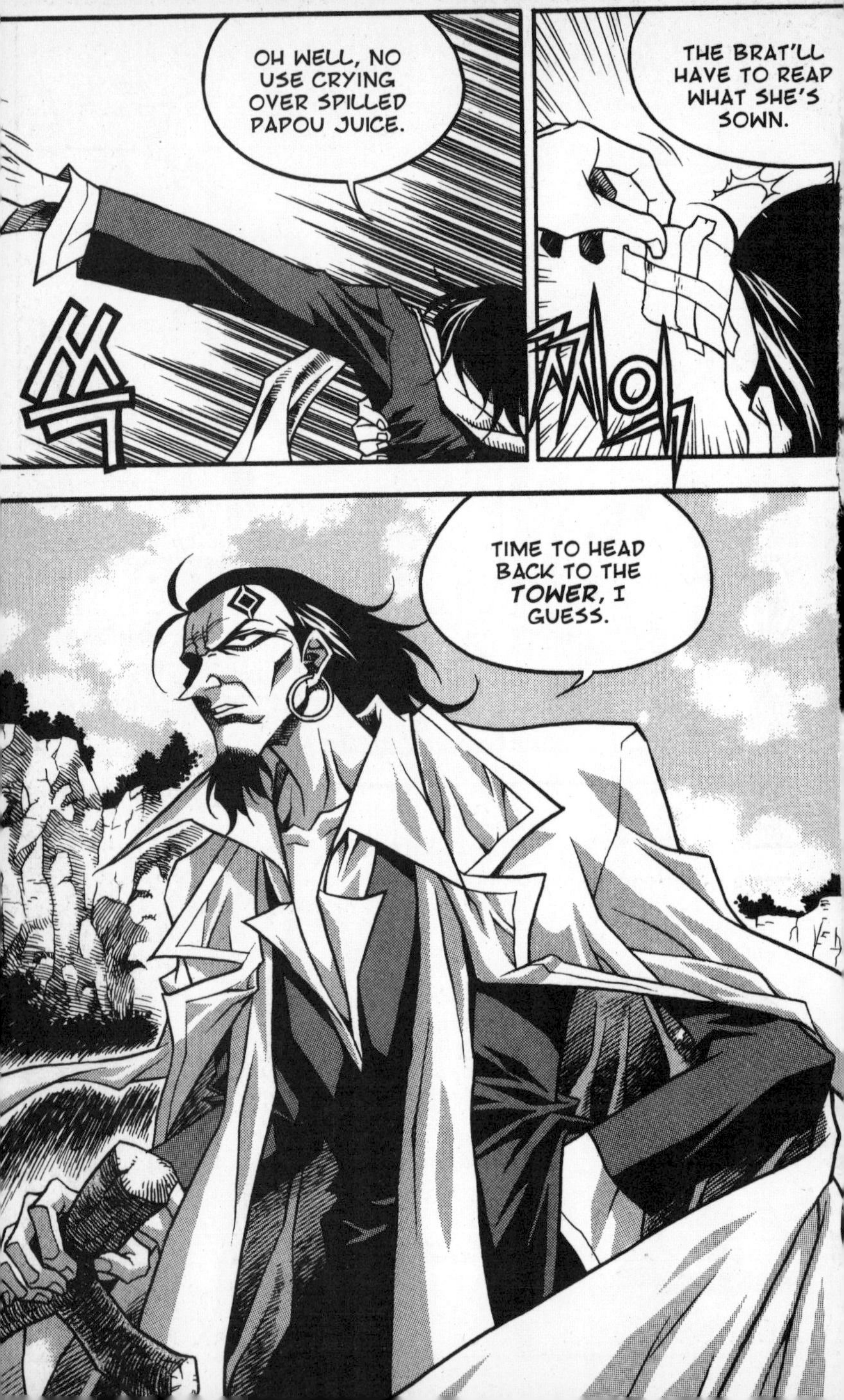
OH WELL, NO USE CRYING OVER SPILLED PAPOU JUICE.
THE BRAT'LL HAVE TO REAP WHAT SHE'S SOWN.
TIME TO HEAD BACK TO THE *TOWER*, I GUESS.

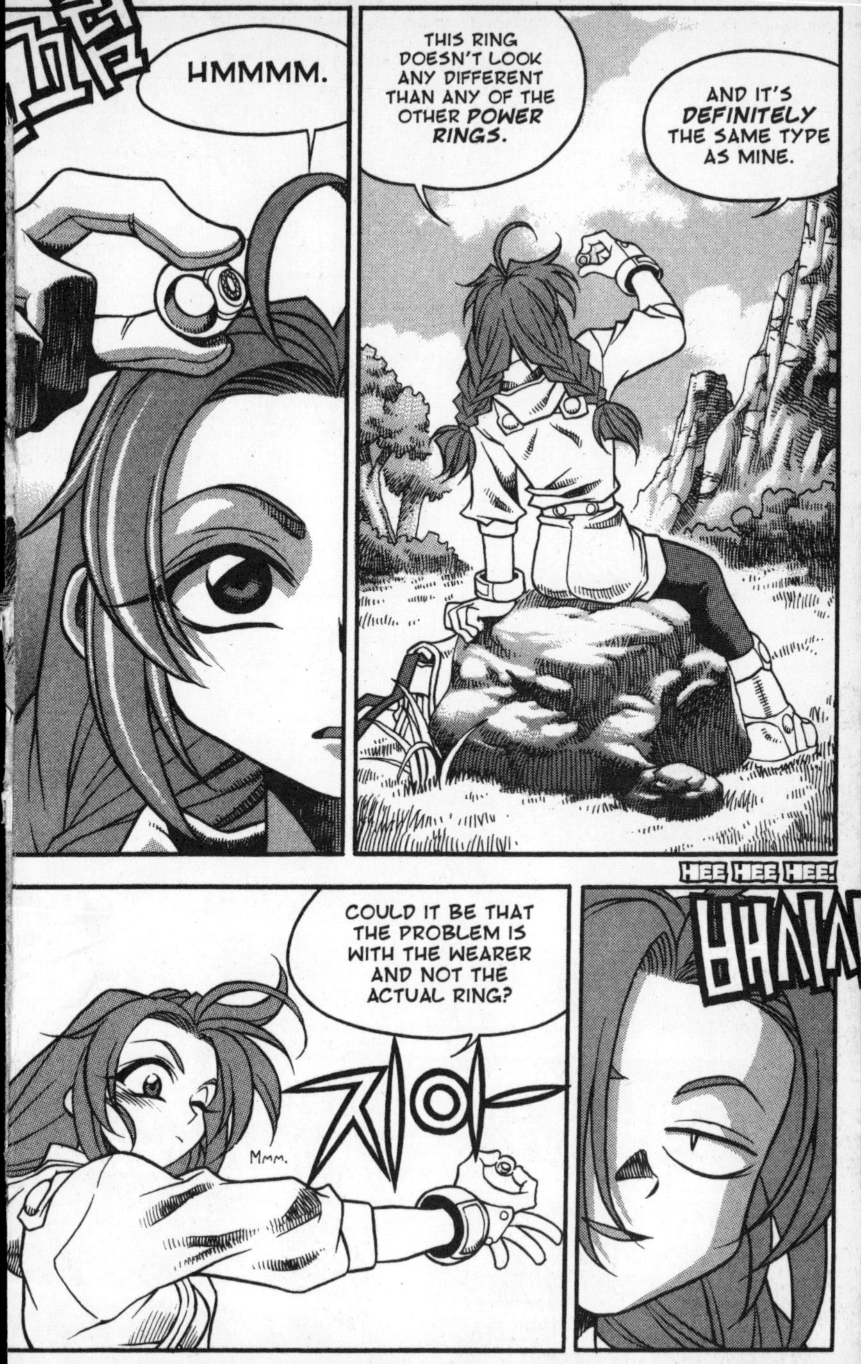
HMMMM.
THIS RING DOESN'T LOOK ANY DIFFERENT THAN ANY OF THE OTHER *POWER RINGS.*
AND IT'S *DEFINITELY* THE SAME TYPE AS MINE.
COULD IT BE THAT THE PROBLEM IS WITH THE WEARER AND NOT THE ACTUAL RING?
Mmm.
HEE HEE HEE!

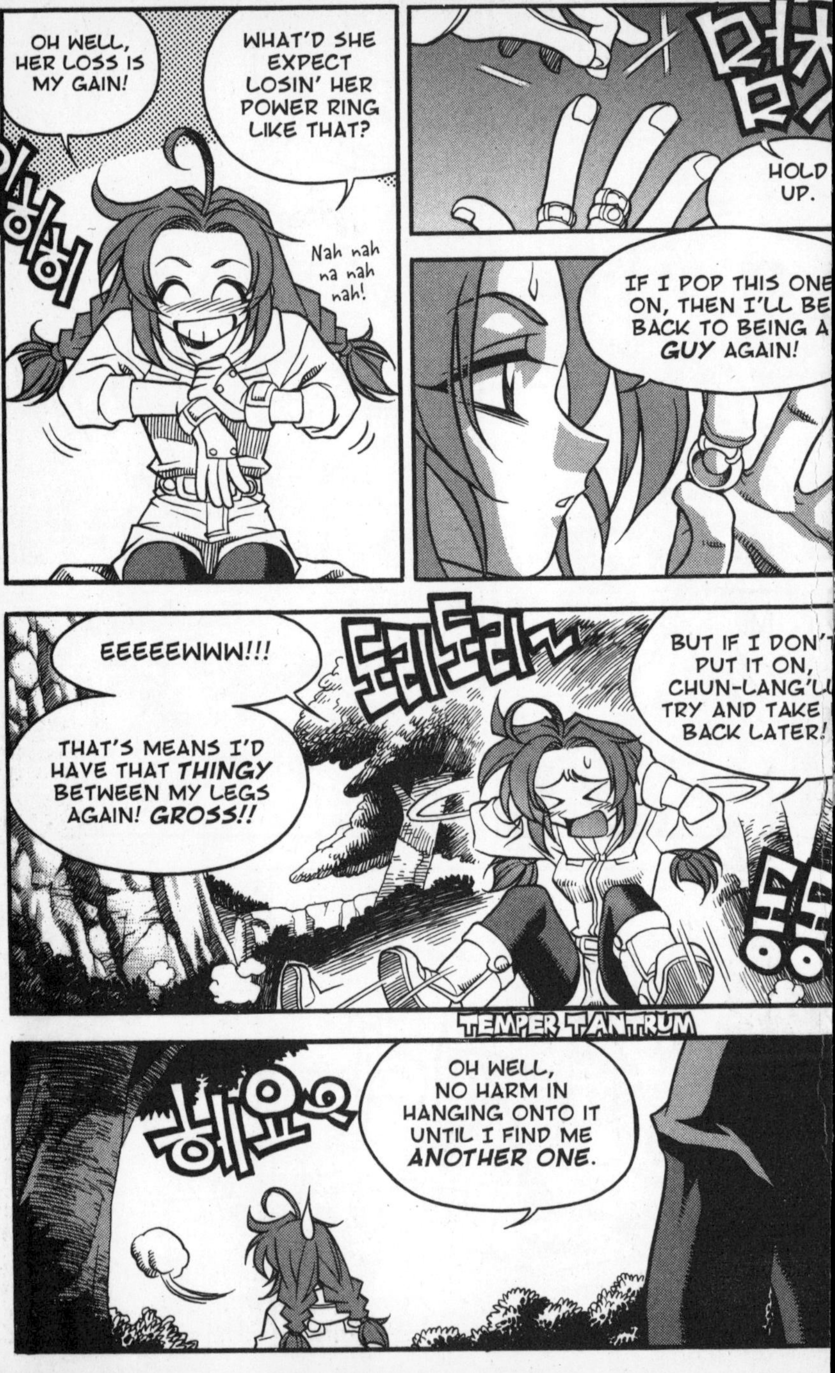
OH WELL, HER LOSS IS MY GAIN!
WHAT'D SHE EXPECT LOSIN' HER POWER RING LIKE THAT?
Nah nah na nah nah!
HOLD UP.
IF I POP THIS ONE ON, THEN I'LL BE BACK TO BEING A GUY AGAIN!
EEEEEWWW!!!
THAT'S MEANS I'D HAVE THAT THINGY BETWEEN MY LEGS AGAIN! GROSS!!
BUT IF I DON'T PUT IT ON, CHUN-LANG'LL TRY AND TAKE BACK LATER!
TEMPER TANTRUM
OH WELL, NO HARM IN HANGING ONTO IT UNTIL I FIND ME ANOTHER ONE.

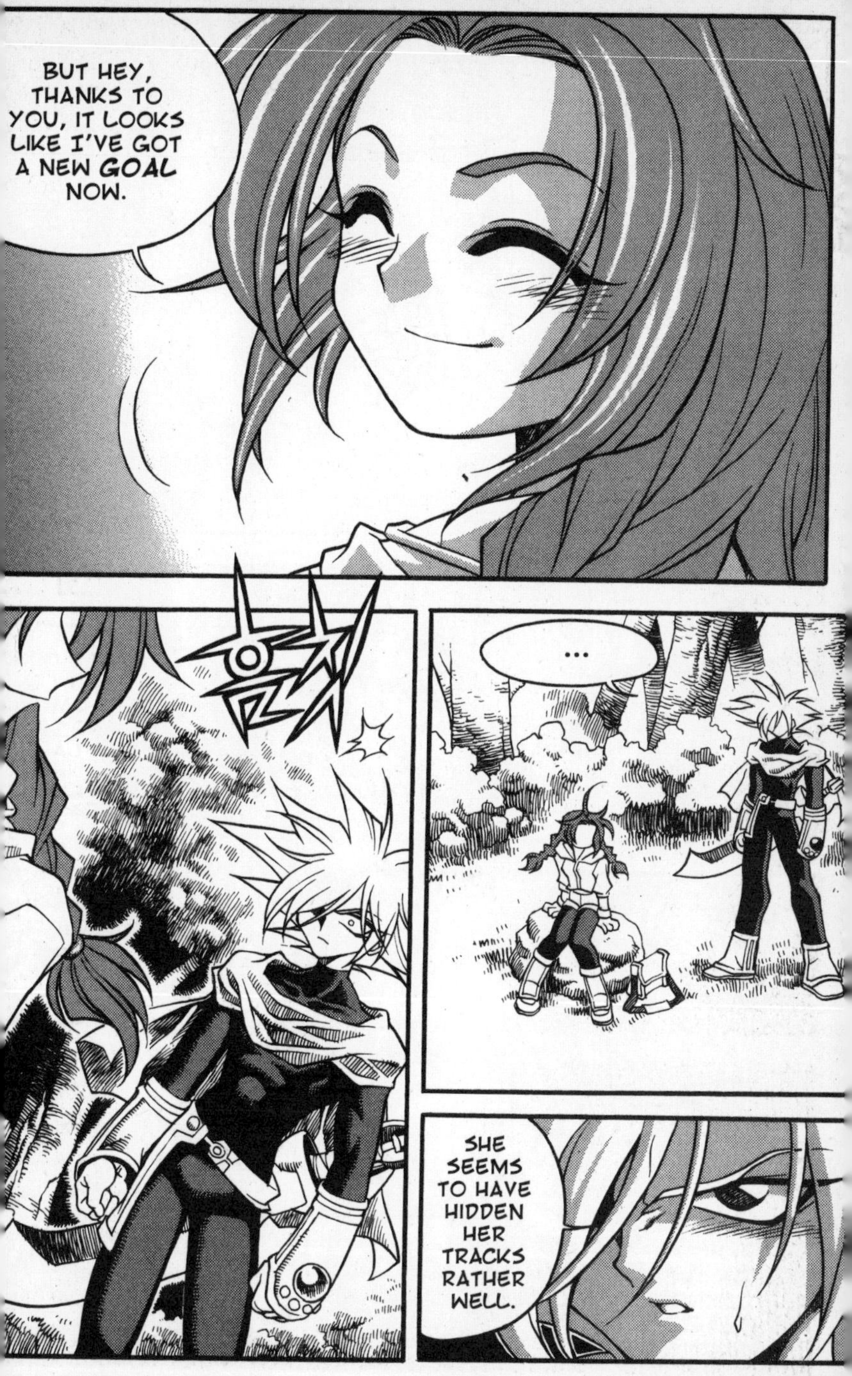
BUT HEY, THANKS TO YOU, IT LOOKS LIKE I'VE GOT A NEW GOAL NOW.
...
SHE SEEMS TO HAVE HIDDEN HER TRACKS RATHER WELL.

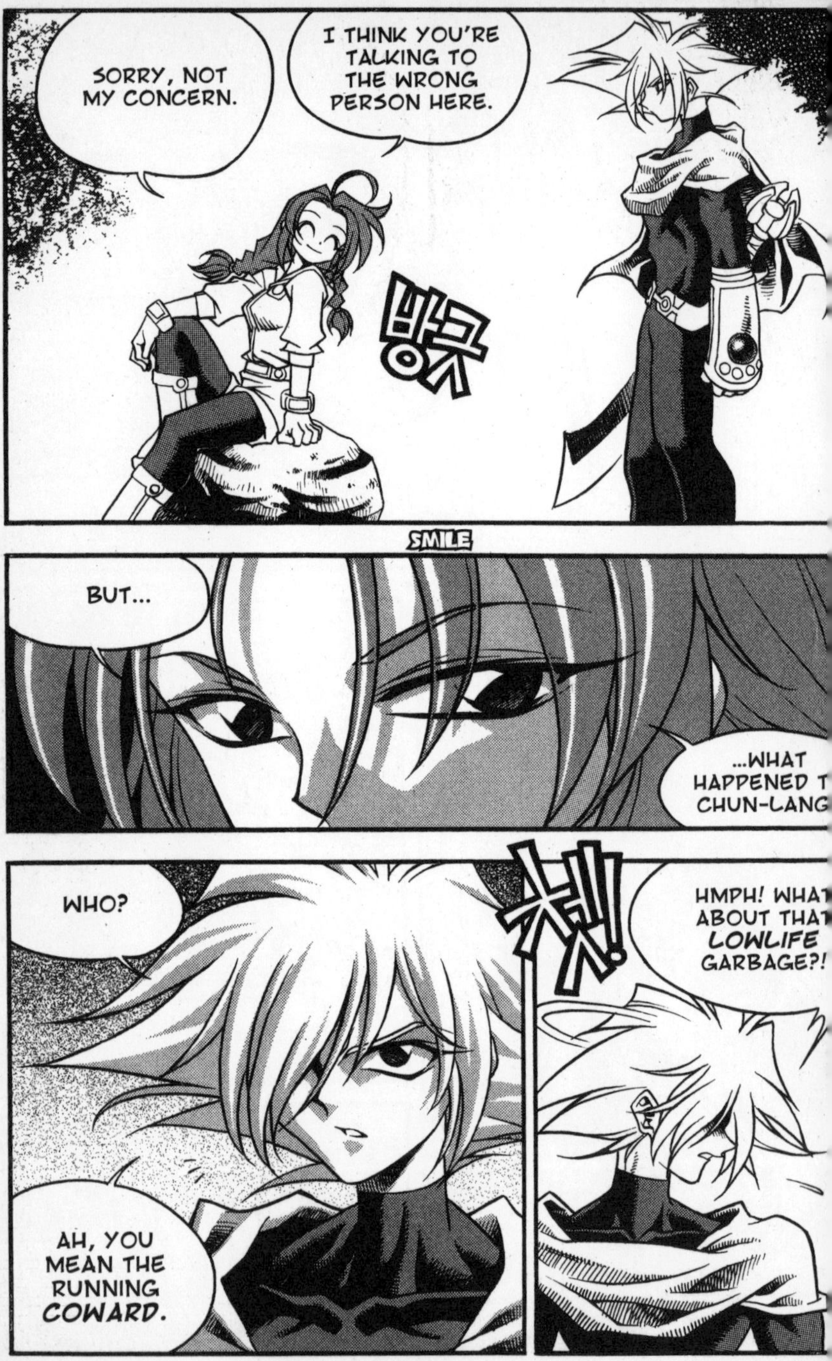
SORRY, NOT MY CONCERN.
I THINK YOU'RE TALKING TO THE WRONG PERSON HERE.
방긋
SMILE
BUT...
...WHAT HAPPENED T CHUN-LANG
WHO?
AH, YOU MEAN THE RUNNING COWARD.
칫!
HMPH! WHA ABOUT THA LOWLIFE GARBAGE?!

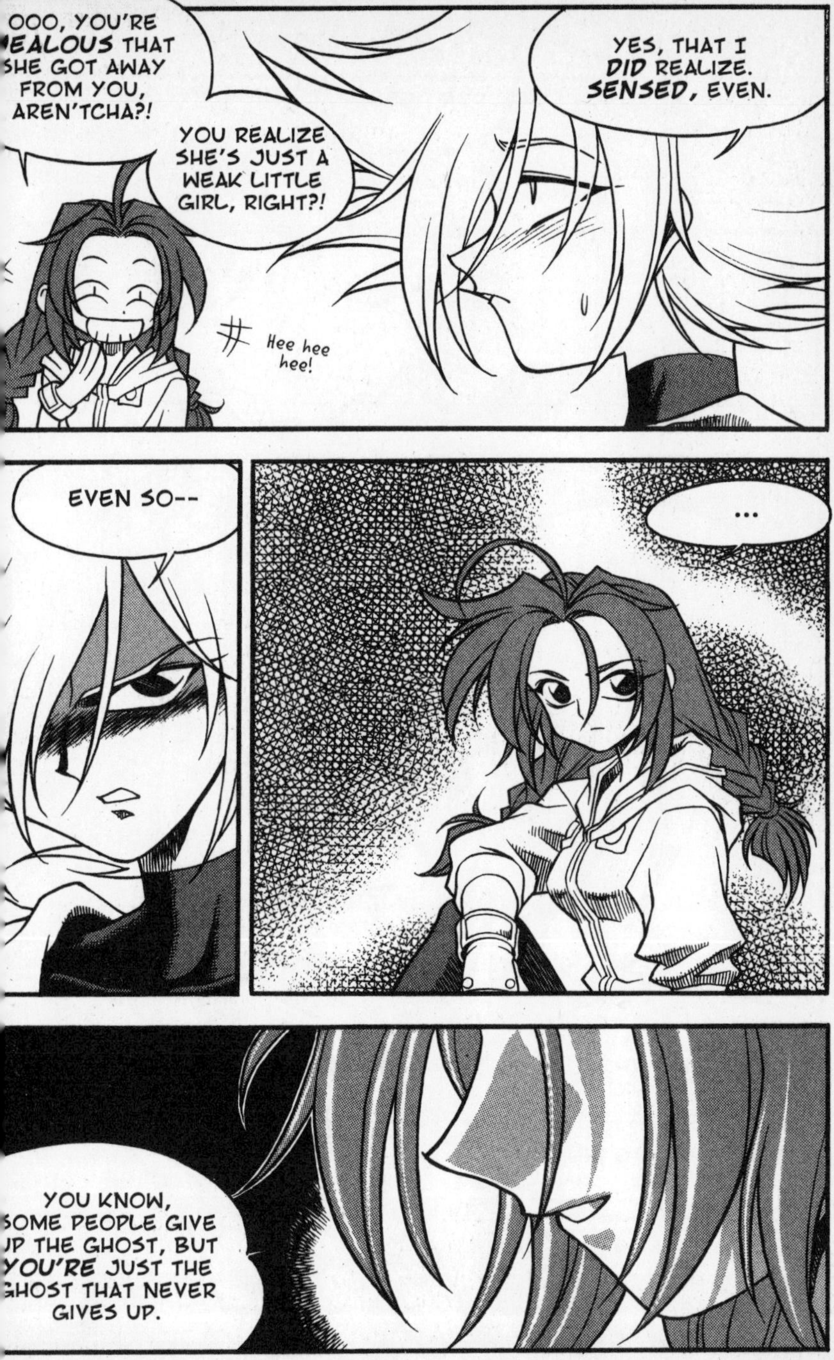
OOO, YOU'RE JEALOUS THAT SHE GOT AWAY FROM YOU, AREN'TCHA?!
YOU REALIZE SHE'S JUST A WEAK LITTLE GIRL, RIGHT?!
Hee hee hee!
YES, THAT I DID REALIZE. SENSED, EVEN.
EVEN SO--
...
YOU KNOW, SOME PEOPLE GIVE UP THE GHOST, BUT YOU'RE JUST THE GHOST THAT NEVER GIVES UP.

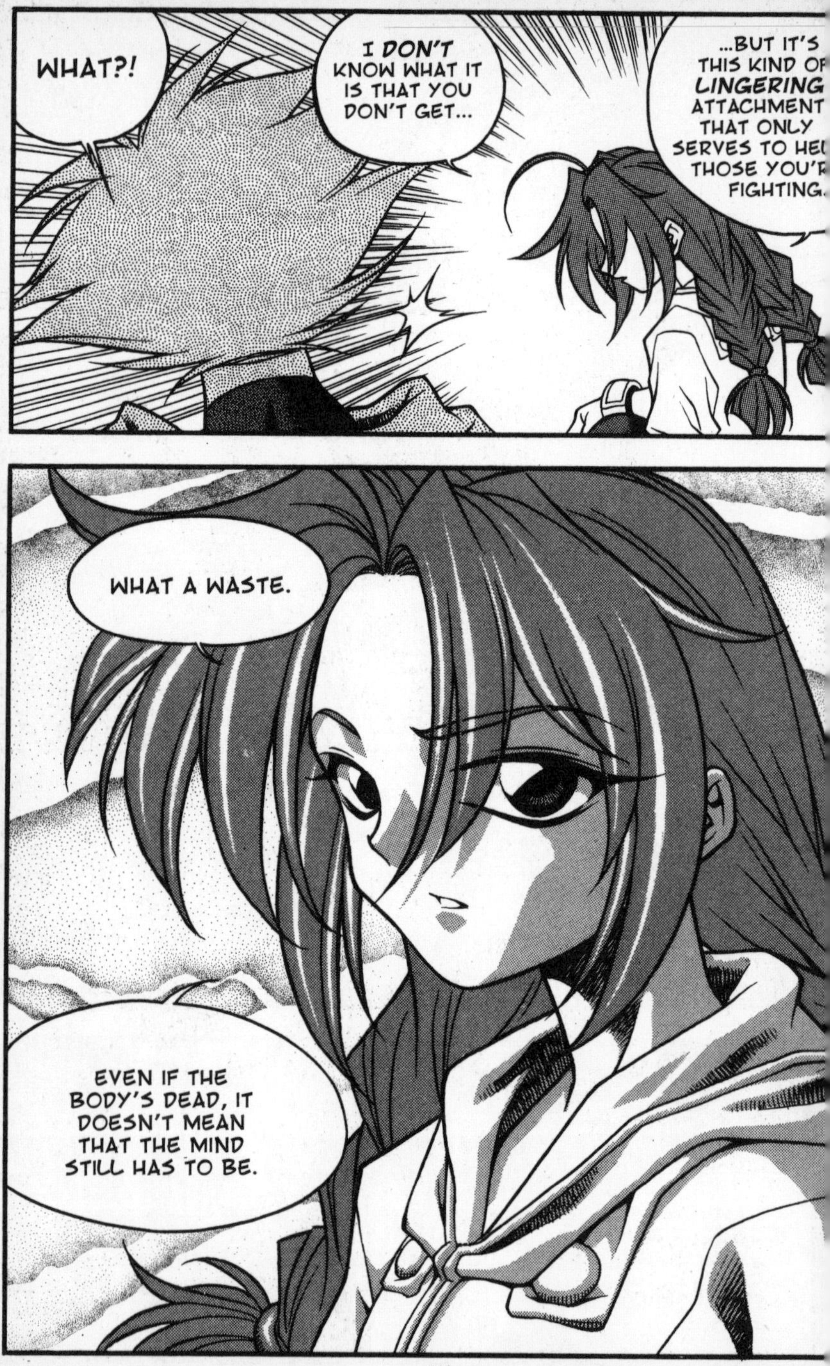

WHAT?!
I DON'T KNOW WHAT IT IS THAT YOU DON'T GET...
...BUT IT'S THIS KIND OF LINGERING ATTACHMENT THAT ONLY SERVES TO HEL THOSE YOU'R FIGHTING.
WHAT A WASTE.
EVEN IF THE BODY'S DEAD, IT DOESN'T MEAN THAT THE MIND STILL HAS TO BE.

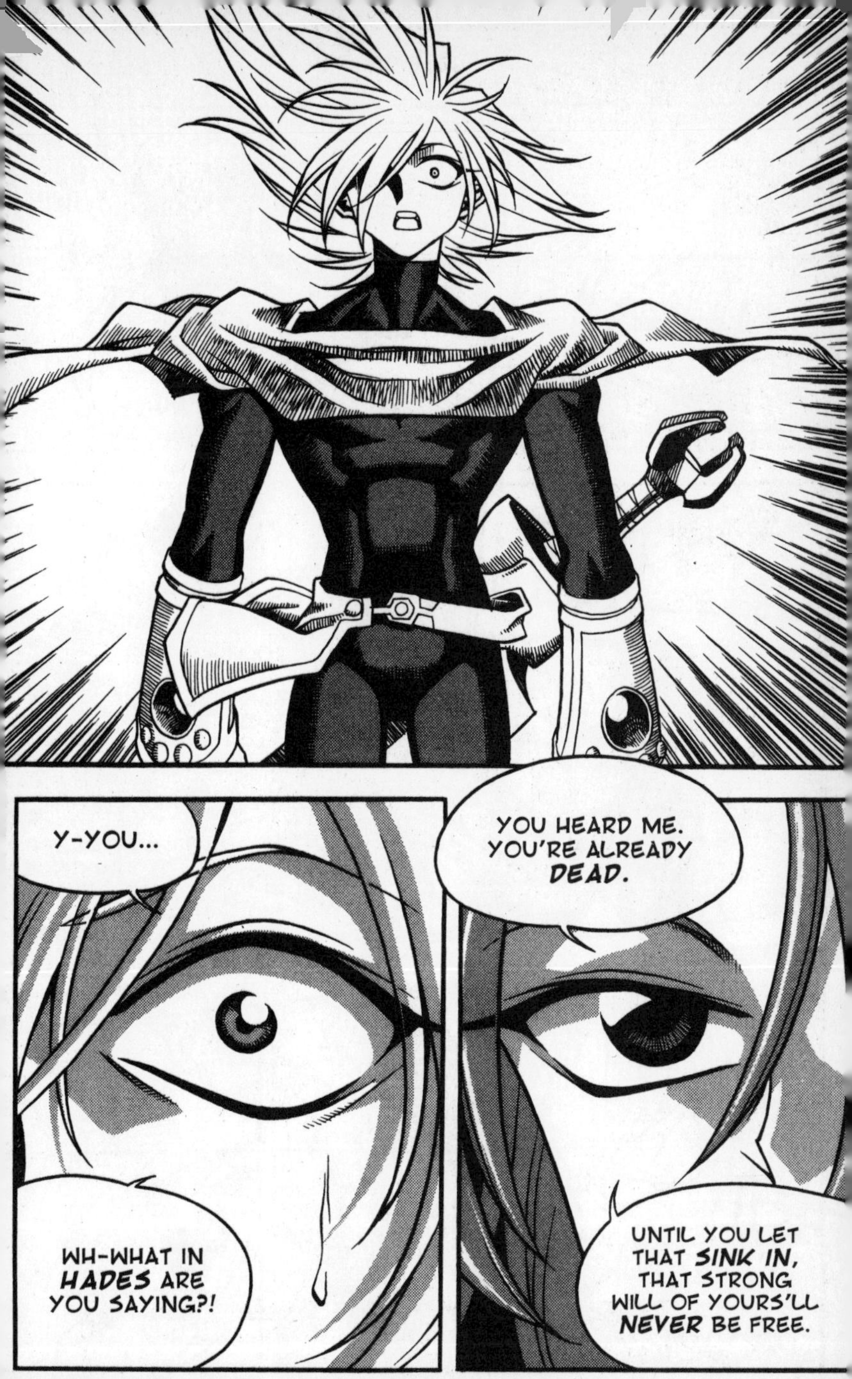
Y-YOU...
YOU HEARD ME. YOU'RE ALREADY DEAD.
WH-WHAT IN HADES ARE YOU SAYING?!
UNTIL YOU LET THAT SINK IN, THAT STRONG WILL OF YOURS'LL NEVER BE FREE.

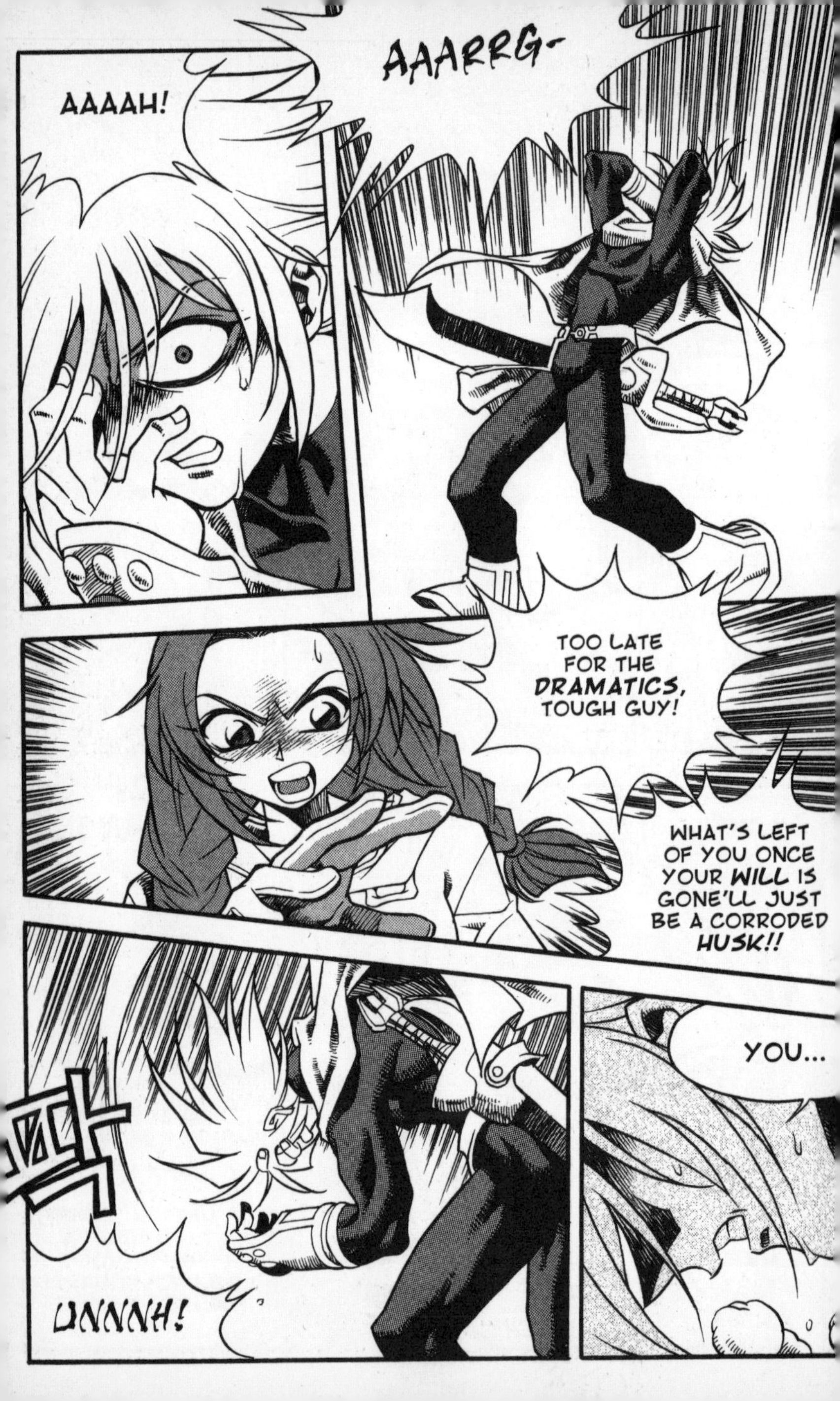
AAAAH!
AAARRG-
TOO LATE FOR THE DRAMATICS, TOUGH GUY!
WHAT'S LEFT OF YOU ONCE YOUR WILL IS GONE'LL JUST BE A CORRODED HUSK!!
UNNNH!
YOU...

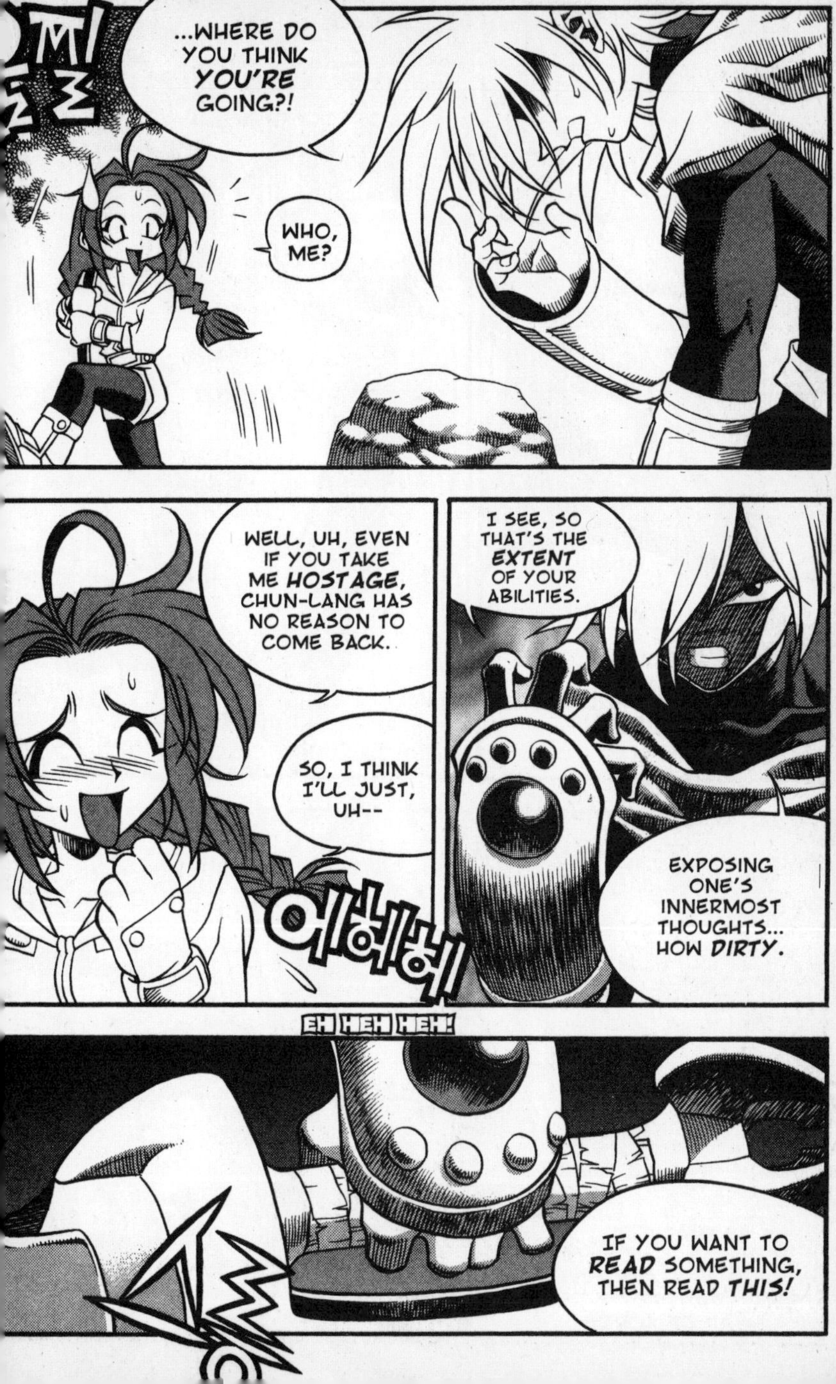
...WHERE DO YOU THINK YOU'RE GOING?!
WHO, ME?
WELL, UH, EVEN IF YOU TAKE ME HOSTAGE, CHUN-LANG HAS NO REASON TO COME BACK.
SO, I THINK I'LL JUST, UH--
에헤헤
EH HEH HEH!
I SEE, SO THAT'S THE EXTENT OF YOUR ABILITIES.
EXPOSING ONE'S INNERMOST THOUGHTS... HOW DIRTY.
IF YOU WANT TO READ SOMETHING, THEN READ THIS!

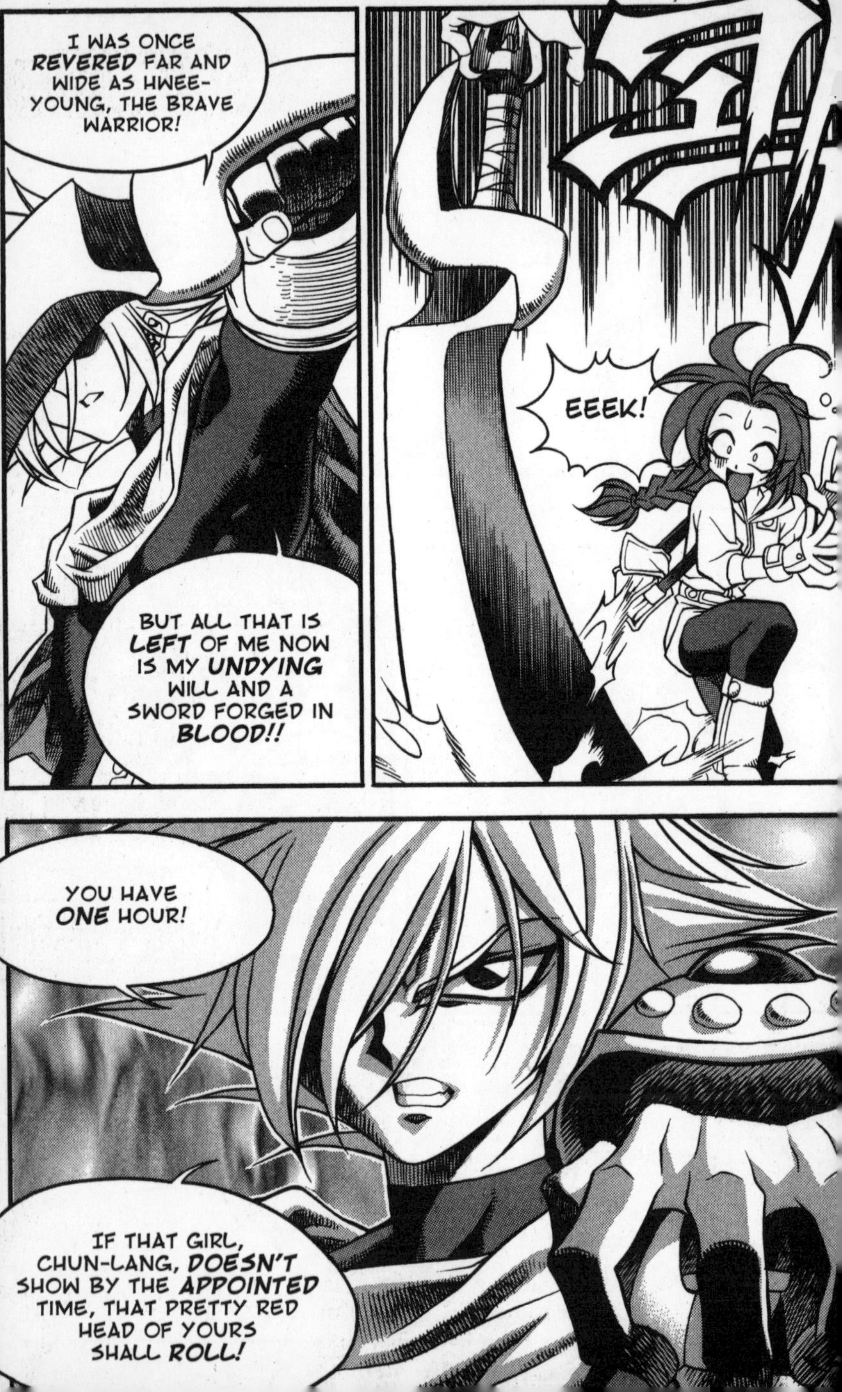
I WAS ONCE REVERED FAR AND WIDE AS HWEE-YOUNG, THE BRAVE WARRIOR!
BUT ALL THAT IS LEFT OF ME NOW IS MY UNDYING WILL AND A SWORD FORGED IN BLOOD!!
EEEK!
YOU HAVE ONE HOUR!
IF THAT GIRL, CHUN-LANG, DOESN'T SHOW BY THE APPOINTED TIME, THAT PRETTY RED HEAD OF YOURS SHALL ROLL!

Quest 30

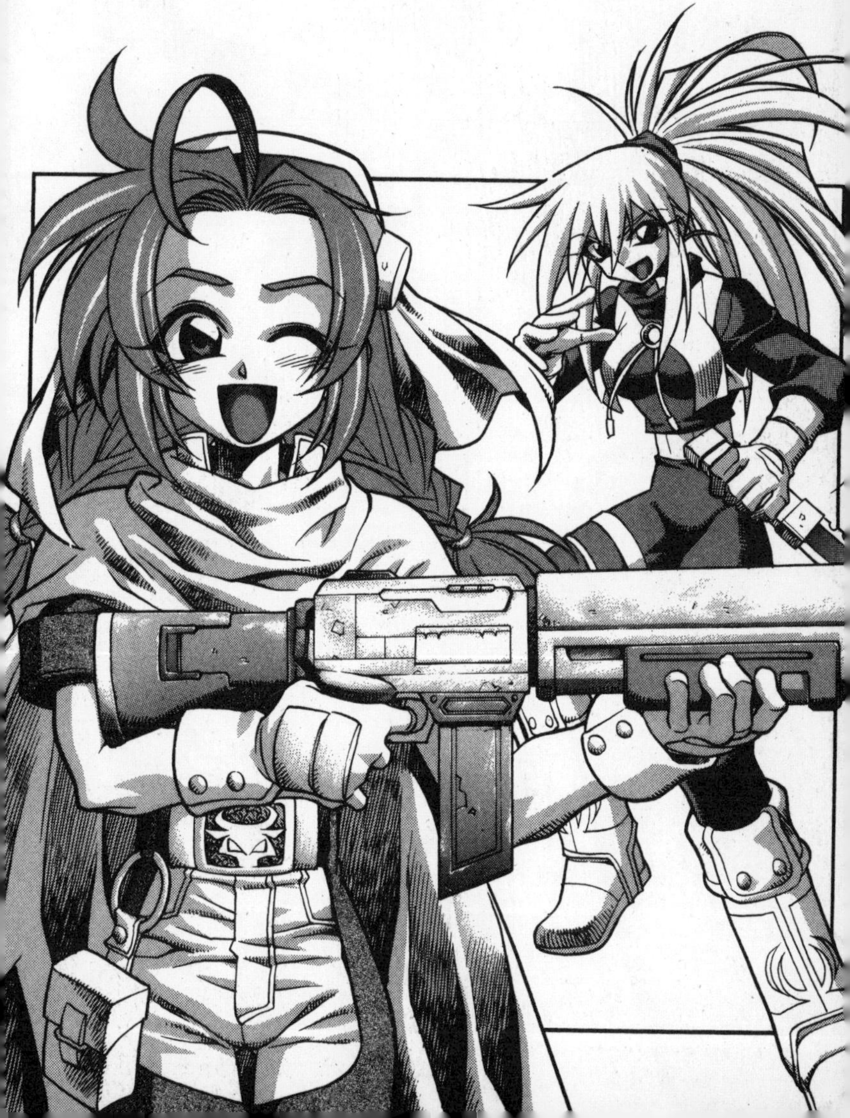

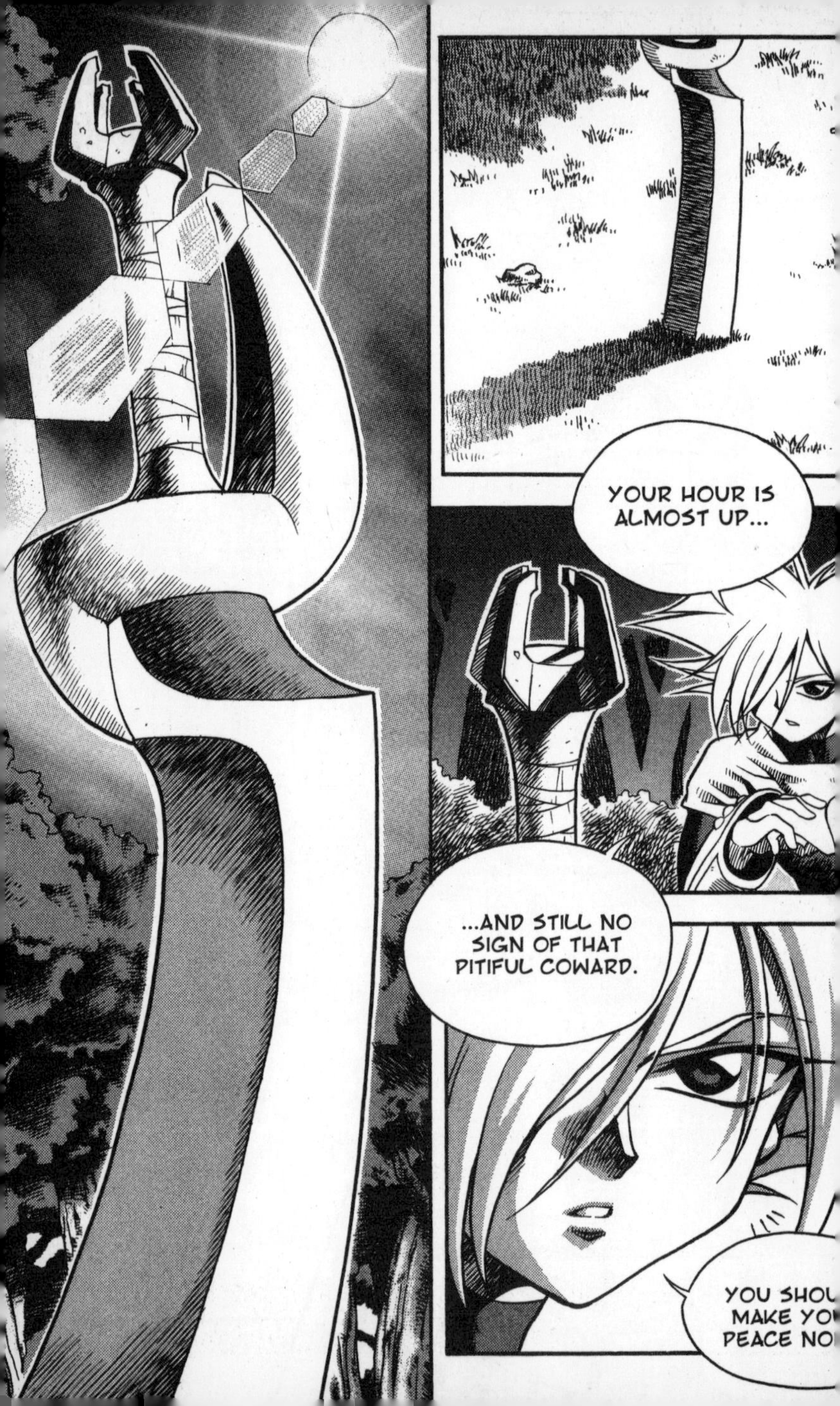
YOUR HOUR IS ALMOST UP...
...AND STILL NO SIGN OF THAT PITIFUL COWARD.
YOU SHOU
MAKE YO
PEACE NO

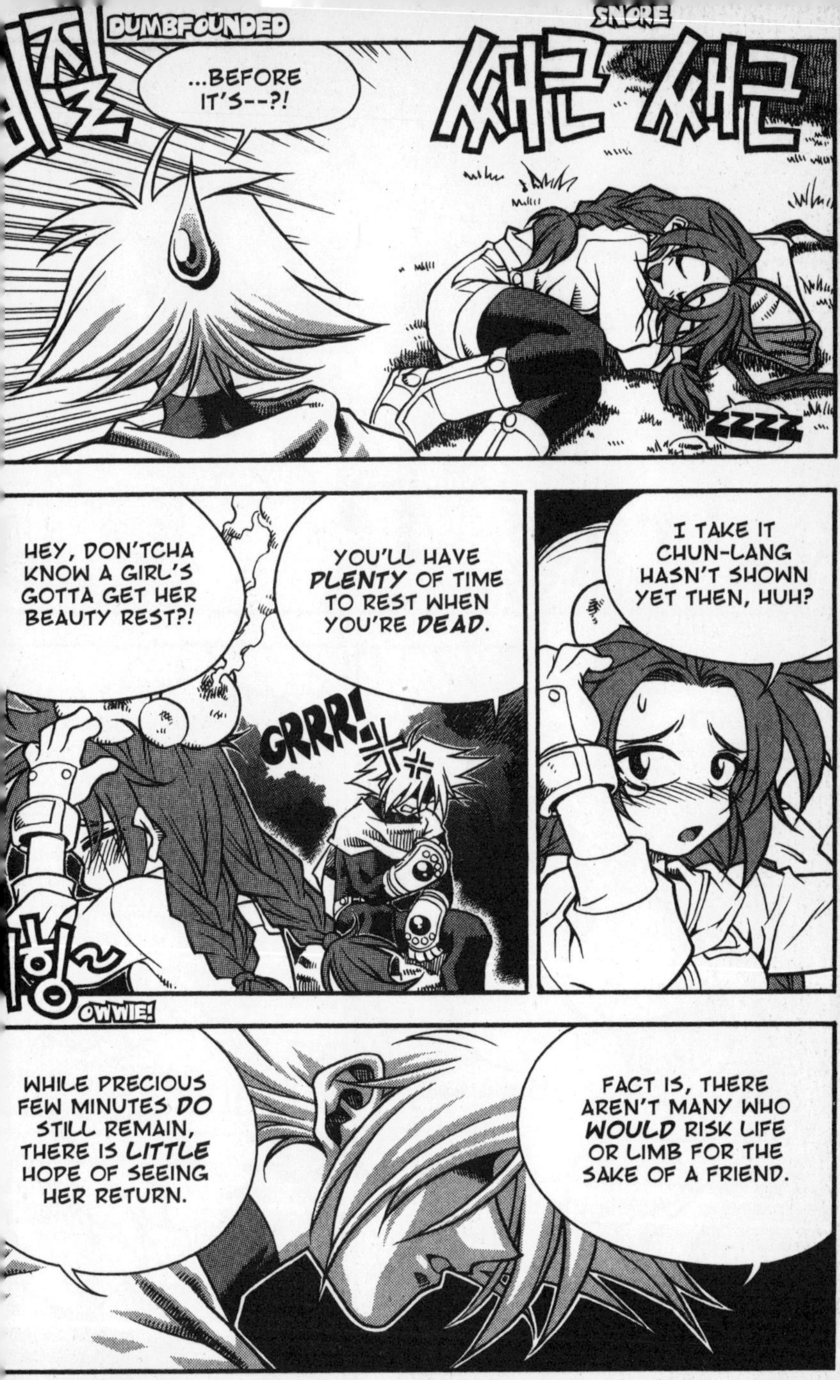
DUMBFOUNDED
...BEFORE IT'S--?!
SNORE
쌔근 쌔근
ZZZZ
HEY, DON'TCHA KNOW A GIRL'S GOTTA GET HER BEAUTY REST?!
YOU'LL HAVE PLENTY OF TIME TO REST WHEN YOU'RE DEAD.
GRRR!
OWWIE!
I TAKE IT CHUN-LANG HASN'T SHOWN YET THEN, HUH?
WHILE PRECIOUS FEW MINUTES DO STILL REMAIN, THERE IS LITTLE HOPE OF SEEING HER RETURN.
FACT IS, THERE AREN'T MANY WHO WOULD RISK LIFE OR LIMB FOR THE SAKE OF A FRIEND.

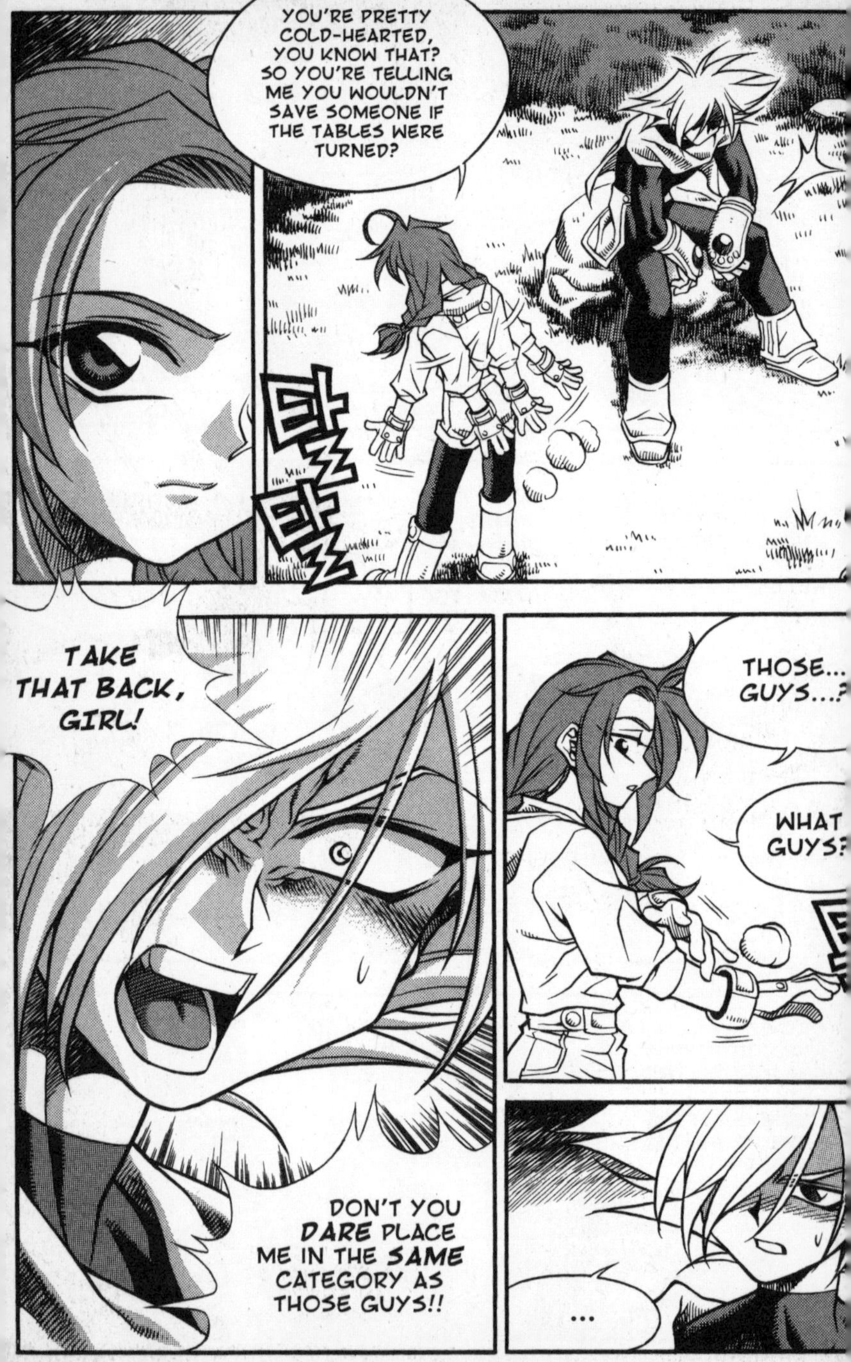
YOU'RE PRETTY COLD-HEARTED, YOU KNOW THAT? SO YOU'RE TELLING ME YOU WOULDN'T SAVE SOMEONE IF THE TABLES WERE TURNED?
TAKE THAT BACK, GIRL!
DON'T YOU DARE PLACE ME IN THE SAME CATEGORY AS THOSE GUYS!!
THOSE... GUYS...?
WHAT GUYS?
...

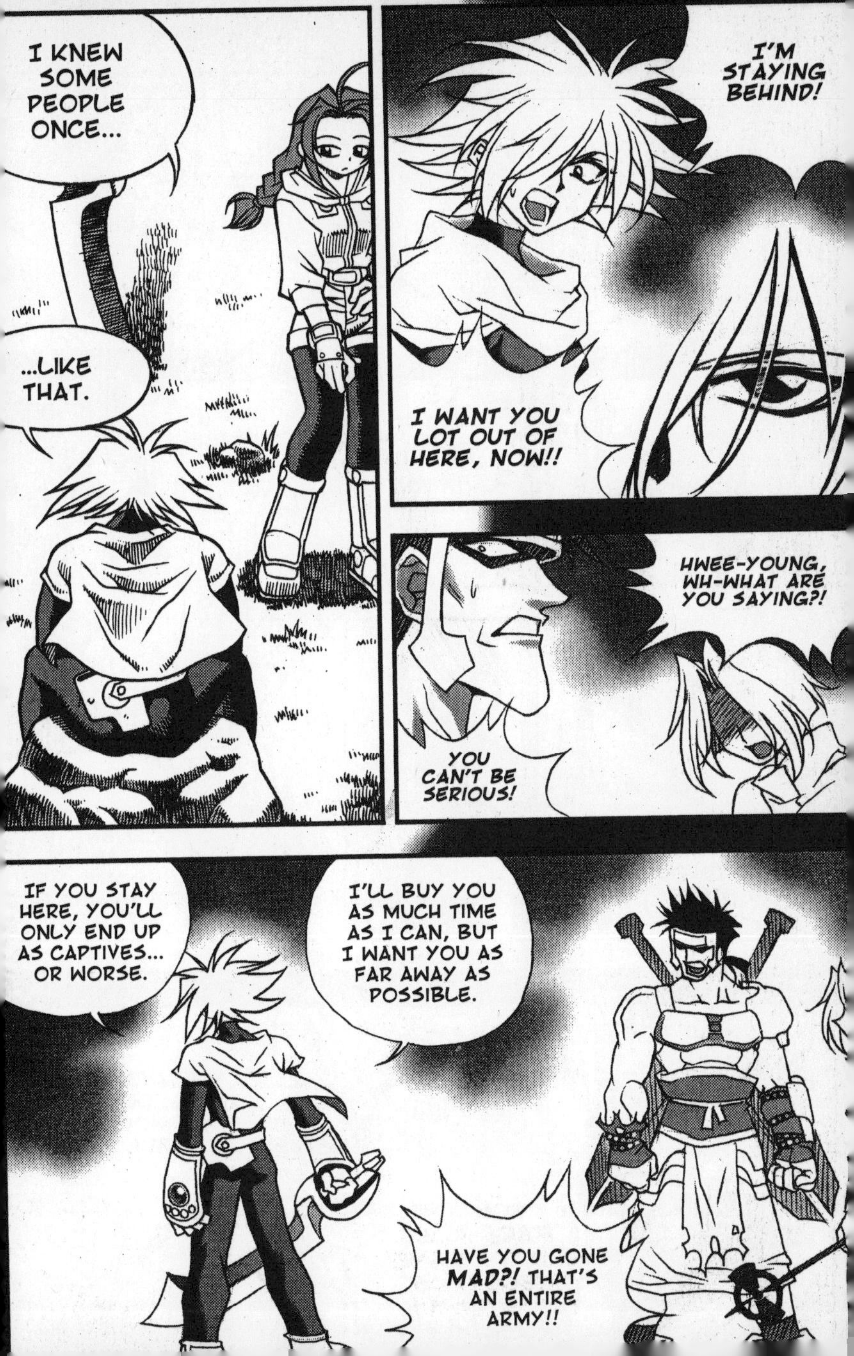
I KNEW SOME PEOPLE ONCE...
...LIKE THAT.
I'M STAYING BEHIND!
I WANT YOU LOT OUT OF HERE, NOW!!
HWEE-YOUNG, WH-WHAT ARE YOU SAYING?!
YOU CAN'T BE SERIOUS!
IF YOU STAY HERE, YOU'LL ONLY END UP AS CAPTIVES... OR WORSE.
I'LL BUY YOU AS MUCH TIME AS I CAN, BUT I WANT YOU AS FAR AWAY AS POSSIBLE.
HAVE YOU GONE MAD?! THAT'S AN ENTIRE ARMY!!

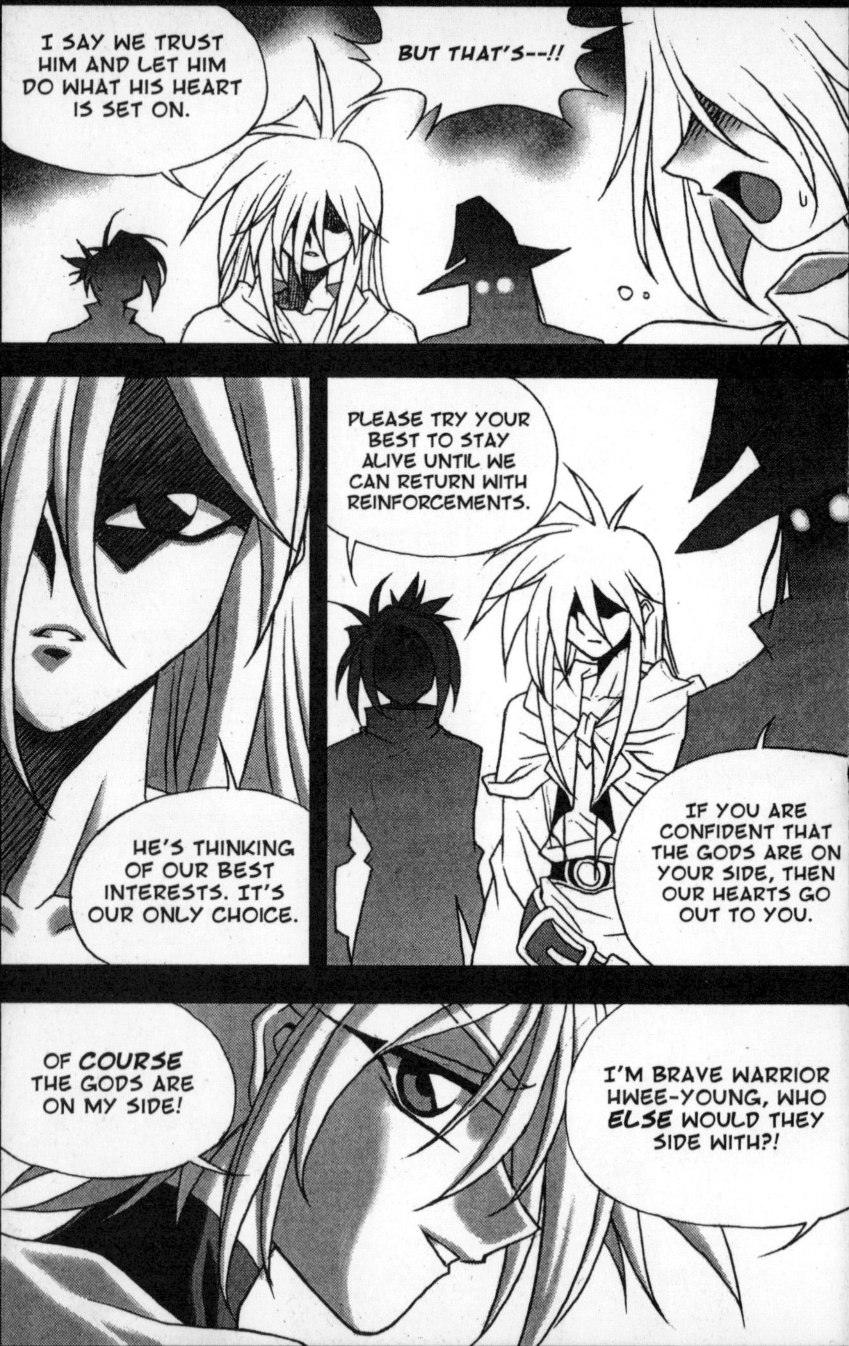
I SAY WE TRUST HIM AND LET HIM DO WHAT HIS HEART IS SET ON.
BUT THAT'S--!!
HE'S THINKING OF OUR BEST INTERESTS. IT'S OUR ONLY CHOICE.
PLEASE TRY YOUR BEST TO STAY ALIVE UNTIL WE CAN RETURN WITH REINFORCEMENTS.
IF YOU ARE CONFIDENT THAT THE GODS ARE ON YOUR SIDE, THEN OUR HEARTS GO OUT TO YOU.
OF *COURSE* THE GODS ARE ON MY SIDE!
I'M BRAVE WARRIOR HWEE-YOUNG, WHO *ELSE* WOULD THEY SIDE WITH?!

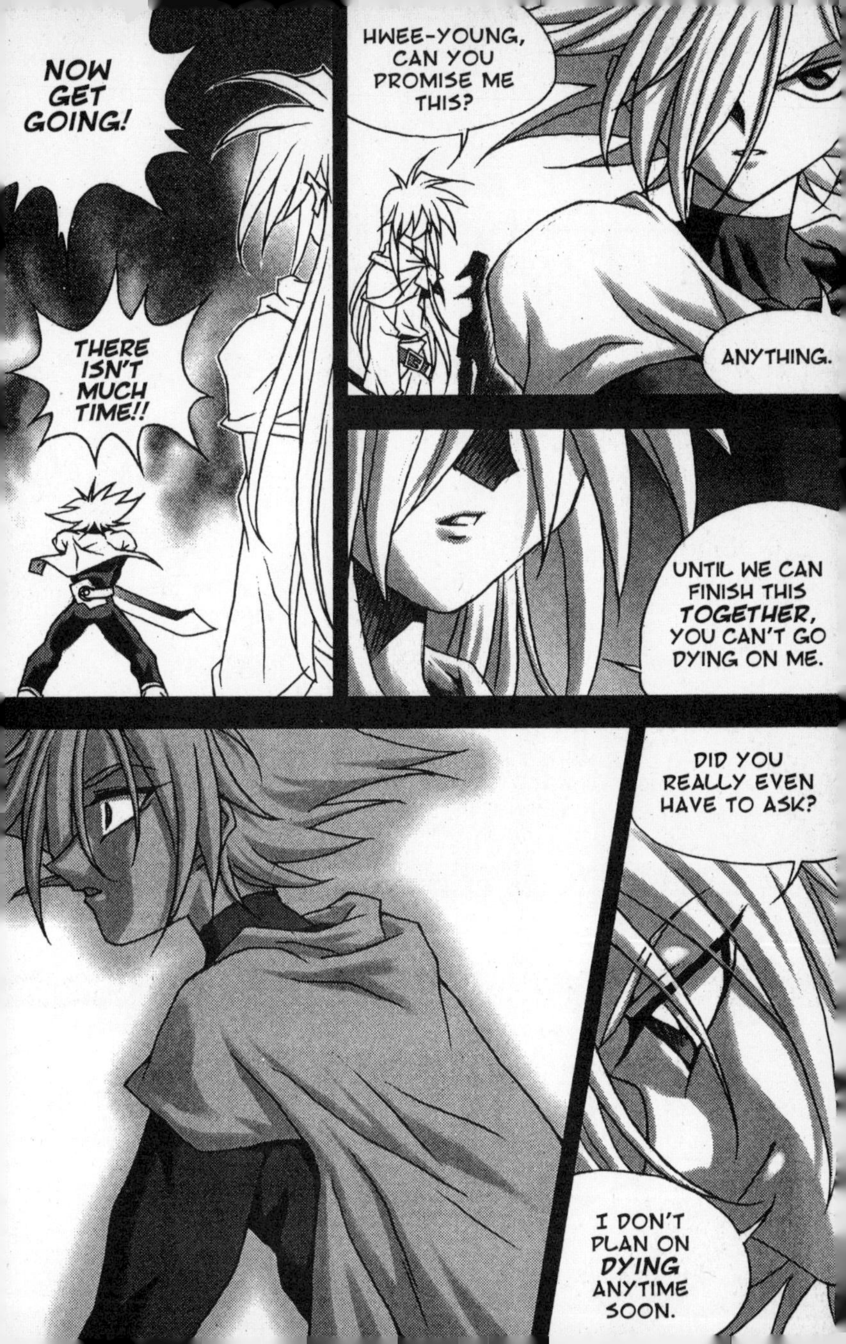
NOW GET GOING!
THERE ISN'T MUCH TIME!!
HWEE-YOUNG, CAN YOU PROMISE ME THIS?
ANYTHING.
UNTIL WE CAN FINISH THIS *TOGETHER*, YOU CAN'T GO DYING ON ME.
DID YOU REALLY EVEN HAVE TO ASK?
I DON'T PLAN ON *DYING* ANYTIME SOON.

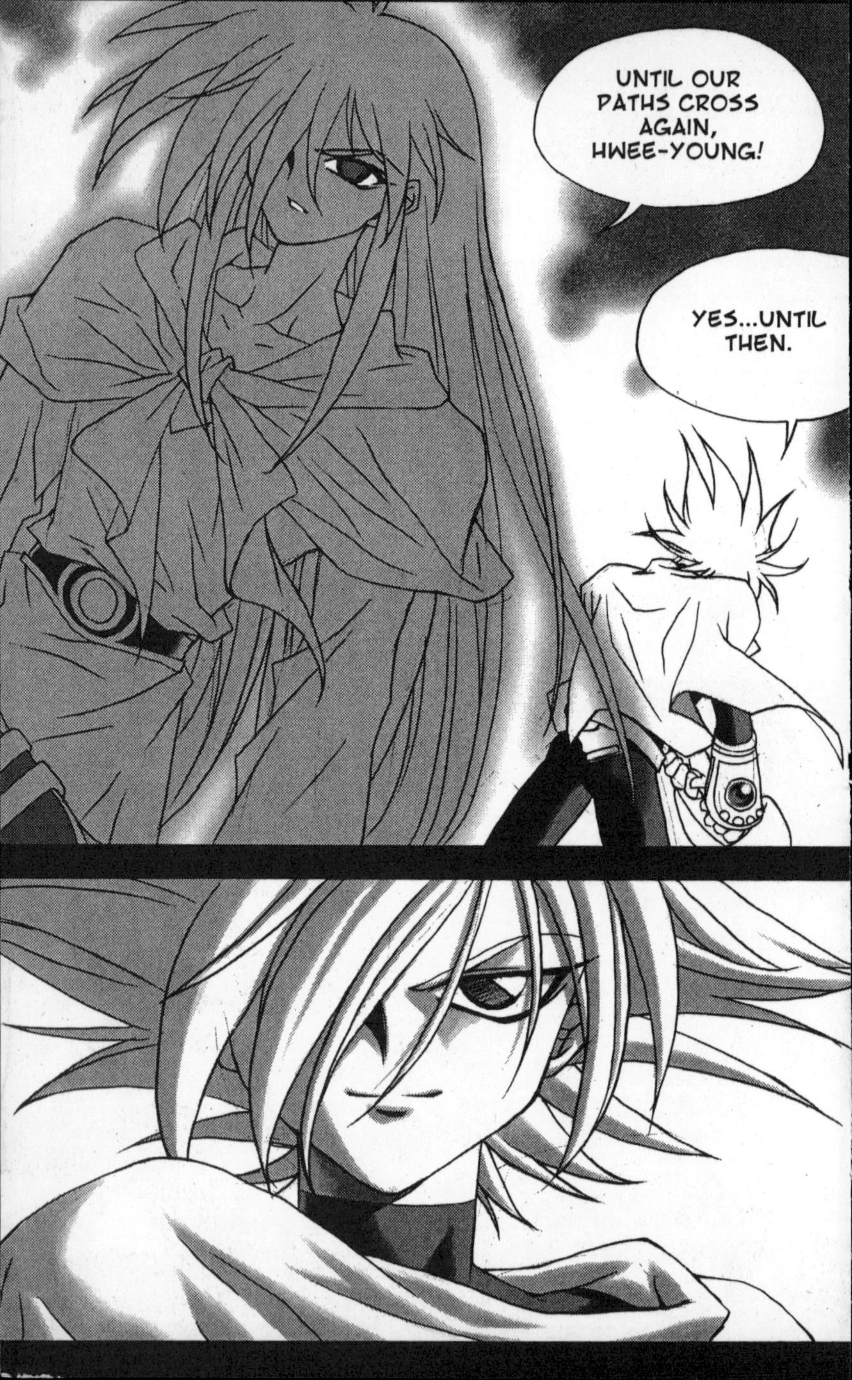
UNTIL OUR PATHS CROSS AGAIN, HWEE-YOUNG!
YES...UNTIL THEN.

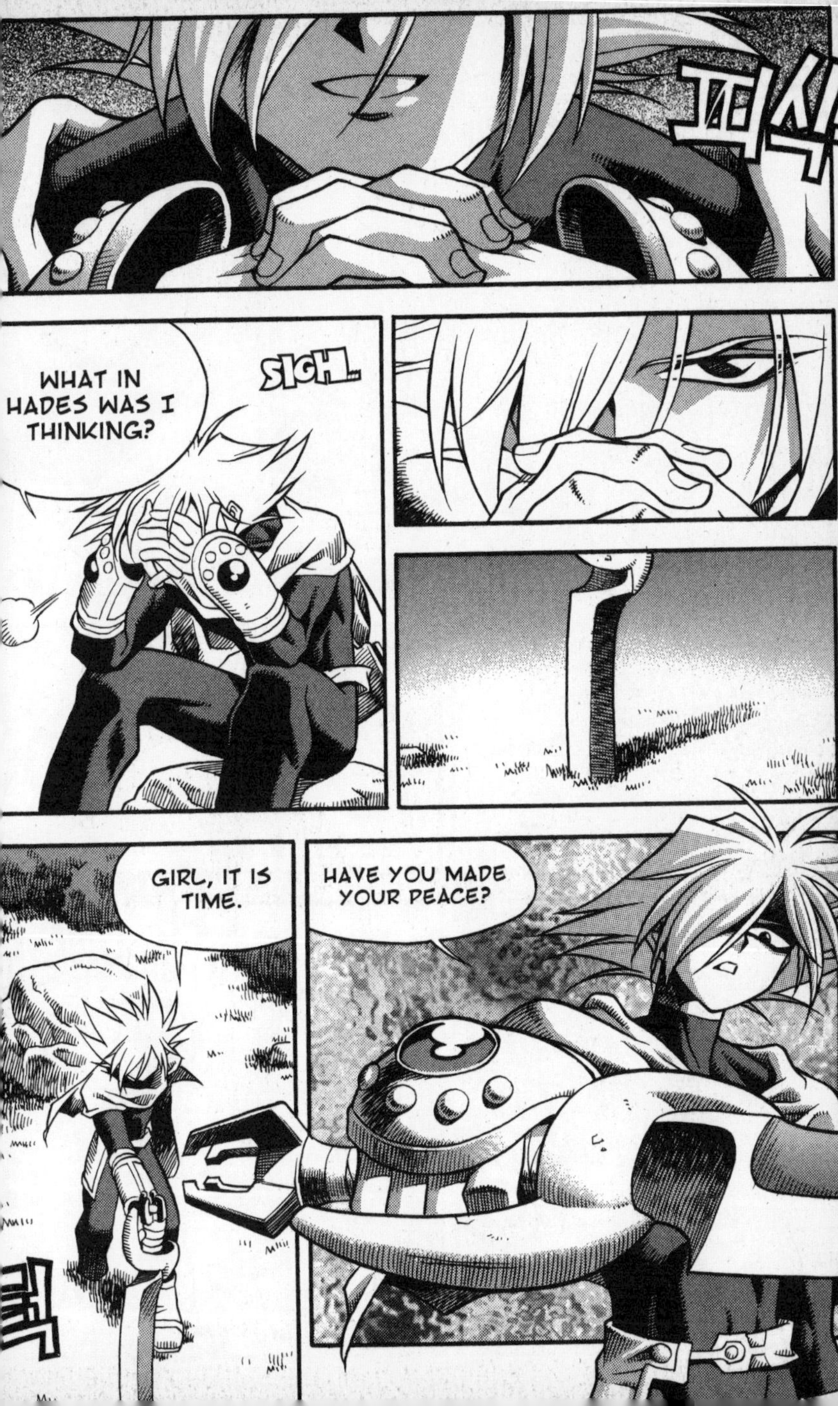
피식
WHAT IN HADES WAS I THINKING?
SIGH...
GIRL, IT IS TIME.
HAVE YOU MADE YOUR PEACE?

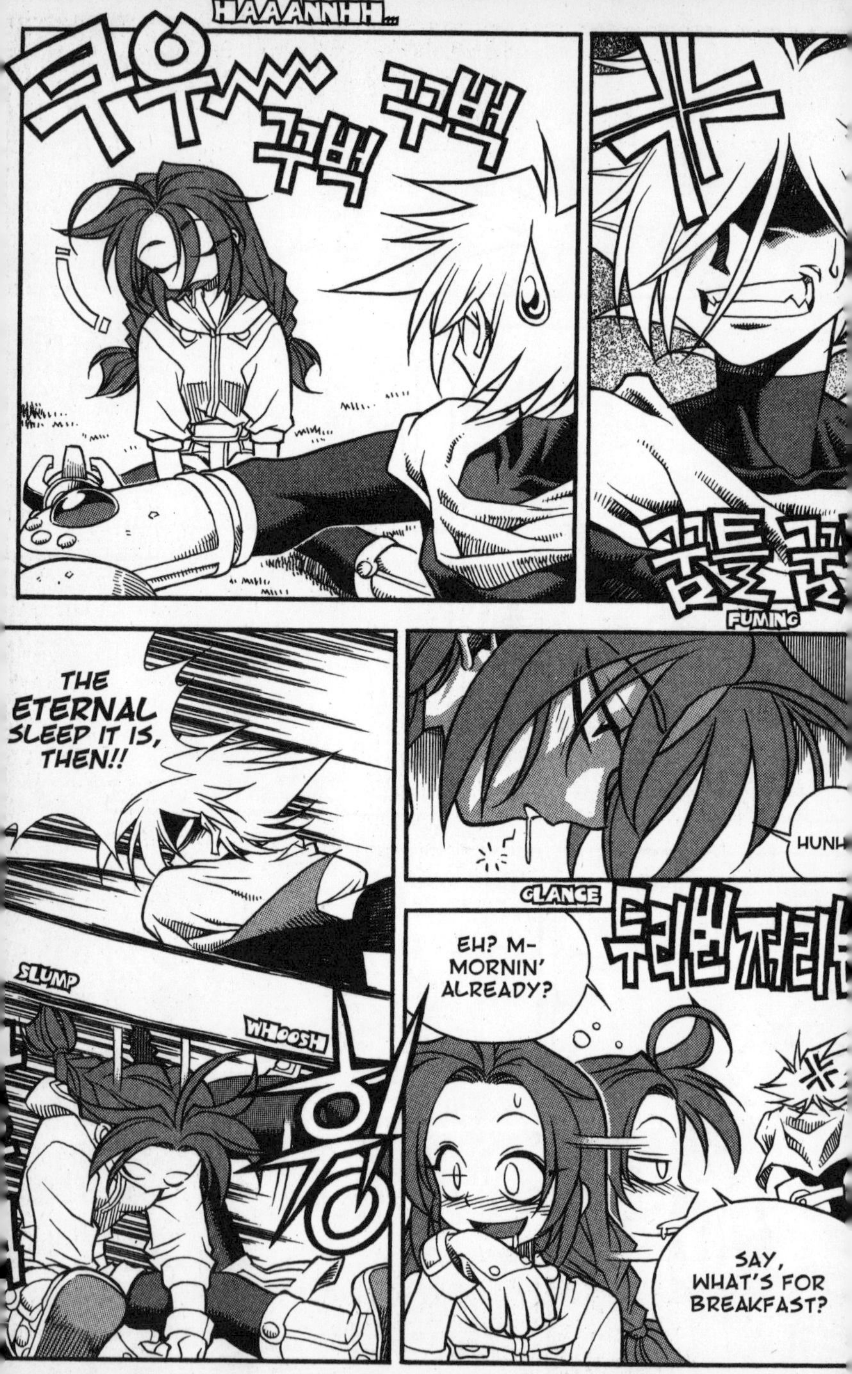
HAAANNHH...
FUMING
THE ETERNAL SLEEP IT IS, THEN!!
SLUMP
WHOOSH
HUNH
GLANCE
EH? M-MORNIN' ALREADY?
SAY, WHAT'S FOR BREAKFAST?

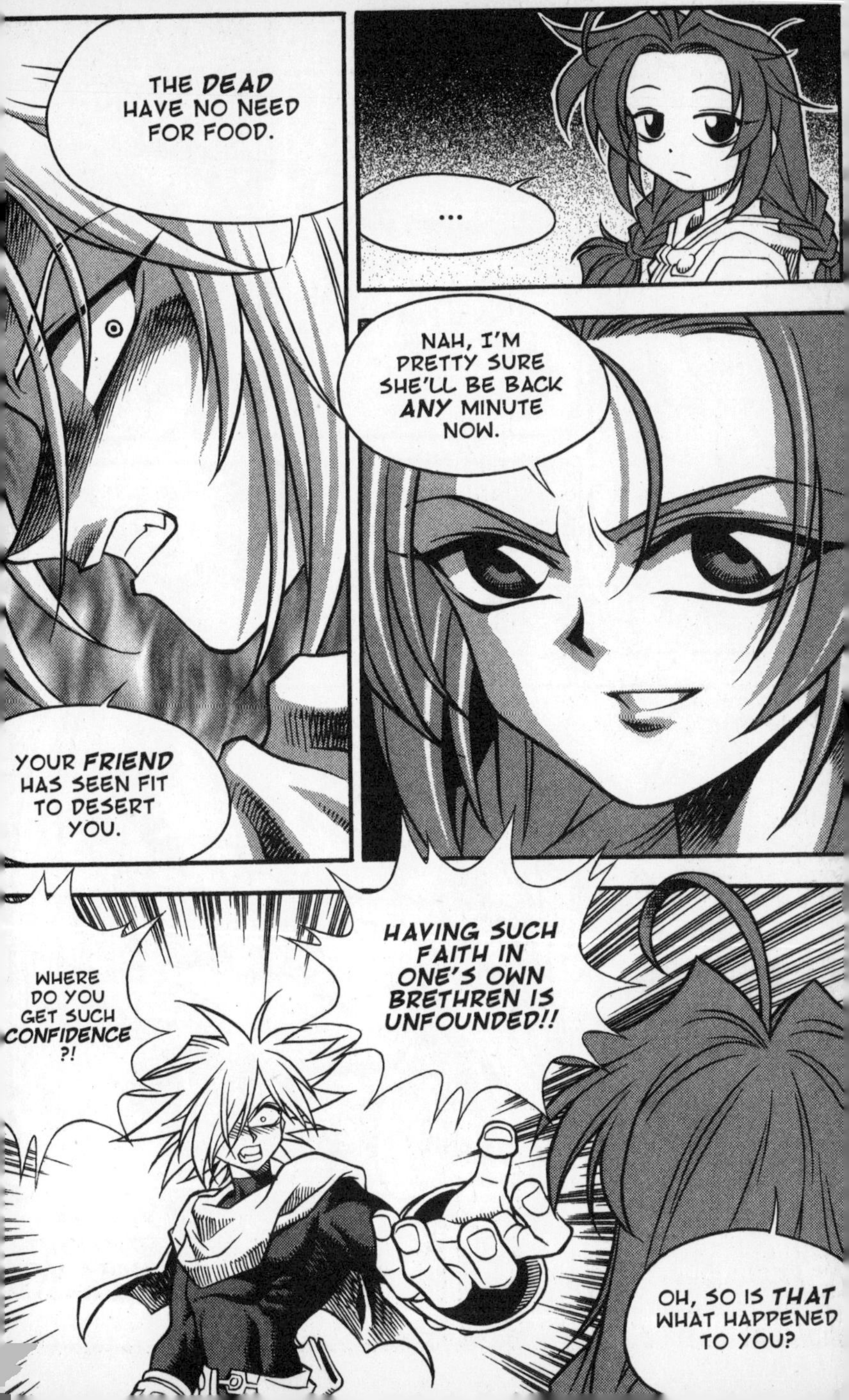
THE DEAD HAVE NO NEED FOR FOOD.
...
YOUR FRIEND HAS SEEN FIT TO DESERT YOU.
NAH, I'M PRETTY SURE SHE'LL BE BACK ANY MINUTE NOW.
WHERE DO YOU GET SUCH CONFIDENCE ?!
HAVING SUCH FAITH IN ONE'S OWN BRETHREN IS UNFOUNDED!!
OH, SO IS THAT WHAT HAPPENED TO YOU?

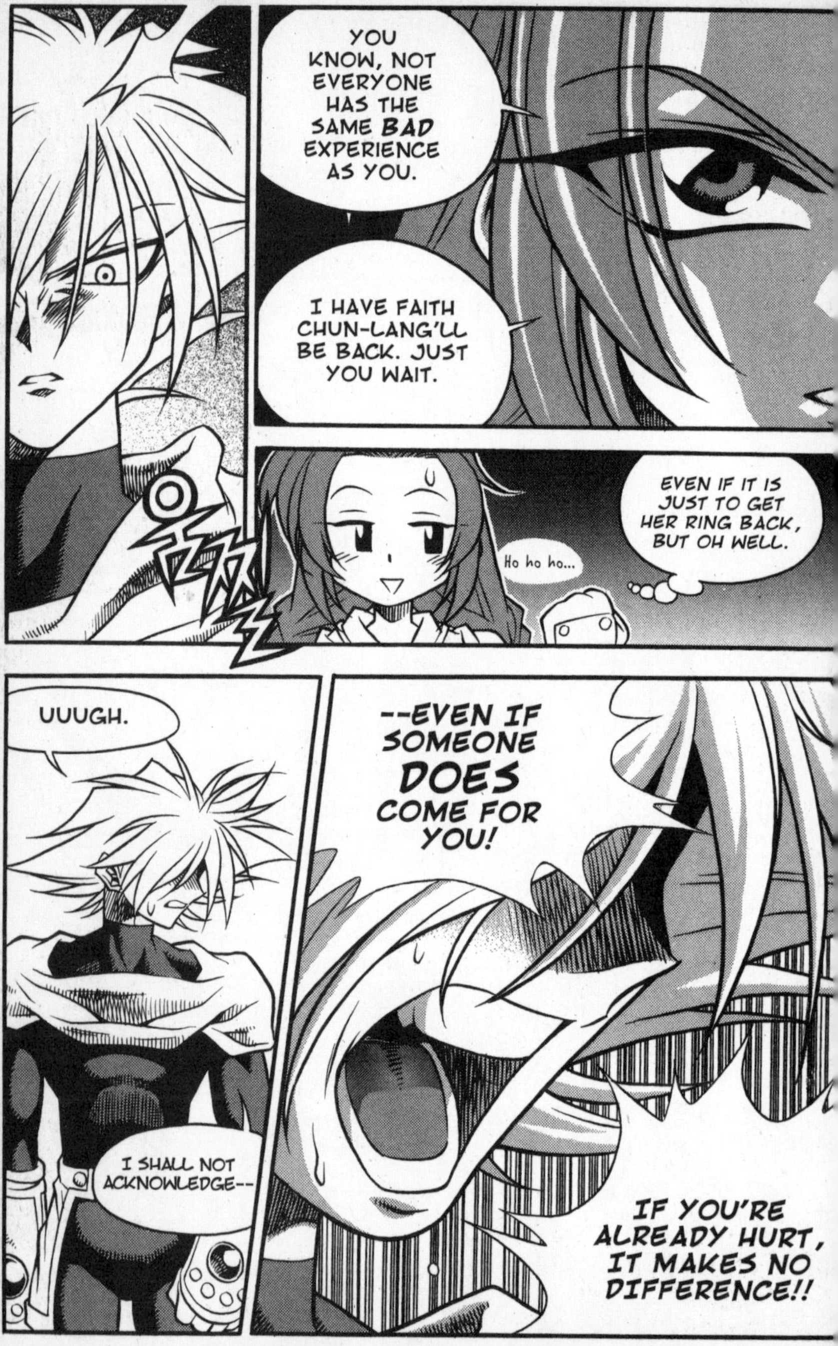
YOU KNOW, NOT EVERYONE HAS THE SAME BAD EXPERIENCE AS YOU.
I HAVE FAITH CHUN-LANG'LL BE BACK. JUST YOU WAIT.
Ho ho ho...
EVEN IF IT IS JUST TO GET HER RING BACK, BUT OH WELL.
UUUGH.
I SHALL NOT ACKNOWLEDGE--
--EVEN IF SOMEONE DOES COME FOR YOU!
IF YOU'RE ALREADY HURT, IT MAKES NO DIFFERENCE!!

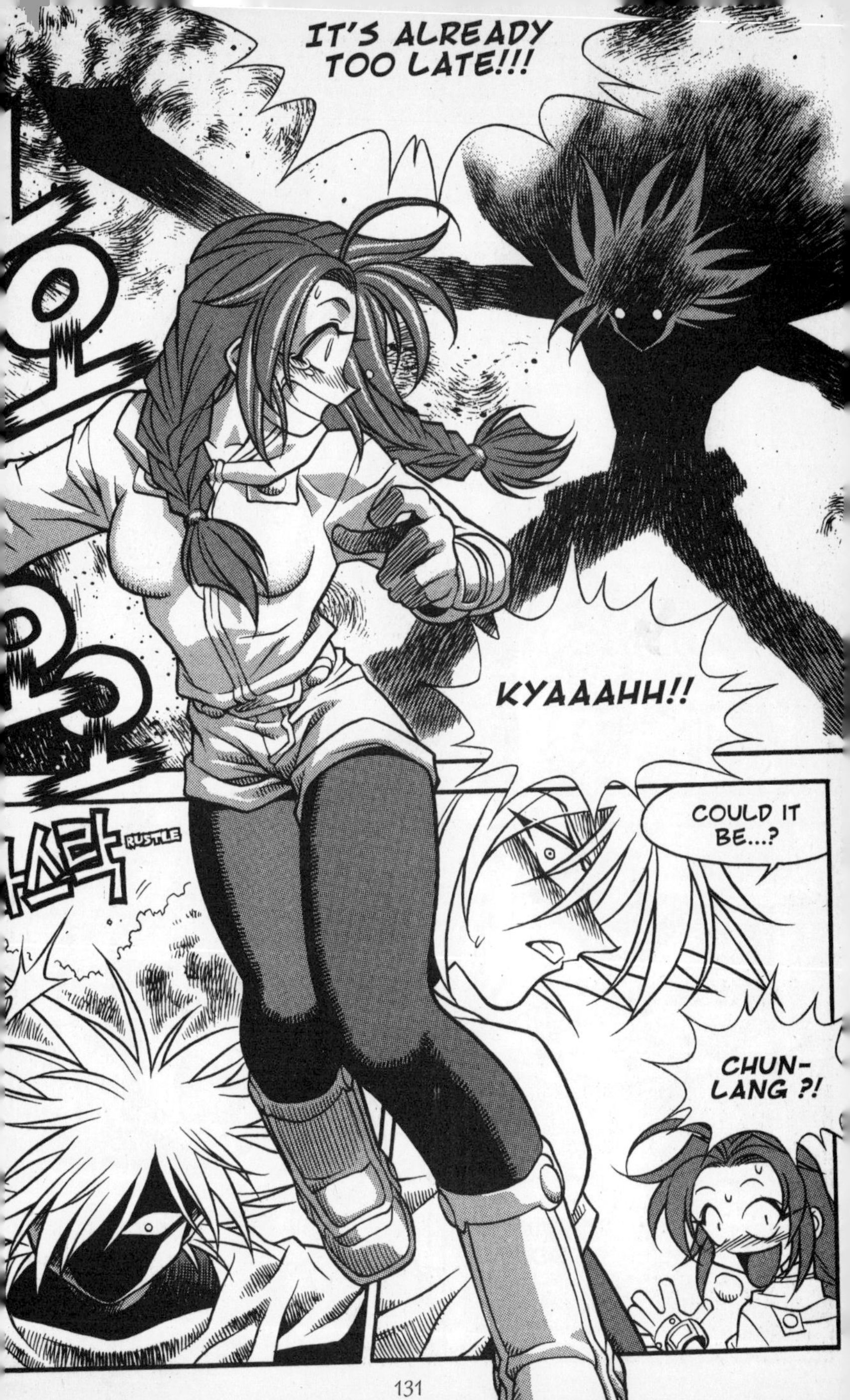
IT'S ALREADY TOO LATE!!!
KYAAAHH!!
RUSTLE
COULD IT BE...?
CHUN-LANG ?!

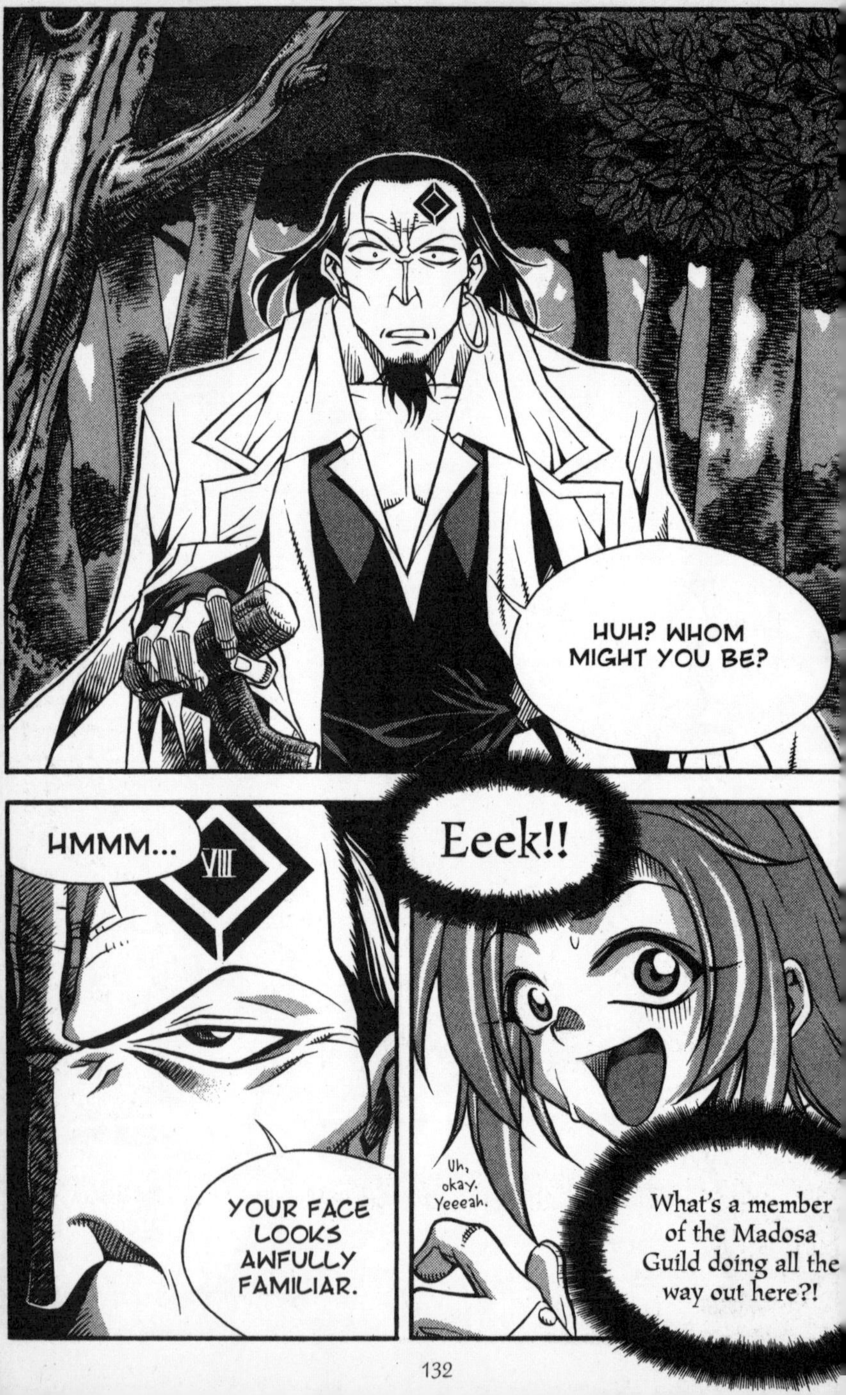
HUH? WHOM MIGHT YOU BE?
HMMM...
VIII
YOUR FACE LOOKS AWFULLY FAMILIAR.
Eeek!!
Uh, okay. Yeeeah.
What's a member of the Madosa Guild doing all the way out here?!

Quest 31

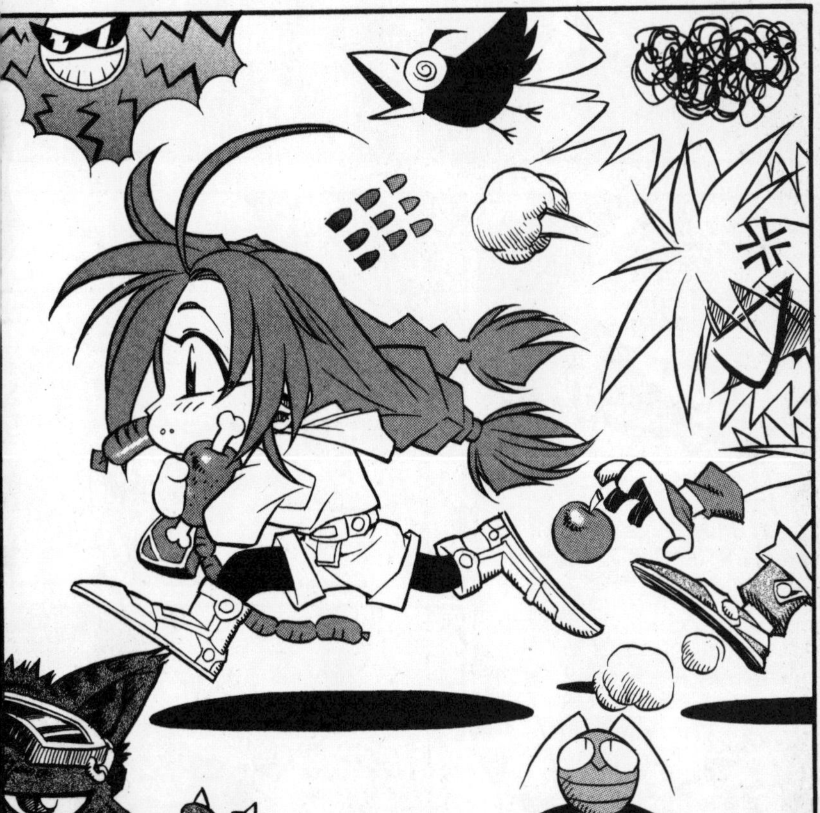

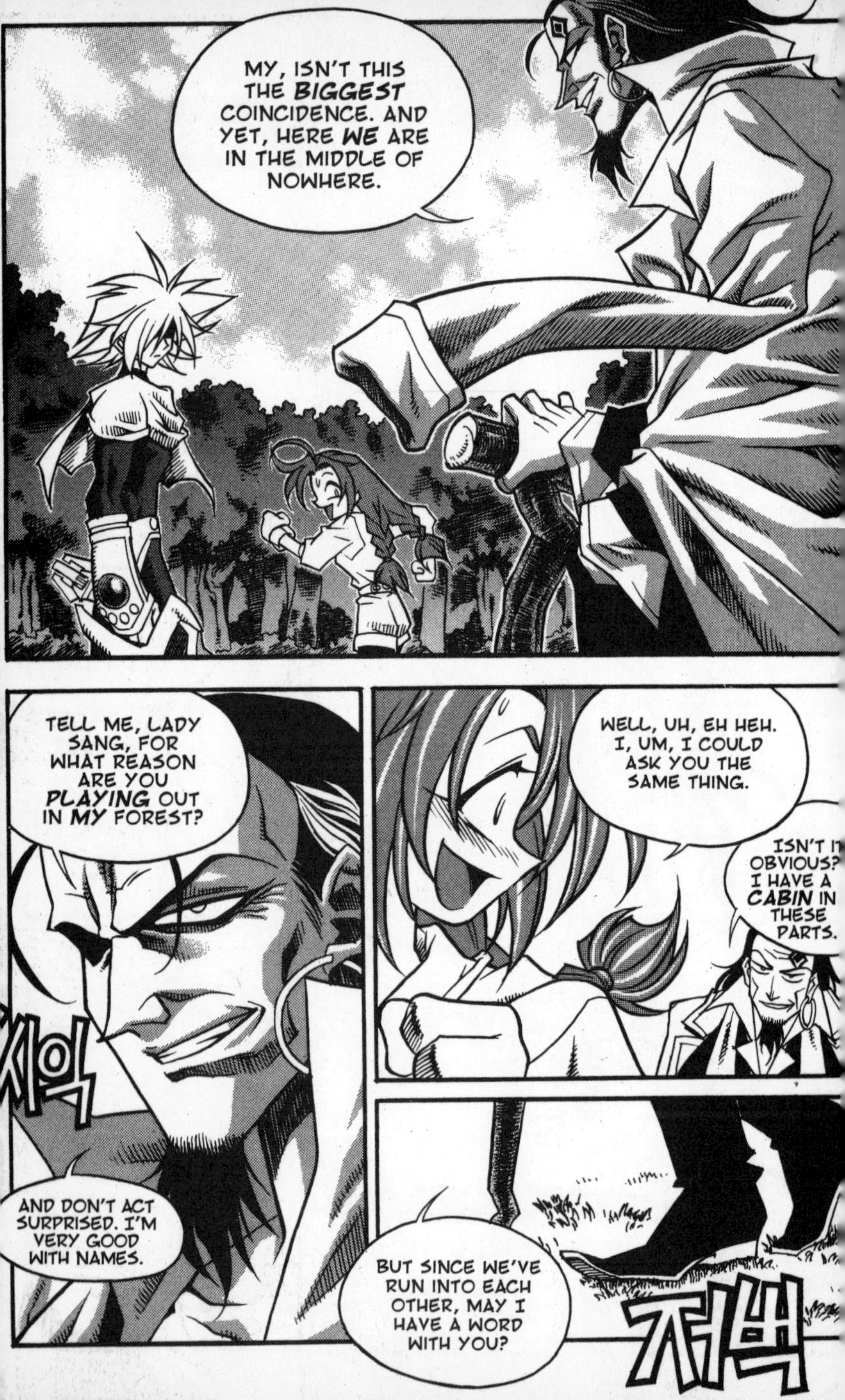
MY, ISN'T THIS THE ***BIGGEST*** COINCIDENCE. AND YET, HERE ***WE*** ARE IN THE MIDDLE OF NOWHERE.
TELL ME, LADY SANG, FOR WHAT REASON ARE YOU ***PLAYING*** OUT IN ***MY*** FOREST?
AND DON'T ACT SURPRISED. I'M VERY GOOD WITH NAMES.
WELL, UH, EH HEH. I, UM, I COULD ASK YOU THE SAME THING.
ISN'T IT OBVIOUS? I HAVE A ***CABIN*** IN THESE PARTS.
BUT SINCE WE'VE RUN INTO EACH OTHER, MAY I HAVE A WORD WITH YOU?
저벅

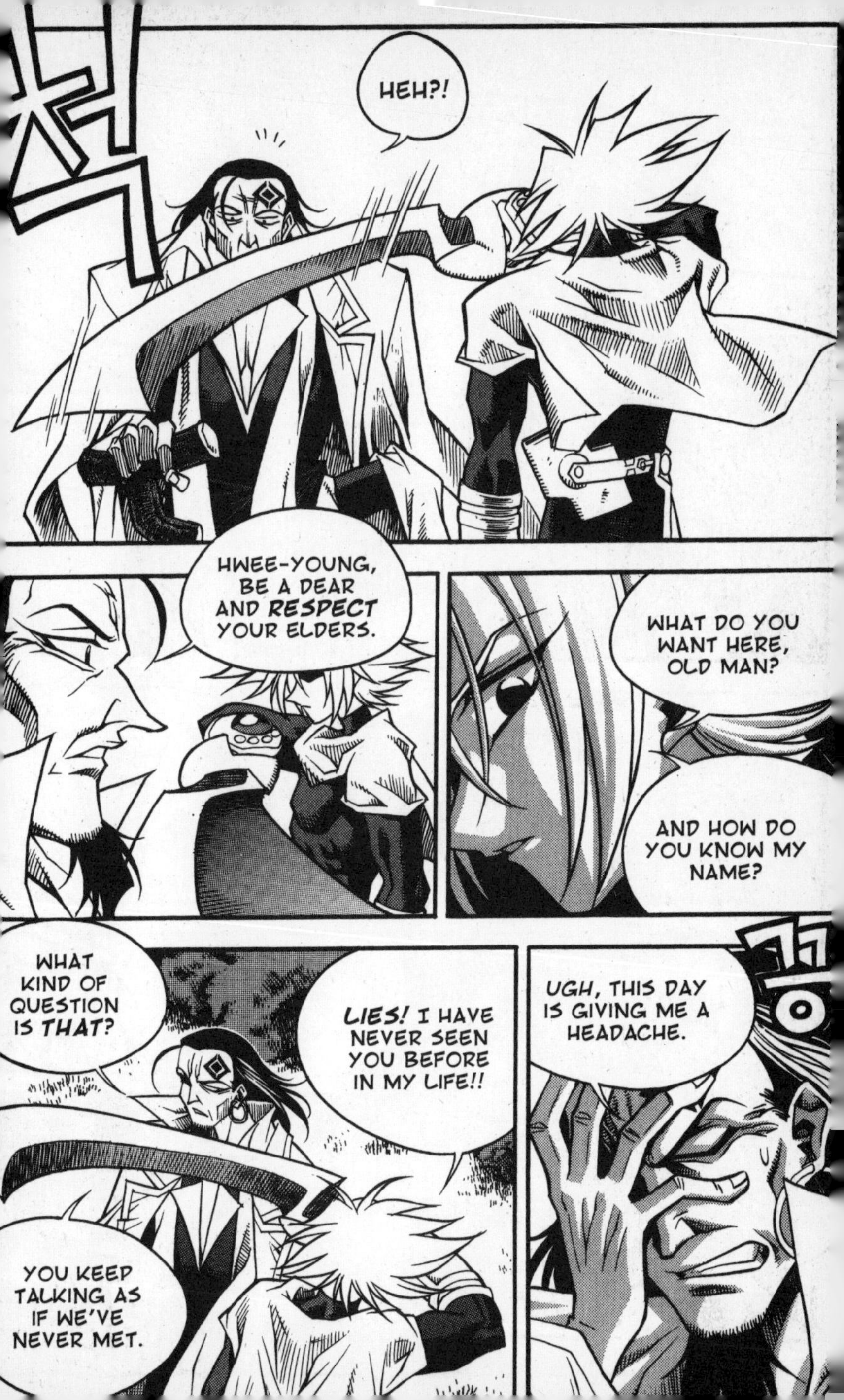
HEH?!
HWEE-YOUNG, BE A DEAR AND *RESPECT* YOUR ELDERS.
WHAT DO YOU WANT HERE, OLD MAN?
AND HOW DO YOU KNOW MY NAME?
WHAT KIND OF QUESTION IS *THAT*?
LIES! I HAVE NEVER SEEN YOU BEFORE IN MY LIFE!!
YOU KEEP TALKING AS IF WE'VE NEVER MET.
UGH, THIS DAY IS GIVING ME A HEADACHE.

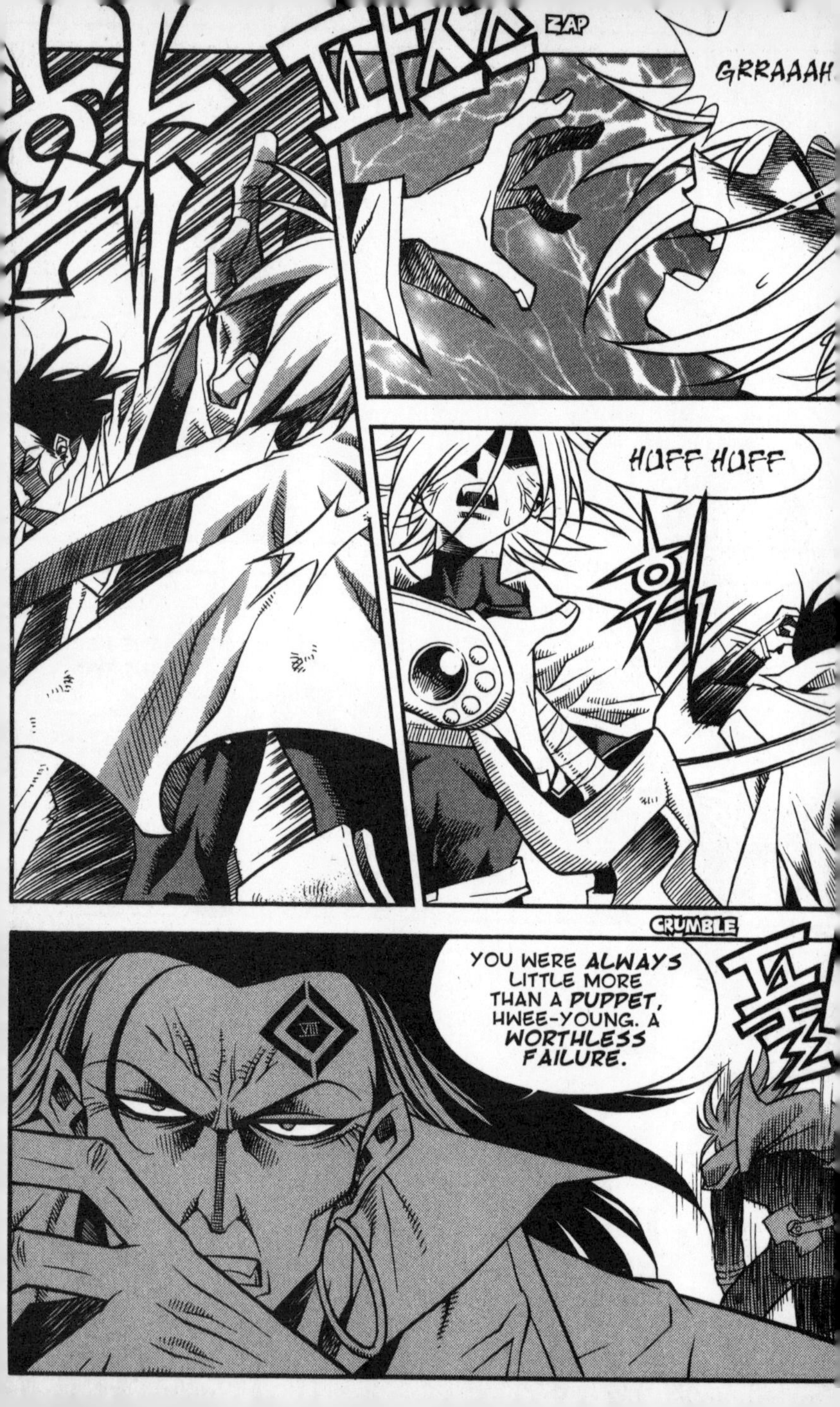
ZAP
GRRAAAH
HUFF HUFF
CRUMBLE
YOU WERE ALWAYS LITTLE MORE THAN A PUPPET, HWEE-YOUNG. A WORTHLESS FAILURE.

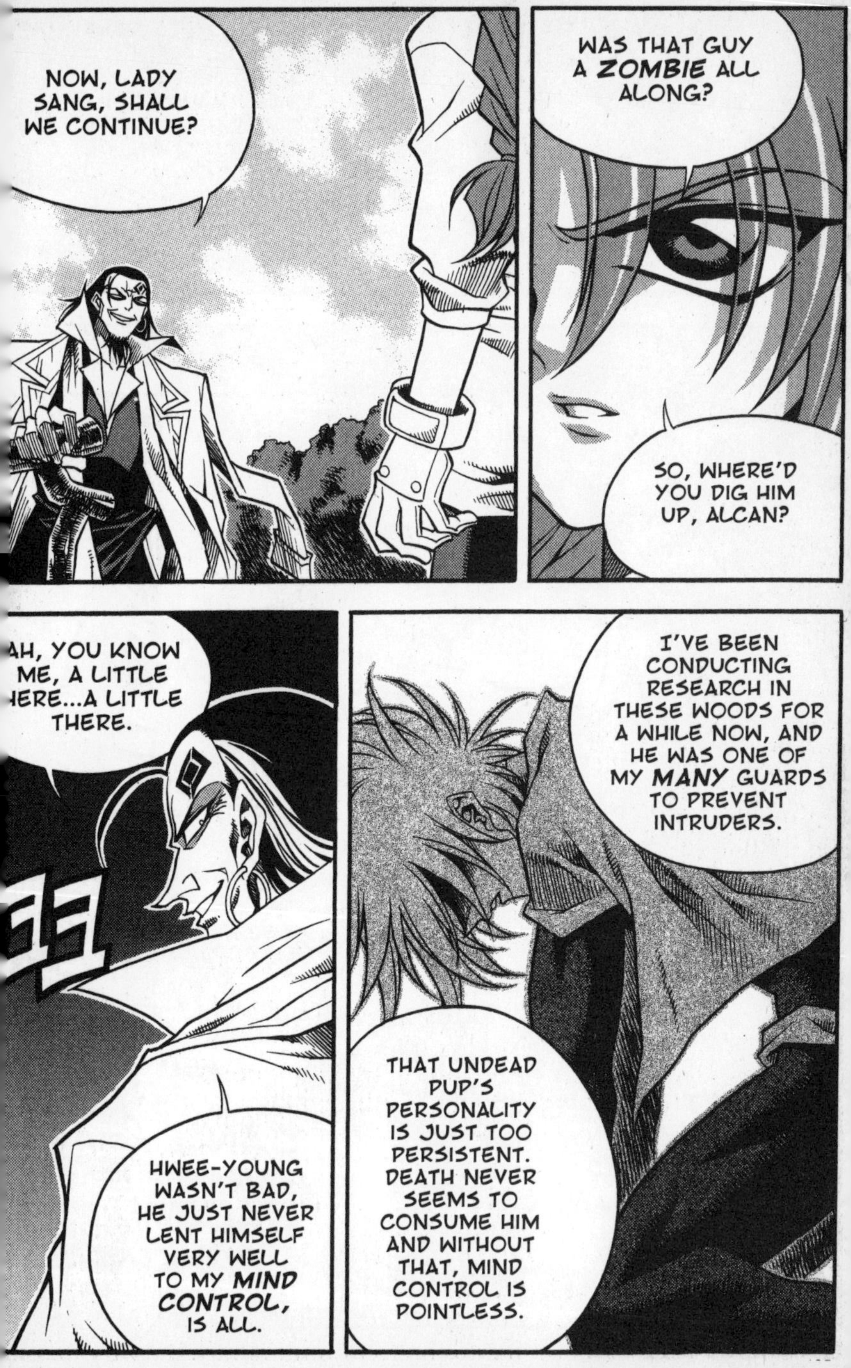
NOW, LADY SANG, SHALL WE CONTINUE?
WAS THAT GUY A ZOMBIE ALL ALONG?
SO, WHERE'D YOU DIG HIM UP, ALCAN?
AH, YOU KNOW ME, A LITTLE HERE...A LITTLE THERE.
HWEE-YOUNG WASN'T BAD, HE JUST NEVER LENT HIMSELF VERY WELL TO MY MIND CONTROL, IS ALL.
I'VE BEEN CONDUCTING RESEARCH IN THESE WOODS FOR A WHILE NOW, AND HE WAS ONE OF MY MANY GUARDS TO PREVENT INTRUDERS.
THAT UNDEAD PUP'S PERSONALITY IS JUST TOO PERSISTENT. DEATH NEVER SEEMS TO CONSUME HIM AND WITHOUT THAT, MIND CONTROL IS POINTLESS.

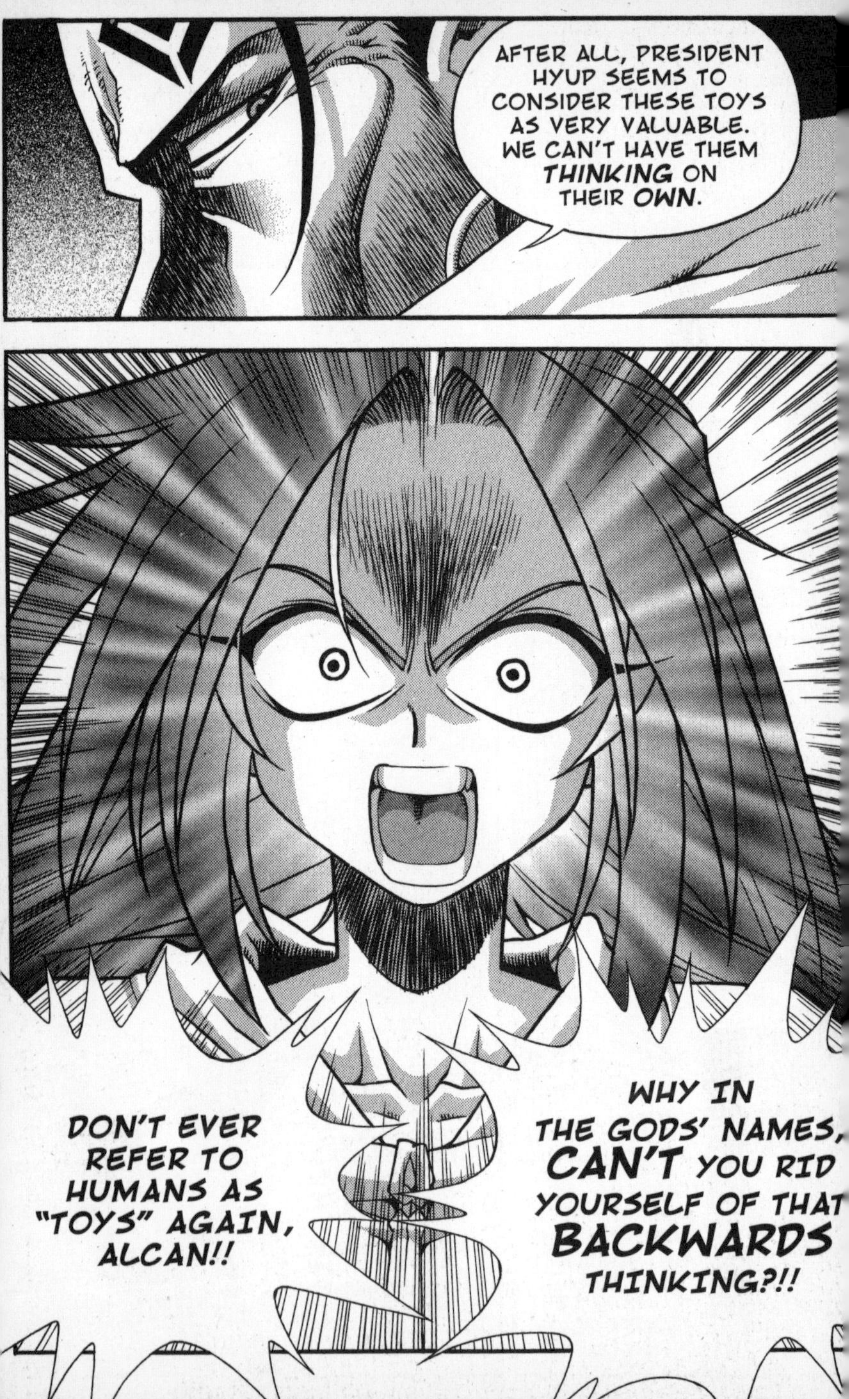
AFTER ALL, PRESIDENT HYUP SEEMS TO CONSIDER THESE TOYS AS VERY VALUABLE. WE CAN'T HAVE THEM THINKING ON THEIR OWN.
DON'T EVER REFER TO HUMANS AS "TOYS" AGAIN, ALCAN!!
WHY IN THE GODS' NAMES, CAN'T YOU RID YOURSELF OF THAT BACKWARDS THINKING?!!

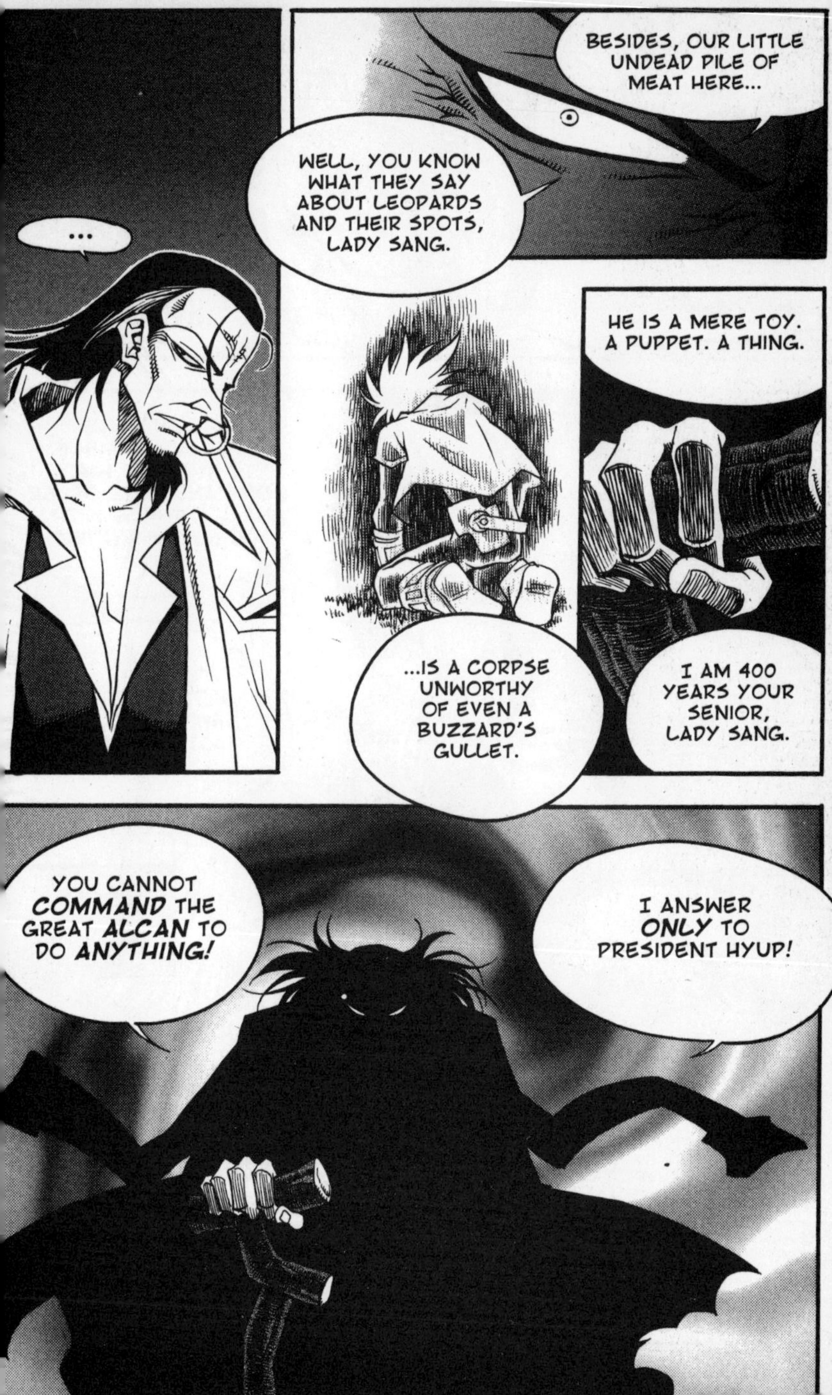

...
WELL, YOU KNOW WHAT THEY SAY ABOUT LEOPARDS AND THEIR SPOTS, LADY SANG.
BESIDES, OUR LITTLE UNDEAD PILE OF MEAT HERE...
...IS A CORPSE UNWORTHY OF EVEN A BUZZARD'S GULLET.
HE IS A MERE TOY. A PUPPET. A THING.
I AM 400 YEARS YOUR SENIOR, LADY SANG.
YOU CANNOT **COMMAND** THE GREAT **ALCAN** TO DO **ANYTHING!**
I ANSWER **ONLY** TO PRESIDENT HYUP!

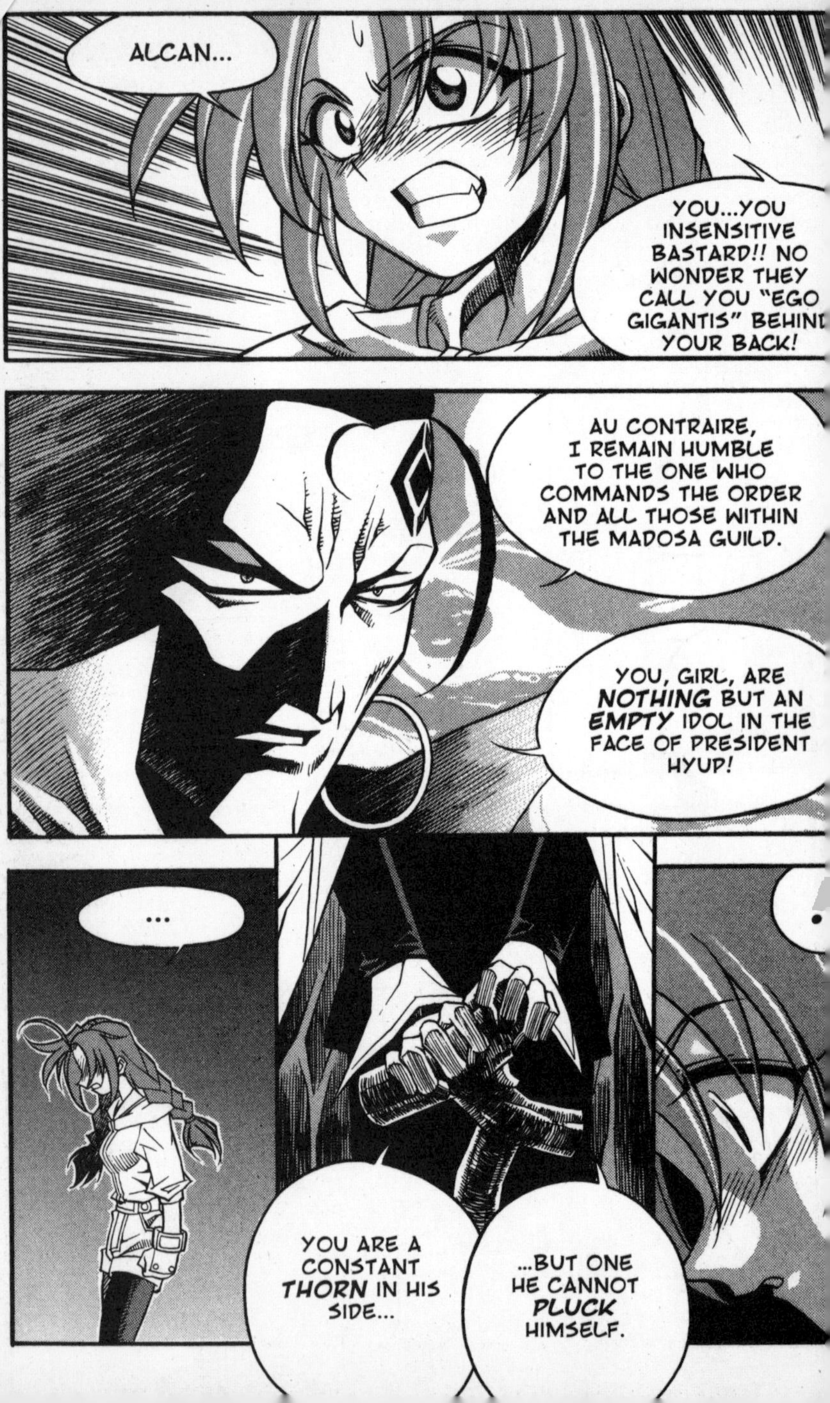

ALCAN...
YOU...YOU INSENSITIVE BASTARD!! NO WONDER THEY CALL YOU "EGO GIGANTIS" BEHIND YOUR BACK!
AU CONTRAIRE, I REMAIN HUMBLE TO THE ONE WHO COMMANDS THE ORDER AND ALL THOSE WITHIN THE MADOSA GUILD.
YOU, GIRL, ARE NOTHING BUT AN EMPTY IDOL IN THE FACE OF PRESIDENT HYUP!
...
YOU ARE A CONSTANT THORN IN HIS SIDE...
...BUT ONE HE CANNOT PLUCK HIMSELF.

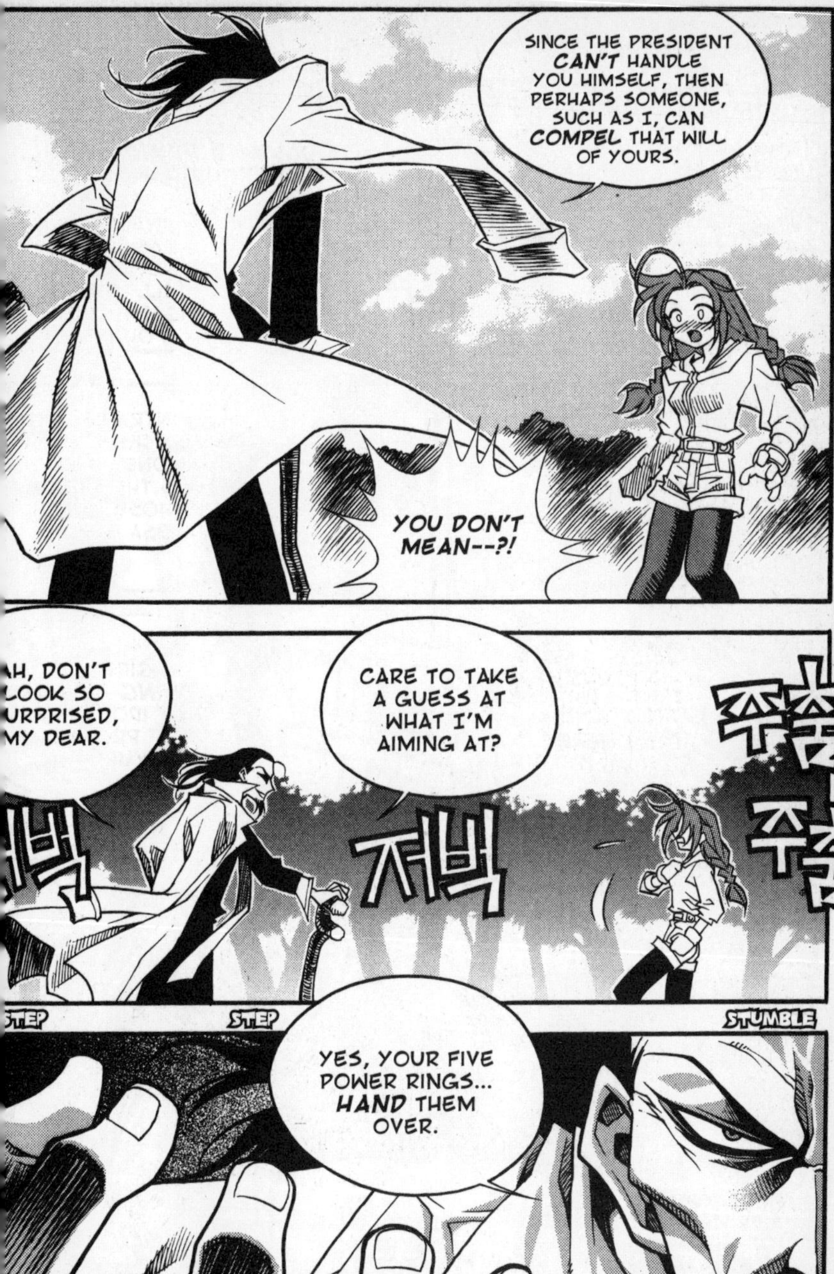
SINCE THE PRESIDENT CAN'T HANDLE YOU HIMSELF, THEN PERHAPS SOMEONE, SUCH AS I, CAN COMPEL THAT WILL OF YOURS.
YOU DON'T MEAN--?!
H, DON'T LOOK SO URPRISED, MY DEAR.
벅
TEP
CARE TO TAKE A GUESS AT WHAT I'M AIMING AT?
저벅
STEP
주춤 주춤
STUMBLE
YES, YOUR FIVE POWER RINGS... HAND THEM OVER.

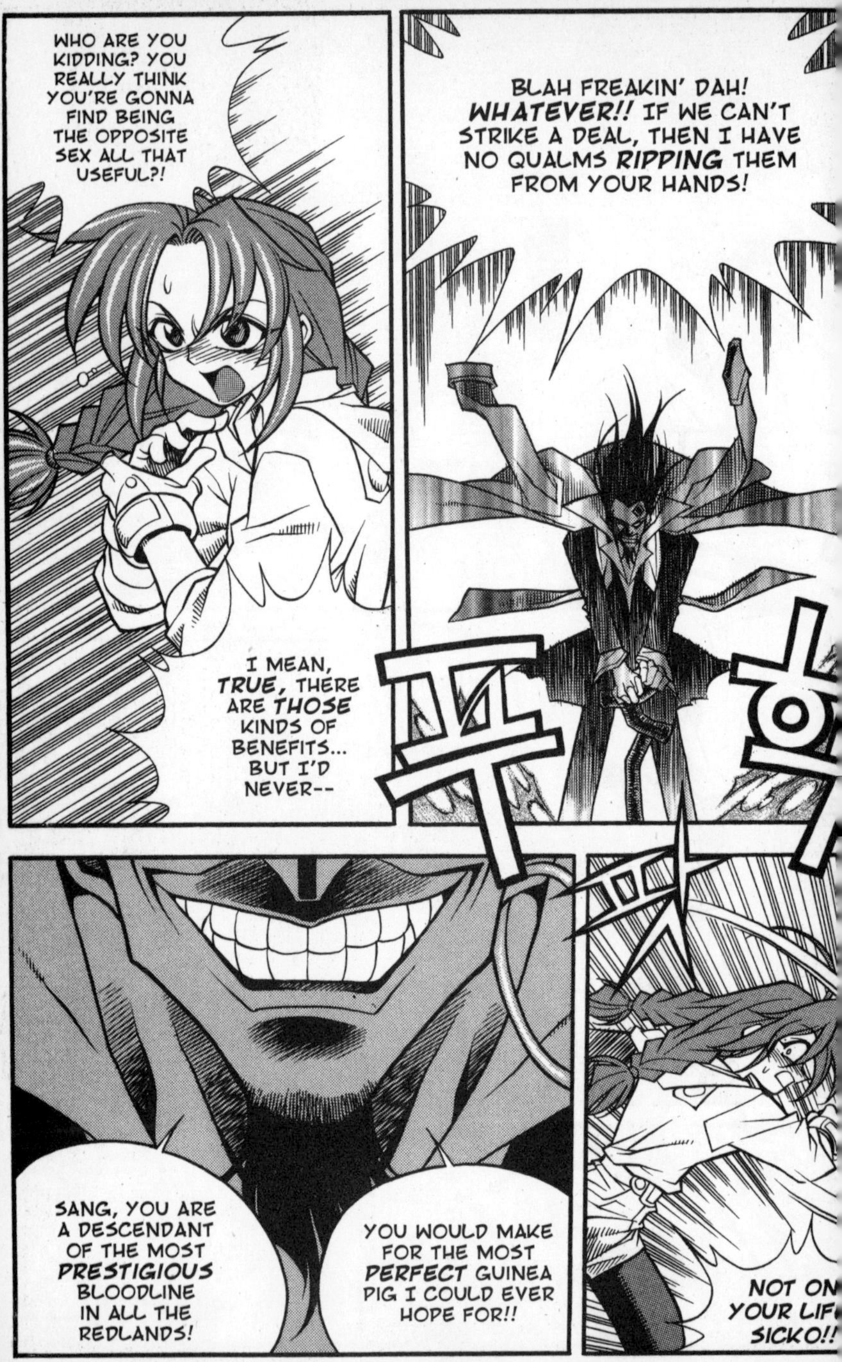
WHO ARE YOU KIDDING? YOU REALLY THINK YOU'RE GONNA FIND BEING THE OPPOSITE SEX ALL THAT USEFUL?!
I MEAN, TRUE, THERE ARE THOSE KINDS OF BENEFITS... BUT I'D NEVER--
BLAH FREAKIN' DAH! WHATEVER!! IF WE CAN'T STRIKE A DEAL, THEN I HAVE NO QUALMS RIPPING THEM FROM YOUR HANDS!
SANG, YOU ARE A DESCENDANT OF THE MOST PRESTIGIOUS BLOODLINE IN ALL THE REDLANDS!
YOU WOULD MAKE FOR THE MOST PERFECT GUINEA PIG I COULD EVER HOPE FOR!!
NOT ON YOUR LIF SICKO!!

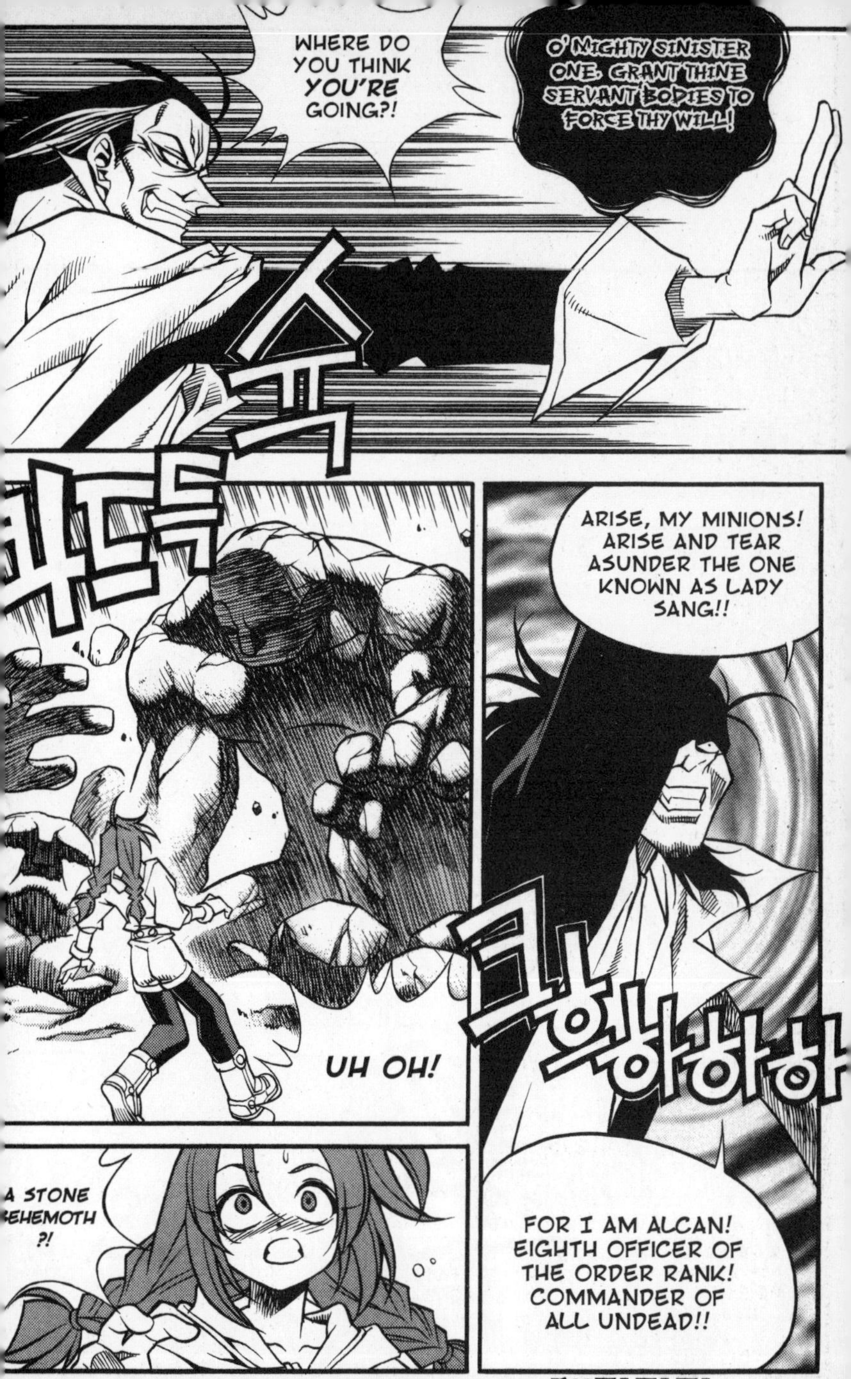
WHERE DO YOU THINK YOU'RE GOING?!
O' MIGHTY SINISTER ONE. GRANT THINE SERVANT BODIES TO FORCE THY WILL!
UH OH!
A STONE BEHEMOTH ?!
ARISE, MY MINIONS! ARISE AND TEAR ASUNDER THE ONE KNOWN AS LADY SANG!!
크흐하하하
FOR I AM ALCAN! EIGHTH OFFICER OF THE ORDER RANK! COMMANDER OF ALL UNDEAD!!

MOO HA HA HA

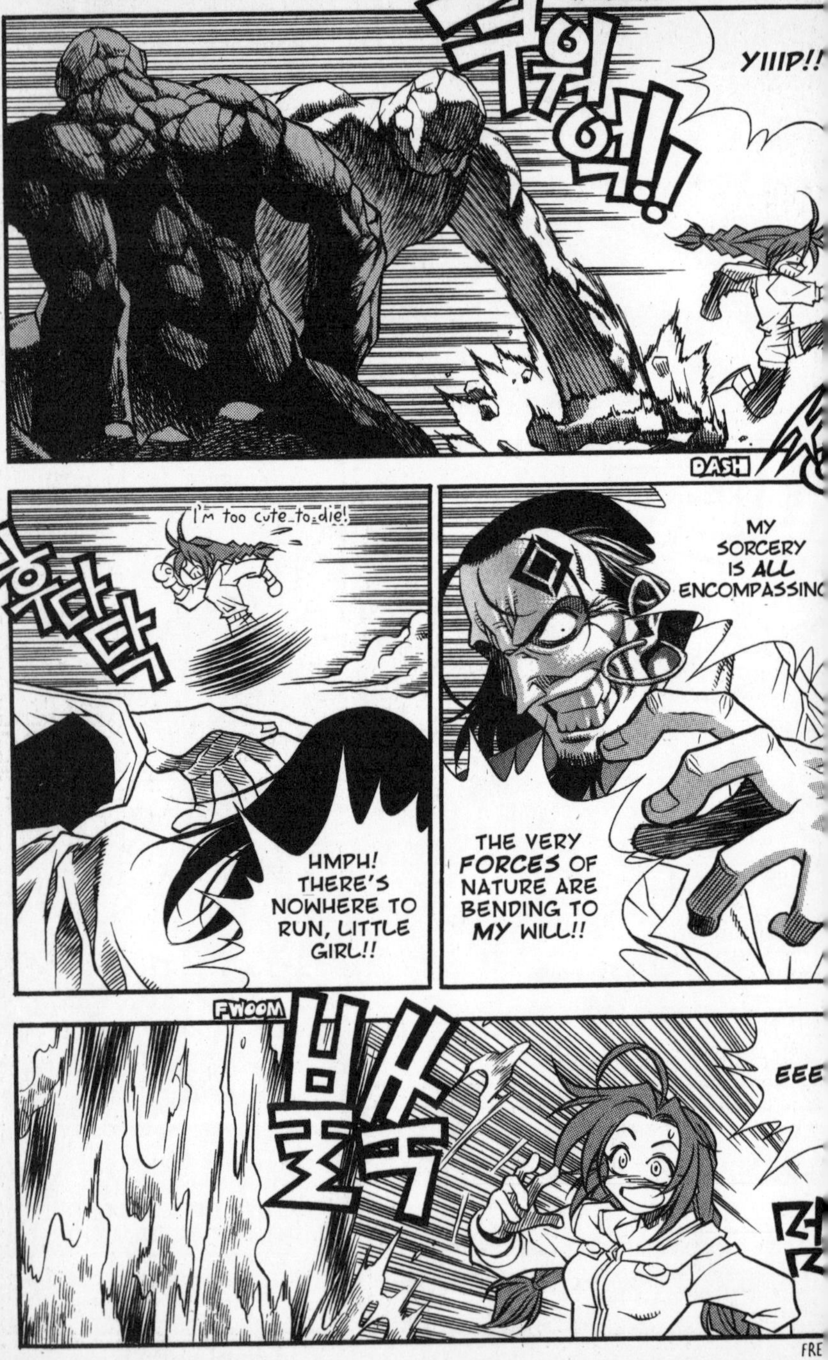
ROOAR!!
YIIIP!!
DASH
I'm too cute to die!
후다닥
HMPH! THERE'S NOWHERE TO RUN, LITTLE GIRL!!
MY SORCERY IS ALL ENCOMPASSING
THE VERY FORCES OF NATURE ARE BENDING TO MY WILL!!
FWOOM
EEE

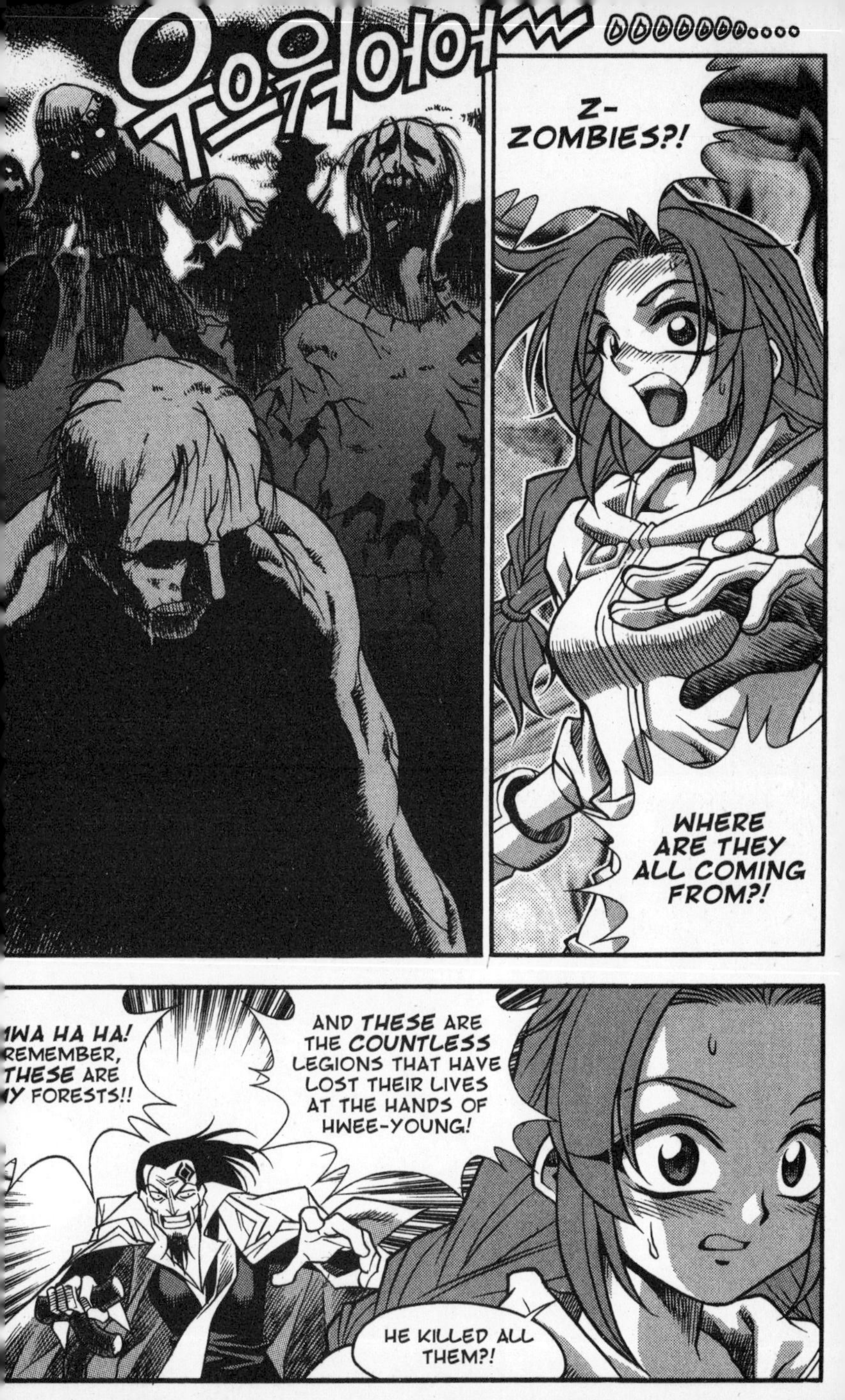

Z-
ZOMBIES?!
WHERE ARE THEY ALL COMING FROM?!
MWA HA HA! REMEMBER, THESE ARE MY FORESTS!!
AND THESE ARE THE COUNTLESS LEGIONS THAT HAVE LOST THEIR LIVES AT THE HANDS OF HWEE-YOUNG!
HE KILLED ALL THEM?!

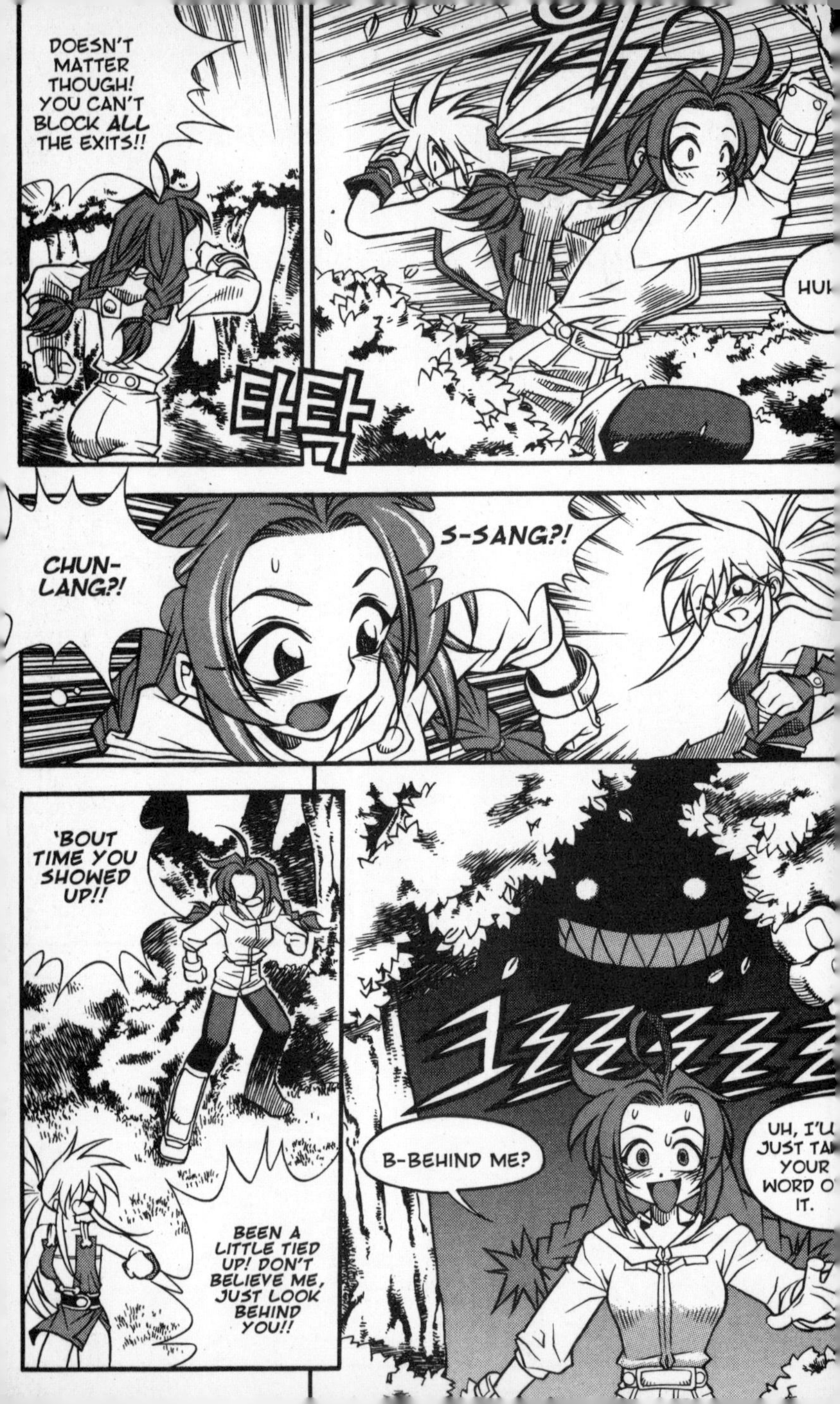
DOESN'T MATTER THOUGH! YOU CAN'T BLOCK ALL THE EXITS!!
타탁
CHUN-LANG?!
S-SANG?!
'BOUT TIME YOU SHOWED UP!!
BEEN A LITTLE TIED UP! DON'T BELIEVE ME, JUST LOOK BEHIND YOU!!
ㅋㅋㅋㅋㅋㅋ
B-BEHIND ME?
UH, I'L JUST TA YOUR WORD O IT.

Quest 32

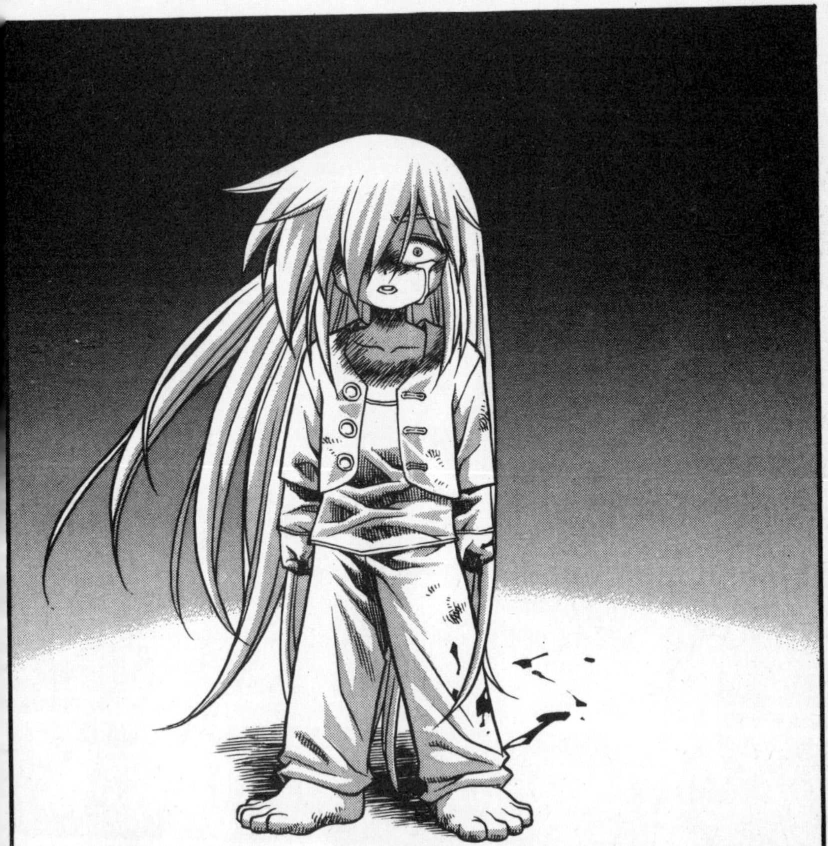

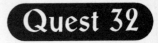

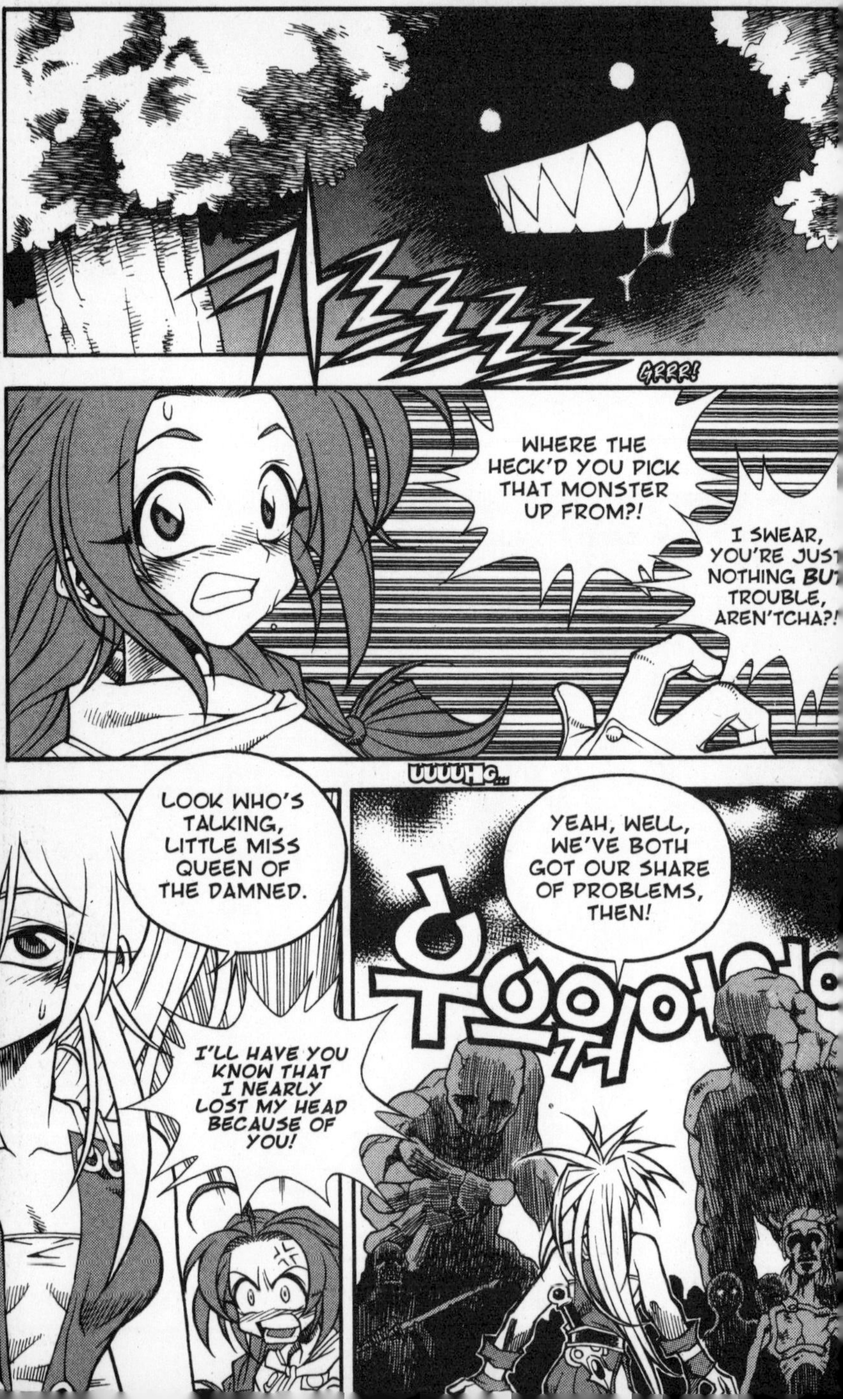
GRRR!
WHERE THE HECK'D YOU PICK THAT MONSTER UP FROM?!
I SWEAR, YOU'RE JUST NOTHING BUT TROUBLE, AREN'TCHA?!
UUUUHG...
LOOK WHO'S TALKING, LITTLE MISS QUEEN OF THE DAMNED.
I'LL HAVE YOU KNOW THAT I NEARLY LOST MY HEAD BECAUSE OF YOU!
YEAH, WELL, WE'VE BOTH GOT OUR SHARE OF PROBLEMS, THEN!

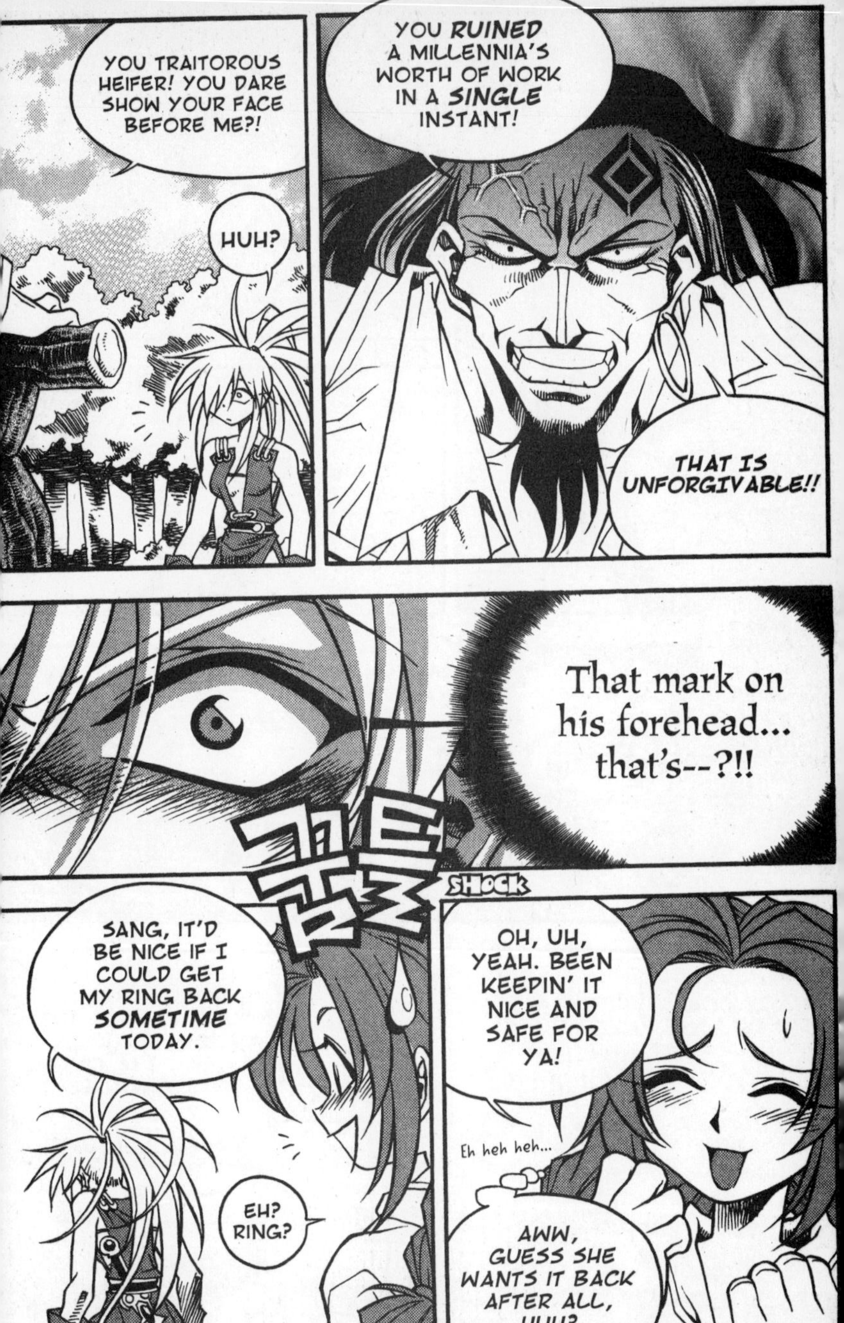
YOU TRAITOROUS HEIFER! YOU DARE SHOW YOUR FACE BEFORE ME?!
HUH?
YOU RUINED A MILLENNIA'S WORTH OF WORK IN A SINGLE INSTANT!
THAT IS UNFORGIVABLE!!
That mark on his forehead... that's--?!!
SHOCK
SANG, IT'D BE NICE IF I COULD GET MY RING BACK SOMETIME TODAY.
EH? RING?
OH, UH, YEAH. BEEN KEEPIN' IT NICE AND SAFE FOR YA!
Eh heh heh...
AWW, GUESS SHE WANTS IT BACK AFTER ALL, HUH?

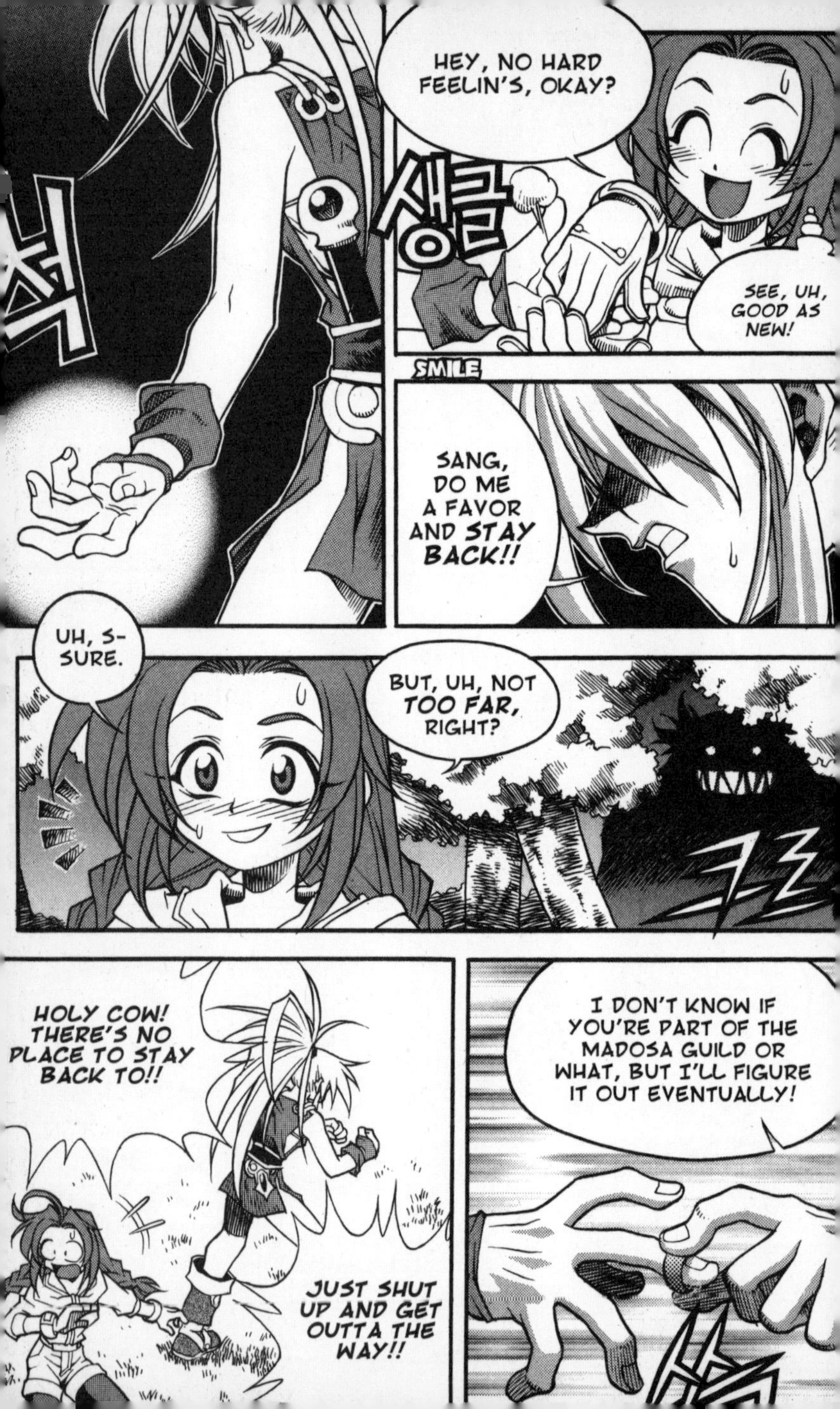
HEY, NO HARD FEELIN'S, OKAY?
SEE, UH, GOOD AS NEW!
SMILE
SANG, DO ME A FAVOR AND STAY BACK!!
UH, S- SURE.
BUT, UH, NOT TOO FAR, RIGHT?
HOLY COW! THERE'S NO PLACE TO STAY BACK TO!!
JUST SHUT UP AND GET OUTTA THE WAY!!
I DON'T KNOW IF YOU'RE PART OF THE MADOSA GUILD OR WHAT, BUT I'LL FIGURE IT OUT EVENTUALLY!

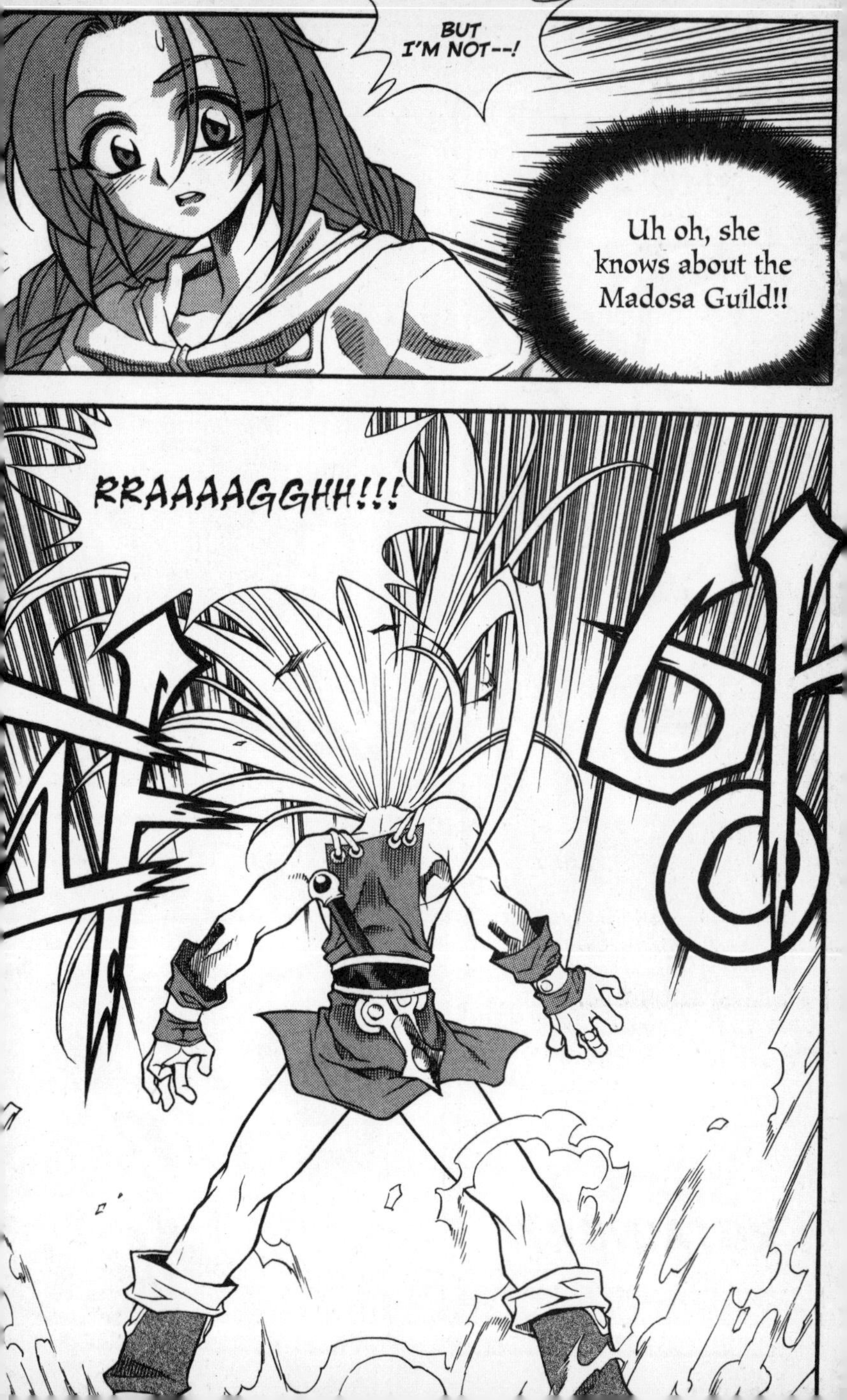
BUT I'M NOT--!
Uh oh, she knows about the Madosa Guild!!
RRAAAAGGHH!!!

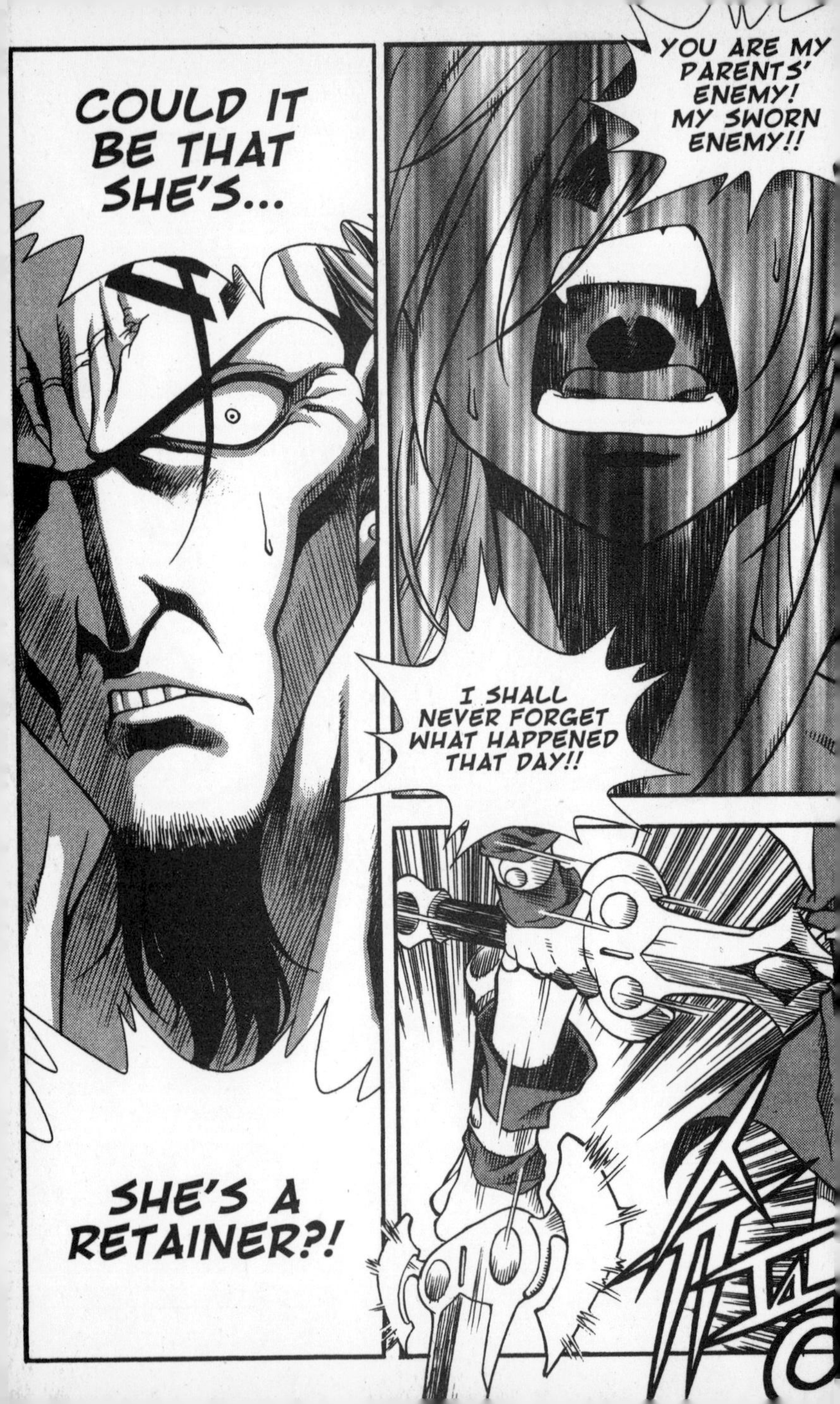
COULD IT BE THAT SHE'S...
SHE'S A RETAINER?!
YOU ARE MY PARENTS' ENEMY! MY SWORN ENEMY!!
I SHALL NEVER FORGET WHAT HAPPENED THAT DAY!!

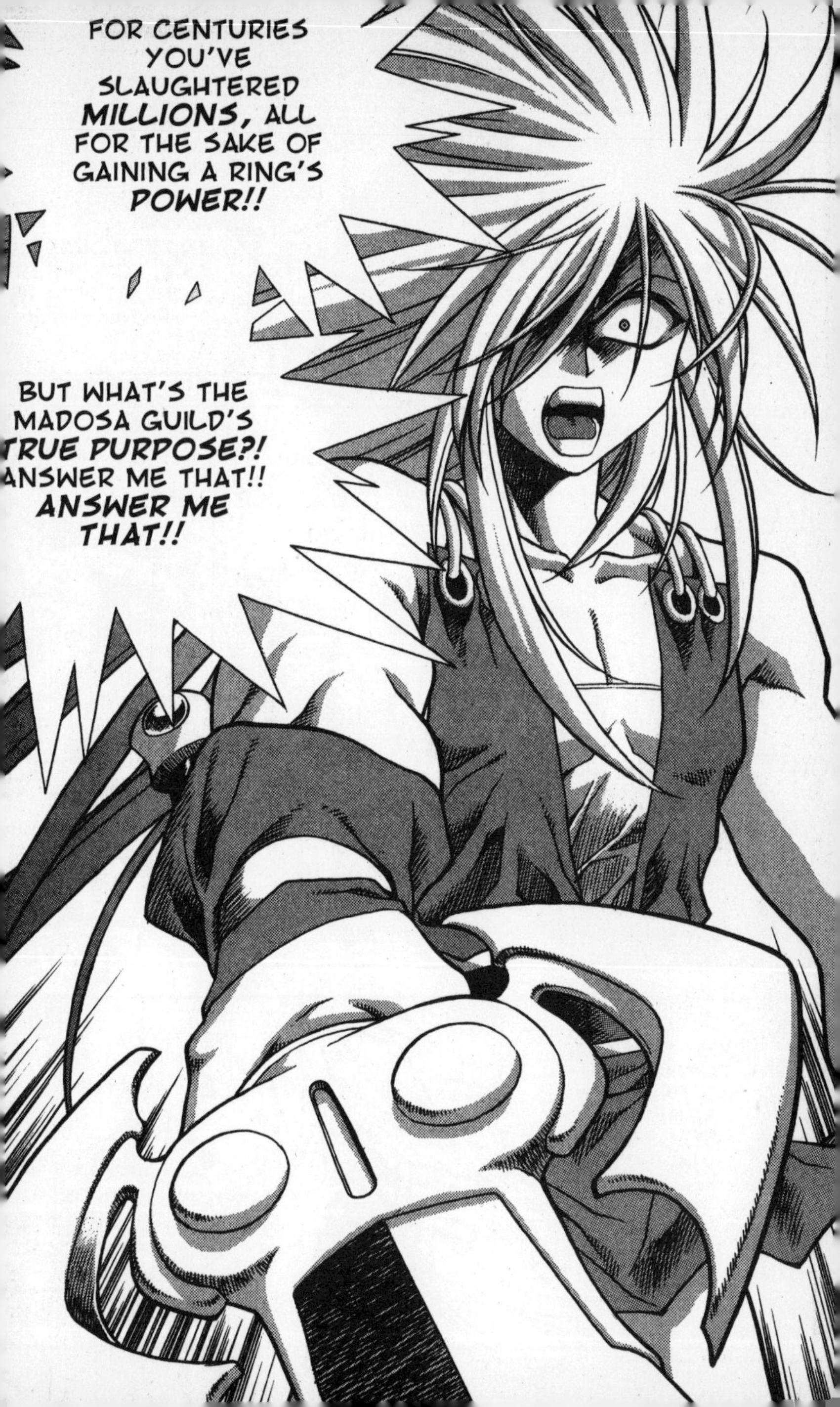
FOR CENTURIES YOU'VE SLAUGHTERED MILLIONS, ALL FOR THE SAKE OF GAINING A RING'S POWER!!
BUT WHAT'S THE MADOSA GUILD'S TRUE PURPOSE?! ANSWER ME THAT!! ANSWER ME THAT!!

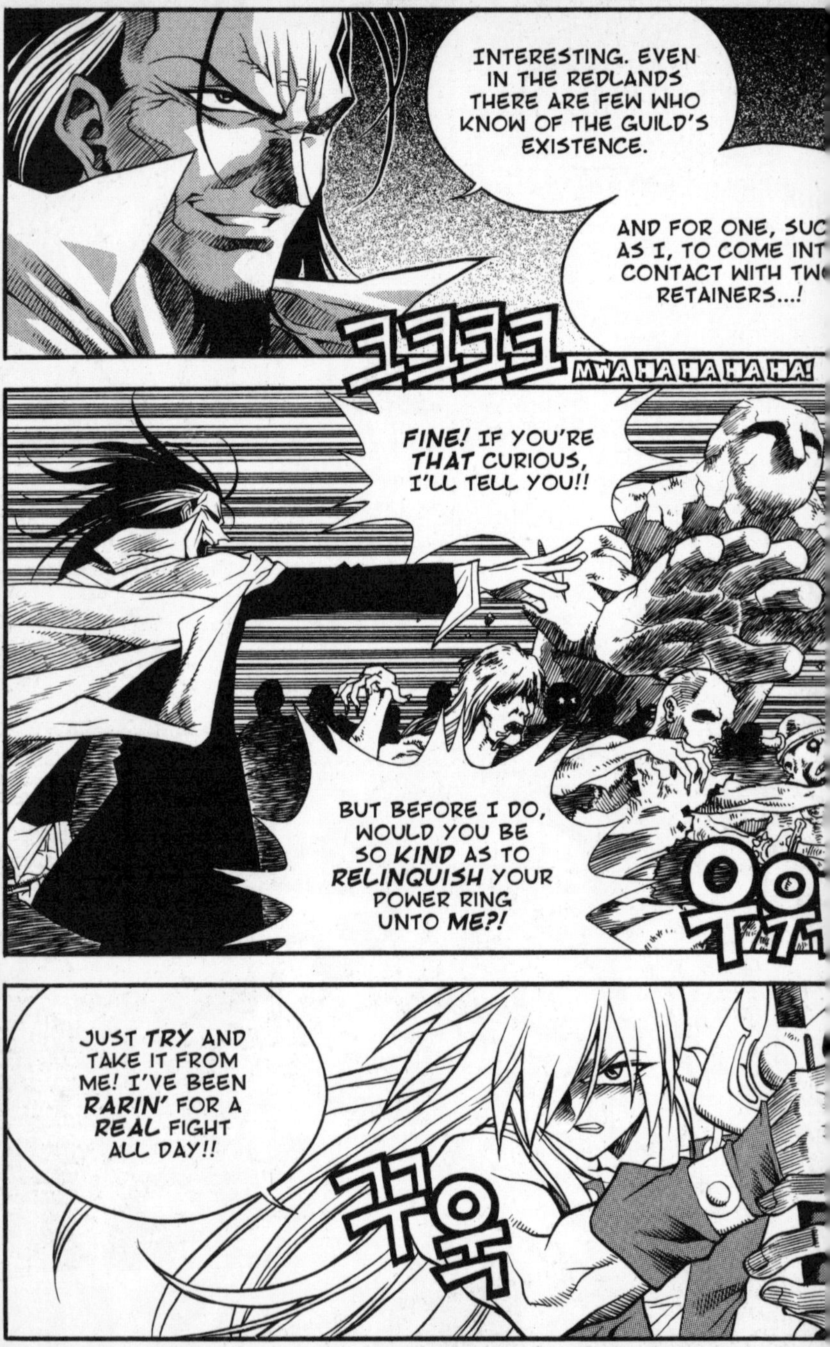
INTERESTING. EVEN IN THE REDLANDS THERE ARE FEW WHO KNOW OF THE GUILD'S EXISTENCE.
AND FOR ONE, SUC AS I, TO COME INT CONTACT WITH TW RETAINERS...!
MWA HA HA HA HA!
FINE! IF YOU'RE THAT CURIOUS, I'LL TELL YOU!!
BUT BEFORE I DO, WOULD YOU BE SO KIND AS TO RELINQUISH YOUR POWER RING UNTO ME?!
JUST TRY AND TAKE IT FROM ME! I'VE BEEN RARIN' FOR A REAL FIGHT ALL DAY!!

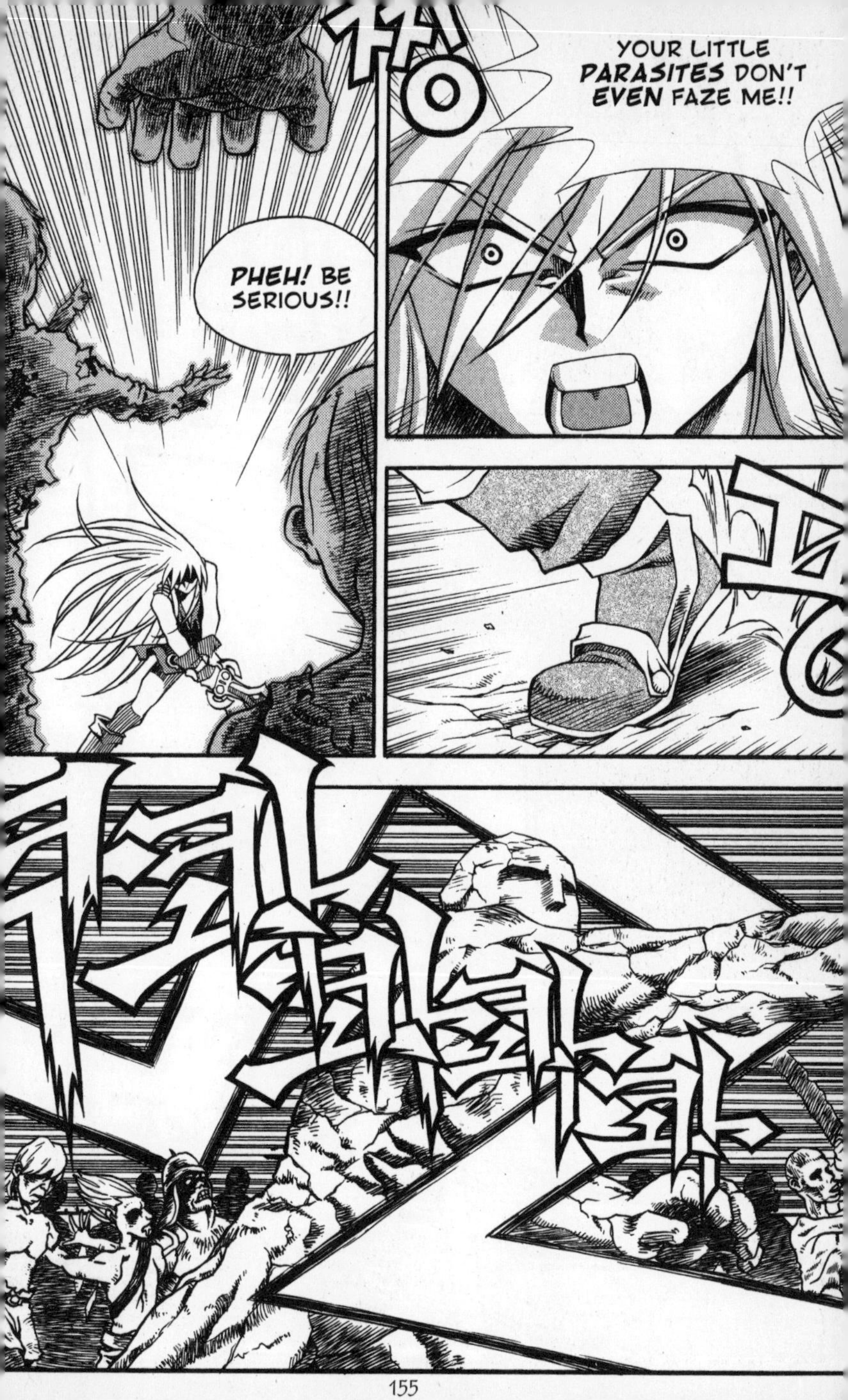
PHEH! BE SERIOUS!!
YOUR LITTLE PARASITES DON'T EVEN FAZE ME!!

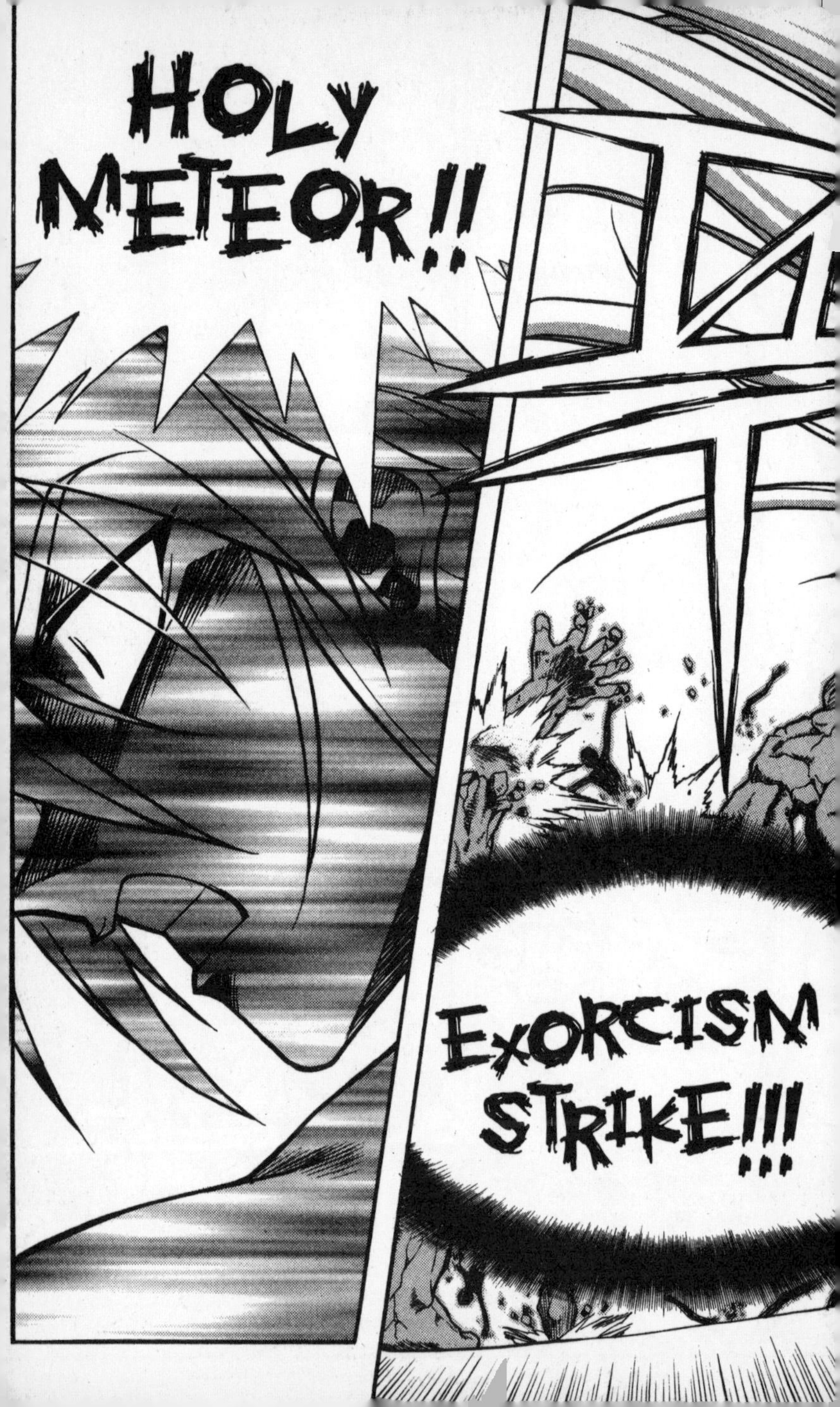
HOLY METEOR!!
EXORCISM STRIKE!!!

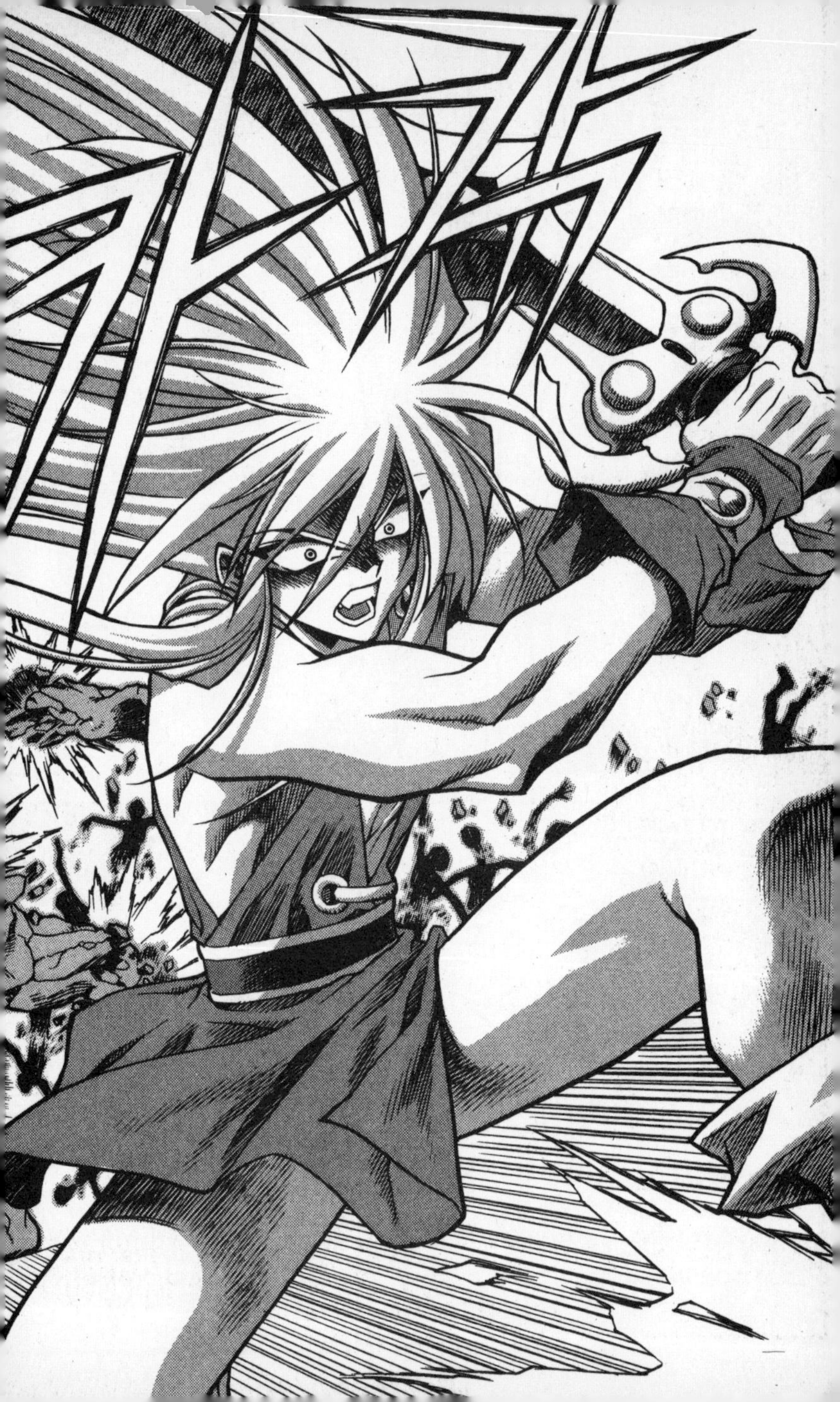

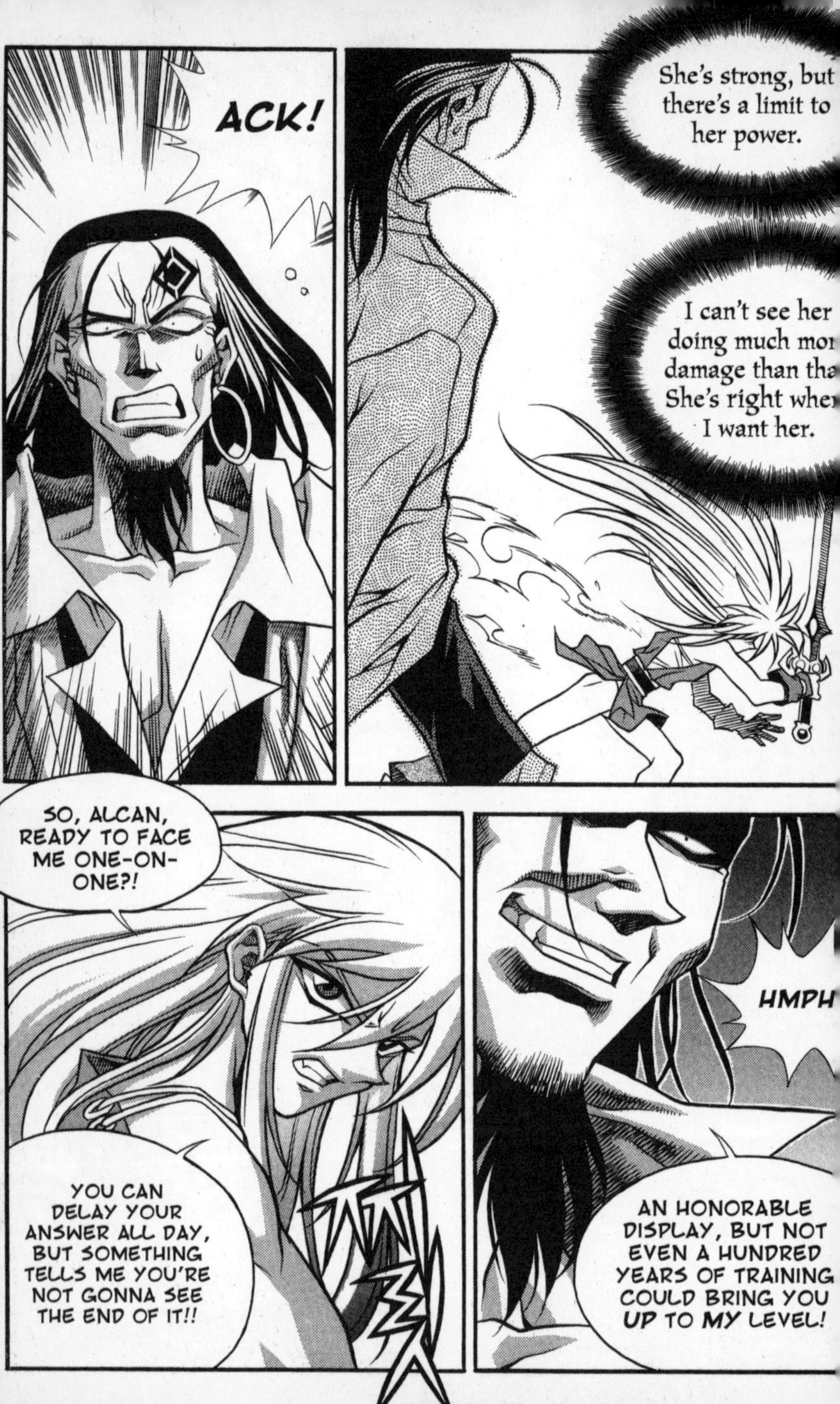
ACK!
She's strong, but there's a limit to her power.
I can't see her doing much mor damage than tha She's right whe I want her.
SO, ALCAN, READY TO FACE ME ONE-ON-ONE?!
YOU CAN DELAY YOUR ANSWER ALL DAY, BUT SOMETHING TELLS ME YOU'RE NOT GONNA SEE THE END OF IT!!
HMPH
AN HONORABLE DISPLAY, BUT NOT EVEN A HUNDRED YEARS OF TRAINING COULD BRING YOU UP TO MY LEVEL!

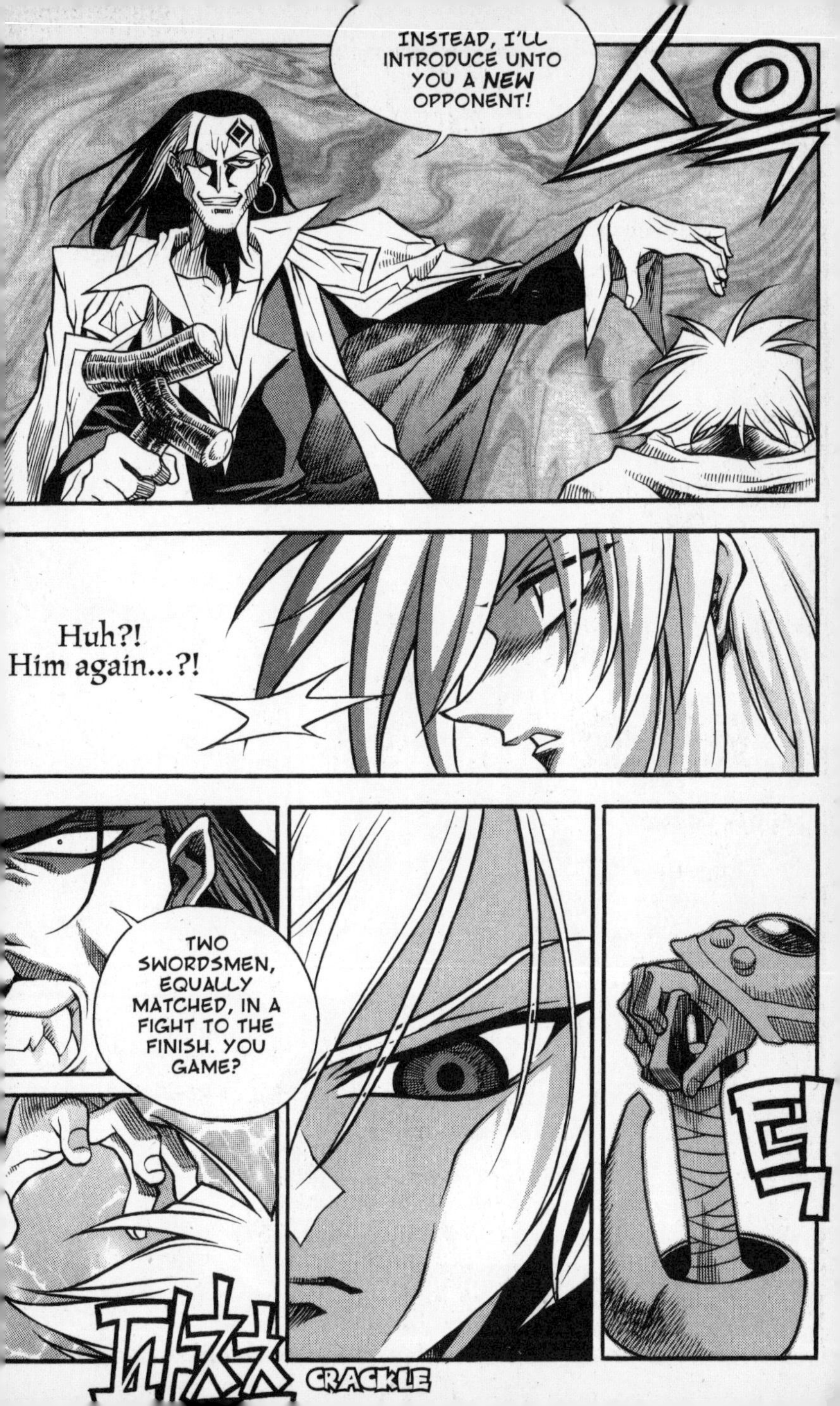
INSTEAD, I'LL INTRODUCE UNTO YOU A NEW OPPONENT!
Huh?! Him again...?!
TWO SWORDSMEN, EQUALLY MATCHED, IN A FIGHT TO THE FINISH. YOU GAME?
CRACKLE

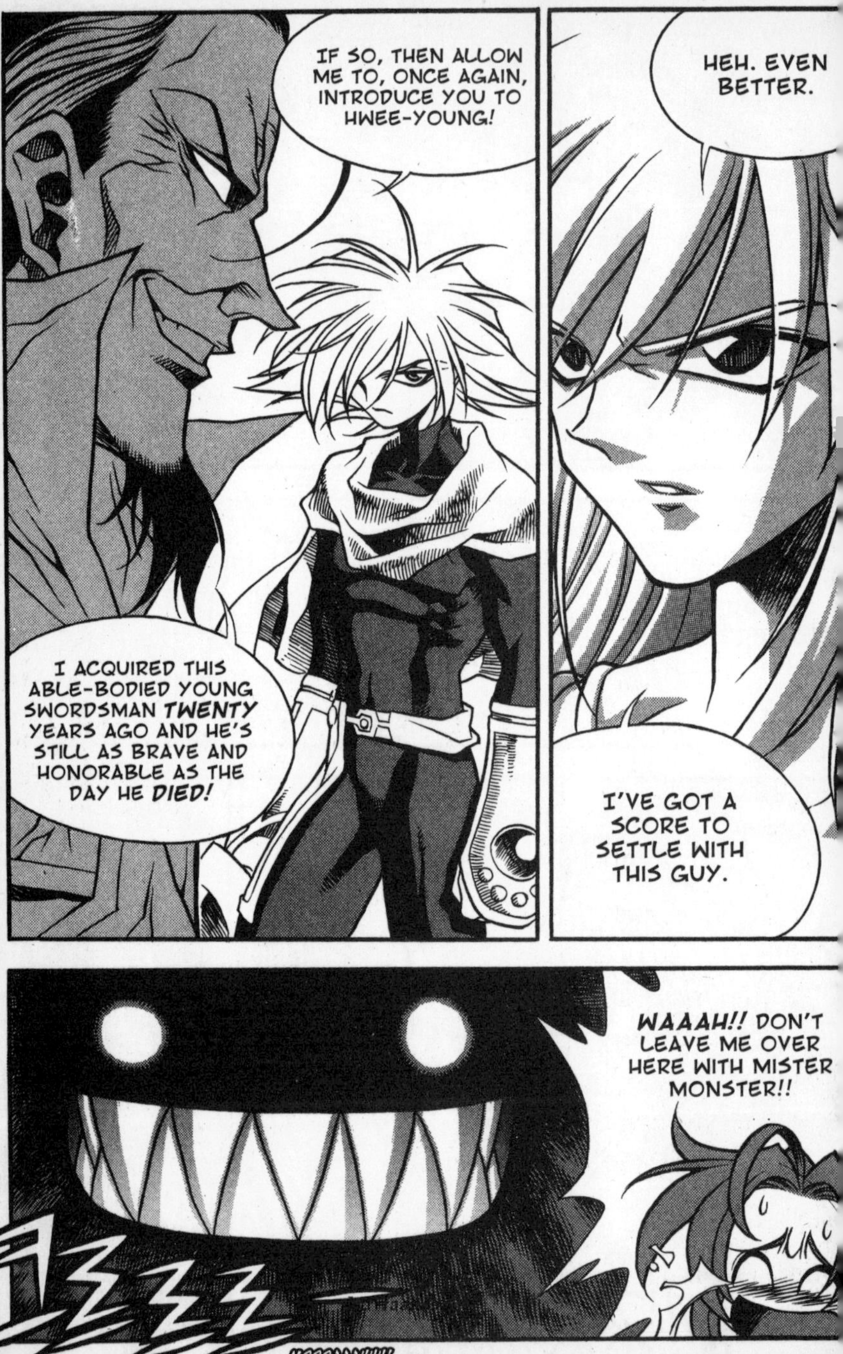
IF SO, THEN ALLOW ME TO, ONCE AGAIN, INTRODUCE YOU TO HWEE-YOUNG!
I ACQUIRED THIS ABLE-BODIED YOUNG SWORDSMAN **TWENTY** YEARS AGO AND HE'S STILL AS BRAVE AND HONORABLE AS THE DAY HE **DIED!**
HEH. EVEN BETTER.
I'VE GOT A SCORE TO SETTLE WITH THIS GUY.
WAAAH!! DON'T LEAVE ME OVER HERE WITH MISTER MONSTER!!
MRRRAAAHHH!

Quest 33

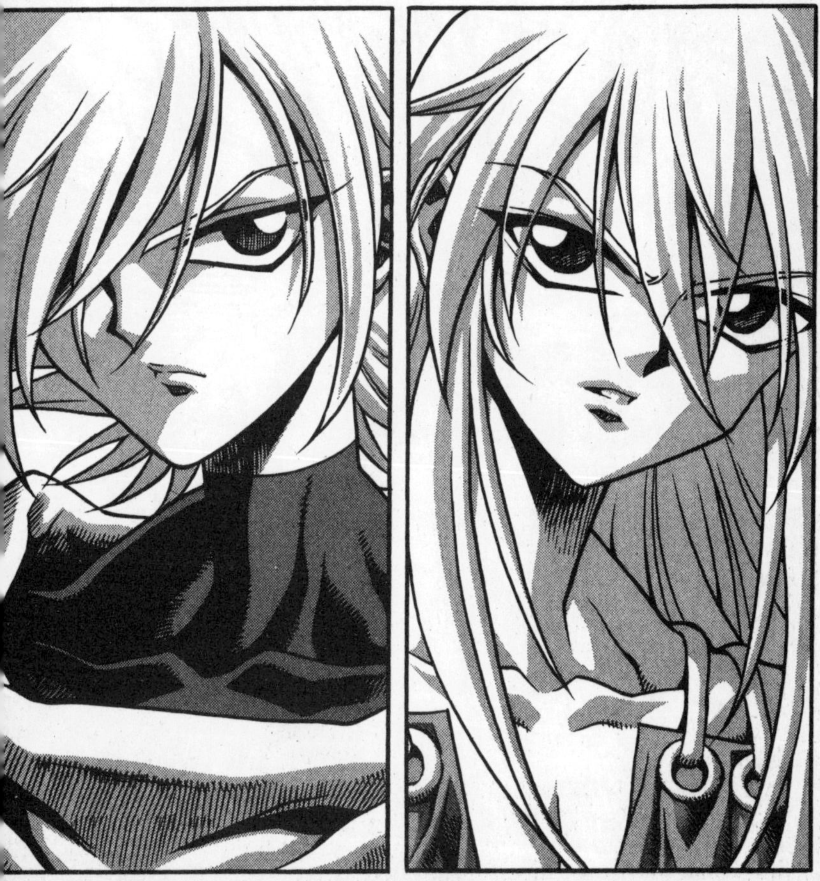

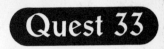

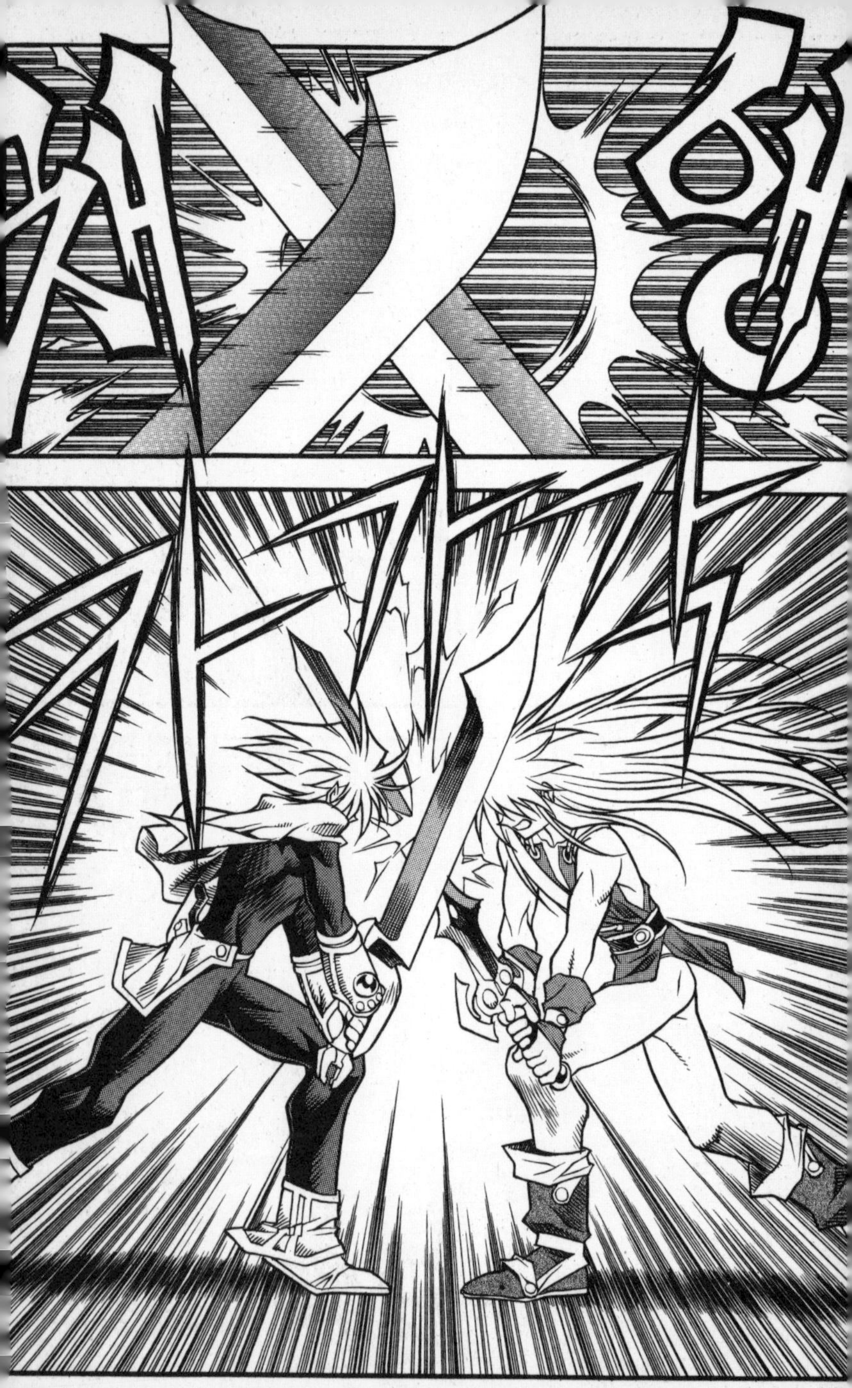

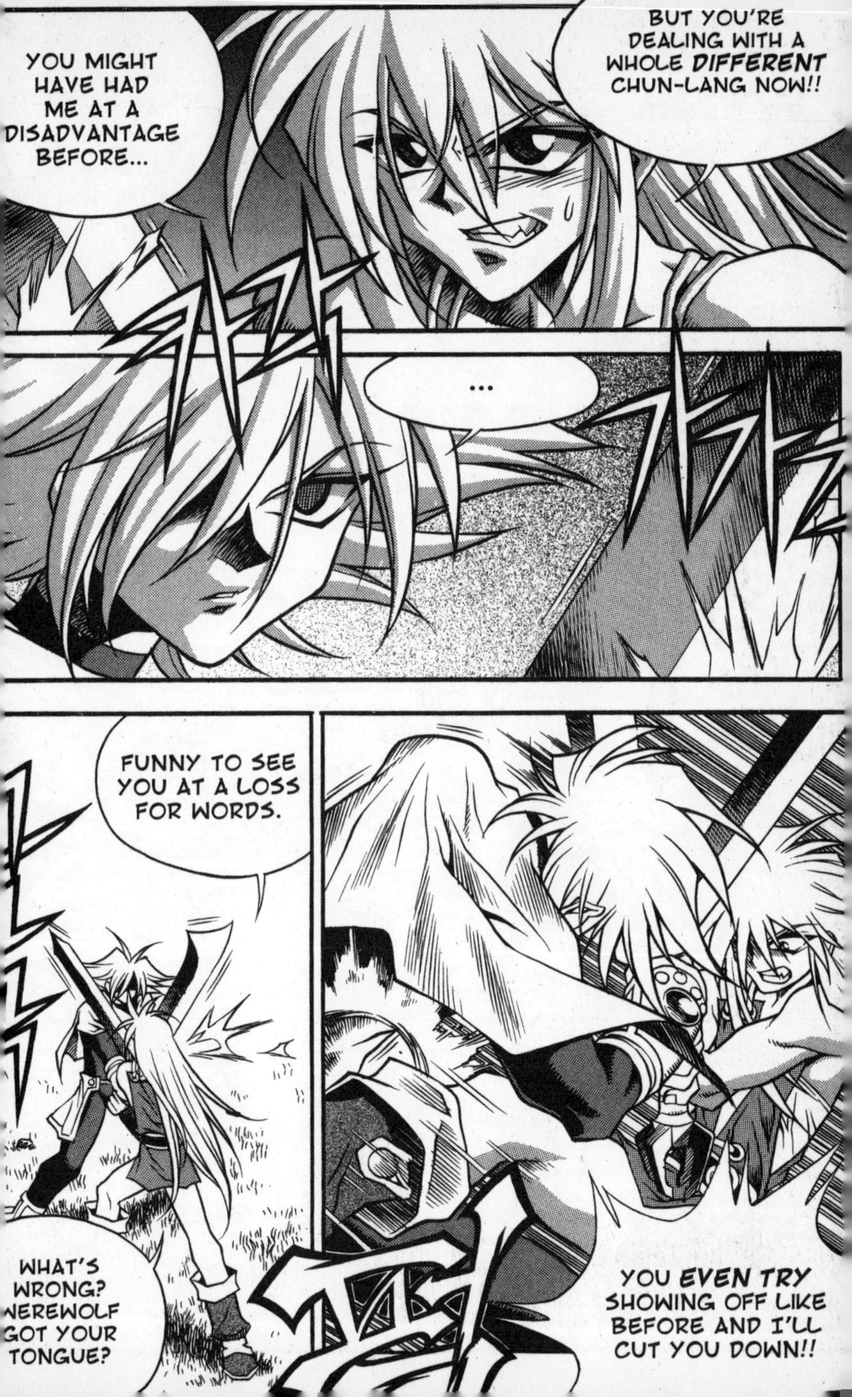
YOU MIGHT HAVE HAD ME AT A DISADVANTAGE BEFORE...
BUT YOU'RE DEALING WITH A WHOLE DIFFERENT CHUN-LANG NOW!!
...
FUNNY TO SEE YOU AT A LOSS FOR WORDS.
WHAT'S WRONG? WEREWOLF GOT YOUR TONGUE?
YOU EVEN TRY SHOWING OFF LIKE BEFORE AND I'LL CUT YOU DOWN!!

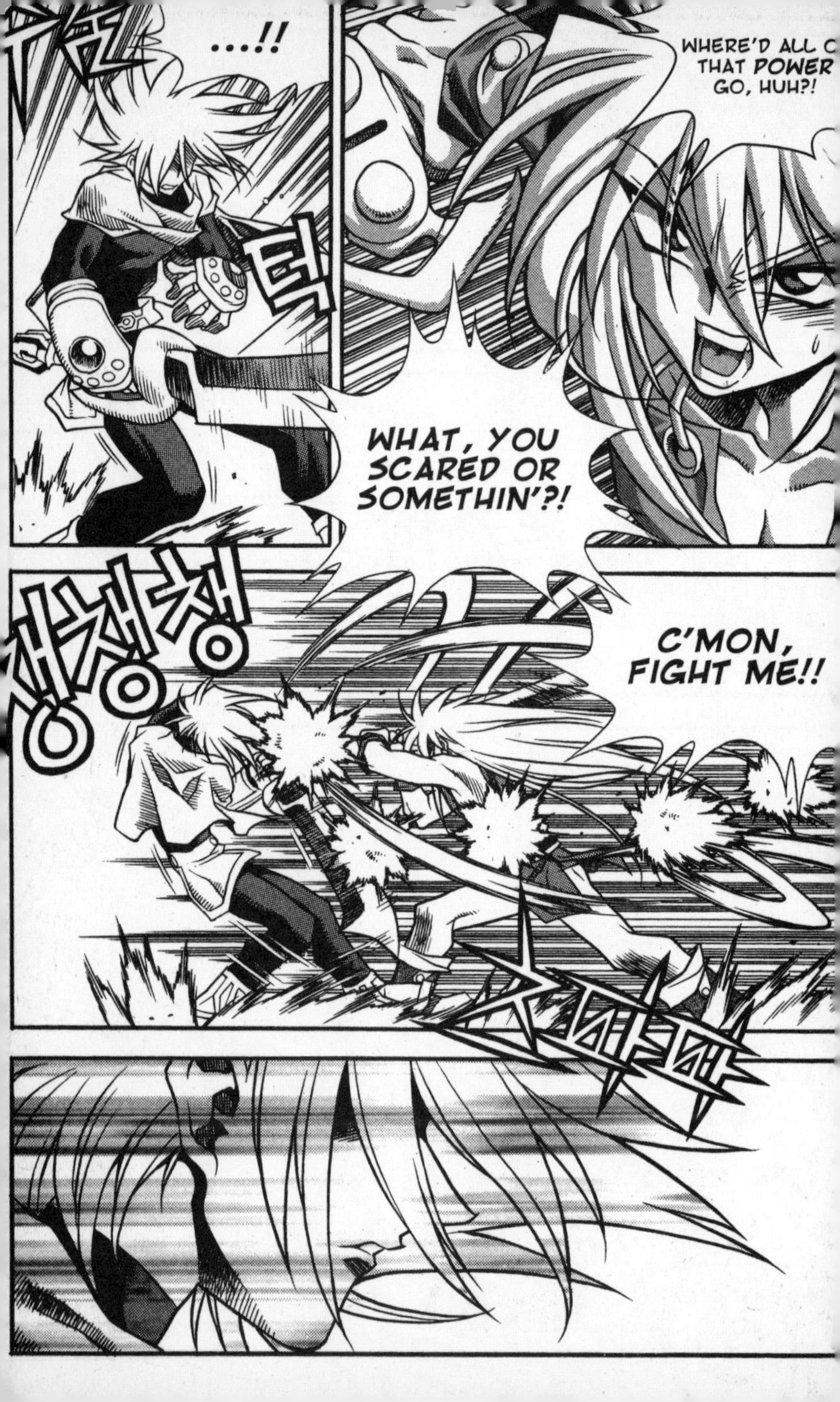
...!!
WHERE'D ALL
THAT POWER
GO, HUH?!
WHAT, YOU SCARED OR SOMETHIN'?!
C'MON, FIGHT ME!!

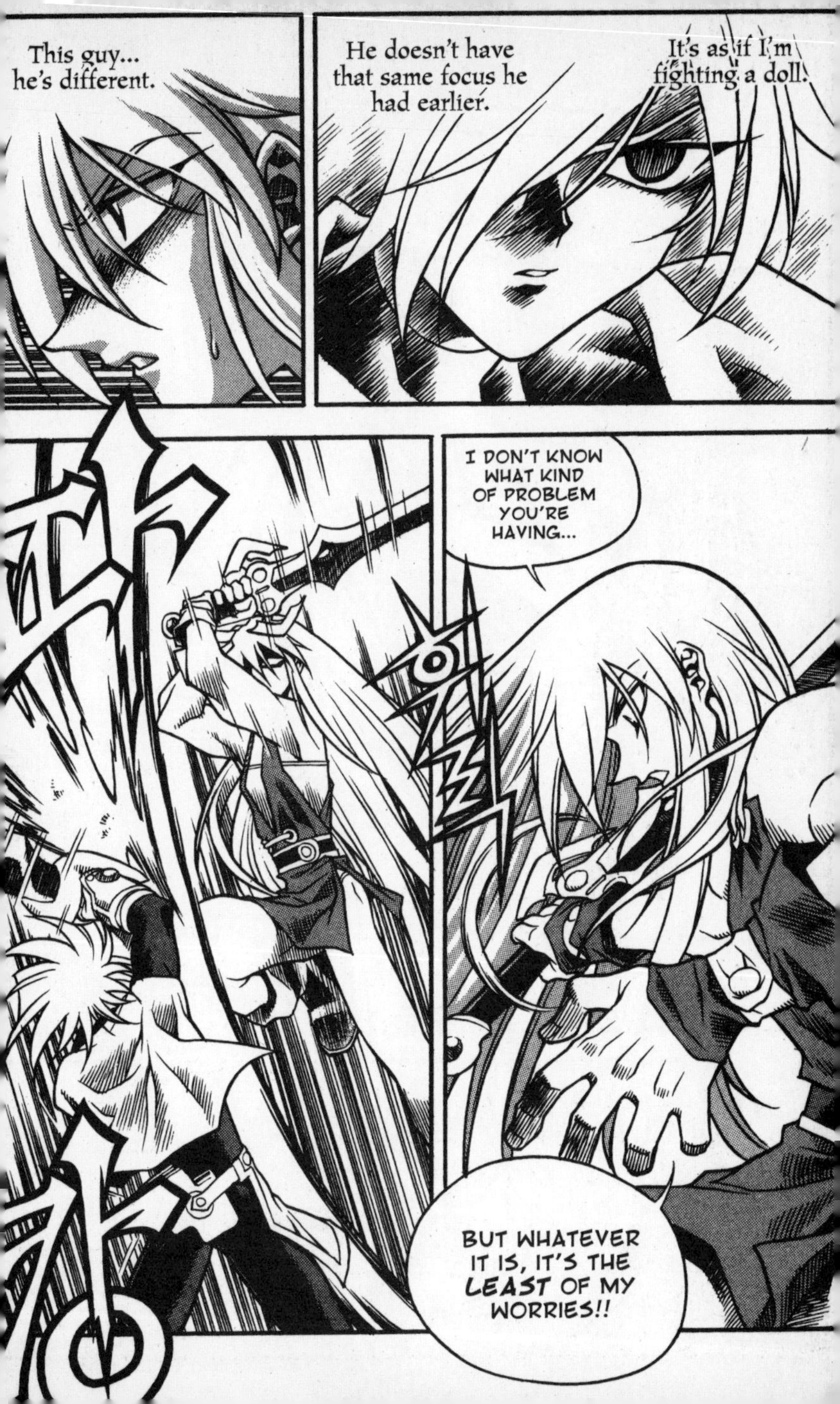
This guy... he's different.
He doesn't have that same focus he had earlier.
It's as if I'm fighting a doll.
I DON'T KNOW WHAT KIND OF PROBLEM YOU'RE HAVING...
BUT WHATEVER IT IS, IT'S THE *LEAST* OF MY WORRIES!!

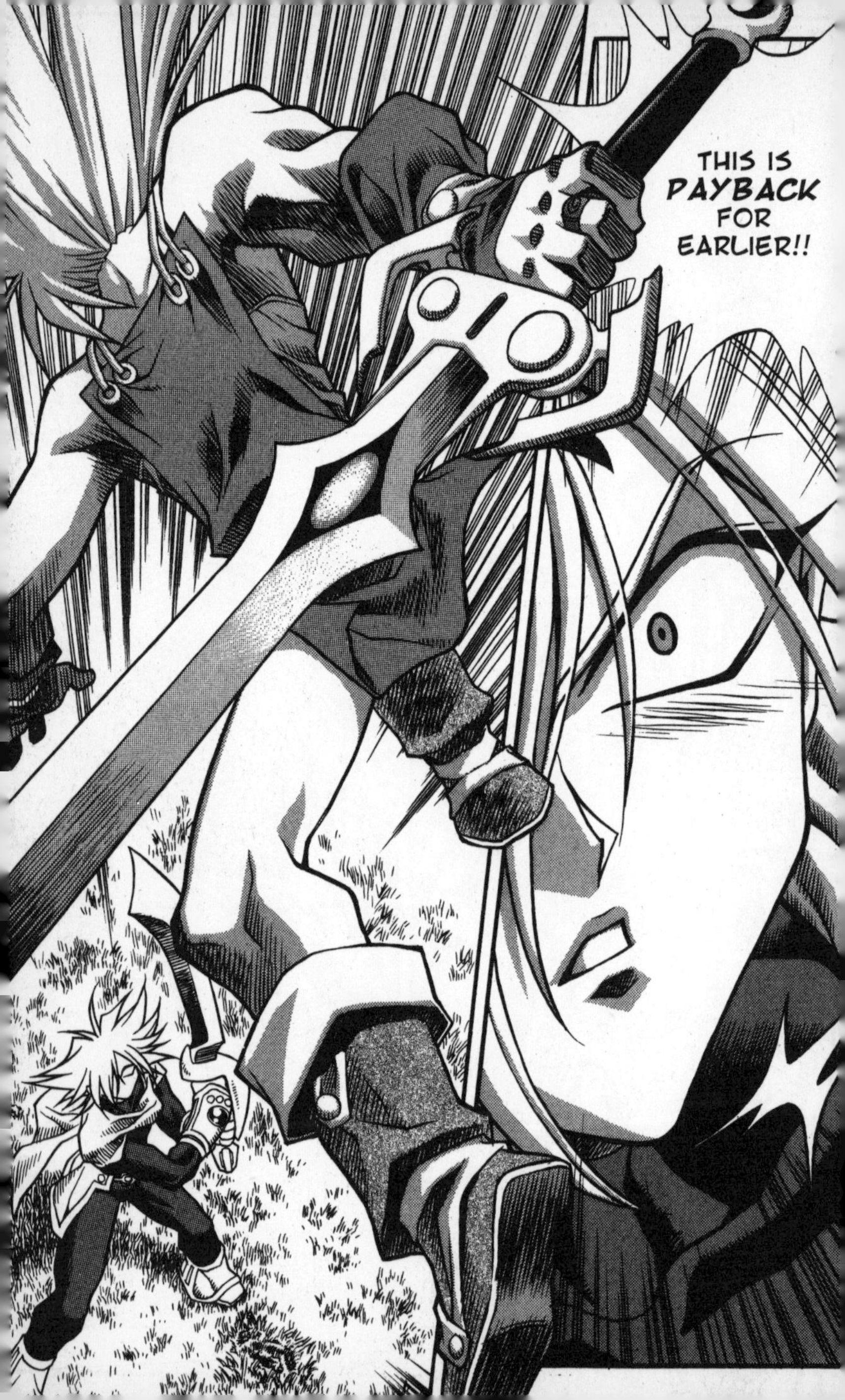
THIS IS PAYBACK FOR EARLIER!!

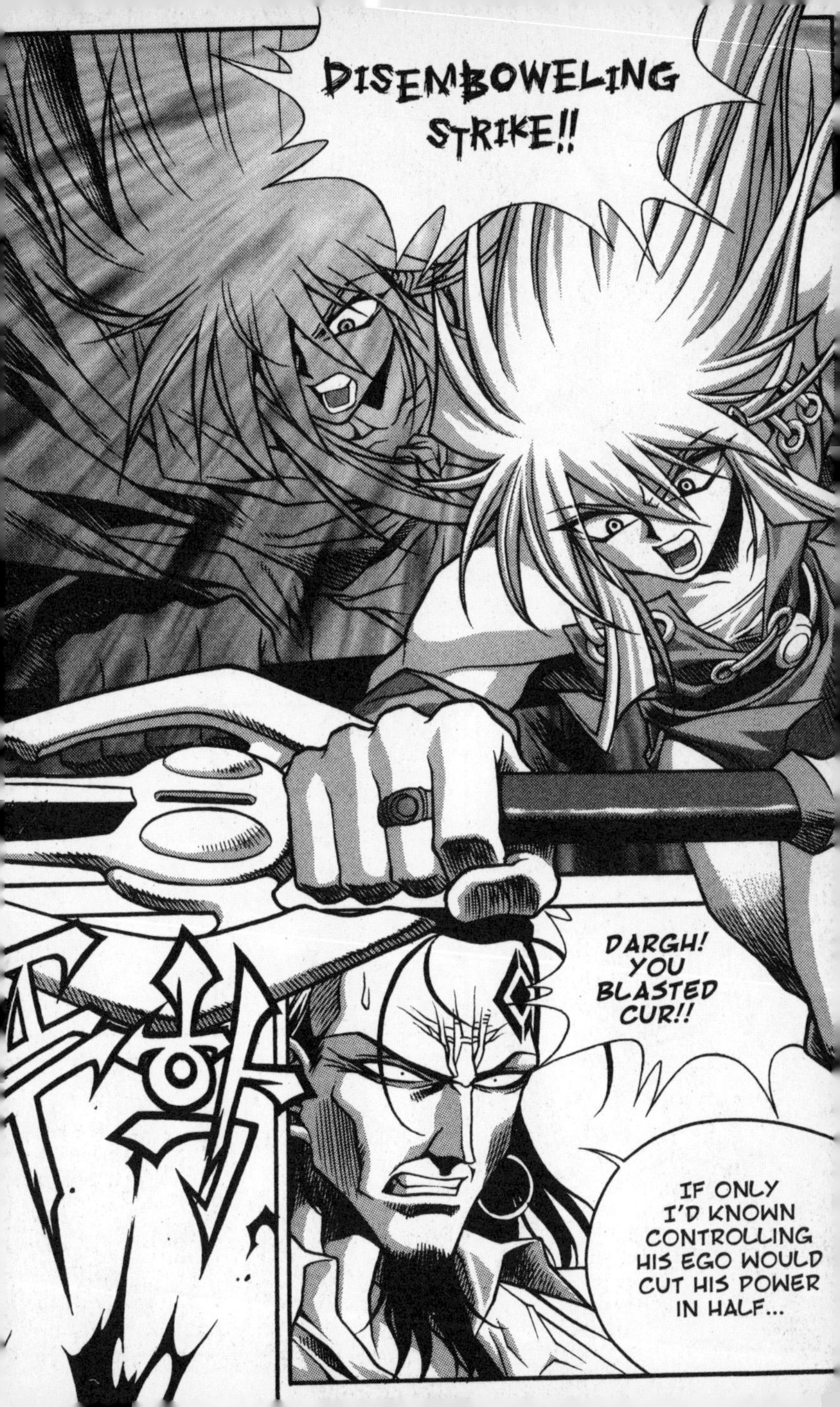
DISEMBOWELING STRIKE!!
DARGH! YOU BLASTED CUR!!
IF ONLY I'D KNOWN CONTROLLING HIS EGO WOULD CUT HIS POWER IN HALF...

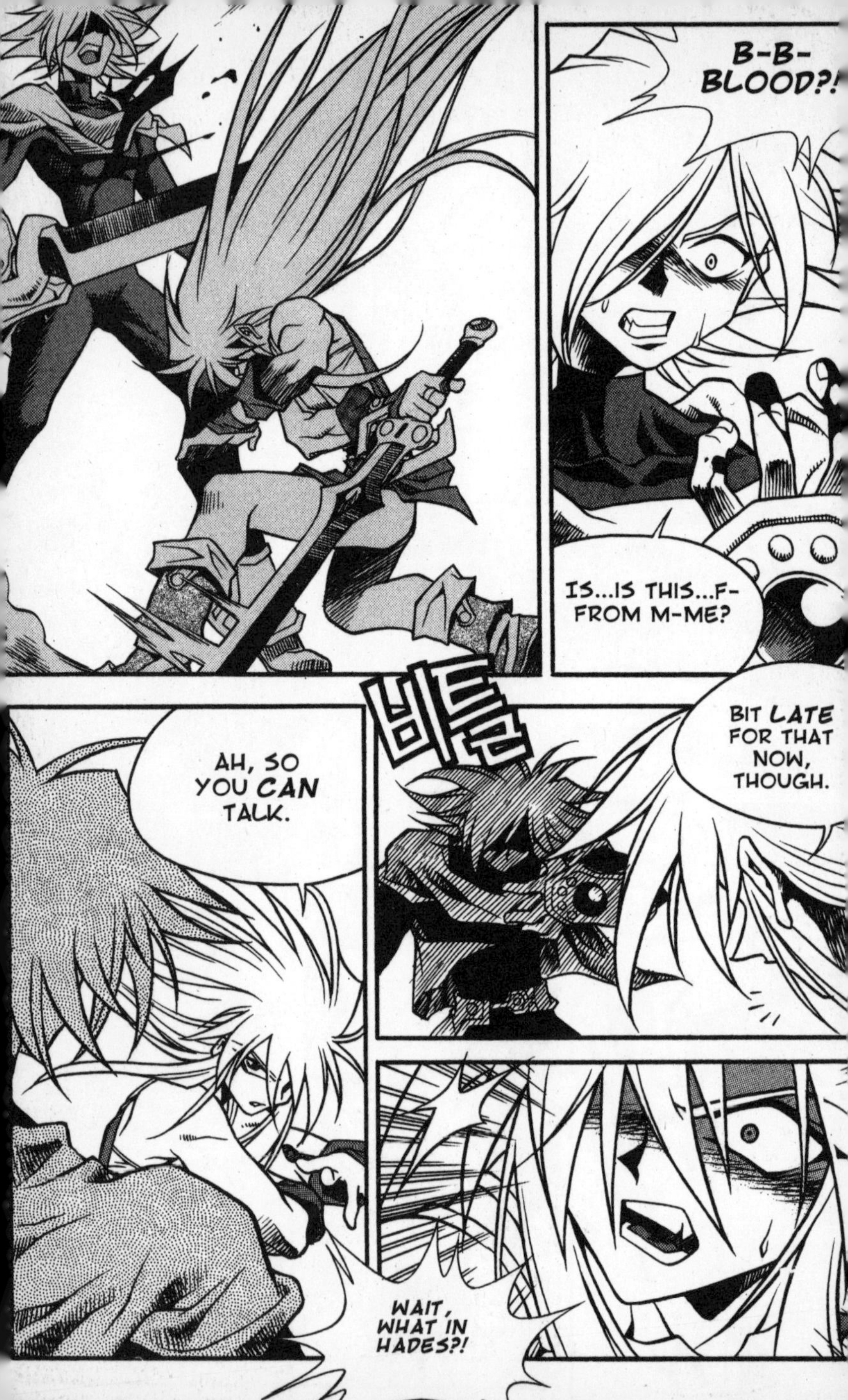
B-B-BLOOD?!
IS...IS THIS...F-FROM M-ME?
AH, SO YOU CAN TALK.
BIT LATE FOR THAT NOW, THOUGH.
WAIT, WHAT IN HADES?!

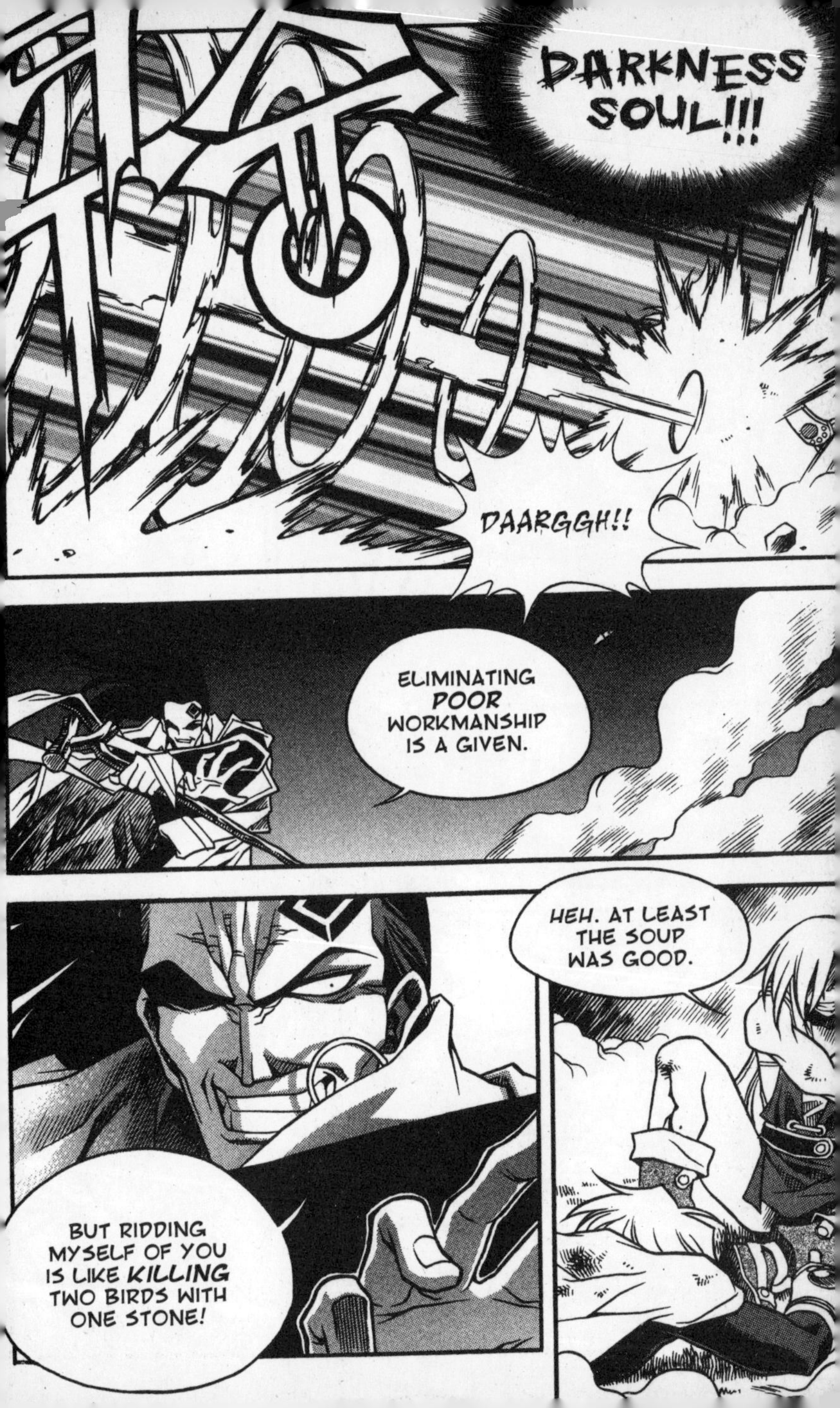
DARKNESS SOUL!!!
DAARGGH!!
ELIMINATING *POOR* WORKMANSHIP IS A GIVEN.
BUT RIDDING MYSELF OF YOU IS LIKE *KILLING* TWO BIRDS WITH ONE STONE!
HEH. AT LEAST THE SOUP WAS GOOD.

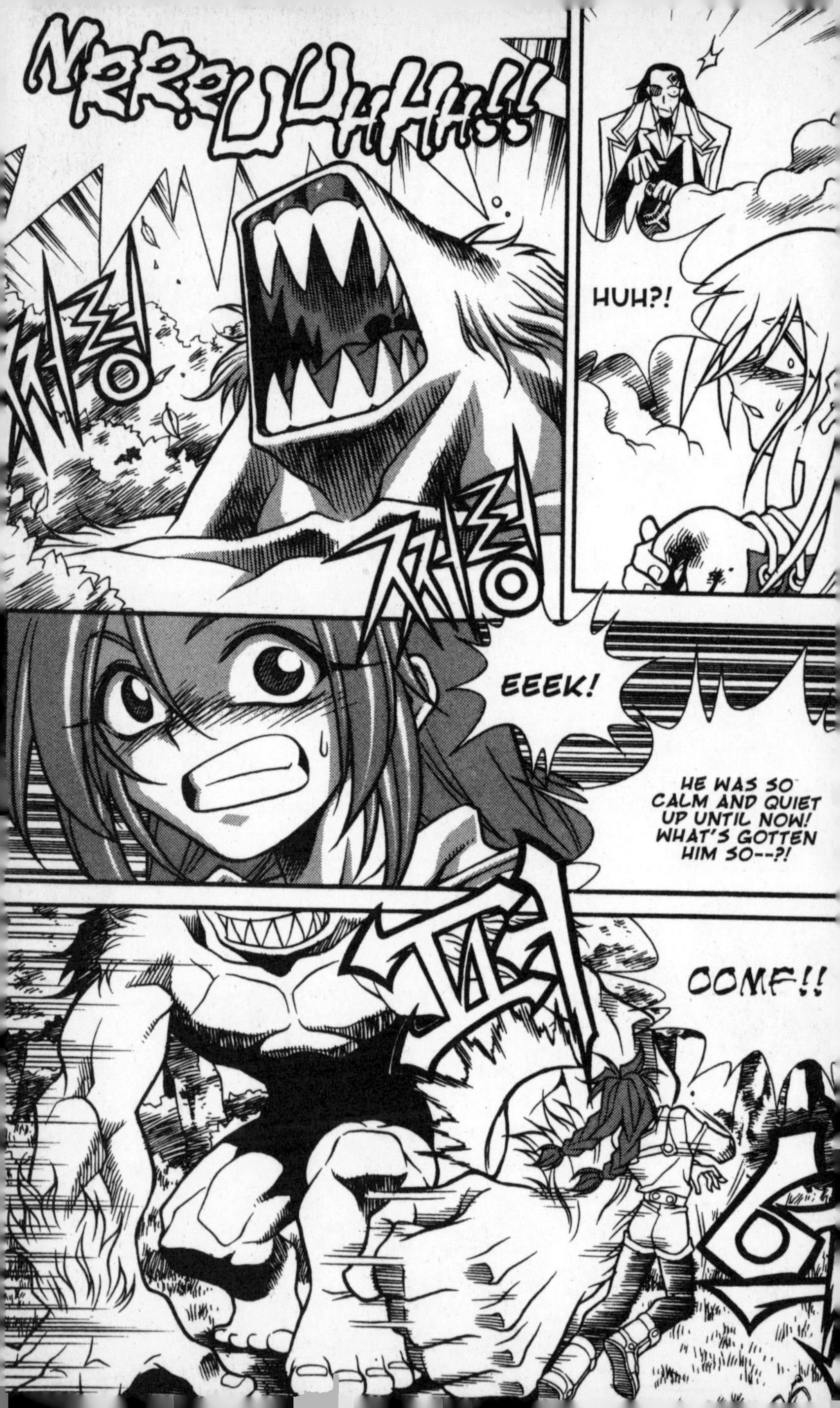
NGRRUHHH!!
HUH?!
EEEK!
HE WAS SO CALM AND QUIET UP UNTIL NOW! WHAT'S GOTTEN HIM SO--?!
OOMF!!

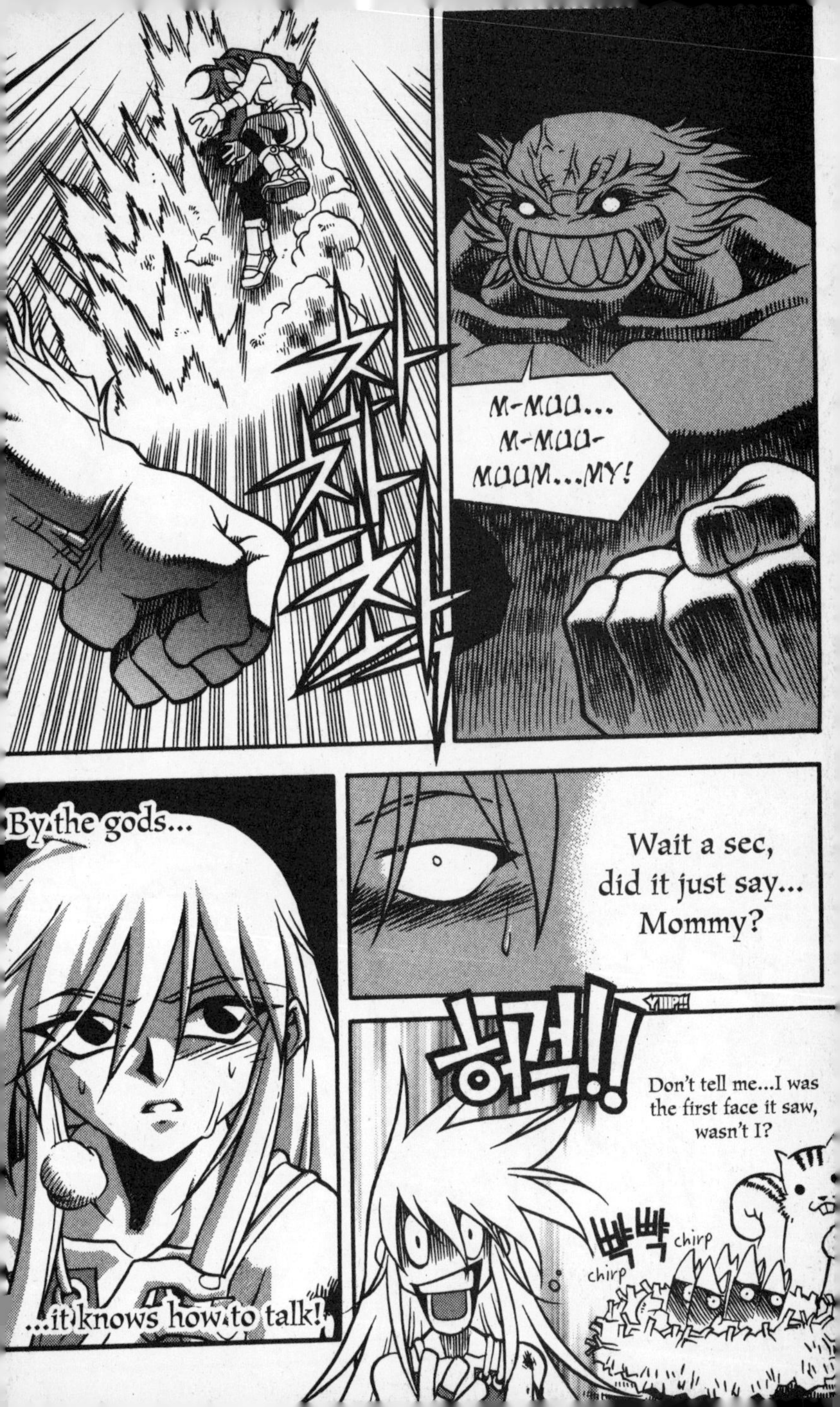

M-MOO...
M-MOO-
MOOM...MY!
By the gods...
...it knows how to talk!
Wait a sec,
did it just say...
Mommy?
헉!!
YIIIP!!
Don't tell me...I was
the first face it saw,
wasn't I?
빽빽
chirp
chirp

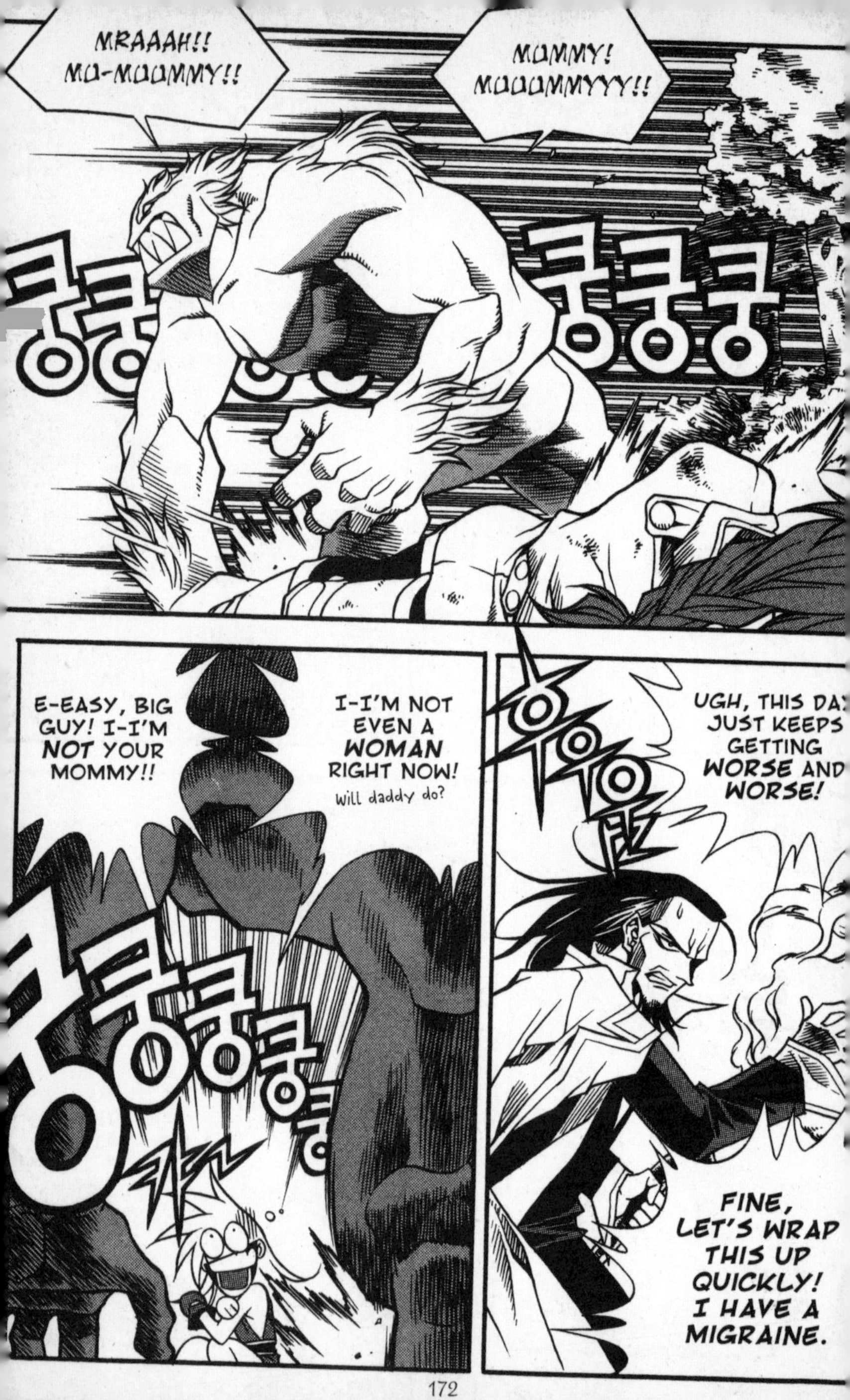
MRAAAH!! MU-MUUMMY!!
MOMMY! MUUUMMYYY!!
E-EASY, BIG GUY! I-I'M NOT YOUR MOMMY!!
I-I'M NOT EVEN A WOMAN RIGHT NOW!
will daddy do?
UGH, THIS DA JUST KEEPS GETTING WORSE AND WORSE!
FINE, LET'S WRAP THIS UP QUICKLY! I HAVE A MIGRAINE.

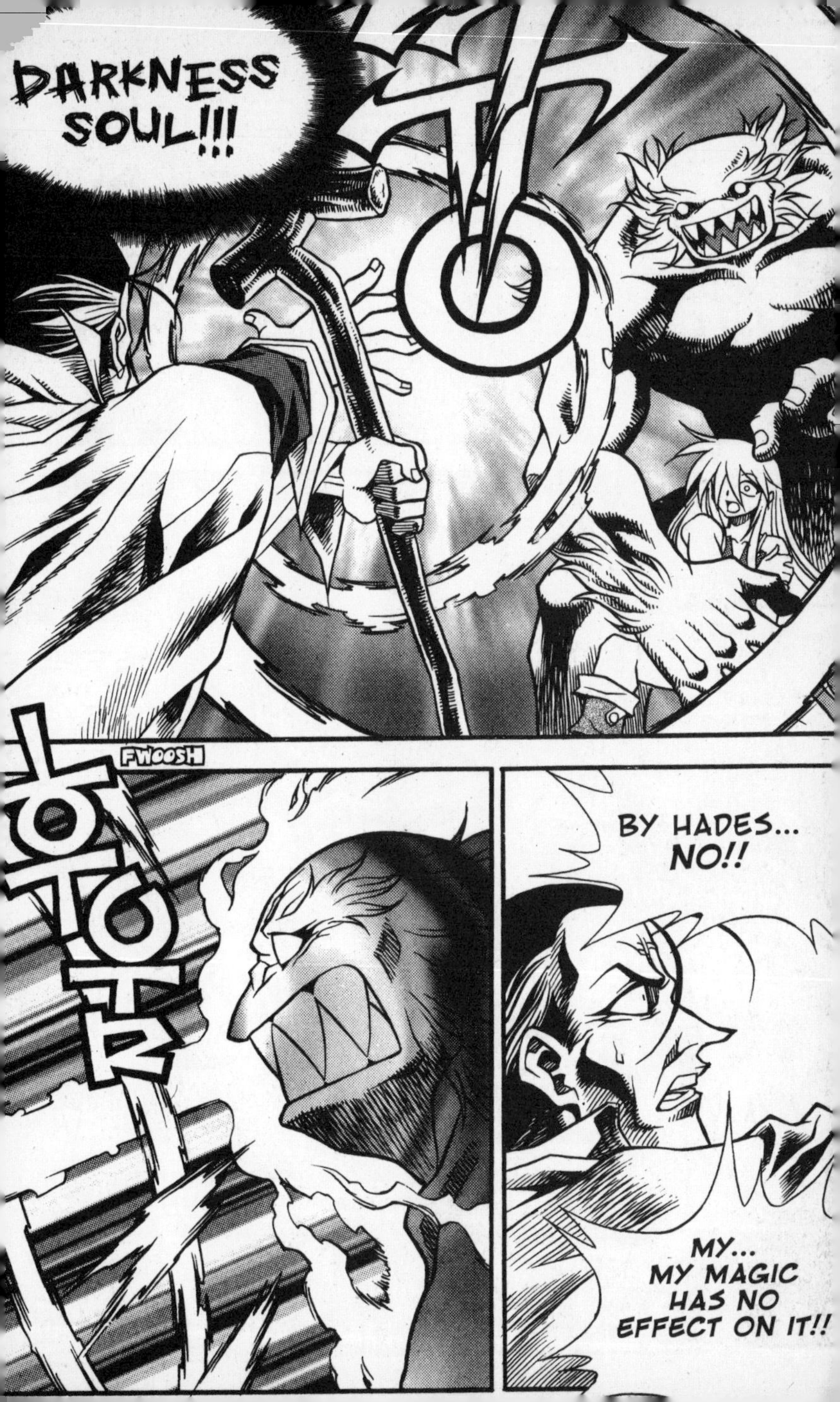
DARKNESS SOUL!!!
FWOOSH
BY HADES... NO!!
MY... MY MAGIC HAS NO EFFECT ON IT!!

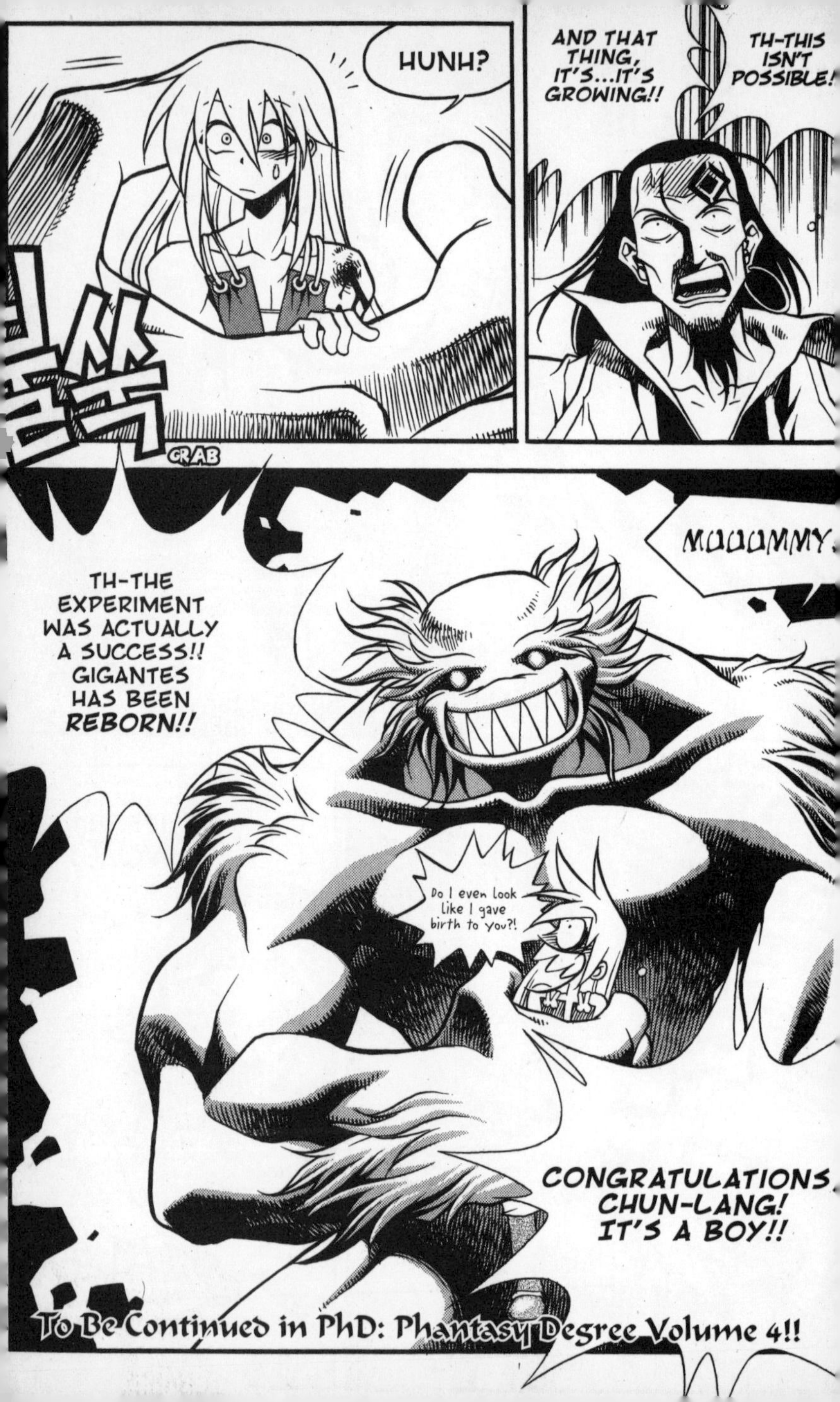
HUNH?
GRAB
AND THAT THING, IT'S...IT'S GROWING!!
TH-THIS ISN'T POSSIBLE!
TH-THE EXPERIMENT WAS ACTUALLY A SUCCESS!! GIGANTES HAS BEEN REBORN!!
MOOOMMY.
Do I even look like I gave birth to you?!
CONGRATULATIONS, CHUN-LANG! IT'S A BOY!!
To Be Continued in PhD: Phantasy Degree Volume 4!!

In the Next Volume of...

PhD
PHANTASY DEGREE

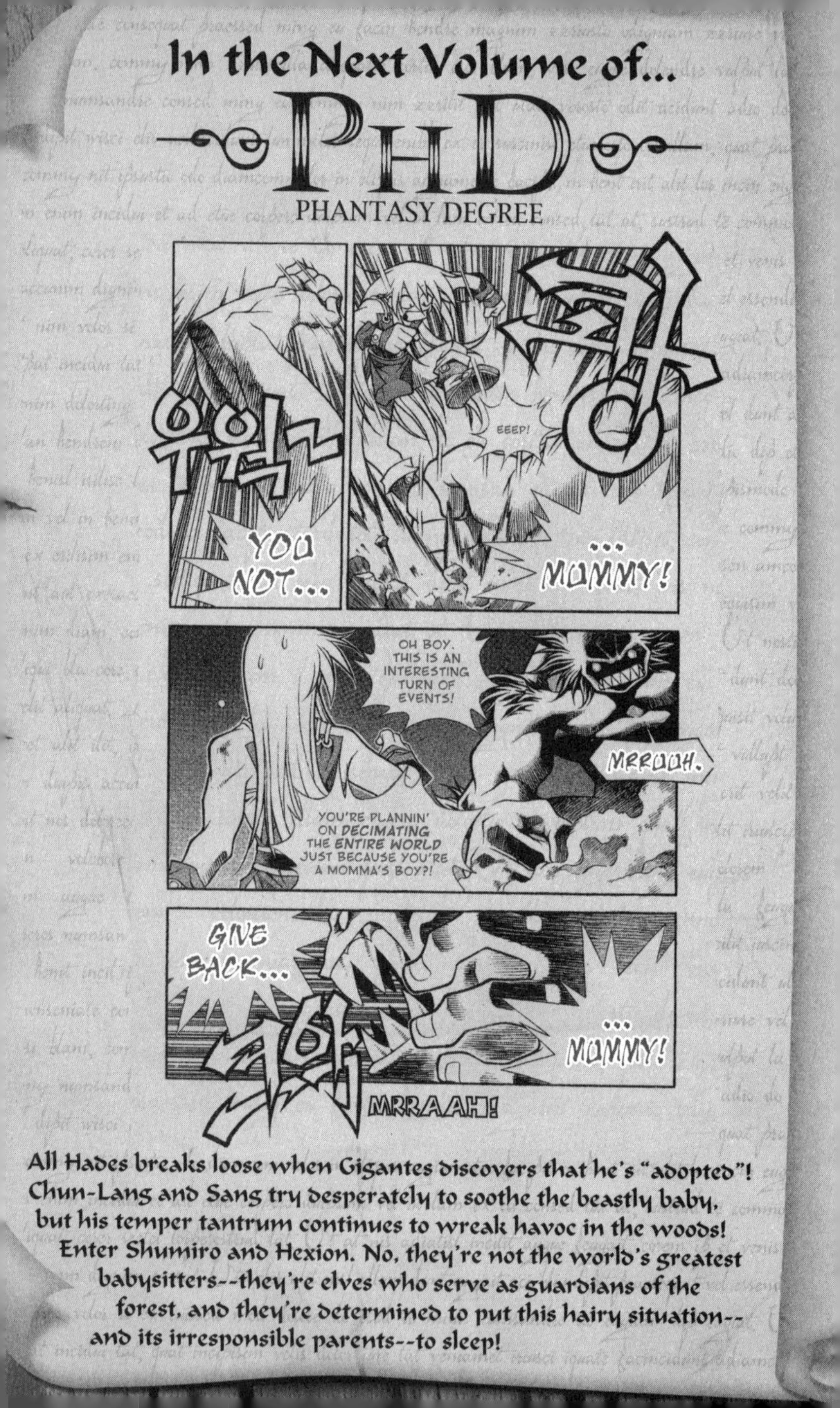

YOU NOT...
EEEP!
...MUMMY!
OH BOY. THIS IS AN INTERESTING TURN OF EVENTS!
MRROOH.
YOU'RE PLANNIN' ON DECIMATING THE ENTIRE WORLD JUST BECAUSE YOU'RE A MOMMA'S BOY?!
GIVE BACK...
...MUMMY!
MRRAAH!

All Hades breaks loose when Gigantes discovers that he's "adopted"! Chun-Lang and Sang try desperately to soothe the beastly baby, but his temper tantrum continues to wreak havoc in the woods! Enter Shumiro and Hexion. No, they're not the world's greatest babysitters--they're elves who serve as guardians of the forest, and they're determined to put this hairy situation--and its irresponsible parents--to sleep!

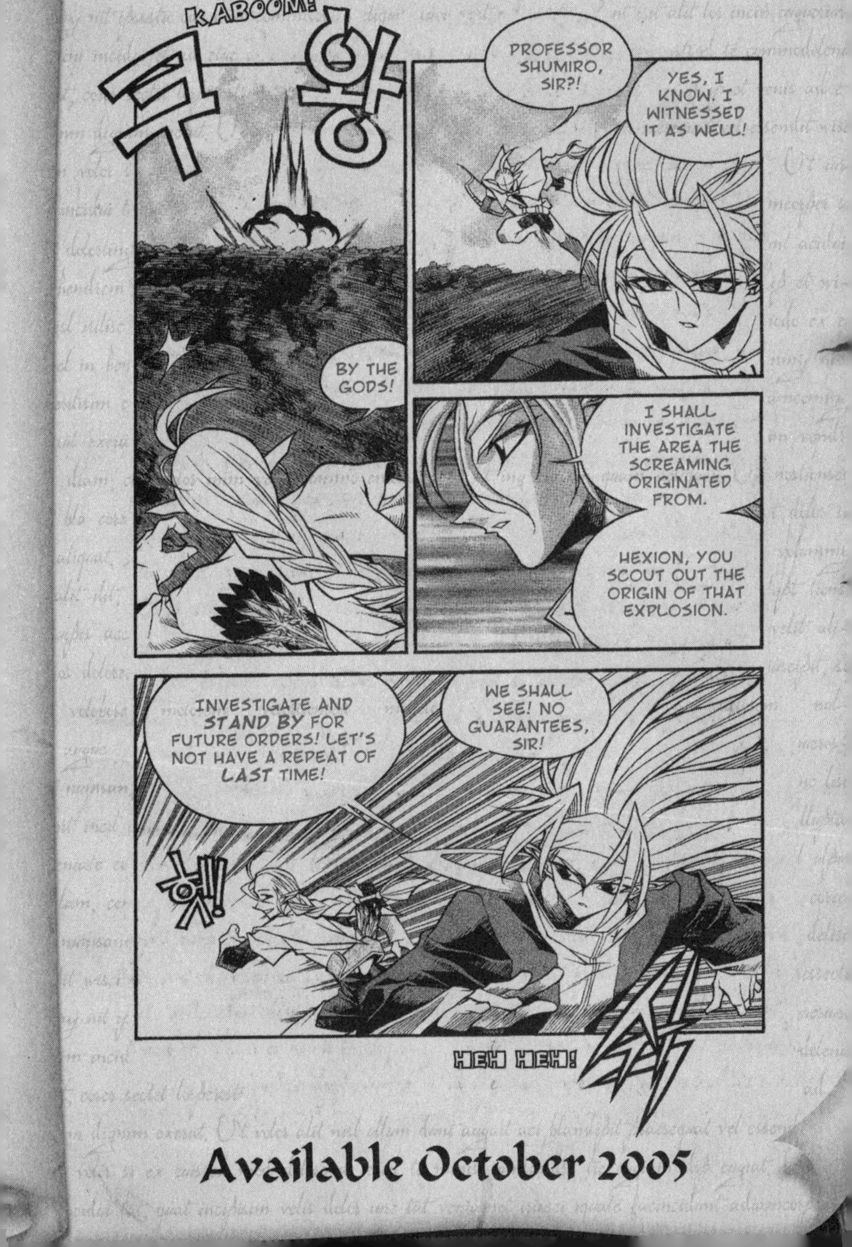
KABOOM!
BY THE GODS!
PROFESSOR SHUMIRO, SIR?!
YES, I KNOW. I WITNESSED IT AS WELL!
I SHALL INVESTIGATE THE AREA THE SCREAMING ORIGINATED FROM.
HEXION, YOU SCOUT OUT THE ORIGIN OF THAT EXPLOSION.
INVESTIGATE AND STAND BY FOR FUTURE ORDERS! LET'S NOT HAVE A REPEAT OF LAST TIME!
WE SHALL SEE! NO GUARANTEES, SIR!
HEH HEH!

Available October 2005

TOKYOPOP SHOP

SPOTLIGHT TOKYOPOP MANGA SUPPLEMENT

SAKURA TAISEN

BY OHJI HIROI & IKKU MASA

SOLDIERS, STEAM ROBOTS, SAMURAI GIRLS... OH, MY!

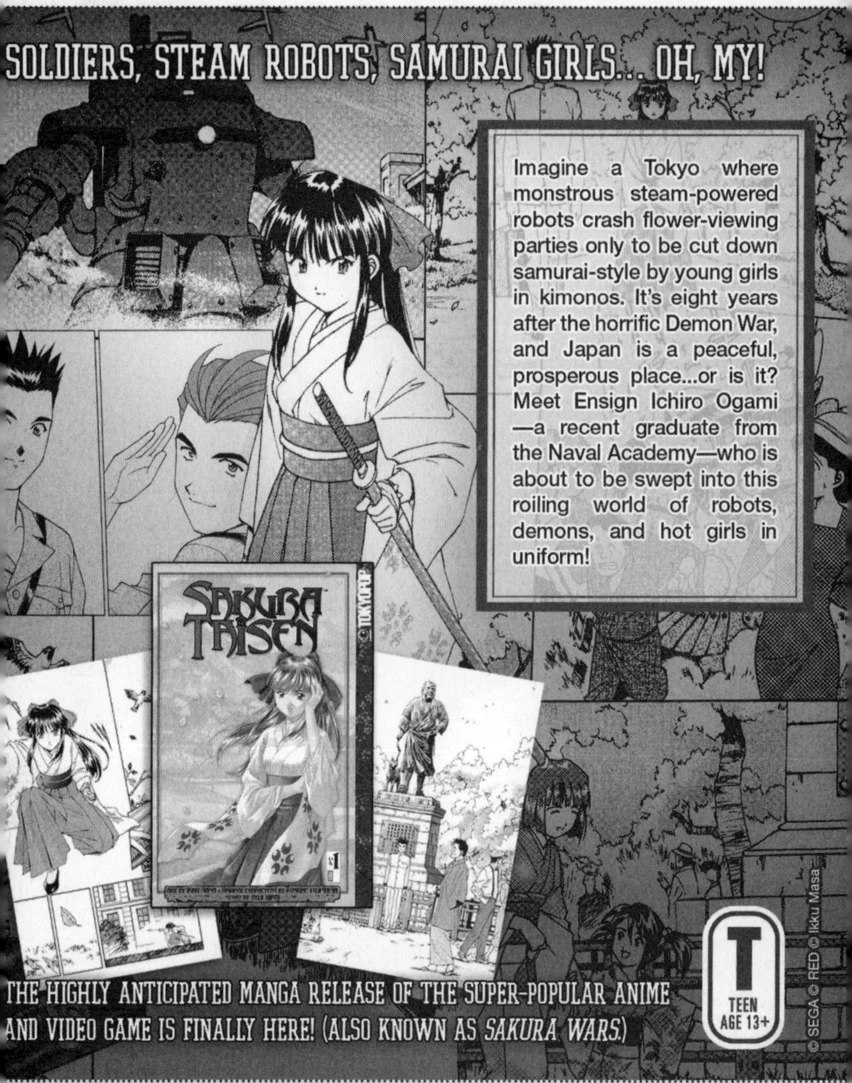
SAKURA TAISEN
TOKYOPOP
1
T
TEEN
AGE 13+
© SEGA © RED © Ikku Masa

Imagine a Tokyo where monstrous steam-powered robots crash flower-viewing parties only to be cut down samurai-style by young girls in kimonos. It's eight years after the horrific Demon War, and Japan is a peaceful, prosperous place...or is it? Meet Ensign Ichiro Ogami —a recent graduate from the Naval Academy—who is about to be swept into this roiling world of robots, demons, and hot girls in uniform!

THE HIGHLY ANTICIPATED MANGA RELEASE OF THE SUPER-POPULAR ANIME AND VIDEO GAME IS FINALLY HERE! (ALSO KNOWN AS *SAKURA WARS*.)

FOR MORE INFORMATION VISIT: WWW.TOKYOPOP.COM

BIZENGHAST

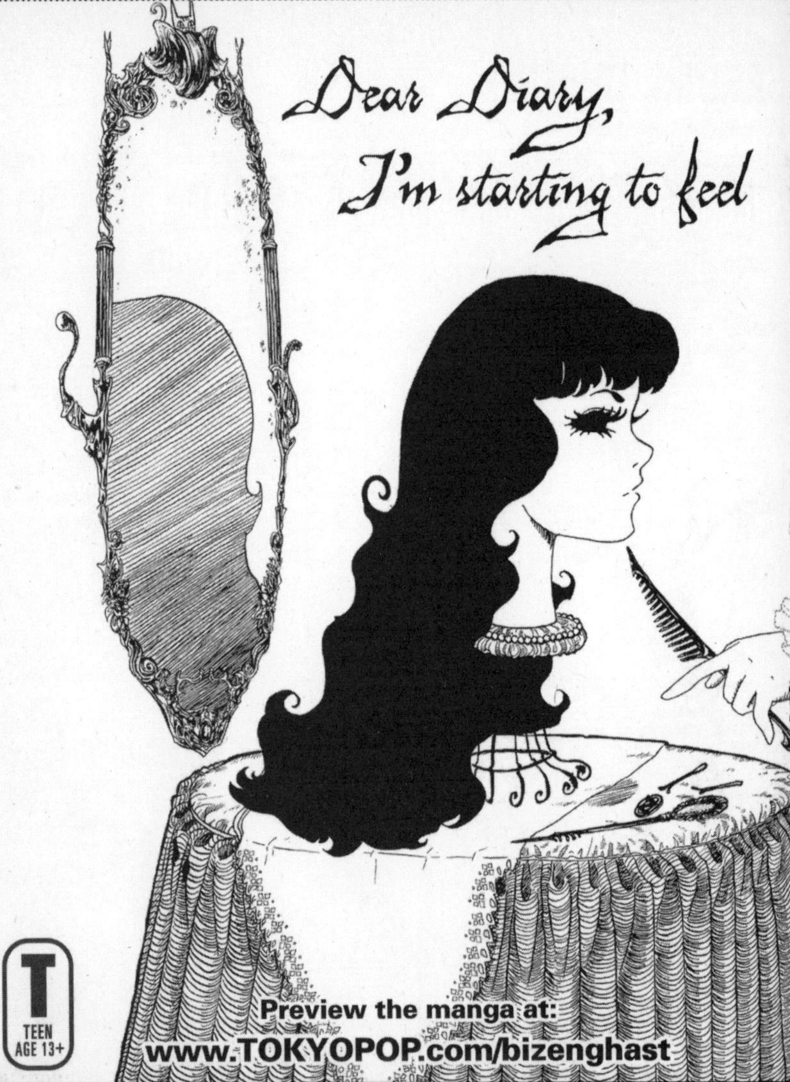
Dear Diary,
I'm starting to feel
T
TEEN
AGE 13+
Preview the manga at:
www.TOKYOPOP.com/bizenghast

When a young girl moves to the forgotten town of Bizenghast, she uncovers a terrifying collection of lost souls that leads her to the brink of insanity. One thing becomes painfully clear: The residents of Bizenghast are just dying to come home.

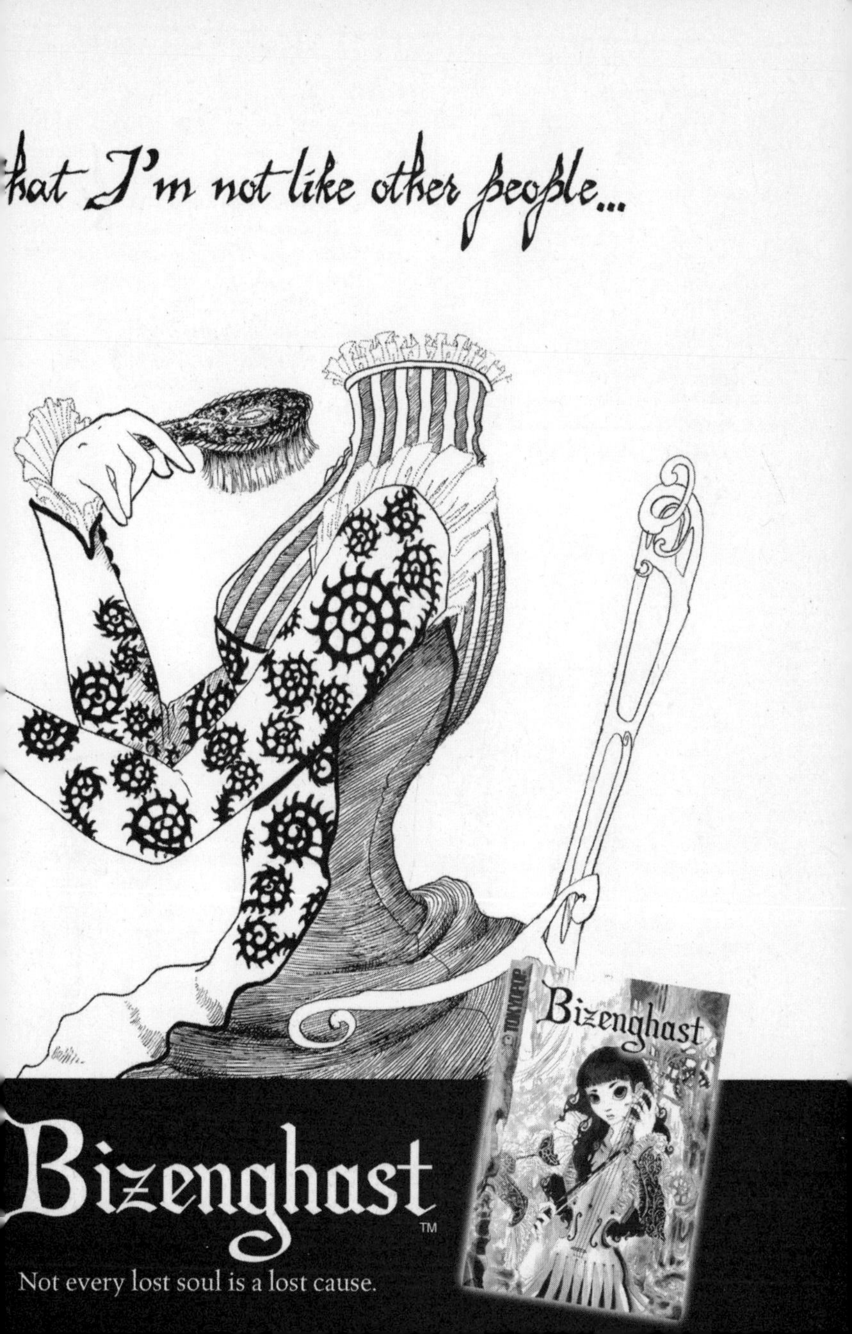
hat I'm not like other people...
Bizenghast
TOKYOPOP
Bizenghast™
Not every lost soul is a lost cause.

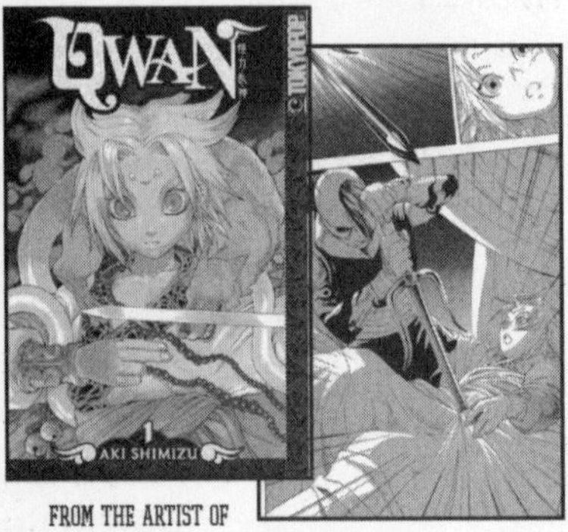
QWAN
1
AKI SHIMIZU
TOKYOPOP

FROM THE ARTIST OF SUIKODEN III

BY AKI SHIMIZU

QWAN

Qwan is a series that refuses to be pigeonholed. Aki Shimizu combines Chinese history, mythology, fantasy and humor to create a world that is familiar yet truly unique. Her creature designs are particularly brilliant—from mascots to monsters. And Qwan himself is great—fallen to Earth, he's like a little kid, complete with the loud questions, yet he eats demons for breakfast. In short, *Qwan* is a solid story with great character dynamics, amazing art and some kick-ass battle scenes. What's not to like?

~Carol Fox, Editor

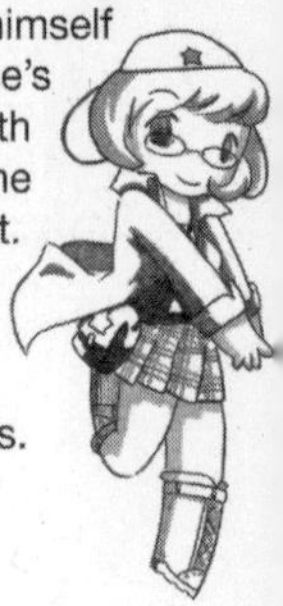

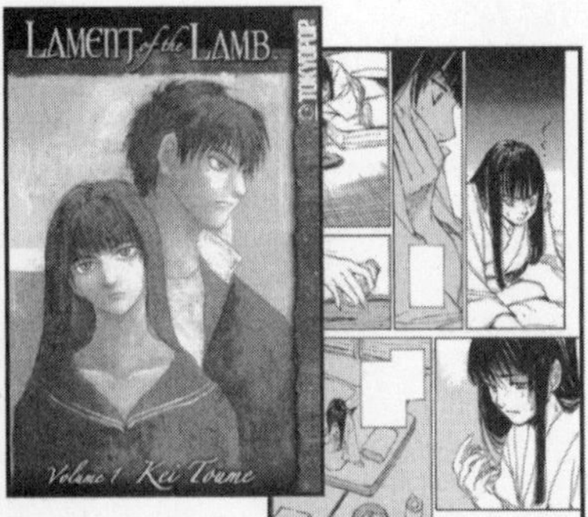
LAMENT of the LAMB
TOKYOPOP
Volume 1 Kei Toume

BY KEI TOUME

LAMENT OF THE LAMB

Kei Toume's *Lament of the Lamb* follows the physical and mental torment of Kazuna Takashiro, who discovers that he's cursed with a hereditary disease that makes him crave blood. *Lament* is psychological horror at its best—it's gloomy, foreboding and emotionally wrenching. Toume brilliantly treats the story's vampirism in a realistic, subdued way, and it becomes a metaphor for teenage alienation, twisted sexual desire and insanity. While reading each volume, I get goose bumps, I feel uneasy, and I become increasingly depressed. Quite a compliment for a horror series!

~Paul Morrissey, Editor

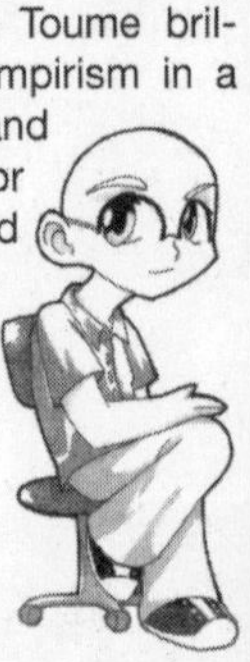

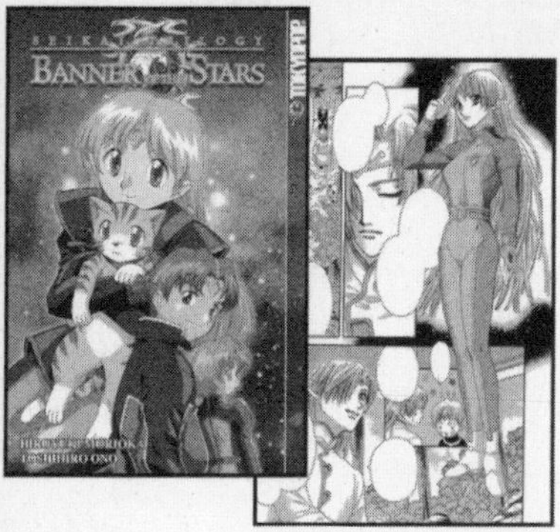

BY AYA YOSHINAGA, HIROYUKI MORIOKA, TOSHIHIRO ONO, AND WASOH MIYAKOSHI

THE SEIKAI TRILOGY

The Seikai Trilogy is one of TOKYOPOP's most underrated series. Although the trilogy gained popularity through the release of the anime, the manga brings a vitality to the characters that I feel the anime never did. The story is a heart-warming, exciting sci-fi adventure epic, the likes of which we haven't seen since *Star Wars. Banner of the Stars II*, the series' finale, is a real page-turner—a prison colony's security is compromised due to violent intergalactic politics. Each manga corresponds to the story from the novel...however, unless you read Japanese, the only way to enjoy the story thus far is through these faithful comic adaptations.

~Luis Reyes, Editor

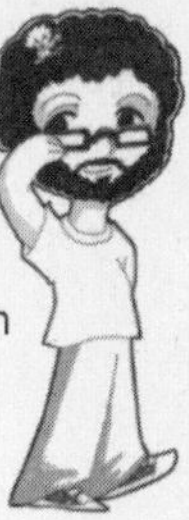

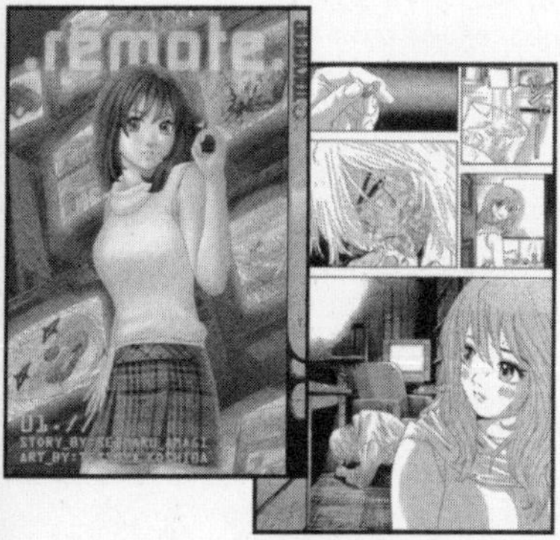

BY SEIMARU AMAGI AND TETSUYA KOSHIBA

REMOTE

Imagine Pam Anderson starring in *The Silence of the Lambs* and you've got a hint of what to expect from Seimaru Amagi and Tetsuya Koshiba's *Remote*. Completely out of her element, Officer Kurumi Ayaki brings down murderers, mad bombers and would-be assassins, all under the guidance of the reclusive Inspector Himuro. There's no shortage of fan-service and ultraviolence as Kurumi stumbles through her cases, but it's nicely balanced by the forensic police work of the brilliant Himuro, a man haunted by his past and struggling with suppressed emotions awakened by the adorable Kurumi.

~Bryce P. Coleman, Editor

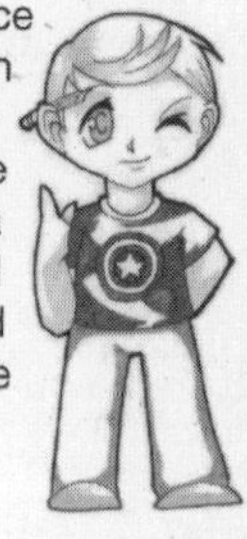

.HACK//AI BUSTER - NOVEL
BY TATSUYA HAMAZAKI

In the epic prequel to *.hack*, the avatar Albireo is a solo adventurer in The World, the most advanced online fantasy game ever created. When he comes across Lycoris, a strange little girl in a dungeon, he soon comes to realize that she may hold a very deadly secret—a secret that could unhinge everything in cyberspace... and beyond!

Discover the untold origins of the phenomenon known as *.hack*!

© Tatsuya Hamazaki © Rei Izumi

CHRONO CODE
BY EUI-CHEOL SHIN & IL-HO CHOI

Time flows like a river, without changing its course. This is an escape from the river's flow...

Three people must cross time and space to find each other and change their destinies. However, a powerful satellite, a secret code and the future police impede their progress, and their success hinges on an amnesiac who must first uncover the true nature of her past in order to discover who her friends are in the future.

© IL-HO CHOI & EUI-CHEOL SHIN, DAIWON C.I. Inc.

SAIYUKI RELOAD
BY KAZUYA MINEKURA

Join Sanzo, Gojyo, Hakkai, Goku and their updated wardrobe as they continue their journey west toward Shangri-La, encountering new challenges and new adventures along the way. But don't be fooled by their change in costume: The fearsome foursome is just as ferocious and focused as before...if not more so.

The hit manga that inspired the anime, and the sequel to TOKYOPOP's hugely popular